Bl # 2/12/2

University of London Historical Studies

XI

UNIVERSITY OF LONDON HISTORICAL STUDIES

MEDIEVAL LONDON

FROM COMMUNE TO CAPITAL

MEDIEVAL LONDON...

From Commune to Capital

by

GWYN A. WILLIAMS

UNIVERSITY OF LONDON
THE ATHLONE PRESS
1963

Published by
THE ATHLONE PRESS

UNIVERSITY OF LONDON
at 2 Gower Street, London WC1
Distributed by Constable & Co Ltd
12 *Orange Street, London* WC2
U.S.A.
Oxford University Press Inc
New York

© *Gwyn A. Williams,* 1963

Printed in Great Britain by
WESTERN PRINTING SERVICES LTD
BRISTOL

TO MY PARENTS

FOREWORD

THIS book is an attempt to use the abundant medieval archives of London to reconstruct the history of the city during its formative years. London won self-government in the late twelfth century and its autonomy was confirmed by Magna Carta; the new order in the city and in Crown-city relationships which took shape in the following century was given legal form by the charters of 1319 and 1327; a few years later came the war with France, the syndicates, and a new phase in English commercial history. These were obvious terminal dates. The method seemed equally obvious. The correlation of material from the city archives and secondary depositories with the royal records and the construction of multiple outline biographies of Londoners should create a mass silhouette of the city population and ground political narrative and constitutional analysis in social reality.

Ecclesiastical affairs, Jewry and the Inns of Court are not touched on except where they impinge directly on the social and political life of the city; in the records of trade and the law, it was possible only to sample. But to the best of my ability, I have tried to see London whole. My debts are many, as bibliography and footnotes make clear. All students of London history are under heavy obligation to Professor Eilert Ekwall, whose thorough work on the city records is a monument to scholarship. To the late Professor George Unwin, my debt is even heavier. There is nothing to equal his buoyancy and grasp of the real. The years add to the stature of his great work on London and its gilds.

To one of those gilds I owe the opportunity to undertake this study. It was made possible by the award of a Studentship by the Goldsmiths' Company of London. My own university, the University of Wales, granted me a Studentship and a Fellowship for the same purpose. My interest in the subject was first aroused at Aberystwyth by the stimulating teaching of Professor R. F. Treharne; it was sustained and educated by my colleague Dr. Edmund Fryde, whose help has been invaluable. At London, I had the exhilarating experience of the seminars of Professor E. M. Carus-Wilson and Mr. T. F. Reddaway, where wide-ranging discussion virtually added a new dimension to every member's own work. I learned a great deal from my colleagues Dr. A. R. Bridbury, Dr. Kevin McDonnell and Miss M. K. James, and I am particularly grateful to Dr. Elspeth Veale, whose work on the fur trade helped materially to shape my thinking, and who freely gave time, thought and assistance of all kinds to a colleague. I owe thanks to Professor M. McKisack for reading the proofs. To my director, Mr. T. F. Reddaway, Reader in the History of London, every student of city history owes a great debt. My own is of the kind Exchequer clerks called 'desperate'—beyond redemption.

I am no less grateful to the staffs of the libraries and archives in which I worked, in particular to the Deputy-Keeper of the City of London Records Office, Mr. Philip E. Jones and his Assistant, Mr. M. J. Chandler, whose kindness never failed. It is to the tradition of which they are the custodians that any worker on city history owes most, to Mr. Jones and his predecessors, Dr. A. H. Thomas and Mr. R. R. Sharpe, who gave us the magnificent series of published London records, and to that long line of archivists, antiquarians and chroniclers which is one of the city's distinctions, stretching back through John Stow and John Carpenter to Andrew Horn who expounded the 1327 charter 'in English', Hugh Waltham who established order by routine as his ironmonger uncle had tried to do by revolution, to the dimmer figures of the dignified and irascible Arnold fitz Thedmar and the rumbustious William fitz Stephen. It is when I look at my own work and realize how much it owes to these men that I am prompted to preface this report on research into the history of their city with another borrowing, this time from Geoffrey Chaucer, in his prologue to the *Treatise on the Astrolabe:*

'I n'am but the lewd compilator of the labour of olde astrologiens and hav it translatid in myn Englissh oonly for thy doctrine.'

Aberystwyth   G. A. W.
July 1961

CONTENTS

ABBREVIATIONS

A.R.	P.R.O. Assize Roll.
Ancient Deeds	P.R.O. Special Collection, Ancient Deeds.
Annales	*Annales d'histoire économique et sociale.*
Ann. Lond.	*Annales Londonienses,* ed. W. Stubbs (1882).
Ann. Paul.	*Annales Paulini,* ed. W. Stubbs (1882).
Beaven	A. B. Beaven, *The Aldermen of the City of London,* 2 vols. (1908–13).
C.C.R.	*Calendar of Close Rolls.*
C. Ch. R.	*Calendar of Charter Rolls.*
C. Chanc. R.	*Calendar of Chancery Rolls, Various.*
C. Lib. R.	*Calendar of Liberate Rolls.*
C.P.R.	*Calendar of Patent Rolls.*
C.R.	*Close Rolls of the reign of Henry III.*
Cal. Coroners Rolls	*Calendar of Coroners' Rolls of the City of London.*
Cal. E.M.C. Rolls	*Calendar of Early Mayors' Court Rolls of the City of London.*
Cal. Inq. Misc.	*Calendar of Inquisitions Miscellaneous.*
Cal. Inq. P.-M.	*Calendar of Inquisitions Post-mortem.*
Cal. Letter-Bk.	*Calendar of Letter-Books of the City of London.*
Cal. of Wills	*Calendar of Wills proved and enrolled in the Court of Husting, London.*
Cat. Anc. Deeds	*A Descriptive Catalogue of Ancient Deeds, P.R.O.*
Chanc. Misc.	P.R.O. Chancery Miscellanea.
Cart. S.M. Clerkenwell	*Cartulary of St. Mary Clerkenwell,* ed. W. O. Hassall (1949).
Chron. Duob. Bell.	*Chronicon de Duobus Bellis apud Lewes et Evesham,* ed. H. T. Riley (1876).
Cur. Reg. Roll	P.R.O. Curia Regis Roll.
Dunstable	*Annales Prioratus de Dunstaplia,* ed. H. R. Luard (1866).
Excheq. Misc.	P.R.O. Exchequer Miscellanea.

Excheq. Plea Roll	P.R.O. Roll of the Exchequer of Pleas.
Feudal Aids	*Inquisitions and Assessments relating to Feudal Aids.*
Flores	*Flores Historiarum*, ed. H. R. Luard (1890).
French Chronicle	*Croniques de London*, ed. G. J. Aungier (1844).
Gerv. Cant.	*Historical Works of Gervase of Canterbury*, ed. W. Stubbs (1880).
Hemingburgh	*Chronicon Walteri de Hemingburgh*, ed. H. C. Hamilton (1848).
Hundred Rolls	*Rotuli Hundredorum temp. Henry III et Edward I* (1836).
Hust. Roll	Court of Husting: Roll of wills and deeds.
Hust. Roll (Common Pleas)	Court of Husting: Roll of Common Pleas.
Hust. Roll (Land)	Court of Husting: Roll of Pleas of Land.
K.R. Acc. V.	P.R.O. King's Remembrancer's Accounts, Various.
K.R. Customs Acc.	P.R.O. King's Remembrancer's Customs Accounts.
K.R.M.R.	P.R.O. King's Remembrancer's Memoranda Roll.
L.T.R.M.R.	P.R.O. Lord Treasurer's Remembrancer's Memoranda Roll.
Lib. Albus	*Liber Albus*, ed. H. T. Riley (1859).
Lib. Cust.	*Liber Custumarum*, ed. H. T. Riley (1859–62).
Lib. de Ant. Leg.	*Liber de Antiquis Legibus*, ed. T. Stapleton (1846).
Lib. Horn	Liber Horn, City of London Records Office.
Lib. Ordinationum	Liber Ordinationum, City of London Records Office.
Lib. Roll	P.R.O. Liberate Roll.
M. Paris	*Matthaei Parisiensis Chronica Majora*, ed. H. R. Luard (1877–80).
Misc. Roll AA, BB, CC	Miscellaneous Roll AA, BB, CC, City of London Records Office.
P. and M. Rolls	*Calendar of Plea and Memoranda Rolls of the City of London.*
Pat. Roll	*Patent Rolls of the reign of Henry III.*

P.R.O. Public Record Office.

Recog. Roll Recognizance Roll, City of London Records Office.

Riley, *Memorials* *Memorials of London and London life in the XIII, XIV and XV Centuries 1276–1419*, ed. H. T. Riley (1868).

St. Paul's St. Paul's Cathedral Chapter Library: deeds and wills.

Select Excheq. Pleas *Select Cases in the Exchequer of Pleas*, ed. H. Jenkinson and B.E.R. Formoy (1932).

Trivet *Nicholas Trivet, annales sex regum Angliae*, ed. T. Hog (1845).

Unwin, *Gilds* G. Unwin, *The Gilds and Companies of London* (1908).

V.C.H. Middlesex *Victoria County History, Middlesex*, ii, ed. W. Page (1911).

W.A.M. Westminster Abbey Muniment Room: deeds, bonds and wills.

W.A.M., Domesday Westminster Abbey Cartulary.

Weinbaum M. Weinbaum, *London unter Eduard I und II* (Stuttgart, 1933).

Wykes *Chronicon vulgo dictum Chronicon Thomae Wykes*, ed. H. R. Luard (1869).

Prologue

'COME what may,' cried Robert Brand in 1193, 'Londoners shall have no king but their mayor!' In that excited spring they had in truth no king; Richard Lionheart lay in captivity abroad. Their mayor, however, was serving as treasurer of his ransom money, in company with Hubert Walter and the earls, exercising an authority which was to some as alarming as it was novel. For it was scarcely eighteen months since John Lackland and the magnates, summoned by the great bell of St. Paul's, had assembled at the Folkmoot site and sworn to maintain the *commune of London*. Not for a million marks, wrote the chronicler Richard of Devizes, would Henry II or the absent Richard have sanctioned this. The dread *commune*, 'terror of kingdoms', had appeared on English soil.[1]

He need not have feared; the monster was soon domesticated. London, after all, was distinctive by tradition. It had occupied a special place in the Anglo-Saxon order; its leader, Ansgar the Staller, had stood at Harold's side. At the Conquest, its status, in essentials, had been preserved, and as the premier urban community of a feudal kingdom, it enjoyed a necessary and distinguished liberty.

London had its own body of peculiar law and custom, expressly confirmed by William I. The citizens, all of the one £5

---

[1] This prologue is a personal interpretation of a confused and controversial period; for the thirteenth-century evidence which supports it, see Chapters II, III, and IV. For the earlier history of London, see *Historical Charters and Constitutional Documents of the City of London*, ed. W. de G. Birch (London, 1887); *Select Charters*, ed. W. Stubbs, 9th edn. ed. H. W. C. Davis (Oxford, 1913); Addit. Ms. 14252 in M. Bateson, 'A London municipal collection of the reign of John', *English Historical Review*, xvii (1902); J. Tait, *The Medieval English Borough* (Manchester, 1936); J. H. Round, *Geoffrey de Mandeville* (London, 1892) and *The Commune of London* (Cambridge, 1899); F. M. Stenton, *Norman London* (London, 1934) and revised version in G. Barraclough (ed.) *Social Life in early England* (London, 1960); W. Page, *London, its Origin and Early Development* (London, 1929); M. Weinbaum, *Verfassungsgeschichte Londons 1066–1268* (Stuttgart, 1929); C. Petit-Dutaillis, *Studies Supplementary to Stubbs' Constitutional History*, i (Manchester, 1908), and *Les communes françaises* (Paris, 1947); W. S. McKechnie, *Magna Carta*, 2nd ed. (Glasgow, 1914).

wergild, were a privileged group. They could not be compelled
to plead outside the city walls except for the most serious
offences, and were quit of toll throughout England. Exempted
from the murder-fine and ordeal by battle, they enjoyed freedom of alienation and bequest, and exercised rights of the
chase in Middlesex, Surrey and the Chilterns. Under the
bishop and the portreeve, they had their general assembly, the
Folkmoot, their weekly court, the Husting, and their twenty-
four administrative wards under aldermen, a traditional and
select group of law-men, to whose authority even the numerous
sokes, or private franchises, were largely subjected.

On this basis of corporate unity the city leaders built, for
in the buoyant twelfth century London's patrician families
grasped at independence. From Henry I they won the privilege
of answering for the £300 farm of both Middlesex and the city
through sheriffs they chose themselves, and were even empowered
to elect their own justiciar. In Stephen's reign, during the
struggle against the Mandeville interest, the *commune* made a
fleeting appearance, to bargain with a king and an empress
and to claim a voice in the selection of the monarch. The accession of Henry II halted this progress. Elective sheriffs and
justiciar were lost, the farm was raised and political life lost
much of its sparkle. In the troubled reigns of Richard and John,
however, the city came into its own.

The struggle for power between Count John and the unpopular chancellor, Longchamp, after the departure of Richard
on crusade, provided the opportunity. In 1190, the hard-
pressed Longchamp restored the city's elective sheriffs and the
old farm of £300, but in the following year, John put himself
at the head of an influential combination against the chancellor,
and in October entered London with an impressive force. A
powerful faction within the city, led by John's personal friend
and financier Richard fitz Reiner, an alderman of long purse and
pedigree, swung the citizens against Longchamp, but as their
price demanded the commune. On 8 October, by a series of
reciprocal oaths on the European model, a commune was
established, subject to the king's pleasure.

The Londoners borrowed French styles and names. They
based their commune on a sworn association of citizens; its

leader, the personification of their community, they called a
mayor. They struck a communal seal, and in the communal
oath which survives from 1193 used the word *échevins* (skivins)
to describe the ruling council which was to assist the mayor.
⸗This was natural; a *seigneurie collective populaire* in the French
manner, a sworn urban community with its own juridical personality, existing in feudal relationship with the monarch, was
the logical end of their endeavour to break out of the shire
system and establish an autonomous régime.⸗The city was regarded as the 'king's chamber'; the citizenry were a tiny élite
of landed and hereditary character. Their acclamation was an
element of the coronation ritual, their tenure was singularly
free, and in the words of chroniclers, because of their wealth
and influence, they were counted aristocrats, *optimates*. They
called themselves *barons*; inscribed the term on their seal.
'Mayor and Barons' was the communal mode of address. And
they took the word seriously. In 1250 they were to claim,
as barons, the privilege of trial by their 'peers', the earls and
barons of England. Implicit in all this was a determination to
break free from the royal demesne, of which London as a
chartered borough formed a part, to break free from the tallage
which the king could levy at will from his own domain and to
assume instead the freewill burden of the aid, the theoretically
voluntary taxation paid by their 'peers'.[1] From this date forward, throughout the thirteenth century, the citizens claimed
that they held the whole city in chief of the king, as a collective
seigneury.[2]

This claim the royal justices never allowed and in the cohesive monarchy of England it could not be made good. The
London commune could survive, as a commune, only by compromise with the established order. This is apparent in internal
affairs no less than external. The creation of the mayoralty
implied the establishment of a communal régime, in particular
of a governing council. When Dublin was granted the right to
elect a mayor in 1229, for example, in direct imitation of London, the appointment of a council of twenty-four followed as a
matter of course. The origin of the London council is obscure.

[1] See the quarrel over taxation in 1255 in Chapter VII.
[2] For example, see *Hundred Rolls*, i, 403–33.

Hard on the heels of the mayoralty came a popular uprising of strongly anti-communal spirit led by the quixotic William fitz Osbert, 'Longbeard', a protest against taxation and oligarchy, suppressed with much cruelty in 1196. Under the year 1200–1, the city chronicler Arnold fitz Thedmar refers enigmatically to a body of 'twenty-five' elected to govern the community along with the mayor; in 1206, after more trouble over tallage, the king himself ordered the replacement of *superiores* by an elected and sworn *societas* of twenty-four. These were evidently troubled and confused times, but it is possible to read into them more confusion than is warranted. The events of 1206, certainly, were very similar to those crises in the thirteenth century when, in analogous circumstances, the king forced a general election of aldermen.｜For the aldermen, the city doomsmen, remained the focus of local power. Every mayor was an alderman; so were all the prominent leaders. There may well have been stresses and strains; by the early thirteenth century the court of aldermen was a uniformly elective body, which it may not have been before the commune.｜But after all the riots, the depositions and the *ad hoc* commissions, it was this court, rooted as it was in civic tradition, which emerged as the central authority.

Within the national community Londoners had to make a similar adjustment. For years their commune inhabited a shadow world of semi-legality. Hubert Walter during the struggle against John in 1193 certainly recognized, and used, the mayor, but Richard never did. His charter, issued on his return to England in 1194, simply repeated his father's; the restoration of elective sheriffs did not itself become fully effective until the same year. The charter which John issued in 1199 confirmed the citizens' liberties but made no mention of mayor or commune. Not until the crisis year of 1215 does the mayor again receive official notice.

Yet throughout this period he was exercising his office. Richard fitz Reiner died at the end of 1191 and the first known mayor was Henry fitz Ailwin, whose ancestors had been important in the London region in Saxon times. He was probably installed in 1192. He was certainly in power early in 1193 and he continued to occupy the chair until 1212, when

he was succeeded by his nephew, Roger Fitz Alan.[1] Already
civic ceremony was beginning to centre on his person; already
the sheriffs were entering their slow decline into dependence
on his council. That council was busy reshaping a building
assize and codifying city custom. The commune was oper-
ative.[2]

It never won official recognition, as a 'commune', from the
monarchy. King John addressed a communication to 'mayor
and commune' in 1200 and the 'commune' was mentioned in
royal orders of 1221 and 1225, but in general the Court was
extremely reluctant to use the word, no doubt mindful of the
threat to the royal demesne and overall royal control. The
Londoners themselves rarely used it, though they frequently
employed such terms as *communauté* and *communitas* virtually as
synonyms, and in the course of internal constitutional con-
troversies the word itself never failed to make an appearance.
'We, we are the commune of the city. To us belongs the election of the mayor!', chanted the crowds in the contested mayoral
election of 1272; 'The commune ought to elect mayors and
sheriffs', said the Hundred jury of Langbourn ward three years
later. The communal spirit was never far below the surface.
In the revolt of 1263 mayor and plebs formed a sworn *societas*,
organized a communal militia with its *cloche* at St. Paul's and
even employed the traditional communal penalty of destruction
of the burgage. The most striking instance was the crisis of
1327 when the Londoners were the close allies of Mortimer and
Isabella in the deposition of Edward II, winning valuable
privileges as reward. The mayor marshalled the citizens into a
sworn association and compelled all magnates who came to the
city to swear to its liberties. When the deposition parliament
reached deadlock, the Londoners, prompted and aided by
Mortimer, held a three-day ceremony at Guildhall in which
scores of barons and prelates were sworn to Isabella's cause
and London's new franchise.[3] The word was never used in
1327, but this was a sworn commune of classical type. By the
turn of the twelfth and thirteenth centuries the term had

---

[1] *Lib. de Ant. Leg.*, p. 23; M. Bateson, *op. cit.*, 726; J. Tait, *op. cit.*, 291, n. 3.
[2] See Chapters II and IV.
[3] For these instances, see Chapters VII, VIII, XI.

acquired alarmist overtones which probably restricted its use, but under any name the commune was a reality.

Its place in the national community was decided by the crisis of 1215. In their attack on John the barons found willing allies among the Londoners. Robert fitz Walter, 'Marshal of the Army of God', was the city's banneret. May was the crucial month. In a last attempt to win the city, John negotiated a charter. The Londoners set out their demands in nine articles, most of which dealt with the Thames, the walls, trade and routine privileges. Two, however, raised fundamental issues. The citizens petitioned to have a mayor, 'year by year', who would be elected by the Folkmoot and swear an oath to the king, and they asked for the abolition of all tallages except those granted by common consent of the kingdom and city. This was a full communal programme. John's response was significant. In the charter he issued on 9 May, there was no reference to tallage. On the other hand, the 'barons' were empowered to elect a mayor and remove him annually, if they wished, and the mayor was to be presented and sworn before the king or his justiciar. The liberties of London were confirmed in general terms, saving the prisage and pre-emption rights of the royal chamberlain.[1] This, in effect, was a royal recognition of a commune, in the sense of a sworn, self-governing community under an elected head who embodied its legal personality, coupled with a refusal to permit this commune to break free from the royal demesne and general royal surveillance. No doubt French lawyers would have found the solution incomprehensible, but the English worked it well enough.

For solution it was. Despite the charter, a city faction committed London to the intransigents and had its demands written into the *Articles of the Barons*. Articles covering measures, alien merchants and the management of the Thames found their way into Magna Carta, but the vital issue was that raised by Article 32. There, tacked on to a petition that no scutage or aid, other than the three provided for in feudal practice, should be levied without common counsel, was a rider that the 'tallages and aids' of London, and of all other cities having liberties in

---

[1] *Select Charters*, ed. W. Stubbs, p. 311; *Historical Charters*, ed. W. de G. Birch, pp. 19–20; M. Bateson, *op. cit.*, 726.

this matter, should be treated in a similar manner, and that London should have its old franchises in full. The royal response in the Great Charter was no different from that in May. Chapter 13 of the Charter confirmed to London all its liberties and free customs, but in Chapter 12, only 'aids' from the city were subjected to the sanction of common counsel, and lesser boroughs were excluded. Tallage was not mentioned.

This was evidently considered policy. In point of fact, the distinction between aid and tallage was losing practical significance. Not until 1237 was the aid firmly re-established as a freewill grant and the complementary concept of the king's ancient demesne, with its tallage, reaffirmed; in a renewed revolt against tallage in 1255 the Londoners were able to use the looser terminology of an earlier period with considerable effect. But if the voluntary nature of the aid was something of a fiction, it was a supremely useful fiction. Henry III treated the city's attempt to refuse tallage in 1255 as a constitutional problem of the first order and this was a permanent royal attitude. No king, not even the prostrate king of Runnymede, would surrender his right to tallage London. It was a matter of status and right. The magnates clearly did not press the matter and, in the Charter, London's ambitions were curbed. Indeed, Chapter 12 was omitted from all subsequent reissues of the Charter. London was at no time to enjoy the feudal and fiscal independence of the greater communes of the continent.

On the other hand, the commune itself had won its place. The mayor, William Hardel, served on the Committee of Twenty-Five which was to enforce the Charter, as the solitary non-baronial representative, and the new status of the city rested henceforth on the authority of the premier constitutional instrument of the kingdom. London rallied to Louis of France in the brief civil war which ensued but in the settlement at the opening of the new reign its liberty was preserved. The Patent Roll of 1221 could refer to the 'mayor and commune of London', city aldermen enjoy eminence and authority during the minority of Henry III. The charter which Henry granted the city after he came of age, in 1227, expressly confirmed all the franchises conferred by his father.[1]

[1] C. Ch. R. 1226–57, pp. 23, 24.

In consequence, London entered the new reign as a chartered and autonomous community. It lacked the full fiscal and seigneurial independence of some of the European communes, but its citizens were a sworn association with a communal seal and its elective mayor took an oath to the king, independently of the sheriffs, as representative of the city. The sheriffs, themselves elective, were falling into dependence upon him and he presided over a community which enjoyed a real freedom in law and administration. The claim that the citizen body, as a unit, was a tenant-in-chief, however frequently it was rejected, had become part of the city's political tradition. This may have been an *English* commune, but a commune nonetheless. It was as a self-governing city with a strong tradition of communal unity and independence that London faced the challenge of the thirteenth century.

CHAPTER I

The Commune

THE century from Magna Carta to the Hundred Years' War was medieval London's age of iron. These were the years in which the city's social and political structure assumed characteristic and distinctive form. For with the establishment of the commune under its mayor, the cluster of bourgeois dynasties which had emerged as the city's directive élite in the twelfth century took control of an autonomous community.

A landed class of merchants and officials, they represented a fusion of the new interests planted in London at the Conquest with an older aristocracy having its roots in the Anglo-Saxon thegnhood. The city they controlled was nucleated around a key strategic site, the point where the Thames could be bridged while it was still tidal. Commanding a wide hinterland and easy communications with the most potent centres of European commerce and civilization, Flanders and the Italian axis, the Île de France, Gascony and the Baltic, London served as a nodal point of both Roman and Norman road-systems, and its patricians had long enjoyed special status within the complex communities of interest which made up the emergent kingdom of England. The removal of the royal court to Westminster under the Confessor weakened that direct contact with the sovereign which buttressed their claim to a voice in his selection, and the Conquest, inserting powerful magnates like the Mandevilles as median authorities, carried further the re-alignment of Crown-city relationships. But, by the reign of Henry I, the dominant families of London were coalescing into an estate. Borne forward by the buoyant expansion of European life and the example of the communal movement across the Channel, the new oligarchs, their social hegemony crystallizing into a

form of dynastic government, bargained and battled with
monarchs and Mandevilles, until their triumph under John
delivered the city into their hands.

Their success was consolidated by Magna Carta, which
opened England's great age of constitutional experiment. For,
with the loss of Normandy in 1204, political consciousness
turned inward, and through the crises of the Barons' Wars, the
legal definition and imperialism of Edward I, the constitutional
struggle of 1297, and the bloody faction war under Edward II,
the realm of England was hammered into an integrated community. Parliament and the merchant class took shape within
the framework of strong monarchical control, and it was a
nation approaching maturity which, in the mid-fourteenth
century, launched on a career of political and commercial
aggrandizement.[1]

London grew as England grew. The accelerating rhythms of
population growth, agricultural production and internal settlement, the rising curve of trading activity, found swift reflection
in city life.[2] Already by 1300 a metropolis inviting comparison
with its continental sisters rather than with the lesser towns of
England, London was drawn into the mainstream of European
commerce. A trade centre since its Roman inception, planted in
the old Danelaw, which remained the most populous and
wealthiest region of the country, it shared fully in the great
expansion of the high middle ages, a growth in terms of population, prices, and trade activity, which sometimes reached
boom proportions.[3] Feeding its staple wool to Flanders, its
grain to Gascony, drawing cloth and wine in return, the English economy, still in its *colonial* phase, operated at the perimeter
of the Flemish-Italian connexion linking the North and the

[1] Most stimulating and thought-provoking studies of the period are those of Sir
Maurice Powicke—F. M. Powicke, *King Henry III and the Lord Edward*, 2 vols.
(Oxford, 1947) and *The Thirteenth Century* (Oxford, 1953).

[2] These problems are analysed in some detail in later chapters, notably Chapters
IV, V, and VI; for a broad survey, see, in particular, the *rapports* by Postan, Sapori,
Cipolla, Dhondt, and Wolff in *Rapports du ixe. Congrès International des Sciences
Historiques 1950* (Paris, 1950), pp. 55–80, 225–41, 280–95.

[3] See H. C. Darby, *The Domesday Geography of Eastern England* (Cambridge, 1952)
and *An Historical Geography of England before A.D. 1800*, ed. H. C. Darby (Cambridge,
1936); F. M. Stenton, 'The road system of medieval England', *Economic History
Review*, vii (1936–7).

Levant, around which Europe's life revolved. The whole period through to the first quarter of the fourteenth century was one of expansion, as the Italians opened up the sea-route to the north (Genoese and Majorcan galleys were lading wool in the Pool by 1281) and the focus shifted to Bruges, where the growing empire of the Hanse found its western outlet.[1]

London stood in the immediate hinterland of three commercial axes. Its natural contacts were across the narrow seas. Regulations for the Lorraine fleet from the Rhine, with its wine, and its goods from Regensburg, Mainz, Novgorod, Persia and Byzantium, are among the earliest city records, and from the twelfth century, industrial Flanders and the basic wool-cloth traffic fill the horizon. The Flemish Hanse of London faded at the turn of the century, but it was this staple which drew the Brabanters, the Dutch, the increasing numbers of Germans, and above all, the Italian companies, whose developed banking techniques and massive resources made them the giants of European commerce. Appearing early in the reign of Henry III, they rose to power under his successors, in the great days of the Riccardi, the Bardi, the Peruzzi, and the Frescobaldi. By 1300, all the important companies were established in London.[2]

Many of them were branches of Parisian concerns, for the Île de France, Picardy, and the whole complex of trading centres from Flanders to the Champagne entrepôts were in the closest rapport with the city. The merchants of the Amiens-Nesle-Corbie hanse, whose woad was vital to the English cloth industry, were one of the first alien groups to win exemption from the city trade regulations, buying the right to warehouse

[1] The literature on this subject is vast. For general accounts, see *The Cambridge Economic History of Europe*, ed. M. M. Postan and E. E. Rich, ii (Cambridge, 1952); H. Pirenne, *Histoire économique de l'occident mediéval* (Bruges, 1951); for the galleys in 1281, see K. R. Customs Acc. E122/68/2; see also A. A. Ruddock, *Italian Merchants and Shipping in Southampton 1270–1600* (Southampton, 1951).

[2] For the Lorraine fleet, see B.M. Addit. Ms. 14252 in M. Bateson, 'A London municipal collection of the reign of John', *English Historical Review*, xvii (1902), 496–502; *Lib. Cust.*, pp. 61–4; for the early Italians, see *C.P.R. 1247–66, passim*. From a great corpus of work on these themes, see, as particularly useful, E. E. Power, *The Wool Trade in English Medieval History* (Oxford, 1941); E. M. Carus-Wilson, *Medieval Merchant Venturers* (London, 1954); R. Doehaerd, *L'expansion économique belge au moyen âge* (Brussels, 1946) and Y. Renouard, *Les hommes d'affaires italiens au moyen âge* (Paris, 1949).

and to long residence with a contribution towards the city's new water-supply. Tournai sent everything from belt-knives to artistic statuary; Parisian merchants in London ranged from wealthy mercers, sometimes of London origin, to humble painters and saddlers. The traffic on these crowded routes remained the most prominent feature of the commercial landscape. As early as 1127, the turn-round of shipping was such that news from Bruges reached London within two days.[1]

The axis to wine-growing Gascony was more characteristically a London trade in the narrower sense. The union with England in 1152 transformed the area into another of the celebrated zones of specialization in medieval Europe, and London was a focal centre of the trade from the beginning. Gascons outnumbered other aliens in its markets; La Réole gave its name to a city street; wine served almost as currency.[2] This connexion, merging with the Italian sea-borne commerce, was strengthened by the marriages of Henry III and Edward I. By 1255, Matthew Paris was complaining that London was 'overflowing' with Poitevins, Provençals, Italians and Spaniards. Along the route came the merchants of Toulouse, Cahors, and Montpellier, of the *maison de Londres* at Narbonne, with their cloth, woad, and above all, their spices and mercery. Far more frequently than the Italians, it was these Cahorsin money-lenders who came into contact with the ordinary citizen, with consequences which differed little from Senlis to Florence, for it was the Cahorsins whom Dante figuratively, and the Londoners literally, consigned to Hell.[3]

[1] See K.R. Acc. V. (Alien Merchants) E101/126/6, 7, 14; *Lib. Cust.*, pp. 64, 68, 69; E. M. Carus-Wilson, 'La guède française en Angleterre; un grand commerce du moyen âge', *Revue du Nord*, xxxv (1938); E. Chapin, *Les villes de foire de Champagne* (Paris, 1937); R. Doehaerd, *op. cit.*, 51, 55.

[2] See, in particular, M. K. James, 'The fluctuations in the Anglo-Gascon wine trade during the fourteenth century', *Economic History Review*, 2nd ser. iv (1951); 'Les activités commerciales des négociants en vins gascons en Angleterre durant la fin du moyen âge', *Annales du Midi*, lxv (1953); 'The medieval wine dealer', in *The Entrepreneur*, papers of the annual conference of the Economic History Society (Cambridge, 1957).

[3] *M. Paris*, v, 531; K.R.M.R. 40–2, *passim*; K.R. Acc. V. (Mint) E101/288/6, m. 1, 3; see F. Lot, *Recherches sur la population et la superficie des cités remontant à la période gallo-romaine* (Paris, 1945–50), ii, 305, iii, 217, 218 and *passim*; A. E. Sayous and J. Combes, 'Les commerçants et les capitalistes de Montpellier au xiiie. et xive. siècles', *Revue Historique*, clxxxviii–clxxxix (1940).

Less unpopular were the Spaniards, established in force from the mid-thirteenth century. The ancient pilgrim route to Santiago awoke to new life as the Reconquista pushed forward the frontier of Europe in the south, and, under Italian stimulus, the merchants of Bilbao and the northern littoral took to the Gascon seas. In the sixties, cargoes of Spanish iron were coming regularly into London; by 1280 it was a staple at Bruges. A generation later, the Spaniards in London were an organized community, and their trade, in wool, olive oil, skins, iron, and the famous Cordovan leather, had transformed the craft structure of an important sector of the city's economy.[1]

Far more important as agents of change were the Germans, who were driving east. Rostock, Danzig, remote Reval, had appeared by the mid-thirteenth century and the basic, bulky trade of the Baltic came flowing back to the foci of European commerce. London, with its English trade oriented towards Boston and East Anglia, had always been in close contact with Scandinavia and the Easterlings. Cologne had its guildhall in the city by 1157, Bergen its Englandfahrer gild. It was in 1250 that Lübeck signed its treaty with Hakon IV. Fifty years later, the Hanse had ousted the English from Bergen, won control of the Skaania fisheries and established itself as the dominant power at Bruges. Lübeck and Hamburg got their English charters in 1266; their trade, if not their traders, swamped the Rhinelanders, and their Steelyard replaced the old guildhall. In 1282 they took over the maintenance of Bishopsgate and won unprecedented liberties in the city. More than any other aliens, the Hansards dominated London in the fourteenth century. They had created a new trading axis for the city, reshaping its patriciate in the process.[2]

---

[1] C. Verlinden, 'The rise of Spanish trade in the Middle Ages', *Economic History Review*, x (1940); M. K. James, 'A London merchant of the fourteenth century', *ibid.*, 2nd. ser. viii (1955–6); see Chapter VI.

[2] See *Lib. Albus*, pp. 485–8; *P. and M. Rolls*, i, 151, 152; *Cal. E.M.C. Rolls*, pp. 140, 182, 183; *M. Paris*, v, 36; on the Hanse in general, see E. R. Daenell, *Die Blütezeit der deutschen Hanse*, 2 vols. (Berlin, 1905–6); F. Rörig, 'Les raisons intellectuelles d'une suprematie commerciale: la Hanse', *Annales*, ii (1930); J. A. G. Gade, *The Hanseatic control of Norwegian commerce during the late Middle Ages* (Leiden, 1951); M. M. Postan, 'The economic and political relations of England and the Hanse from 1400 to 1475', *Studies in English Trade in the Fifteenth Century*, ed. E. E. Power and M. M. Postan (London, 1933).

Overshadowed by these aliens in early years, the Londoners, as the century progressed, significantly increased their stake in Flemish and Brabantine cloth, English wool, Gascon wine, the spices and mercery of the Mediterranean, and won their share of the new and growing commerce of Spain and the Baltic. At all times, their progress was directed and punctuated by the operation of the monarchy, with its wool staples of 1294 and 1313, its massive Wardrobe markets, its incessant demands for goods, money and contractual service, and its migrations, which tapped a reservoir of provincial mercantile enterprise and fed it into the city. By the middle of the fourteenth century, London was rapidly becoming the focus of the English merchant class. Its leading men were moving into finance and war purveyance, stood ready to take their place at the head of the syndicates and merchant companies of Edward III.[1]

The whole complex of interests which constituted the medieval state played upon the city. So many magnates held land in or near it that the disposal of the urban property of intestate non-citizens became a problem to be interminably discussed at royal Iters. In 1306 there were said to be over a thousand *knights* in London.[2] Much of its land was owned by the Church. With St. Paul's and 110 parish churches, Holy Trinity and several collegiate foundations within the walls, fashionable nunneries and priories and Westminster at hand, the ecclesiastical order, with its courts, gilds, ordinances, and its offer of a career open to the talents, was a formative factor of considerable importance.[3] No less significant was the proximity of the royal courts and administrative services at Westminster, models and objects of alarm, as the city painfully created its own bureaucracy and equipped itself with a legal establishment to meet the demands of the new Edwardian order.[4]

More immediate was the direct impact of the monarchy, the

---

[1] See Chapters V and VI.

[2] Misc. Roll AA, p. 68; *Ann. Lond.*, p. 146; the Iters were periodic visitations by royal justices on circuit, who heard Crown pleas and conducted searching enquiries, generally of a fiscal nature.

[3] For a useful sample of ecclesiastical transactions in city property, see Ancient Deeds A 13700–13800; and *The Records of Merton Priory*, ed. A. Heales (London, 1898), p. 176 and *passim*.

[4] This subject is treated in some detail in Chapter IV.

controlling factor in all social evolution. As soon as he came of age, Henry III resumed the Angevin drive, and the commune came under attack. What made royal pressure more dangerous was the almost simultaneous irruption of internal discontent. For expansion was breeding new interests, to whose absorption the oligarchy proved resistant, conditioned as it was by a quasi-feudal tradition, of which William fitz Stephen's topography and Arnold fitz Thedmar's chronicle were classic expressions. The interplay of internal and external hostilities culminated, during the Barons' Wars, in the explosion of 1263, when a popular insurrection overthrew the aldermanic régime and created a revolutionary commune under the aegis of Montfort. Montfort's downfall ended it, but there was a recrudescence of revolutionary action in the early years of Edward I, and the restored patricians were given barely a decade of peace before the liberties of their city were again threatened, this time by the aggression of the strongest king medieval England ever knew. In 1285, after a head-on collision between king and patriciate, London's fragile freedoms were annulled.

The national crisis of 1297 prised the city free from Edward's grip, but in the intervening thirteen years, the social pressures which had been building up since mid-century had been given free play, and London plunged into the bitter struggles of Edward II's reign torn by partisan conflict. After 1263 there were two generations of virtually continuous political upheaval, in which inherited institutions and modes of thought dissolved, a turmoil stilled only by the royal charters of 1319 and 1327, which finally integrated London into the national community. In the 1330's London society stabilized itself and acquired a political form which proved enduring. The commune had given place to the capital.

For London, then, as for England, growth was the century's theme, in terms of communal rents which increased by a half between 1234 and 1307, of food prices which rose by two-thirds between 1212 and 1280, in terms of the physical expansion of the city itself.[1] London grew around the wharves and

[1] The rise in food prices is inferred from the variation in allowances for *table* in building workers' wages fixed by the council; see also the rise in poultry prices between 1274 and 1321—*Lib. Cust.*, pp. 82, 83, 86–8, 99–100, 206; for communal rents, see *Cal. Letter-Bk. C*, 237, 238 and St. Paul's A/17/540.

the Bridge.[1] The riverside wards were the wealthier, Billingsgate and Bridge, the natural harbour of fishmongers and woolmongers, Dowgate, the international entrepôt, and, upstream
across Walbrook, the Vintry, heart of the wine trade, with
Queenhithe and its corn market, Castle Baynard and the
Thames fisheries lying beyond. Here were the wharves, the
gangs of porters, the hostels, warehouses and cellars of alien and
citizen. From the Steelyard at Dowgate, barge traffic could
penetrate up Walbrook into the heart of the city, where the
skinners of Walbrook ward looked on Cheap, the commercial
hub. There at Woolchurchhaw was the great weigh-beam for
wool and the Stocks fish market. To the west, behind Vintry
and Queenhithe, was congested Cheap, with the mercers,
goldsmiths and drapers, and, leading off the central market, the
streets of the pepperers and the cordwainers. To the north
lay Jewry and the administrative nucleus around Guildhall,
to the west, the open Folkmoot site and the muster-ground,
soon to be swallowed up in St. Paul's Churchyard. The foci
of the city were the river, the centre and the west. East Cheap
had been built over, and population thinned out towards the
marshy ground on both sides of the eastern wall. Beyond, in
Portsoken and Bishopsgate, the people were poor. Westwards,
however, the suburb grew rapidly, spilling over the Fleet into
Westminster, whose parishes were almost as urban as London's,
a thickening belt of houses forming around the mansions of
nobles and prelates, the houses of nuns and friars, and cutting
into the great gardens.

In the thirteenth century, pigs roamed the streets and city
ordinances dealt with the rearing of cattle in houses. The famine
of 1258 administered a grim rebuke to urban over-confidence.[2]
The semi-rural atmosphere of other English towns, however, is
absent. London was intensely urban. The city's assize of building

[1] This section is based mainly on the subsidy rolls of 1292, 1319 and 1332; the
latter is printed in M. Curtis, 'The London lay subsidy of 1332', *Finance and Trade
under Edward III*, ed. G. Unwin (Manchester, 1918); the two earlier rolls appear in
M. Weinbaum, *London unter Eduard I und II* (Stuttgart, 1933), ii, 203–42, but by far
the best version is that found, together with notes on individuals and a valuable
introduction, in E. Ekwall, *Two Early London Subsidy Rolls* (Lund, 1951).

[2] W.A.M., Domesday, fo. 621–622b; *Cal. Letter-Bk. A*, 183, 184, *C*, 5; *Cal.
E.M.C. Rolls*, pp. 98, 157, 158; *Lib. Albus*, pp. 257–60; *Lib. de Ant. Leg.*, p. 37;
M. Paris, v, 693–712.

in John's reign is the earliest English building legislation known. Supplemented by much special ordinance, it countered the perennial danger of fire by ordering the replacement of wood with stone and thatch with tile. Skilled and exclusive crafts of masons, carpenters, tilers and glaziers developed rapidly, under strict municipal control.[1] The new fabric was not indestructible. In 1271 the steeple of Bow Church suddenly collapsed and crushed the big house nearby. In 1306–7 depreciation rates were running at 16–18 per cent.[2]

This in itself was a measure of growth, for building, rebuilding, enclosure and sub-division was a continuous process. Husting rolls, St. Paul's deeds, Westminster Abbey muniments, are loud with the clamour of expansion, that expansion which was building new walls, creating new parishes and peopling the suburbs of every European town of importance.[3] London began to dig a city ditch in 1275, but its wall was a gesture rather than a necessity; it curved to admit Blackfriars in these years, but otherwise there was no change.[4] By 1381 three new parishes had been added, but the city, whose basic street-plan had been laid down in Saxon times, was already equipped with a parochial framework perfectly adaptable to growth.

Within the walls, deed after deed testifies to the intensification of settlement. There was continuous sub-division. One communally owned tenement rented at 10s. early in the reign of Edward I had become two shops at £1 each by 1304, and this was typical.[5] Waste sites were taken up wholesale. St. Paul's, when leasing such sites, made their immediate development a condition of tenure.[6] Enclosures of streets and lanes by ecclesiastical corporations, followed by intensive building, reached such proportions that they ate into highways and common land,

[1] See, for example, *Lib. Albus*, pp. 319–22; *Lib. de Ant. Leg.*, pp. 206–11; *Cal. Letter-Bk. C*, 105; W.A.M. and St. Paul's, *passim*.

[2] *Ann. Lond.*, p. 81; depreciation rates calculated from extents made in execution of debt recognizances in *Cal. Letter-Bk. C*, 242–48.

[3] See F. L. Ganshof, *Étude sur le développement des villes entre Loire et Rhin au moyen âge* (Paris, 1943), especially pp. 47 ff.

[4] *Ann. Lond.*, p. 85; *C.P.R. 1272–81*, pp. 147, 148, 258; *Cal. Letter-Bk. C*, 71, 72; Weinbaum, ii, 146.

[5] *Cal. Letter-Bk. C*, 237, 238; St. Paul's A/17/540; see Hust. Rolls and St. Paul's deeds, *passim*.

[6] See, for example, St. Paul's A/4/690, A/17/542, A/24/1495 and *passim*.

C

and provoked a violent reaction in the revolution of 1263. By 1279, in Bridge ward, there were apparently no vacant sites left to develop.[1]

Population spilled over into the western suburb. Nowhere was development so intense; no other district is so heavily represented among the enrolled deeds.[2] New units of jurisdiction, the extra-mural appendages of intra-mural wards, made their appearance. Cripplegate Without was in existence by 1244, and the extra-mural sectors of Aldersgate, Bishopsgate and Ludgate-Newgate (Farringdon) were all functioning before the end of the century, bringing the new populations safely within the shelter of the franchise.[3]

Much of that new population was drawn from the English counties, for London, with its numerous but mobile colonies of aliens, was peopled by immigrants from almost every corner of England. From the last quarter of the thirteenth century, there was an unusually heavy influx from the east Midlands. Norfolk alone gave the London mercers a hundred new recruits over two generations, for the immigration was peculiar also in that it was almost exclusively mercantile. For a variety of reasons, the rich, commercialized provinces of the east were pumping new blood into the city. It was in this period that the London dialect changed from East Saxon to East Midland.[4] At the same time, under the stimulus of Scottish wars and Household migration, the northern counties were sending their ambitious young men into London to capture the Wardrobe market and the city's legal plums. By the date of the first surviving register of citizenship admissions in 1309 and the early tax rolls of 1292–1332, the bulk of the city's apprentice population was country-born.[5] A good half came from the Home Counties and the immediate vicinity, a strong and socially important influx from the eastern shires and a steady flow from the north; small

[1] Weinbaum, ii, 150, and see Chapter VII.

[2] See Hust. Rolls, *passim*, and, for Westminster, W.A.M. and A.R. 543, for example.

[3] Misc. Roll AA, p. 76; Misc. Roll BB; K.R. Acc. V. (Army and Navy) E101/13/39; Ekwall, *op. cit.*

[4] See E. Ekwall, *Studies on the Population of Medieval London* (Stockholm, 1956), pp. 1–207 and xlii–lxxii; the movement is treated in some detail in Chapter V.

[5] See *Cal. Letter-Bk. D*, 35–179; A. H. Thomas, *P. and M. Rolls*, ii, introduction; S. L. Thrupp, *The Merchant Class of Medieval London* (Chicago, 1948), chapter 5.

numbers entered from the west and south-west, and there were surprisingly few from the south-east. They came in to replenish a city which no doubt suffered from the customary urban death and replacement rates, to reinforce whatever natural increase there may have been in those buoyant years.

The size of that increase, however, is a matter of pure conjecture.[1] The nearest anchorage is the poll tax of 1377. Its returns suggest that London was then three times as large as York or Bristol, five times as large as Coventry, six times Norwich. Certainly, to the Italians, apart from York and Bristol, there was nothing in England outside the city.[2] The returns themselves point to a resident population of between 35,000 and 40,000, in a period of relative stagnation during the pestilence. In the years before the plague, the number of taxpayers in the subsidies of 1292, 1319 and 1332 remained fairly uniform, allowing for faulty documentation and fluctuation in the exemption level, at 1,700, 1,900 and 1,600. Behind them stood the shadowy army of kinsfolk, dependants, paupers, technical and real, and the non-citizens who formed the majority of London's inhabitants. The population, at the crest of an economic and social expansion which had probably doubled it over a century, could scarcely have been less than 40,000.

Paris in 1328 had 200,000 inhabitants, but this was the continent's capital. Much later, Venice, Naples and Milan reached the 100,000 mark; other large Italian cities seem to have been around 50,000 in the early fourteenth century. Ghent had at least 40,000, Bruges and Brussels over 30,000, Toulouse and the towns of southern France under 20,000.[3] Despite the curious reluctance of some English historians to admit it, there seem to be no *a priori* grounds for believing that London was any smaller than Brussels or even Ghent.

This is speculation. What is certain is that from the reign of

[1] The argument on which this estimate of population is based is set out in detail in the 'Note on the Population of London' in the Appendix.

[2] S. L. Thrupp, *op. cit.*, 1, and see *The Italian Relation of England*, quoted as title-motto in E. M. Carus-Wilson, 'The overseas trade of Bristol', reprinted in *Medieval Merchant Venturers*.

[3] F. Lot, *op. cit.*, i, 24–204; ii, 337–405; iii, 144–603; *Rapports du ixe. Congrès International des Sciences Historiques 1950*, p. 65.

John to that of Edward II, London was growing and, in thirteenth-century terms, growing rapidly, absorbing an increasingly heavy intake of immigrants and possibly maintaining a respectable natural increment. Its growth cannot be measured in precise quantitative terms, but probably the population doubled, rising from somewhere around 20,000 in the early thirteenth century to somewhere around 40,000 in the early fourteenth.

This was the basic problem which confronted Londoners in their new-found autonomy, the problem of growth, of adaptation to a new and rapidly changing community in a nation which was approaching maturity. The mental equipment they brought to the task was at once complex and crude. Pride, certainly—this is writ large across custumal and chronicle. 'Among the noble cities of the world that are celebrated by Fame', proclaimed fitz Stephen, 'the CITY OF LONDON, seat of the monarchy of England, is one that spreads its fame wider, sends its wealth and wares further, and lifts its head higher than all others.'[1] The matrons of London are very Sabines, the city itself far older and more venerable than Rome—sentiments which would have appeared equally self-evident to that fifteenth-century tailor who assumed as a matter of course that possession of the London franchise was a fact to which the Almighty should give serious attention.[2]

Yet, allied to it were a cat-like caution in the face of royal authority, a shrewd, subtle and cynical calculation, which at times approach servility and double-dealing. No less paradoxical was the co-existence, sometimes in the same person, of that sophistication which graces their custumals and legal processes with that capacity for direct and even brutal simplicity which sent fraudulent fishmongers parading through Cheap with their rotten fish slung underneath their miscreant noses, which burdened one respectable family with the official patronymic Never-at-Home, and which identified the potent aldermanic dynasty of Bucointe by its founder's 'oily mouth'. Arnold fitz Thedmar the chronicler, embodiment of the bourgeois virtues,

[1] William fitz Stephen's description of London, translated by H. E. Butler, is printed in F. M. Stenton, *Norman London*, pp. 25–32.
[2] Will of Richard Chalkhill, quoted in S. L. Thrupp, *op. cit.*, 1.

solemnly recounts the miracles which appropriately attended his birth; the knowing author of the *French Chronicle* explains the popular attack on the queen in 1263 in terms of the Fair Rosamunde; the rector of St. Margaret Lothbury, in 1300, imports four putrid wolves in a cask to cure an unknown disease, called *le Loup*, from which no-one is suffering.[1]

Their aldermen wore the scarlet, were clad in awesome majesty and vested with terrifying power, but that did not save them from rude, derisive and 'English' snorts of 'Trrphut! Trrphut!' from the incorrigibly vulgar. The very conservatism for which the Londoners were renowned was not really conservatism at all, but the almost instinctive reaction of an insecure and cosmopolitan community set in a feudal environment of headstrong barons and aggressive kings. To the Londoners, every archaic word of a dusty charter was a shield against oppression and disinheritance. And this siege mentality was complemented by a capacity for reckless violence which is their most immediate and vivid characteristic. Trivial quarrels over chequers and ale degenerated with unnerving speed into brawls of fatal consequence, as ill-paid and idle private chaplains so often took the lead in a kind of chain-development of violence which sometimes did not stop short of mass riot.[2] William Woodcock, the tailor who turned up at Guildhall on election day in 1384, armed with sword, buckler and pole-axe, '*hoping* that a riot would arise', had plenty of spiritual brethren in the previous century.[3]

Violence was endemic. Tourneys were the most popular sport, on land, water or ice; two held at Fulham in 1305 stopped all work in London for a week. Wrestling matches at Clerkenwell wrecked the priory wall. The public disputations of scholars, where 'enthymemes were hurtled in a wrestling bout of wit', were as popular as the cock-fights. 'The only plagues of London', said fitz Stephen, 'are the immoderate drinking of fools and the frequency of fires.' For the former there was certainly ample scope. In 1309 there were 354 taverns

---

[1] See Misc. Roll AA, p. 7; *Lib. de Ant. Leg.*, pp. 238, 239; *French Chronicle*, pp. 3–5; Riley, *Memorials, passim.*

[2] For one example, in 1305, see *Cal. Coroners Rolls*, pp. 28–30.

[3] *P. and M. Rolls*, iii, 67; my italics.

and 1,334 brew-shops in the city.[1] The smallest liquor measure in the civic records is a quart.

Indeed, there is a quality of almost juvenile inebriation about their violence, as there is about their politics, which were often simply another expression of it. London was not a large town in any absolute sense. Everyone knew everyone else. The social unit was easily comprehended and every institution was represented by people to whom the Londoner could give a personal name. In consequence, their political conflicts were as bitter and yet as ephemeral as their brawls. There was little ideological content and a compensatory abundance of energy. For the men of London, whether they were court scriveners decorating the margin of the record with caricatures of lawyers with ever-open mouths, uproarious apprentices rolling barrels full of stones down Dowgate hill, or outraged aldermen lecturing the king on his duties to his face, were men of vitality.

Vitality was curbed and channelled by the traditions they had inherited from a feudal and paternalistic past, and by the influence of the Church, in its doctrine, its practice and its ritual. There were no heretics, no Brethren of the Free Spirit. One witch was a sensation.[2] Among the moneyed classes, in particular, preoccupation with life after death, intensive application to formal ritual, and an overriding concern with atonement were almost obsessive, as was perhaps natural, given the current canonical ambiguities on wealth, trade and usury. Personal chaplains were common earlier in London than elsewhere in England; chapel-building was an aldermanic duty, chantry-endowment a fashion, and bequests to the Church munificent.[3] With it went a creditable care for the poor, for widows, who had a legal right to a third of a husband's property, if they had not been dowered with a specific 'free-bench' on marriage, and for orphans, whose funds were administered by the council. There was much diffused poor-relief. Women enjoyed status, could manage a business, and no doubt much

[1] See *Ann. Lond.*, pp. 138–57; *Ann. Paul.*, p. 267; *Cart. S.M. Clerkenwell*, p. 260; F. M. Stenton, *op. cit.*, 28, 30.

[2] *Ann. Lond.*, p. 236; *Ann. Paul.*, pp. 275, 276.

[3] There is an excellent specimen of a *bien-pensant* aldermanic testament in Ancient Deeds E 16; see also *Cal. of Wills*, i, 239, 328, 603, 649, 651 and *passim*, and J. R. H. Moorman, *Church Life in England in the Thirteenth Century* (London, 1946), pp. 15–18.

besides, if Chaucer be any warrant. The city cared for its children. The parish gild was an instrument of civilization. So were those craft gilds which often grew out of them and whose multiplication was the most striking social phenomenon of the period. Whatever their economic function, the poor-box of the gilds, their fraternities, their imposition of professional standards and their co-operative ethos were civilizing influences.

For what could be more civilized than the Feste du Pui?[1] With all the paraphernalia typical of a gild, the annual mass at St. Helen's, the light in St. Martin-le-Grand, the poor-box, and the private Guildhall chapel of St. Mary, its functions were primarily musical and convivial. Its objects were 'bon amour, joly desport et curtais solas joie et doucour entre gent norir et enhauncer', aims achieved by communal feasts, at which members presented songs of their own composing, to win the title of 'Prince' for the year. A crown was awarded to the best song, a copy of which was attached to the new prince's arms in hall. The old prince paraded the hall, crowned and singing, and presented a gilded cup of wine to the new, as a sign of election. After the feast, members rode through London, escorting the new prince to his home, where they drank and danced as farewell. No gluttony was tolerated. Each of the *amerous compaignoun* was served with good bread, ale and wine, then potage, one course of solid meat, a double roast in a dish, and cheese—and no more. From this frugal repast, ladies were excluded, so that members might learn to 'honour cheir et loer trestotes dames, totes houres en tous lieus, au taunt en lour absence come en lour presence'.

The Pui, however, was a patrician society. Its members were 'marchaunts hauntauns les feires'. A man could join only 'sil soit suffisaunt'. Sufficiency was the key to the good life, to public respect, rights and responsibilities, and sufficiency it-self, though breeding counted, rested in the last analysis on the ultimate sanction of wealth. For London was a hierarchical society, class and sub-class spaced out along the spectrum of

---

[1] The ordinances of the Pui are set out in *Lib. Cust.*, pp. 216–28; a similar type o society, under the same name, existed in many towns—see L. Verriest, *Les lutte^s sociales et le contrat d'apprentissage à Tournai jusqu'en 1424* (Brussels, 1912), pp. 8, 9' on the gilds in general, see G. Unwin, *The Gilds and Companies of London* (London' 1908).

minutely graded landed and monetary substance. With the exception of Bridge and Billingsgate, where middle class fishmongers were numerous, the tax returns of 1292–1332 reflect a society in which inequality was rooted. *Potentiores, mediocres, populares,*[1] the submerged population of non-citizens and paupers, shading off into the large and mobile underworld of displaced and endemic criminality, were clearly differentiated. Alderman John Wade had one of the great houses built around a square, with a grand hall, wings to street and rear, and warehouses to complete the pattern, but many shops measured as little as five or six feet by ten, with a living-room above; thousands lived, ate, worked and slept in an airless solar in some alley tenement. Katherine de la Ryole could cherish her hallchest of ivory garnished with silver, Juliana Russel her tapestries and silver cups of Tours, but the majority, in their rough burel, ate off wooden dishes and counted themselves lucky if they owned the tools they worked with. In 1257 the aldermen claimed that many in the city simply did not possess goods to the value of one of the king's new golden pennies, and for many Londoners, their only epitaph was the refrain monotonously reiterated by the coroners' rolls—'Chattels and goods had he none.'[2]

The acceptance of inequality was rooted no less firmly in men's minds, in the recognized vocabulary of political discourse. The adjustment of political to social realities was the prime public task, and during the thirteenth and early fourteenth centuries, it became a task of increasing difficulty and urgency. As social horizons broadened, new groups and interests jostled for supremacy, new families climbed the social scale, and new forms of economic organization strove to establish themselves, against a background of intensifying population pressure. Within a generation, the structure of the new commune was feeling the strain. For, ultimately, most social problems resolved themselves into questions of political rights and duties, of constitutional order. Autonomous London had to resolve those contradictions, even as it had to find and keep

[1] These terms, the more powerful, the middling people, the populace, were typical of the conventional vocabulary of social discourse.

[2] See, for example, A.R. 541b, m. 23; *Cal. of Wills*, i, 173, 174; *Lib. de Ant. Leg.*, p. 30; *Cal. Coroners Rolls*, pp. 5, 8, 10, 11, 12, 13, 18 and *passim*.

its place in the new community of the realm of England, which was rapidly taking shape. This is the question which lies at the heart of London's history in the years between Magna Carta and the Hundred Years' War. Could the city find an adequate response to the challenge implicit in fitz Stephen's ambiguous salutation—'In truth a good city when it has a good lord'?'

CHAPTER II

The Structure of Government

THE London which achieved self-government in the early thirteenth century was a community intensely conscious of itself. Its institutions were complex and its population heterogeneous, but a long tradition of concerted action had imbued its citizens with an acute sense of the personality of their city. A fourteenth-century clerk could call it a *respublica*.[1]

The independence of the Londoners, however, was strictly limited. They were still subject to the justices itinerant and the justices of appeal at St. Martin-le-Grand, to the royal power of taxation and the overall jurisdiction of the king and his council. Their mayor had to be presented and sworn in the royal presence; not until 1253 were they allowed to present him to the Exchequer in the king's absence.[2] The position of the sheriffs was ambiguous and there was plenty of scope for disagreement. For three generations, London's liberty was fragile, subject to frequent suspension by Henry III and a resolute attack by Edward I. Feudal authority itself proved remarkably persistent. Montfichet and Castle Baynard, fitz Stephen's 'two strong castles in the west', were strongholds of seigneurial jurisdiction. The lord of Castle Baynard was the city's *Procurator*, commander of the city host and banneret of London. His soke enjoyed wide privileges and he sat beside the mayor in the Husting; and in the person of Robert fitz Walter, the *Procurator* was still in full possession of his powers in 1215.[3]

Throughout the thirteenth century, the governing groups in the city represented a political interest which was chronically insecure. There was an obsessive preoccupation with measures

---

[1] *P. and M. Rolls*, ii, 291. [2] *Lib. de Ant. Leg.*, pp. 19–20.
[3] *Lib. Cust.*, pp. 147–51; M. Bateson, *op. cit.*, 485–6; W. Page, *op. cit.*, 138, 139; F. M. Stenton, *op. cit.*, 7, 8, 27.

designed to deflect royal wrath. City clerks faithfully recopied John Carpenter's slightly shame-faced recitation of the elaborate precautions to be taken at the Iters, and the fear of a public display of faction which might provoke royal intervention affected the temper of political life, strengthening the trend towards oligarchical forms of government.[1] Perhaps for this very reason, the communal council was remorseless in its ambition, jealously extending its authority, reducing the sokes to its instruments, provoking the royal justices to the loud complaint in 1244, 'quod maior et cives semper calumpniaverunt set nichil profuit!'[2] Nothing is heard of the *Procurator* in the wars of mid-century, and in 1275 Castle Baynard and Montfichet passed to the Dominicans to become the house of the order at Blackfriars.[3] With every year, London's autonomy became more secure. By the reign of Edward I, its liberties were hardening into a tradition. The king's destruction of the franchise in 1285 was widely regarded as an affront to the great charters. It was reversed during the crisis of 1297 and thirty years later, Edward III, as a reward for the Londoners' support in the rising of 1326, granted them a charter whose liberal terms swept away insecurity for many years.[4]

Of crucial importance, therefore, was the character of the ruling council. The years following the creation of the commune in 1191 were years of high political temper, but when the dust had settled, it was the court of aldermen which emerged as the centre of control.[5] They had long exercised jurisdiction in the wards and guided proceedings in the Husting. Power in the commune passed to them and the class from which they were drawn. The mayor, elected on 28 October, was invariably an alderman. Re-election was frequent, and before 1340 no more than fifty men held office.[6] The two sheriffs, usually chosen on

[1] See, for example, *Lib. Albus*, pp. 54 ff.
[2] Misc. Roll AA, p. 69.
[3] *C.P.R. 1272–81*, pp. 96–8 and *passim*; *Cal. Letter-Bk. C*, 71–2; Weinbaum, ii, 146.
[4] See Chapters IX and XI.
[5] On this period, see *Lib. de Ant. Leg.*, p. 2; M. Bateson, *op. cit.*, 507–11; J. H. Round, *The Commune of London*, pp. 235–45; W. Page, *op. cit.*, 116–18; J. Tait, *op. cit.*, 266 ff., 288.
[6] A. B. Beaven, *The Aldermen of the City of London*, 2 vols (London, 1908–13), ii, xxiii, xxvii; *Lib. de Ant. Leg.*, *passim*; the one exception, Henry le Waleys in 1298, was a special case—see Chapter IX.

the Monday before Michaelmas, were also re-elected from time to time, despite the prohibition of this practice in 1230. Not all were aldermen when elected, but many joined the council after their tour of duty and there was no difference socially between the sheriffs and the aldermen themselves.[1] The central political fact of independence was the elevation of the aldermanic court, with its senior member the mayor, into the sovereign council of the city.

An immediate consequence was a striking decline in the relative importance of the sheriff. In the twelfth century, he had dominated the scene. As the Husting was the city equivalent of the county court, so the ward, with its alderman, corresponded to the hundred. To fitz Stephen, the aldermen were senators, the sheriffs consuls.[2] Even at this date, however, aldermen hardly ranked as mere reeves. They were the dooms-men, *judices*, and long before autonomy, it was they who decided in a case of affray whether the suit was a crown plea or not. All disputed points of law were referred to them, and, even in the sheriffs' court, it was they who pronounced judgment.[3] Self-government brought its own problems. The farm, no burden in itself, could be made intolerable by an unforeseen disaster, and to the sheriff a royal Iter was one long agony of amercements. The Exchequer was implacable, pursuing defaulters and their descendants even into France. When the sheriffs failed, the citizens were made responsible. They resisted, levying the debts forcibly from the property of three former sheriffs in the twenties and, in 1296, paying the arrears of a sheriff who had died seventy years before only when bludgeoned into it by a process in the Exchequer. In 1299 they ordered the imprisonment of any sheriff in default at a preliminary audit of the farm and the unfortunate Martin de Aumbresbury spent most of the time between 1299 and 1303 passing in and out of prison under this rule.[4] In sheer self-defence, the Londoners were driven to

[1] *Lib. de Ant. Leg.*, p. 6 and *passim*; *Cal. Letter-Bks.*, *passim*.

[2] A. H. Thomas, *P. and M. Rolls*, iv, xxx; F. M. Stenton, *op. cit.*, 10, 30.

[3] Lib. Ordinationum, fo. 173b; *Lib. Albus*, p. 214; M. Bateson, *op. cit.*, 487–8.

[4] Misc. Roll AA; Misc. Roll BB; Lib. Ordinationum, fo. 174; L.T.R.M.R. 4, m. 13d; 13, m. 4d; *Select Cases in the Exchequer of Pleas*, ed. H. Jenkinson and B. E. R. Formoy, Selden Society (London, 1932), pp. 136–8; *C.P.R. 1272–81*, p. 431; *Cal. Letter-Bk. B*, 85, *C*, 34–9, 62–4; *Lib. Cust.*, pp. 91–2, 285 ff.; amercement was a payment for pardon made to the king when an offence had put the transgressor 'in mercy'.

bring the sheriffs under civic control. Their dual status caused
further trouble. Time and time again they were called upon to
execute royal writs known to be contrary to the city's liberties,
forced to make defiant or ambiguous returns according to the
political climate of the moment. As a safeguard, the council
ultimately compelled all sheriffs' officers to swear an oath of
obedience to the mayor, and the law-books held that this oath
took priority over their oath to the sheriffs themselves.[1]

Mayoral and aldermanic control was rapidly established.
From a very early date, the council was supervising the disposal
of shrieval records. In 1283 they forbade the leasing of Middlesex.[2] Appeals against the sheriff went to the mayor's court, and
even in the Husting, the 'county court', the sheriff was reduced
to the status of a 'minister' of the mayor, 'nientcountreestaunt',
as the law-book put it, 'qe le brief originale soit direct au Mair
et viscountz en comune'.[3] By the time John Carpenter compiled
his *Liber Albus* from fourteenth-century records, their subjection
was complete. The London sheriffs were no longer the right
hand of the king. They were the 'eyes of the mayor'.[4]

For it was the mayor who assumed the premier rank. He
was the personification of the city. All courts, even the ancient
wardmoots, were considered to be held by his warrant. All
officials derived their authority from him. By his oath a delegate of the king, he promulgated all civic ordinances, for no
legislation was valid without his presence. His court became the
most powerful urban tribunal in the realm. He had a guard of
honour, a personal sword-bearer well-versed in the etiquette of
chivalry; his Common Crier and staff of serjeants were horsed
for the honour of the city. His name was linked to that of the
old justiciar and as chief 'baron' of the city, he ranked as an
earl, his sword borne ceremonially before him. He was the
central figure in the complex and colourful rituals which the
city had evolved for itself, when at All Saints, Christmas, Cir-
cumcision, Epiphany, Purification and Whitsun, he led great
processions representing the city, Middlesex and Essex to

---

[1] *Cal. Letter-Bk. C*, 178, 179; *Lib. Albus*, pp. 45, 46 and *passim*.
[2] Lib. Ordinationum, fo. 172b; *Cal. Letter-Bk. A*, 206; *Lib. Cust.*, p. 91.
[3] *Lib. Albus*, pp. 183, 184, 219; see *Cal. E.M.C. Rolls, passim*.
[4] *Lib. Albus*, p. 42.

solemn services of dedication at the mother cathedral of St. Paul's and at St. Thomas Acon in Cheap, raised to the memory of Thomas Becket, a martyr London claimed as its own. The most important day of the political year was 28 October, when the new mayor took the oath at Westminster in solemn ceremony. After a brilliant pageant, he gave a banquet at his home, offered prayers in St. Paul's for Bishop William, who had preserved London at the Conquest, led the aldermen in ritual chant at the Becket grave and in a torchlight procession through Cheap to the house of St. Thomas.[1] So was the mayor identified with and assimilated into the body of civic tradition, which became a living reality in his person.

But what was the mayor save the chosen leader of his colleagues? London was governed by the aldermen, 'seniores non propter senectutem sed propter sapientiam', as the author of *Liber Ordinationum* optimistically remarks.[2] The office was of great antiquity.[3] The first direct reference occurs in the middle of the tenth century; aldermen appear in conjunction with the wards in 1111; all twenty-four had probably made their appearance before the early twelfth century. In essence, they were lawmen. As the compurgators testified, so the aldermen gave judgment. Their presence was required in every court and they had a special responsibility for land and tenurial relationships. Keeping of the peace was a prime duty. In London, the king made use of the city's own officers and the powers extended to the keepers in the counties after 1332 seem to have been granted to the city many years earlier. More and more, aldermen tended to act as justices themselves and in 1299 one of them could be officially described as 'justice and guardian of the vill'.[4]

Key figures in the military organization of the city, they supervised the assize of arms and led out the parish contingents

---

[1] See Lib. Ordinationum, fo. 174; *Lib. Albus*, pp. 12, 13, 23–30, 49.

[2] Lib. Ordinationum, fo. 194b–195.

[3] There is a thorough and sometimes entertaining account of the office in Beaven, ii, xi–lx; see also A. H. Thomas, *P. and M. Rolls*, iv, xxx–xli; F. M. Stenton, *op. cit.*, 10–13, 15–16; W. Page, *op. cit.*, 173–229.

[4] *Lib. Albus*, pp. 67, 114, 182, 189, 190, 214; Misc. Roll AA, pp. 50–1; *Cal. Letter-Bk. C*, 108; M. Bateson, *op. cit.*, 487, 488, 491, 506, 708, 715–18, 726–8; A. H. Thomas, *P. and M. Rolls*, iv, x–xii; *Cal. E.M.C. Rolls*, p. 6.

under the banners of their wards. The maintenance of order, the endless wardmoot inquests, indeed, the whole apparatus of administration was under their control.[1] As city governors they were omnicompetent, and when one of them was robbed in 1304 the court roll gives a vivid picture of his ward treasure chest, crammed full with charters, letters obligatory, tallies, rolls and memoranda, all the documentary witnesses to the intense and ceaseless administrative life of his ward.[2]

Such judicial, military, police and administrative power was naturally invested with awful dignity. The pride of these men is writ large across record and chronicle. They wore the robes of justice, their funerals were pageants. Their names were prefixed by 'Dominus' or 'Sire', their wives were 'Dames'. In 1302 a man was accused of abusing the tax-collectors and the aldermen, thus insulting king and commune respectively. It was proved that he had in fact berated the collectors, but not the aldermen—and the case against him was promptly dismissed. In 1298 Alderman Adam de Rokesle, as *minister pacis*, intervened in a brawl in Thames Street, and in the fracas which followed, one misguided wretch, not content with cursing Adam, struck him in the face. To atone for this enormity, he was compelled to walk in penance, clad only in a tunic, from the place of offence to Guildhall. In his hand he carried an axe to signify his liability to the ancient penalty for striking an alderman, the loss of the offending hand.[3] Clearly the nature of aldermanic office and the method of recruitment were issues of crucial importance.

Aldermanic office was certainly attractive. Its prestige and power were very real. Nominally unpaid, an alderman was allowed to enrol his deeds and recognizances free of charge. He received a two-shilling fee on all land transactions in his ward, fourpence for every baker's stamp registered with him and three-farthings of the fourpence fine paid by wardmoot defaulters.[4] The perennial concern with food prices made

[1] See *Lib. Albus*, pp. 36–9, 257–60, and *Cal. Letter-Bks.*, *passim*.

[2] *Cal. E.M.C. Rolls*, pp. 164, 165.

[3] For these cases, see *Cal. E.M.C. Rolls*, pp. 6, 7, 255.

[4] Lib. Ordinationum, fo. 173; *Lib. Albus*, pp. 35, 38; M. Bateson, *op. cit.*, 491; *Cal. Letter-Bks.*, Hust. Rolls and Recog. Rolls, *passim*, for marginal entries 'nil quia aldermanus'.

aldermanic participation in the retail grain trade suspect and brewing for the retail market was specifically forbidden. Some trades were regarded as too inferior socially, but there was no hard-and-fast rule. Wit, wealth and wisdom were Carpenter's requirements.[1] Inevitably, office fell to rich men of known character and ability and, in the earlier half of the thirteenth century, to members of great civic dynasties.

Under the commune, aldermanic office was elective, but there was evidently a strong tradition of proprietary jurisdiction. Portsoken was a case apart, for when the extramural estate of the *cnihtenagild* of prominent Londoners was granted to Holy Trinity in 1125, the new soke of the priory became the only extramural ward, and the prior the only soke-lord who was *ex officio* a ward alderman, presumably in succession to the aldermen of the gild.[2] More striking is the example of Ludgate-Newgate. In 1265, after the Barons' Wars, its Montfortian alderman Michael Tovy was imprisoned, and the ward passed, probably by royal grant, to Thomas de Arderne, a Middlesex landowner, who leased the aldermanry to a kinsman of Tovy's. After the death of the incumbent, Arderne sold the office to Ralph le Fevre, whose son John passed it on to William de Farndon. In 1294 John's brother Nicholas, who had married Farndon's daughter and taken his name, received it from his father-in-law and forty years later bequeathed the aldermanry, now bearing the name of Farringdon (Farndon) to John Pulteney. Pulteney never held this ward and it passed to Richard Lacer, after which aldermen were elected in the usual way. The persistence of proprietary attitudes in this case, which proved no less puzzling to the contemporary Husting, may have owed something to the fact that the ward was coterminous with the ancient soke of the king of Scotland, granted to Roger fitz Reinfred by Henry II.[3]

There were plenty of other proprietary echoes in the political discourse of the thirteenth-century Londoner. Most of his

---

[1] Lib. Ordinationum, fo. 173b; *Lib. Albus*, p. 33.

[2] Hust. Roll (Common Pleas) 6, m. 1d; F. M. Stenton, *op. cit.*, 13–15; W. Page, *op. cit.*, 181; Beaven, ii, xvi; the gild appears to have been a social and religious association.

[3] Hust. Roll 13(57); Hust. Roll (Land) 2, m.5; *Cal. of Wills*, i, 398; A.R. 543, *passim*; Beaven, ii, xvi–xvii; W. Page, *op. cit.*, 181–4.

aldermen in the early years of the century were provided by a handful of rooted civic dynasties who exercised an almost hereditary authority. The early ward lists designate most wards by personal names. There are some curious instances of wards being identified by the names of parishes. The first completely territorial list is that of 1285 and even so, tax-returns of the nineties use both methods and Ludgate-Newgate took the name of Farringdon as late as the fourteenth century.[1] There were so many sokes, so many proprietary churches. In 1244 an alderman's ward was called his 'soke' and thirty years later the prior of Merton's soke-reeve was described as his 'alderman'.[2]

Nine other wards beside Portsoken and Farringdon were coterminous with ancient sokes,[3] and the strength of the proprietary tradition probably derives from the very mixed origin of the wards themselves. Their topography is extremely varied. Some peculiarly tortuous boundaries were probably fixed by property limits. Other wards were formed around axial thoroughfares, gates and street-markets. The form of some has no apparent meaning.[4] The most credible explanation of this variety is that which places their period of growth, if not of origin, in the Danish wars. Trade centres and settlements of craftsmen on the one hand, sokes of land-owners on the other, formed natural units for the supply of men and were the nuclei of the wards.[5] In the conditions of the time, soke-wards would have provided hereditary aldermen, the others aldermen selected from their leading families. In all probability, the change to uniform electoral practice coincided with the estabment of the commune.[6] New council may have been nothing but old judiciary writ large, but theoretically, it marked a clean

---

[1] *Cal. Letter-Bk. A*, 209; Ekwall, *Two Early London Subsidy Rolls*, pp. 139–204; *Pipe Roll 14 Henry III* (Princeton, 1927); J. Tait, 'Two unknown names of early London wards', *London Topographical Record*, xv (1931), 1–3.

[2] Misc. Roll AA, p. 55; Hust. Roll (Land) 1, m.9; see also W.A.M. 25372; Cur. Reg. Roll 191, m. 6d; K.R.M.R. 40, m.12.

[3] Queenhithe, Castle Baynard, Aldersgate, Cripplegate, Cornhill, Bishopsgate, Aldgate, Tower and Walbrook—W. Page, *op. cit.*, 173.

[4] There is a good topographical analysis of the wards in H. A. Harben, *A Dictionary of London* (London, 1918), pp. 610–11; see also W. Page, *op. cit.*, 173–6.

[5] A. H. Thomas, *P. and M. Rolls*, iv, xxxiii–xxxiv.

[6] Fitz Thedmar's reference, under 1201, to the election of a body of 'twenty-five' to govern the city may be a garbled account of the process (*Lib. de Ant. Leg.*, p. 2).

D

break with the past. The commune carried with it the ideal of responsibility and the practice of election. The change would make little real difference, would represent, basically, a re-organization of the old governing body into more coherent form. Social inertia would account for the persistent confusion of private and public jurisdiction and for the relapse into pro-prietary modes in Farringdon. It took time for the electoral tradition to strike root.

Certainly by 1249, date of the earliest recorded aldermanic election, it was firmly established.[1] The practice was for the *probi homines* of the ward to make their choice and present him before the mayor and aldermen in Husting. If acceptable, he was sworn and admitted. He could resign if he wished, and in times of crisis he could be deposed, by king or colleagues, but he was undisturbed by the painful necessity to present himself for re-election. Annual election of aldermen, when it came in 1319, came as a victory for a reforming movement and did not last long. The demand was renewed in 1376, with equally ephemeral success. Carpenter states unequivocally that alder-men were not removable except for some grave misdemeanour and in 1394 an edict which made an aldermanry tenable till death was described as a reversion to traditional custom.[2] Aldermen were elected for life unless they gravely offended king, colleagues, or public morality.

Announcements of elections in the rolls are terse and unin-formative.[3] Only for one brief moment in 1298 is it possible to glimpse something of the reality behind them. In that year, the city recovered its franchise after it had been lost for thirteen years, and the aldermen took the opportunity to purge their ranks of king's men. A veritable spate of elections ensued and as the scattered announcements are pieced together a remark-able picture emerges of eleven weeks of continuous shuffling and re-shuffling of seats.[4] At nearly all the elections, the *probi*

---

[1] *Lib. de Ant. Leg.*, p. 15.

[2] See Hust. Rolls, *passim*; *Lib. Cust.*, p. 269; *Lib. Albus*, pp. 35–6; for some depositions, see *Lib. de Ant. Leg.*, pp. 15, 33 ff., 168–9; for a resignation, *Ann. Lond.*, p. 50; see also R. Bird, *The Turbulent London of Richard II* (London, 1949), pp. 30–1.

[3] For an example, see Hust. Roll (Common Pleas) 2, m.1.

[4] The story may be reconstructed from announcements of elections in Hust. Roll (Common Pleas) 24, interlocutaria, m. a, b dorse and c and the evidence of tenure cited in Beaven, i, 375–80.

presented two alternative candidates. Final choice remained with the council. Translations were frequent, and in face of them, the elections assume an unreal air. Bishopsgate provides the most striking example, for this poverty-stricken ward had four different aldermen in eleven weeks. On 5 May, after the removal of their alderman, the *probi* presented Ralph de Honilane and John de Storteford. Honilane was admitted. But on 2 June, Bread Street fell vacant and Honilane was elected to it. Bishopsgate promptly presented his former rival Storteford, but the presentment was ignored, Nicholas Picot being sworn alderman a week later. On 7 July, however, Picot, with John le Chaucer (a rejected candidate for Billingsgate) was presented for Coleman Street. Picot was sworn and he promptly left Bishopsgate vacant once more. At last, on 21 July, no doubt to the final despair of Storteford, John de Northampton, a rejected candidate for Cheap, was sworn.

The opinion of the council was decisive. Chaucer and Storteford were evidently unacceptable, whatever the wishes of the *probi*. In *Liber Albus*, Carpenter gives a detailed account of fourteenth-century practice. It was the mayor who ordered the election and who summoned the 'maiorem et saniorem partem' of the *probi* to take part. They were given two weeks of grace. If an unsuitable person were presented, the council could refuse him. If the ward persisted in its bad taste, power of nomination passed finally to the mayor and aldermen.[1] The grip of the council must have been even closer in more uninhibited times, before the joint pressure of royal and popular discontent had somewhat diminished the joys of aldermanic immunity. The commune, after all, owed its existence to its directive élite of patrician families. They would decide who were to be admitted to their select circle.

The power of their council rested on the consent of the politically important, for they could not govern without support, at least among the articulate classes. It was the city's apparatus of courts and assemblies which supplied the instruments of political action and which was, in the last resort, the only internal check to aldermanic authority. The oldest assembly in the city and the premier in dignity was the Folkmoot, the

[1] *Lib. Albus*, pp. 39–40.

original 'thing', the primitive gathering of burgmen. By the thirteenth century, it had become the great formal gathering of the citizens, meeting three times a year at St. Paul's Cross. The moot was the proper setting for a proclamation of out-lawry. Attendance was compulsory for all freemen who heard the great bell of St. Paul's and a fine of £2 was inflicted on absentees. Even here, however, the record speaks of *prud-hommes* being summoned by ward beadles, for the complicated life of a great city could hardly be regulated by a mass-meeting.[1] This was the function of the courts, the specialized sheriffs' and chamberlain's tribunals, and, above all, of the great central court of Husting. The Husting was probably as old as the Folk-moot itself and had long been the city's major tribunal. During the thirteenth century, personal actions and actions by plaint tended to pass to the new mayor's court and the Husting, meet-ing on the Monday and later the Tuesday also, at Guildhall, became a formal court concerned primarily with land.[2] But administrative business continued to occupy it and, indeed, in their administrative functions, it is often impossible to dis-tinguish between mayor's court, court of aldermen and the Husting itself. The increasing complexity of public business, the difficulty of identifying freemen in mass-meetings and the establishment of the commune stimulated the development of these administrative assemblies and the Folkmoot lost much of its vitality. By mid-century, it seems archaic and moribund and in 1285 its very site disappeared into the churchyard of St. Paul's.[3]

What replaced it as a communal organ was the admini-strative assembly, the *congregatio*, as it was called later. From the outset, selected citizens had been associated with the aldermen in the government of the city. The communal oath of 1193 en-joined obedience to *probi homines* bracketed with the mayor and aldermen and the earliest known collection of civic ordinances took pains to exclude undesirables from counsel. It was in-tolerable that 'passim et indifferenter', anyone should intrude

[1] Lib. Ordinationum, fo. 194b–5; *Lib. Albus*, pp. 118–19; M. Bateson, *op. cit.*, 502–5, 708.
[2] *Lib. Albus*, pp. 181–99; *Lib. Cust.*, p. 39; *Lib. de Ant. Leg.*, pp. 45 and *passim*; see Chapter IV.
[3] St. Paul's A/70/1756; *Lib. Cust.*, pp. 338–44.

into the council chamber, so a guard was placed at Guildhall and no-one was allowed to enter unless he were 'de consilio sive vocatus ad consilium'.[1] At the Iter of 1221, the jurors drew a sharp distinction between this council and the Folkmoot. No fines were paid by absentees and the council's decisions had force of law no matter what the number of defaulters. An identical verdict was given a hundred years later.[2]

In law, the will of the suitors of the Husting, whatever their number, was regarded as the will of the conscious citizenry, and the prevalence of this same attitude among the administrative assemblies is a clear pointer to their source of origin. Within the Husting, there was a body of men of superior status, the famous occupiers of the 'four benches', traces of whose elusive fraternity have been left in ordinance and law-book. They were the law-men, the worthy, 'better' citizens, learned in the lore of city custom, who formed the nucleus of the court. They were reinforced by selected *probi* regularly summoned from the wards, to provide jurors and pass upon inquests. For the common pleas, the wards sent six men; for land pleas, twelve. All had to be freeholders of the 'more sufficient' sort.[3]

The pattern of the administrative assembly was similar. There is evidence of an inner council. In later years, for example, at the coming of an Iter, preparations were made by the mayor and aldermen together with a select group of twenty-four elected out of Common Council.[4] The first register of councillors to survive dates from 1285 and it is in many respects unusual. It refers to an oath sworn by councillors, unique for this period, and the basic number of ward representatives is two, a quota encountered again in an assembly of 1322, when to manage a tax assessment the *probi* elected a committee of two men from every ward, 'to save the commonalty trouble'.[5] The 1285 list

---

[1] Lib. Ordinationum, fo. 173b; *Lib. Albus*, p. 51; and see M. Bateson, *op. cit.*, 510–11, 719–30.

[2] *Lib. Albus*, pp. 69–70; *Cal. Letter-Bk. E*, 147.

[3] See M. Bateson, *op. cit.*, 489, 499; *Lib. Albus*, pp. 182, 189, 190.

[4] *Lib. Albus*, pp. 51, 55.

[5] *Cal. Letter-Bk. A*, 209–10, *E*, 174. J. Tait, *The Medieval English Borough*, p. 308, misinterprets the election of the committee in 1322. It did not imply the general grant of power to elect assembly-men to the wards; councillors in general continued to be nominees.

may have been a register of this inner council, a standing body constantly at hand, to be reinforced whenever necessary by summons to the wards.

For the majority of known administrative assemblies consisted of gatherings of ward-representatives similar to those which met for the pleas of Husting. Proportional representation by wards was of course an obvious method, one used constantly for all manner of purposes.[1] Administrative assemblies were regularly recorded only after 1285, when royal officers took over the government of the city. The regularity they imposed survived the recovery of the franchise, but from the middle of the reign of Edward II, when a reform movement remodelled the civic constitution, assemblies tended increasingly to be blanketed under the stock formula, 'Mayor, Aldermen and Commonalty'. Altogether, between 1291 and 1331, thirty administrative assemblies are recorded in some detail.[2] In a number of cases, councillors are hidden under the general description 'others'. For one or two assemblies a simple list of names is given, but close scrutiny of personnel reveals that these, too, represent fixed numbers of men from the wards.[3] Most give the names of representatives by ward. One to four were the most common quotas. More important decisions, the levy of a tax or the preparation of accounts, called for six representatives. London's parliamentary members were chosen by a similar assembly, which nominated either two individuals or a panel, sometimes as numerous as ten, who would select two of their number, presumably at their convenience. Aldermen, and lawyers in particular, were generally chosen, though sometimes an assembly-man was picked. Occasionally, aldermen on the one hand and councillors on the other would nominate separate individuals or panels. Six ward-

---

[1] See, for example, *Pat. Rolls 1225–32*, p. 132; *Lib. de Ant. Leg.*, p. 32; *Cal. Letter-Bk. A*, 211–12.

[2] For these assemblies, see *Cal. Letter-Bk. B*, 236–46, *C*, 3–143, *D*, 231–52, *E*, 80–254, *passim*.

[3] For example, in an undifferentiated list at Easter 1296 (*Cal. Letter-Bk. C*, 23–4), the first seven names represent four sets of ward representatives, the first for Queenhithe, the three following pairs for Cheap, Cordwainer and Bassishaw. For confirmation, see *Cal. Letter-Bk. A*, 210, *B*, 235–9, 246, *C*, 1; K.R. Acc. V. (Alien Merchants) E101/126/6, m.1, 2, 3d; K.R. Acc. V. (Army and Navy) E101/13/39, m.3; Weinbaum, ii, 213, 215.

representatives was the usual quota for the assembly, though
by the reign of Edward II it may have increased.[1] In no case,
however, were more than twelve men called from each ward.
On such occasions the 'whole commonalty' or 'a very great
commonalty' were said to attend.

In the city of Norwich, which had been granted the customs
of London by Richard I, the common assembly was attended
by twelve, ten or eight men from each of its leets. These figures
are the twelfth-century watch-quotas of London wards. They
were later reduced by city sheriffs but the older figures reappeared in late fourteenth-century London, then as ward-
quotas for electoral meetings of the common assembly. In
London as in Norwich, there were references to 'panels', sug-
gesting fuller lists from which the *somoniti* were drawn.[2] The
administrative assemblies which met in the outer chamber
of Guildhall were composed of carefully selected *probi*, summoned and chosen in a system obviously derived from Husting
practice.

Before 1285, however, it is difficult to speak of a 'system'.
There was a great deal of informality. The 1285 list itself illustrates this in a striking manner. It was appended to a register
of aldermen, and while both are undated, internal evidence
enables them to be placed fairly accurately. They were presented some time between June 1285 and January 1286, and
were almost certainly prepared for the royal warden who took
over the city in July 1285.[3] Ten names on the list of councillors
are erased. Seven of these men never appeared in the records

[1] There are numerous records of assemblies called to eiect parliamentary representatives in *Cal. Letter-Bks. D* and *E, passim.*

[2] *Records of Norwich,* ed. W. Hudson (1906), i, 191; see *Cal. Letter-Bk. C,* 4, 175,
and J. Tait, *op. cit.,* 306.

[3] The aldermen named first appeared together as a court in January 1286 and
the latest date of accession is that of Martin Box, first described as an alderman on
26 June 1285 (Hust. Roll 19(19)(20); Beaven, i, 121). Both Beaven, i, 370 and R. R.
Sharpe, *Cal. Letter-Bk. A,* xi, n.3, suggest that the latest date possible is March
1287, when John de Northampton was replaced. Sharpe misdates the appearance
of Northampton's successor (see Hust. Roll 17(22)), but in any case, one of the
listed aldermen, Henry de Frowyk, was dead by 13 May 1286 (St. Paul's A/66/8),
his last appearance as an alderman being on 18 January 1286 (Hust. Roll 19(20)).
Sharpe himself suggested July 1285 as a probable date for the presentation of the
lists (*Cal. Letter-Bk. A,* xi). The lists may be found in *Cal. Letter-Bk. A,* 209–10; a
similar list was prepared for a new warden in 1293 (*Cal. Letter-Bk. C,* 11).

after 1282. In all probability, they were dead. This was certainly true of an eighth man, Osbert de Suffolk, for his will was proved on 8 May 1284.[1] There was thus a gap of one year and one month at least between the preparation of the list and its presentation. The two remaining erasures are startling, for both Richard Eswy and Thomas Box were included in the very list of aldermen to which this supposedly contemporary register was attached. Box became alderman of Walbrook late in 1284; Eswy was elected to Castle Baynard as early as March 1280.[2]

The formalism of royal agents was evidently something of a bureaucratic innovation to the Londoners. In earlier days, there was probably little regularity or systematic record. They were hardly necessary. Aldermen and *probi* were similar folk and much city business must have been decided over the wine at a fraternity dinner or a meeting of the Pui. This is not to say that consultation was infrequent. In a single month in 1297 as many as 128 different citizens were called to assemblies.[3] This was admittedly in a period of profound social and political change, but at all times, the aldermen must have kept in close touch with those important groups to which they themselves belonged. Consultation at a certain level was essential to sound opinion and keep tempers sweet. Indeed the entire apparatus of aldermanic and consultative councils was basically nothing more than the patriciate in committee.

More controversial was the application of the system to elections of mayors and sheriffs. Constitutional conflict in London centred on these elections, particularly the mayoral, and it was not until the reign of Edward II that the dissidents turned baleful eyes upon the snug confederacy of administrative councils. The electoral assemblies were far more dramatic, and nowhere do opposing conceptions of the commune find more forceful expression. For the elections had been managed from the beginning. Fitz Thedmar regarded the intervention of lesser citizens as a revolutionary heresy and at the disputed election of 1272, the aldermen claimed electoral rights as their exclusive privilege. They were judges and had precedent

---

[1] *Cal. Letter-Bk. C*, 119, 120.
[2] Beaven, i, 88, 216, 376.
[3] *Cal. Letter-Bk. B*, 236–9.

behind them, while most of the populace were landless and often servile in origin, caring nothing for the city's welfare.[1] In mid-fourteenth century they added the rather ingenious rider that they, too, were members of the commonalty and should not be overridden merely because they held office.[2]

There seemed little danger of the latter. Carpenter gives a brief historical sketch of the process of restriction. Rallying the Fathers to the cause, he stresses the need to avoid tumult, 'quia collectio populi sicut testatur Sapiens, Ecclesiastici, xxvito capitulo est timenda ratione que leviter tunc evenire poterunt murmuris et tumultus'. Elections in the early days of the mayoralty had been marred by such outbreaks and the council decided to limit electoral assemblies to a number of carefully chosen *discretiores*.[3] This account may be accurate, for the original petition for the annual mayoralty in 1215 had asked for election by open Folkmoot.[4] The populace, unencumbered with the Biblical scholarship of Common Clerks, would have proved troublesome. The electoral assembly which replaced the moot, the *magna congregatio*, met by individual summons at Guildhall.

In essence, it seems to have been simply a full-scale administrative assembly. The terms 'whole' or 'immense' commonalty were applied in the same sense as in the *congregatio*. In 1293, for example, the clerk writes, 'The whole commonalty of the city aforesaid was assembled, namely from each ward the wealthier and wiser men.'[5] This meant, as an abundance of record makes clear, an assembly of the mayor, aldermen and twelve men from every ward.[6] The role of the *somoniti* was not important. Elections were made by the aldermen, 'in the presence of' the *probi*, who were called to 'receive' the elected. By the late fourteenth century, the commons were claiming the right not only of *election* but of *nomination*. Their role was evidently to acclaim and confirm in the proper Thomist manner.[7] Trouble could certainly arise, but in that event, the whole

---

[1] *Lib. de Ant. Leg.*, pp. 55, 58, 80, 149, 150.
[2] *Lib. Albus*, p. 20.
[3] *Lib. Albus*, pp. 18, 19.
[4] M. Bateson, *op. cit.*, 726.
[5] *Cal. Letter-Bk. C*, 11.
[6] See, for example, *Cal. Letter-Bk. A*, 196–8, *B*, 213, *C*, 8, 79, 80, 101, 102, 114, 173–80.
[7] *Cal. Letter-Bk. C*, 101, 102, 114, 173, 174; *Lib. Albus*, p. 20.

procedure was disrupted. In normal times, a preliminary consultation of aldermen, as in the administrative assemblies, was
decisive. 'The Mayor and Aldermen retired to the chamber,'
says a court record in 1328, 'to make the election for themselves
and the Commonalty according to custom.'[1]

Evidently, attendance at electoral and administrative assemblies was regarded as a duty, like the watch itself, to be imposed
upon or shouldered by the wealthier and most respected men
of each ward. Individuals selected from them, to the maximum
number of twelve, assisted at all functions which required
communal participation. In all probability, the personnel of
panels for pleas and for administrative assemblies were identical.
Probi as councillors were indistinguishable from *probi* as law-
men. They were a distinctive group within the wardmoot,
where the alderman sat 'cum valentioribus Wardae' to hear
pleas and prepare panels.[2] Damages in the courts were assessed
by clerks and councillors; important juries were staffed by
them; the Hundred and Iter juries contain many councillors'
names and were probably composed of assembly-men. In fact
they formed a type of administrative estate, a key executive
class beneath or alongside the aldermen.[3] Indeed, it is possible
that such terms as 'commonalty' or 'probi homines de warda'
were in fact precise descriptions of a panel of twelve selected
men in each aldermanry, called to council in varying numbers
according to the importance of the matter under discussion.
When the issue was fundamental, as in a mayoral election, the
'whole commonalty', that is, all twelve of them, would be
summoned.[4] At all events, this pattern of consultation and
control, based on the Husting, was the natural consequence of
the assumption of autonomous power by the city's leading

---

[1] *P. and M. Rolls*, i, 72–3.   [2] See, for example, *Lib. Albus*, pp. 36–9.

[3] For some examples, see W.A.M., Domesday, fo. 504b–5; K.R. Acc. V.
(Alien Merchants) E101/126/6, m.4; *Hundred Rolls*, i, 403–33; St. Paul's A/16/246;
Cal. E.M.C. Rolls, p. 204.

[4] In September 1305, a mayor's court roll used the expression 'The good men
of the Ward of Chepe, namely . . .' followed by a complete list of twelve names
(*Cal. E.M.C. Rolls*, p. 225). Panels of possibles from whom vestries selected con-
stables were still in use in the nineteenth century and the number twelve with its
multiples had almost a mystic significance in eighteenth-century local government.
I am grateful to Mr. T. F. Reddaway for drawing my attention to these intriguing
parallels.

families. For a citizen body which was itself an élite, it was admirably suited.

This, however, was precisely its weakness, for the keynote of the thirteenth century was growth. In the early years of autonomy, the identification of aldermen and *probi* was wellnigh complete. But the growth of population and the impulse towards stricter definition brought changes of qualitative significance. The aldermen tended to draw apart as a separate estate, the commons to acquire a juridical personality, a condition typified in the mayoral elections of the late fourteenth century, when the Common Pleader acted as a spokesman from the commonalty to the council.[1] The assemblies attracted the attention of reforming groups, came to embody the ideals of responsible and representative government, wresting many powers from the aldermen, until in the thirties of the fourteenth century they call to mind not so much the four benches as the Common Council. Popular reform movements and royal interventions were important stimuli, but they themselves were largely the consequence of what was the central and decisive factor, the sheer growth of the city, quantitatively and qualitatively. For, in the process, citizenship itself was transformed.

Citizenship was the basis of public life. The primary distinction between London's inhabitants was that between citizens who were of the freedom on one hand, county or London-born 'foreigns' and overseas 'aliens' on the other. Only the citizens bore the burden of civic duties, but only they enjoyed political rights and the cherished freedoms. No foreign could buy wares for which a citizen had offered an equal price or prove his case against a citizen by foreign witnesses alone. Above all, only citizens could open shops for the retail trade and traffic with non-citizens.[2] The London citizen stood to the London foreign as the *bourgeois* to the *manant* in Flanders and Brabant, as the privileged citizenry of all the cities of Western Europe to their far more numerous fellow-inhabitants.[3]

[1] *Lib. Albus*, p. 21.

[2] See, for example, *P. and M. Rolls*, i, 27; M. Bateson, *op. cit.*, 713, 718.

[3] See Marc Bloch, 'Les éléments de la société urbaine mediévale', *Annales*, ii (1930), 439–40; F. Favresse, *L'avènement du régime démocratique à Bruxelles pendant le moyen âge, 1306–1423* (Brussels, 1932), pp. 18–22.

Fitz Thedmar, describing the settlement of his German grandparents in London about 1180, said of them, 'ementes sibi domicilium in Civitate Londoniarum facti sunt Cives Londonienses'.[1] Burgage-tenure was not in itself sufficient; a citizen had to be in scot and lot, to share in the financial obligations of his city, but based on the burgage and scot and lot, it was freedom by patrimony, by inheritance, which was the original, basic form of citizenship. The commune created the citizen's oath, but not until 1387 was the oath made compulsory for citizens by patrimony and even then no payment was exacted.[2] These were the citizens with the highest prestige, the 'old standards'. Royal charters conferred liberties on citizens and their 'heirs' and the first comprehensive civic legislation on the subject in 1275 called for no compulsory register of patrimonies. Freemen by birth were probably well known.

Small wonder that in the early thirteenth century, they called themselves 'barons'. *Sigillum Baronum Londoniarum* proclaimed the original common seal; it was by his fellow barons that the mayor was elected. The Londoners' fondness for the title could have surprising consequences, as in 1250, when they claimed the privilege of trial by their 'peers', the earls and barons of England. They enjoyed great freedom in the tenure of their land and claimed to hold the whole city in chief of the king, and, generally speaking, in the early thirteenth century they used *barones, cives, probi homines* as synonymous terms.[3]

Probably it was always possible to buy citizenship and since the exercise of the retail trade was a function of the franchise, apprenticeship was another route. The increase in the number of this type of citizen seems to have become a problem of political importance in the early years of Henry III, for it was then that the earliest civic ordinances on the subject were promulgated. Because large numbers of Londoners travelling in England and abroad were claiming the liberty, the city proclaimed that in future it would defend as a freeman no foreign

---

[1] *Lib. de Ant. Leg.*, p. 238.

[2] M. Bateson, *op. cit.*, 723; J. Tait, *op. cit.*, 257–8; *P. and M. Rolls*, ii, xix–xx, 10–11; *Cal. Letter-Bk. G*, 179, *H*, 310.

[3] See *Lib. de Ant. Leg.*, pp. 16, 23; Ancient Deeds A 1477; *Hundred Rolls*, i, 403–33; M. Bateson, *op. cit.*, *passim*; A. H. Thomas, *P. and M. Rolls*, ii, xxi–xxiii; F. M. Stenton, *The First Century of English Feudalism* (Oxford, 1932), pp. 85–90.

or apprentice quitting his master, unless he had been enrolled in the city's books. Half a mark was the fee, though wealthy men were to pay more. Enrolment of apprenticeship covenants was ordered, compulsory for foreign-born apprentices, permissive for the others.[1]

In 1275 fresh legislation was necessary, for in the turmoil of mid-century, foreigns and lesser citizens had collaborated with the organized crafts in support of the popular mayors of the revolutionary commons. In reaction, the qualifications for citizenship were formally reaffirmed—inheritance from a citizen father by a legitimate son born in the city; service as an apprentice to a freeman for at least seven years; purchase of the freedom from the chamberlain before the mayor and aldermen. Registration of apprentices and redemptioners was again made compulsory.[2]

The newer methods became increasingly important with the rise of the crafts. Apart from the patrician fraternities of drapers, pepperers, goldsmiths, mercers and vintners, the number of recognized, semi-autonomous misteries was small at first but their multiplication is one of the most characteristic phenomena of the century.[3] In the reign of Edward I, they at last triumphed over aldermanic resistance, and the threat to their position from the king's free trade policy drove them into political action. In 1294, the keeping of craft registers was made compulsory. Repeated proclamations insisted that only free masters should take apprentices, who were to be sworn to the freedom and enrolled before taking up trade, and in 1300, a committee of aldermen was appointed to enforce these rules. By this time the chamberlain was handling litigation over apprenticeship covenants by the light of an established body of law and custom.[4] The climax came in the early years of Edward II when, for a variety of economic and political reasons, the leading misteries made an organized drive for citizen rights. The chamberlain's registers for 1309–12 reveal a great rush of people taking up the franchise in unprecedented numbers. Over 250 of the new

---

[1] Lib. Ordinationum, fo. 173. [2] Ann. Lond., pp. 85, 86.
[3] The crafts are examined in some detail in Chapter VI.
[4] Lib. Albus, p. 272; Lib. Cust., p. 93; Cal. Letter-Bk. B, 241, C, 78; Cal. E.M.C. Rolls, pp. 46–8.

citizens were ex-apprentices and a further 294 apprenticeship covenants were enrolled. No term was for less than seven years and premiums were stiff. Apprentices were qualifying for the enfranchised aristocracy of the city.[1] Craft control was rapidly established. In 1319 the misteries won a recognized place in the civic constitution. Numbers of craft ordinances increased rapidly, and by 1364 the gild-wardens had the decisive voice in the admission of apprentices to the freedom.[2]

More important is the fact that the craft drive of 1309–19 was directed largely towards control of redemptioners. Early civic ordinances had fixed a scale, but allowed the mayor and aldermen much latitude in the admission of wealthy foreigners. The lorimers made foreign craftsmen pay £2 to the commune and wealthy alien merchants, like the vintner from Toulouse admitted in 1284, generally paid stiff sums and brought guarantees of good treatment for Londoners in their native city.[3] In 1285 Edward I ordered the city to admit alien merchants of good character, and six years later, a committee was appointed to supervise such admissions.[4] The crafts viewed the uncontrolled sale of the franchise to alien merchants with the utmost suspicion and throughout the century made repeated demands for prior communal consent. In any case, they had to take account of the continuous inflow of unenfranchised men. In the turbulent years from 1309 to 1312 no fewer than 646 men purchased the freedom at fees varying from 5s. to £5, and large numbers of them were men of the trades taking up the freedom in organized groups. In the reform movement of 1309–19, the crafts, with their authority now vastly extended, carried their demand for control over redemptioners. By the great charter of 1319 no stranger was to be admitted to the franchise until he had been accepted by six men of the mistery he wished to join, or by the commonalty, if he wished to follow no trade.[5] Mistery

---

[1] For these admissions, see *Cal. Letter-Bk. D*, 35–179; A. H. Thomas, *P. and M. Rolls*, ii, xxxii–xxxiv, xxxvi–xxxviii, lii; G. Unwin, review of *Cal. E.M.C. Rolls* in *History*, n.s. x (1925–6); the returns are subjected to more detailed analysis in Chapter VI.

[2] See A. H. Thomas, *P. and M. Rolls*, ii, xxxvii–xxxviii and Chapter VI.

[3] *Lib. Cust.*, pp. 78–9; *Cal. Letter-Bk. B*, 281.

[4] *Cal. Letter-Bk. C*, 23; *Lib. Albus*, p. 287.

[5] These events are treated in Chapters VI and X.

control became permanent. In 1364 one extreme measure ordered that no redemptioner was to be admitted at all unless he had served seven years in a trade, thus equating him with an apprentice. This was repealed, but the consent of the craft remained essential. Indeed by the mid-fourteenth century, citizenship and craft-membership had been virtually identified, a condition which created that peculiar half-world of legal fiction in late medieval London, when men simply used the crafts to acquire the franchise and when craft-membership itself became almost meaningless as an economic category.[1]

The governing factor was the increase in population and trade competition, which transformed the citizen body out of all recognition. Multiplication of numbers would itself have reduced the relative importance of citizenship by patrimony. The vast majority of the new citizens of 1309–12 were immigrants. There seems to have been little direct replenishment from hereditary citizen families. Of the apprentices of those years, some seventy or so can be identified as the sons of citizens. A citizen's son who became an apprentice lost the right to claim the franchise by patrimony, a rule which, in a time of increasing mistery control of the more important trades, must have led to the virtual 'disappearance' of many hereditary freeman families.[2] Citizenship by patrimony withered away as London grew to an intensely commercial capital, drawing on all England for its citizens.

In the sixties, a distinction between *barones* and *cives* begins to creep into royal writs. From 1298, the 'heirs' of royal charters is replaced by 'successors'.[3] The position in 1364 was remarkable. A plaint was made in that year that citizens by patrimony were prevented from enjoying the franchise unless they had also served an apprenticeship or paid a redemption. The aldermen proclaimed that anyone born free was to enjoy the same privileges as other citizens, if he could prove his freedom. If challenged, freemen by apprenticeship and redemption were to produce their record, freemen by birth to put themselves on a jury

[1] See *Cal. Letter-Bk. G*, 180; A. H. Thomas, *P. and M. Rolls*, ii, liii–lvii; S. L. Thrupp, *The Merchant Class of Medieval London*.

[2] A. H. Thomas, *P. and M. Rolls*, ii, xxix.

[3] For example, see *Historical Charters*, ed. W. de G. Birch, p. 43; *C.P.R. 1258–66*, p. 613.

of their birthplace. Gradually the oath was imposed on them.[1]
Within eighty years of the ordinance of 1275, hereditary citizens
had become slightly eccentric survivors.

By 1321 the term 'baron' was restricted to the aldermanic class.
Carpenter grants the patricians sole title to its use, quoting the
example of the baronial funerals of aldermen in the fourteenth
century, with their heraldic trappings.[2] The aldermen, drawing
apart as a political class, adopted, by a curious parallelism, the
title of the old landed citizenry. There is a striking similarity
in the urban evolution of the Low Countries. At Dinant during
the thirteenth century, the term *bourgeois* became more restricted in meaning until in the end it applied only to the patriciate. The word *poorter* in Flanders went through a similar
change. As opposed to the town oligarchs, the rest of the citizens
were dubbed *commun* or *communauté* after the fashion of the
London *commonalty*. In fact, in these towns, the early citizen
body was nothing more than the patriciate itself.[3]

The patrician government of London lacked the strict legal
definition sometimes encountered on the continent, but the
similarity is too close to be fortuitous. There was the same virtual
identification of aldermen and *probi* in the early days, the same
small, landed, hereditary core of citizens. That core must have
been very small. In the far more mobile London of the sixteenth
century, citizen families numbered a quarter of the population,
citizens themselves less than one-twentieth. A generous estimate puts them at a third in the fourteenth century, and the
proportion of those who were citizens by birth would have been
smaller still.[4] In the early thirteenth century, the citizens must
have been a select group indeed.

Among them, aldermen, with their kinsfolk and their dependants, formed the controlling élite. For the communal
régime marked, in reality, the climax of a century of political
development. With the establishment of the commune, the
great twelfth-century families consolidated their position, ela-
borating a system of government based on the Husting of their

---

[1] *Cal. Letter-Bk. G*, 179; *Lib. Albus*, p. 206; *P. and M. Rolls*, ii, 10–11.
[2] *Lib. Albus*, pp. 32, 33, 51; J. Tait, *op. cit.*, 258–9.
[3] H. Pirenne, *Les villes et les institutions urbaines* (Paris, 1939), ii, 27, 28.
[4] A. H. Thomas, *P. and M. Rolls*, ii, xxx, lxii.

little landed oligarchy of hereditary citizens. As the city grew and its life became more complex, the hereditary and proprietary character of citizenship was eclipsed. There was a shift away from proprietary modes of thought in the field of aldermanic authority and, as the wards acquired a territorial nomenclature, the assemblies of the *probi* assumed the character of a representative estate. Accelerated and directed by the stimuli of royal intervention and popular protest, the process ultimately destroyed the organic unity of earlier days and made necessary a readjustment of political society, which was not effected without travail.

Through all the changes, however, there was one constant. Never was there any permanent displacement of political power. The governing factor in the life of London remained what it had always been, the character of the aldermanic class.

E

CHAPTER III

The Ruling Dynasties

I N 1222 Richard Renger became mayor of London. He held office almost continuously until 1229 and within two years was succeeded by Andrew Bukerel, who remained mayor until his death in 1237. Between them, these men, who had both reached the aldermanic council in the early years of Henry III, monopolized the mayoralty for almost two decades; between them, also, they personify the first autonomous patriciate of the commune.[1]

Both, in particular, were the heirs of 'illustrious ancestors'. The Bukerels stemmed from an Italian pepperer who had settled in London after the Conquest; Renger's family, the fitz Reiners, descended from Berengar, servant and compatriot to the first Norman bishops of London. Bukerels had produced aldermen in every generation from about 1100 onward. The fitz Reiners had been equally prominent; Renger's uncle, Richard fitz Reiner, had been a personal friend of King John. Naturally, both were buttressed by great inherited wealth. Bukerel's property is poorly documented, but must have been considerable, with the family manors in Kent and Middlesex and the concentrated holdings around Guildhall and in Cripplegate. It was his father, Andrew Bukerel I, who had alienated the original *caput* of the family holding, the great fortified mansion of Bucklersbury (Bukerels' Burh) to Hasculf de Tania before setting out, in 1183, on the pilgrimage to Jerusalem from which he never returned. Renger fell heir to massive dynastic properties in Hertfordshire, Essex, Middlesex and Suffolk, for on the division of Richard fitz Reiner's estate in 1191, the lion's share fell to Richard's brother William, the mayor's father. Within the

---

[1] Outline biographies of these men, with references, may be found in the Appendix.

city, he owned much property in Vintry and Bridge, including the cellars used by the Lorraine fleet.

They inherited also that establishment at Court and in the royal household which was so characteristic of their class in the early days of autonomy. Bukerel was serving as royal chamberlain of London, the king's butler, at Henry's accession and actually covered the Coronation expenses out of his own pocket. In 1218 he bought, for 4,000 marks, a three-year lease of the Exchange, with the right to traffic in the goods of arrested aliens. Renger followed as Master of Exchange from 1226 to 1233. In 1238 he was a keeper of the royal treasure, and both men were prominent in Court society during the Minority and in the early thirties. Renger served as justice itinerant in Surrey, with Stephen Segrave, performing many personal services for the king, and both he and Bukerel were notable members of the commissions which presided over the fall of Peter des Rivaux. Renger, indeed, enjoyed a peculiar prestige. A friend of the Marshals, from whom he bought corn in bulk, he witnessed the charters of the archbishop of Canterbury and acted as attorney to Robert fitz Walter. In city deeds, he sometimes took precedence over mayor and sheriffs, and in 1232 an Italian creditor of the king, professing himself dissatisfied with the bishop of Chichester as sole surety for the debt, insisted that Renger's name be added to the bond.

For, however substantial their inherited property and however secure their status at Court, both men, like most of their fellows, committed their fortunes to trade. Indeed both, at one time or another, were mortgaging their lands to the Jews. Renger went further. He became an intimate of the notorious Cahorsin financiers, trading in partnership with Peter Beraud at Bristol in 1230, chartering a ship with Arnold Beraud seven years later. Bukerel was active on the Irish and Scottish trade routes. In 1220 he tried to have £100 transmitted to his agents in Dublin by the Exchequer; ten years later, one of his ships was en route from Scotland with a cargo of hides. Nominally a pepperer, he was exporting wool at the end of his life, trading with Caen merchants in particular. In 1230 he was selling his hides to an alien in exchange for wine. In truth, as with most of their colleagues, it is as vintners that these men figure in the commercial records. Safe-conducts were issued for Bukerel's ships in 1224 and 1225; Renger got a general safe-conduct in 1224, sent two ships abroad the following year and used Dunwich craft in 1230. Both sold wine to the Household in a type of transaction which was to loom increasingly large in aldermanic enterprise.

Throughout their lives, they went from success to success, Renger adding much property in Suffolk and Essex to his patrimony. They were untypical in that they left no direct heir to follow in aldermanic office. Andrew died without issue and his brother Thomas inherited. But two of the alderman's brothers served on the council with him and a third married an alderman's daughter. His kinsmen, Stephen and Mathew, and their descendants Stephen II and William followed in office with the customary regularity, and the Bukerels had a clear run in the aldermanic class through to the end of the thirteenth century, a record which only the fitz Ailwins, the oldest family in the city, could rival. Some of Andrew's property indeed passed to the Rengers, for the families intermarried. Renger's son John, an Exchequer official, became a well-endowed country gentleman, but his daughter married into the Hadestoks, and his grandchildren linked the family to the Hardels and Frowyks. In both men the tradition of government by patrician dynasties was maintained and enhanced.

⌐Their careers suffice to expose the inadequacy of any over-simplified theory of the nature of urban élites, whether it be Pirenne's concept of successive waves of rootless new rich, Lestocquoy's of an urban squirearchy or even Unwin's suggestion of a gradual shift from a characteristically 'knightly' to a characteristically 'bourgeois' class.[1]⌐The peculiar strength

---

[1] For Pirenne's famous theory, see his seminal essay on the social stages of capitalism in *Bulletin de l'Académie Royale de Belgique*, v (1914), and also *Les villes et les institutions urbaines*, i, 215–22; a classic exposition is his *Medieval Cities*, trans. F. D. Halsey (Princeton, 1925). For his most effective critics, see J. Lestocquoy, *Les dynasties bourgeoises d'Arras du xie. au xve. siècle* (Arras, 1945) and *Les villes de Flandre et d'Italie sous le gouvernement des patriciens* (Paris, 1952). Unwin's ideas may most easily be assessed from Unwin, *Gilds*, pp. 55–6 and his article on 'Social evolution in medieval London', *Finance and Trade under Edward III*, ed. G. Unwin (Manchester, 1918). The most useful works from a corpus of European studies are listed in the Bibliography. Little work of this nature has been done on English towns, but for some evidence, see A. B. Hibbert, 'The origins of the medieval town patriciate', *Past and Present*, iii (1957).

of the English monarchy was a prime differentiating factor; there was the local power, tenurial and social, of the Church; London was growing into one of the foci of European commerce, and its status had been miraculously preserved at the Conquest. Inevitably, its patriciate had many roots.

The names are known of ninety-five aldermen and non-aldermanic sheriffs who held office between the establishment of the commune in 1191 and the outbreak of the popular revolt in 1263.[1] Three-quarters of them belonged to families which had been established in the aldermanic class since the early twelfth century or even earlier and the proportion was greater still among the thirty-three known to have been elected before 1230.[2] Naturally, it is as an hereditary and landed aristocracy that they figure in city records. Whatever the provenance of the original capital, the founders of these dynasties had created a landed establishment which left a permanent impress on the city's topography. London was full of streets bearing family names, Bat's Lane, Hadestok's Lane, Basing Lane. St. Martin Orgar probably took its name from the fitz Ailwin family and it was but one of many proprietary churches. The Aldermanbury soke, for example, included the advowsons of three.[3] Sokes themselves were numerous. Joce fitz Peter of the fitz Ailwins acquired the soke of the Norman William Martel and passed it on to his alderman son Nicholas. Bukerels, Bucointes, Cornhills and Steperangs possessed them; William Eswy had two.[4] A seld, an indoor market-cum-warehouse, may well have been the original nucleus of an estate. The great mansions, really considerable blocks of property built around an enclosure with many dependent shops and tenements, certainly were, and

---

[1] For the names, see the massive and authoritative compilation in Beaven, i and ii. On the difficulties and rewards of a biographical approach, see R. L. Reynolds, 'In search of a business class in thirteenth-century Genoa', *Journal of Economic History*, v (1945) and E. M. Carus-Wilson, review of S. L. Thrupp, *The Merchant Class of Medieval London* in *Economic History Review*, 2nd. ser. ii (1949).

[2] Basic information on the structure of the aldermanic class in terms of trade designations, interests and origins is given in tabular form in the Appendix. This chapter should be read in conjunction with those tables.

[3] *C.Ch.R. 1226–57*, pp. 313, 314; St. Paul's A/16/141, 1206, 1282; W. Page, *op. cit.*, 248–52; T. Stapleton, preface to *Lib. de Ant. Leg.*

[4] Hust. Roll 2(10); St. Paul's A/4/692; Misc. Roll AA, pp. 45, 65, 66; *Cal. of Wills*, i, 1; *C.P.R. 1247–58*, p. 583; *C.Ch.R. 1226–57*, p. 290; W. Page, *op. cit.*, 146–7.

both selds and mansions were largely aldermanic preserves.[1] Such block holdings sometimes persisted even into the mid-thirteenth century. Mathew Bukerel's property all lay in three neighbouring parishes, while the estate of Arnold fitz Thedmar the chronicler comprised a great hall and capital messuage, rents, tenements and a wharf in Haywharf Lane, shops and houses in Gofair Lane, Bow Lane, Ropers Street, Wendegos Lane, all within the one parish of All Hallows Haywharf.[2]

When aldermanic property comes into the light of evidence, however, it is generally widely diffused. The vintner dynasty of Hardel, which gave London the mayor who sealed Magna Carta, had a concentrated riverside holding in Vintry and Billingsgate, supplemented by rents, some as valuable as sixteen marks, scattered over the city;[3] another vintner, Henry de Coventry, as well as his mansion in St. James Vintry and the new house he had built for himself in All Hallows Haywharf, had property in eight parishes, with gardens in the suburb.[4] Edward Blund, who owned three selds, John Norman, who held important market-sites in Cheap, Laurence de Frowyk with his palatial hall at Holborn, Isabella Bukerel, who owned most of the Drapery, Ropery, Saddlery and Peltry in Cheap and Walbrook, had houses, tenements or rents in anything from ten to twenty parishes,[5] while the scattered and poorly documented property of some of the earlier generation, men like Solomon de Basing, Serlo le Mercer and Simon fitz Mary, was massive indeed.[6]

[1] For example, see St. Paul's A/4/273, A/14/1258, A/24/263, 713, 1725, A/71/1818; Hust. Roll 2(137); Hust. Roll (Land) 1, m.10; Cal. of Wills, i, 62, 63, 192, 275.

[2] Bukerel: Hust. Roll 4(63); 12 (31) (62) (63); St. Paul's A/15/204, 284; Misc. Roll AA, p. 54. Fitz Thedmar: Cal. of Wills, i, 22, 50, 147, 239, 435.

[3] Hust. Roll 1 (27); 2 (146); St. Paul's A/15/1410; Cal. Letter-Bk. A, 170; Ancient Deeds D 4603; Cal. of Wills, i, 3–4.

[4] Hust. Roll 2 (3); 4 (93); 5 (58); 9 (54) (55); 13 (173); Cal. of Wills, i, 62–3.

[5] Norman: Hust. Roll 2 (24) (81); W.A.M. 13789; St. Paul's A/24/267; Misc. Roll AA, p. 79; Cal. of Wills, i, 5, 31; Frowyk: St. Paul's A/9/293–5, A/70/1763; Cal. Letter-Bk. A, 157–60; Cal. of Wills, i, 26–8; Blund and Bukerel: Cal. of Wills, i, 30, 31, 49, 50.

[6] Basing: Hust. Roll 2(41); C.Ch.R. 1226–57, p. 202; Cart. S.M. Clerkenwell, pp. 106, 107, 225, 226; Mercer: W.A.M., Domesday, fo. 369b; C.Ch.R. 1226–57, pp. 68, 201–2; Fitz Mary: Ancient Deeds D 3160; St. Paul's A/17/214, A/25/1070; C.Ch.R. 1226–57, pp. 202, 207; C.Ch.R. 1257–1300, p. 38.

In fact there is some evidence of the existence of a class of men, similar to the *otiosi* and *lediggangers* of the continent, who lived as rentiers. A third of the aldermen elected before 1263 carried no trade designation. In many cases, this meant nothing. Neither Renger nor William Joynier, for example, carried a trade name, but both were merchants. Evidence on trading activity itself is circumscribed. If an alderman had no contact with the royal administration, his commerce could escape record altogether. Even fitz Thedmar, the prototype of a rentier-administrator, owned several shops. Nevertheless a substantial number of men remain for whom there is no evidence of any commercial activity. They were particularly numerous among the earlier generation who took office before 1230.[1]

Thomas de Haverhill, for example, held a great fee in Honey Lane, scattered rents in six parishes and property in Middlesex. His father had been an alderman, a soke-reeve and a patron of St. Paul's; his grandfather had served as chamberlain to Henry II, Thomas himself on the committee which assessed the dower of Berengaria, widow of Richard I.[2] The fitz Alulfs were similar. Arnulf, alderman son of the influential patrician Fromond, had four sons, all of whom served as aldermen and sheriffs in the late twelfth and early thirteenth centuries. His sons Arnulf and Constantine were administrators, lucratively propertied, particularly around Guildhall and St. Paul's. Their nephew Peter, who inherited estates at Acton and acquired the manor of Fulham, was a protégé of the bishop of London. By mid-century, the family was in difficulties. Constantine was hanged for sedition in 1222, one of his nephews was under pressure from the Jews in 1236, another compelled to sell out to Giles de Cambrai.[3] This family, like the Haverhills rentiers in close rapport with the Church and the royal administration, like

---

[1] See table of trade designations in the Appendix.

[2] W.A.M., Domesday, fo. 483b; A.R. 536, m.5; *Cart. S.M. Clerkenwell*, pp. 156–58, 176; *Pat. Rolls 1216–25*, p. 265; *C.Ch.R. 1226–57*, p. 202; *C.Ch.R. 1257–1300*, p. 256; W. Page, *op. cit.*, 264–65.

[3] For the Fitz Alulfs, the key references are W.A.M., Domesday, fo. 483b–4, 491–1b; St. Paul's A/12/291, A/13/1258, A/17/229, 1321, A/26–40/1463 (154) (231) (409); *C.R. 1227–31*, p. 122; *C.R. 1231–4*, pp. 195, 484, 490, 491; *C.R. 1234–7*, pp. 140, 298; *C.R. 1242–7*, pp. 496, 530; *C.Ch.R. 1226–57*, pp. 322, 336; *Cal. Inq. Misc.*, i, 580.

them also, faded out as a patrician family, but both were, after all, the last members of a very long line.

Nevertheless, there was little rigidity. The Londoners enjoyed unusual freedom of bequest and alienation and there was a constant movement of capital into and out of real estate and mercantile enterprise, a surprising number of extents for debts to the Jews. Patricians like Renger and Bukerel freely mobilized their assets and, as the years pass, land figures more frequently in the records as one of the sinews of commerce. A widow's legal right to one-third of her husband's property made marriage a matter of moment and there was a constantly shifting pattern of ownership between families. The old Aldermanbury soke with its three churches and £40 rent-roll, for example, nourished successive generations of patricians, Basings, Eswys and Bedyks in turn.[1] Nowhere was this mobility more notable than in county property. Estates in the counties were coveted as commercial assets, residences and badges of status. Neighbouring areas such as Edmonton and Enfield were very popular and must have fulfilled many of the functions of a nineteenth-century residential suburb. Patrician estates and minor holdings lay thick around the city and Middlesex and Essex were far and away the most heavily colonized counties.[2] Many of the rooted patrician families, of course, were closely integrated into the structure of shire society. People like the fitz Ailwins were as much men of Hertfordshire or Surrey as of London. As the years passed, this connexion grew stronger, as immigrants from the provinces came to assume social supremacy in London. In earlier years, many of the established city families followed the opposite and traditional route from trade into the gentry, though, to judge from available evidence, on nothing like the same scale as became common in the fourteenth century. For, in the early thirteenth century, county estates, coveted and widespread as they were, figured as something external in more than a topographical sense.

Of the aldermen elected before 1263, at least a half were the

---

[1] St. Paul's A/16/141, 206, 1282.

[2] There are examples in abundance in A.R., W.A.M., St. Paul's, Ancient Deeds, *C.Ch.R.*, *C.P.R.*, *C.R.*, *Cal. Inq. Misc.*, etc., *passim*; see also S. L. Thrupp, *The Merchant Class of Medieval London.*

possessors of substantial holdings in the counties.[1] Many, like the fitz Reiners', were inherited. All were cherished. But they were disposed of quite freely and they seem to have been regarded primarily as the object and reward of mercantile endeavour. Most, indeed, were acquired in this period by commercial and financial transactions with the baronage and knighthood or by royal favour. In 1228, for example, Roger le Duc, a city rentier who dealt with Italians and Jews and paid the king's debts, received from the prior of St. Vaast, Romilly, the thirty-mark farm of the town of Fobbing, together with a life-interest in three Hampshire and Dorset manors, almost certainly in consequence of a loan. Two years later, John fitz Robert leased him another manor for five years.[2] He was typical of many. William Joynier, an important city financier who was rescued from prison in 1216 because of the enormous debts King John had owed him, built himself into a city magnate in this fashion.[3] A vintner, who in 1226 and 1233 freighted three ships with his cargoes, including a Flemish craft at St. Savinien in Poitou, Joynier was a Wardrobe merchant. It was he who supplied the vestments, chasubles and albs for the royal chapel at Oxford in 1226, a quilt of silk for Queen Eleanor at Bristol seven years later.[4] He made loans to the earl of Winchester and the countess of Pembroke, received many gifts from William Marshal. Between 1228 and 1238, when he met most of the expenses of the Seneschal, Henry de Turberville, his money was a factor in Gascon administration. The consequences were familiar. He acquired temporary control of the Turberville estates; from Saer de Quincy he got the rents of Brackley, from the Marshals, lands in Cambridgeshire.[5] Throughout the period, landed wealth was a characteristic of the aldermanic class, particularly among its earlier representatives, when inherited property loomed large on the social horizon.

[1] See table of interests in the Appendix.

[2] W.A.M. 1117; *C.R.1227–31*, pp. 383, 384; *C.Ch.R. 1226–57*, pp. 85, 121, 238; Beaven, i, 371.

[3] *Pat. Rolls 1216–25*, p. 13.

[4] *Pat. Rolls 1216–25*, p. 493; *Pat. Rolls 1225–32*, pp. 17, 18, 40; *C.Lib.R. 1226–40*, pp. 2, 226, 227, 284, 332; *C. Lib.R. 1240–5*, p. 29; *C.R. 1227–31*, p. 301; *C.R. 1234–7*, p. 72; *C.P.R. 1232–47*, pp. 14, 99.

[5] K.R.M.R. 2, m.13d; *Pat. Rolls 1225–32*, pp. 274, 275; *C.P.R. 1232–47*, pp. 83, 137, 139; *C.R. 1234–7*, p. 152; *C.Lib.R. 1226–40*, pp. 94, 289, 300, 317; *C.Ch.R. 1226–57*, p. 124.

More typical, perhaps, of later generations was William de Durham, who had a holding at Edmonton, land in Hertfordshire and property in the trade centre of Boston, all acquired during his life-time.[1] For in mid-century, it was generally the successful merchants who were the big landowners.

There was, of course, a limit to this mobility. It had free play only within the restricted group formed by the established families and their fringe of wealthy newcomers. Those newcomers multiplied as England grew and by the last quarter of the century quantitative changes became qualitative as new men climbed to power on the disintegrating patrimonies of declining families. Well into the century, however, the twelfth-century dynasties were able to maintain themselves. Newcomers were few; they were generally immigrants and almost invariably, indeed necessarily, highly successful merchants. They were rapidly assimilated, usually by marriage, and absorbed into the traditional tenurial pattern. For while commercial success made them suitable husbands for patrician daughters, they did not arrive until their wealth had been grounded.

The career of one of the later generation, Philip le Tailor, illustrates the process.[2] He was unusual in that he sprang from an established, if relatively obscure London family, for the dynasties generally looked outside the walls for their new recruits. Philip, nominally a mercer, was handling cloth in 1275, grain in 1276. As with so many in these years, it was the wine trade which made him. He and his partner were buying quittances of prise on cargoes of 120 and 150 tuns in the early fifties, and by 1256 he was selling wine to the royal household. In 1259 his sales to the Court topped the £100 mark and he began to number important people among his customers— Adam Despenser, John de Burgh, William Bagod. In the same year, he began to buy land, in St. Michael Paternoster. The impetus of commercial success carried him into the patriciate. Between 1260 and 1263, when his sales to the Court were running at the peak level of £240 a year, he served as sheriff and became alderman of Billingsgate. Within a year, he brought off

---

[1] W.A.M. 283; *C.R. 1251–3*, p. 209; *C.C.R. 1296–1302*, p. 590.
[2] An outline biography, with references, may be found in the Appendix.

a brilliant marriage. For his wife was Sabine, daughter of Peter fitz Alan the mercer. Fitz Alan, whose brother was a canon of Holy Trinity, was the great-grandson of Alan, brother of the first mayor Henry fitz Ailwin, and as marriage-portion, Sabine brought with her not only the prestige of her name, but a great block of the fitz Ailwin property in five parishes.

Henceforth Philip's success was assured. By 1280, when the record ceases, he had supplied the Court with wine worth £1,625, an annual average over a quarter-century of £68; his customers now were Roger de Clifford, the earl of Pembroke and the earl of Oxford. The king declared him exempt from prise and tallage, confirmed him in the tenure of his lands. His rent-roll grew. Within the walls, he had scores of holdings in twenty-three parishes, some individual tenements bringing in £4 a year and more. Outside, John de St. John sold him the manor and church of Crayford and leased him that of Erith, and he died in 1291 one of the most powerful city landowners in London and Kent. His sons Henry and John retained much Kentish property and married into the rising families of Picard and Paris; a daughter Sabine was given to John le Mire, a substantial councillor. Three other daughters became nuns at fashionable Clerkenwell, while a fifth, Matilda, married Philip de Beauvais, apothecary son of the King's Surgeon, who by 1293 had succeeded his father in office. Their daughter married an Essex knight. Philip's widow carried on his business for a while, and, a typical patrician lady with her own private chaplain, was one of London's highest taxpayers in the last years of her life. Small wonder that Philip le Tailor emerged in mid-century as a patrician champion in the struggle with the *populares*.

It was his success as a wine merchant which took him into the élite, for however strong the proprietary and curial tradition of the London patriciate, its power in the last resort was rooted in the city's commerce. The English economy, a vital sector of the basic Flemish-Italian connexion, was lively and expansive, London a key distributive centre. It was at an earlier peak of the trade expansion that the city's leaders had won autonomy, and expansion was virtually continuous up to the early fourteenth century. After 1230, the number of aldermen not identified with a trade fell sharply. At least two-thirds of those elected before 1263 carried a trade name and there cannot have been many who did not venture into commerce at some stage of their life.

The range of patrician enterprise was distinctive. At least twenty-one of them were drapers, at least twenty, vintners. The Flemish cloth and wool traffic and the close English-Gascon connexion absorbed most of them who were committed to trade. The remainder serviced those luxury trades which were so lucrative—eight were goldsmiths, seven mercers, and five pepperers.[1] Already these crafts were organized in tight and exclusive fraternities. Goldsmiths and pepperers were among a number of adulterine city gilds amerced in 1180, the former paying forty-five marks, the latter, eighteen.[2] When evidence becomes available from 1272, the goldsmiths' fraternity of St. Dunstan was rooted in patrician society; they were already owning or at least managing land as a gild.[3] The pepperers were acting as an organized group throughout the century. They controlled the Small Beam and their fraternity, which sponsored the creation of the Grocers' Company in 1345, was strong and well-established. At the Iter of 1244 the drapers were treated as a corporate body; by 1257 the vintners' election of two wardens to supervise the trade had become a tradition; the weigher at the Great Beam was elected by a collective of wool merchants.[4] When the mercers' fraternity emerges into the light of evidence in the late thirteenth century, it is a powerful and highly cohesive organization, intervening decisively in mayoral elections and treating the Guildhall chapel of the Pui as its private chantry.[5] None of these gilds ever followed the common mistery pattern of supplication to the aldermanic council for ratification of ordinances and legal power to enforce a monopoly. They were that council. Fully articulated misteries from their first

[1] See tables of designations and interests in the Appendix.

[2] Unwin, *Gilds*, p. 50; adulterine because organized without royal permission.

[3] Hust. Roll (Common Pleas) 2, m.4, 5; A.R. 543, m.12; Recog. Roll 3, m.2; St. Paul's A/13/1128, A/19/207; W.A.M., Domesday, fo. 494b; Unwin, *Gilds*, p. 58.

[4] Misc. Roll AA, p. 73; *Lib. de Ant. Leg.*, pp. 25, 26; *Cal. Letter-Bk. C*, 153; *C.P.R. 1247-58*, p. 585; S. L. Thrupp, 'The Grocers of London', *Studies in English Trade in the Fifteenth Century*, ed. E. E. Power and M. M. Postan, pp. 247-92.

[5] St. Paul's A/22/1632, 1633; *Cal. Letter-Bk. C*, 138, 139; see Chapter X.

appearance in the records, they fulfilled in London the function that the Gild Merchant fulfilled in lesser towns.[1] For these were the fraternities of London's merchant aristocrats, nesting on the central focus, drawing their wealth from the staple wine, cloth and wool of England's economy and from the distribution of expensive products among the upper classes which was their prime function.

William fitz Richard, for example, served as cloth supplier to a great range of knights and barons.[2] The draper, grandson of an Essex immigrant, mayor, bailiff and royal officer, sold the Court cloth worth over £100 for the marriage of the duke of Brunswick in 1263 and on his death eight years later his executors were pursuing debtors in fifteen counties, ranging from Cumberland to Kent. Geoffrey Giffard, bishop of Worcester, and Imbert de Montferrant were among them; James de Audley owed him £30, John de Courtenay, John Comyn and Roger de Somery £40–50. Among his debtors were William de Braose, Robert Aguillon, Laurence de Balliol and William de la Zuche. John de Muscegros owed £101. In all, thirty-eight men were still in debt to the draper to a total of over £610.[3]

His colleagues William Viel, John Norman and John Adrien, one of the most important cloth-sellers in the city listed at the Iter of 1276, dealt continuously with the county aristocracy. Stephen Bukerel supplied Eleanor, countess of Pembroke, with her scarlet; his son William bought from Brabanters and Cahorsins, sold to Sir William de Percy and financed the operations of lesser fellows. At least eighteen aldermen were selling cloth in London in 1276.[4] The complementary trade in wool is very poorly documented. For the earlier generation, only two transactions are recorded, a sale to a Caen merchant and the lading of a ship at Sandwich, but in the early customs accounts and

[1] See Chapter VI.

[2] On this man, see *C.P.R. 1258–66*, pp. 166–516, *passim*; *C.P.R. 1266–72*, pp. 28, 733; *C.P.R. 1272–81*, p. 381; *C.R. 1264–8*, p. 206; *C.Ch.R. 1257–1300*, p. 79; K.R.M.R. 41, m.2; Ancient Deeds E 16; W.A.M. 3912; St. Paul's A/17/1308; *Cart. S.M. Clerkenwell*, p. 132.

[3] The debts may be found in Exchequer Plea Roll 1E; a few of them are indicated in E. F. Jacob, *Studies in the Period of Baronial Reform and Rebellion 1258–67* (Oxford, 1925), p. 33, n.3.

[4] Misc. Roll BB, m.3, 5; *Cal. Letter-Bk. A*, 3, 7, 12, 23, 40; *C. Lib. R. 1245–51*, p. 318; *C.C.R. 1272–9*, p. 44.

the licences of the seventies, some of the later men appear, William de Durham, William Bukerel, John Norman.[1] At Montreuil in 1274, Henry de Coventry was claiming £128 compensation for twenty-four sacks shipped to Bruges, and some were clearly wool merchants of the first order. Thomas de Durham handled 'wool of Morgan' on a large scale, and the draper John Adrien junior, who married Cicely, sister of Laurence de Ludlow, the greatest wool merchant of England, bought up the entire clip of the Warenne estates in Surrey, in 1288, for 600 marks.[2]

Few branches of commerce are adequately documented, but the chancy royal records hint obliquely at intense activity in all fields.[3] For the earlier generation, a stream of safe-conducts points to a brisk maritime traffic, on the Gascon route in particular; agents and factors appear at Boston, Stamford, Bristol and Ireland.[4] Their successors, men like Philip le Tailor, John Norman, Henry de Coventry, were familiar figures at Bruges, Rouen, Amiens as they were at the English fairs.[5] William de Durham took the king's money and messages to Paris and Toulouse and a cluster of merchants followed the Court.[6] For it was Household business which bulked largest. From the thirties, the scale and importance of this traffic increased perceptibly. Hugh Blund, who was supplying jewels for Gascony, silver cups for Rochester Abbey and Marlborough church in the forties, Richard de Walbrook, who was selling ginger and Alexandrine sugar ten years later, were typical.[7]

As the years pass, the range of enterprise widens. By mid-century, stone, tiles, lead, a wide variety of goods were handled.

[1] K.R. Acc. V. (Alien Merchants) E101/127/3; K.R. Customs Acc. E122/68/8, 9; *C.R. 1227–31*, p. 356; *C.R. 1231–4*, pp. 79, 148, 149; *C.P.R. 1266–72*, pp. 688, 704; *C.P.R. 1272–81*, pp. 25–6.

[2] Excheq. Misc. E163/5/17; *C.R. 1242–7*, p. 181; *C.Lib.R. 1240–5*, p. 308; *C.Lib.R. 1245–51*, pp. 364, 370; *C.C.R. 1279–88*, p. 527; *Cal. of Wills*, i, 70, 71.

[3] All the royal records yield evidence, but see, in particular, *C.Lib.R. 1226–60* (final volume, *1251–60*, in P.R.O., printed but not published).

[4] See, in particular, *Pat. Rolls 1216–32*, *C.R. 1231–7* and *C.Lib.R. 1226–40*, *passim*.

[5] See K.R. Acc. V (Alien Merchants) E101/127/2, 3; and *C.R. 1237–72*, *C.Lib.R. 1240–60*, and *C.P.R. 1232–72*, *passim*.

[6] *C.R. 1231–4*, p. 564; *C.P.R. 1258–66*, p. 569; *Hundred Rolls*, i, 411, and *C. Lib.R.*, *passim*.

[7] For these transactions, typical of many, see *C.Lib.R. 1240–5*, p. 174; *C.Lib.R. 1245–51*, pp. 3, 36, 46; *C.Lib.R. 1251–60*, pp. 55, 190, 192.

Richard de Hadestok, who leased his ships to fishmongers, was supplying herrings in 1245; Peter fitz Alan and Adam de Basing handled barley and butter. In the fifties, the first known fishmonger to hold aldermanic office reached the council, in the person of Adam Bruning, who sold sturgeon to the Court and supervised the royal prise of fish.[1] He was accompanied in the same decade by the first alderman skinner, John de Northampton, a merchant with several factors, who married into the Viels and founded a new dynasty. Drawing heavily on the Baltic merchants in London, Northampton fed the Household with furs, supplying consignments at £200 a time. Between 1252 and 1280 his sales averaged £54 a year and in the decade 1250–60 they were running at the annual average of £240.[2] Both he and Bruning were new men of the Baltic connexion, precursors of that powerful mercantile group which grew out of the victualling and industrial crafts under the stimulus of the booming German trade and which climbed into the patriciate at the end of the century.[3]

Before 1263, however, they were isolated figures, for it was the traditional trades which filled the records. Dwarfing all others, even the cloth-wool traffic, was London's own staple, wine. At least twenty-nine aldermen, of all misteries, were engaged in it and these wine merchants were easily the strongest single interest. Fourteen men are known to have handled cloth, eleven to have exported wool. Spices and victuals took five each.[4] At least a third of the aldermen were committed to the wine trade, and these were simply the men who happened to appear in royal records. The real strength of wine traders among patricians must have been greater still. If it were at all possible to characterize the early patriciate in a single phrase, a patriciate of vintners would be the obvious choice.

Moreover, there is probably more evidence of direct and wholesale import by Londoners for the early thirteenth century

---

[1] Lib. Roll 48, m.8; *C.Lib.R. 1226–40*, pp. 258, 377; *C.Lib.R. 1251–60*, pp. 200, 378, 446; *C.R.1254–6*, pp. 175, 176; *C.R. 1256–9*, p. 330.

[2] Lib. Roll 36, m.1; *C.Lib.R. 1251–60*, pp. 29, 53, 145, 153, 186, 190, 192, 409, 447, 448; K.R.M.R. 42, m.7; *C.P.R. 1272–81*, p. 202; *C.C.R. 1272–9*, p. 123; *C.C.R. 1279–88*, p. 24; and see genealogical tables in the Appendix.

[3] See Chapter VI.

[4] See table of interests in the Appendix.

than for any period before the mid-fourteenth. The sheriff
Ralph de Ely, for example, went to Gascony as his father's
agent in 1221 and bought safe-conducts for three of his ships
between 1224 and 1230.[1] William Hardel, the mayor who sealed
Magna Carta, bought wine from a Dunwich shipper in 1218,
brought in his own wine ship in 1224, and in the following year,
imported three shiploads under royal safe-conduct, using his
craft later to bring herring from Yarmouth.[2] From 1217 to the
late twenties, safe-conducts and licences went to a score of
London patricians with craft, their own or those of the Cinque
Ports or Channel towns, on the Biscay route. Between 1224 and
1227 three of them went to John Travers, who also traded with
Yarmouth, and it was this man who partnered Renger, in
1230, in the shipment to London of a thousand crannocks of
corn from the Irish estates of Earl William Marshal.[3] A group
of aldermen, including Bukerel and Joynier, were established in
the Irish trade as they were in the Scottish. Bukerel, Joynier,
Gervase le Cordwaner, fitz Thedmar's brother-in-law Walter
de Winton and many others bought Irish grain and Scottish
hides in the exchange pattern with Gascony which became
traditional.[4] Richard de Hadestok had a Gascon partner; two
of the early aldermen were themselves Gascon immigrants.[5]

In mid-century, there is less evidence of direct import as safe-
conducts become rare, though certainly men like Ralph Hardel,
John Norman and Richard de Hadestok had their craft on the
route. It is sales to the Household which fill the rolls now.
Coventrys, Durhams, Aungiers and the rest throng in the
records, enmeshed like their predecessors in the complementary
Irish and Scottish trade.[6] William Hardel's sons Robert and

[1] *Pat. Rolls 1216–25*, pp. 284, 494; *Pat. Rolls 1225–32*, pp. 268, 334.

[2] K.R.M.R. 1, m.1d; *Pat. Rolls 1216–25*, pp. 467, 468, 499, 510, 554.

[3] *Pat. Rolls 1216–25*, pp. 470, 511, 526; *Pat. Rolls 1225–32*, pp. 18, 109; *C.R. 1227–31*, p. 291.

[4] *Pat. Rolls 1216–25*, pp. 275, 493; *Pat. Rolls 1225–32*, pp. 17, 18, 40, 241, 261; *C.R. 1227–31*, pp. 210, 356; *C.R. 1231–4*, pp. 79, 148, 149; *C.R.1234–7*, p. 72; *C.P.R. 1232–47*, pp. 14, 99.

[5] For these instances and other characteristic examples of wine trade enterprise, see *Pat. Rolls 1216–25*, p. 467; *Pat. Rolls 1225–32*, pp. 65, 319; *C.R. 1234–7*,
pp. 232, 485; *C.R. 1237–42*, p. 433; *C.P.R. 1232–47*, p. 92; *C.P.R. 1247–58*, p. 27;
C.P.R. 1258–66, p. 21; *C.Lib.R. 1226–40*, pp. 57, 92, 115, 256.

[6] See, for example, Lib. Roll 36, m.1; Misc. Roll BB, m.2, 3; *C.Lib.R. 1251–60*,
pp. 204 and *passim; C.R. 1251–3*, p. 99; *Cal. Letter-Bk. A*, 15.

Ralph became important royal merchants, the latter buying safe-conducts for two shiploads in 1235 and supplying the Household at up to £100 a time in the forties and fifties.[1] Andrew Bukerel's nephew, John Blund, served as taker of the king's wines at Southampton and trafficked with the Gascons established there.[2] Men like Philip le Tailor and John de Gisors were shipping in cargoes of 150 tuns and selling to the Court at a rate which sometimes approached £300 a year for decades at a time.[3] As late as 1285, when the disgruntled Cinque Portsmen protested against the wine merchants, the two men they singled out by name as leaders were the Londoners Henry le Waleys and Gregory de Rokesle.[4] Both men recorded individual purchases of 200–300 tuns at a time; both shipped Libourne and St. Emilion claret direct from Gascony to London and Boston. Waleys was at one time mayor of Bordeaux itself; he got £548 for his wine in 1261, and over twenty years averaged £100 annually in sales to the Household.[5] The early sixties, indeed, were a climax for London's wine patricians. Waleys's average then was running at £300 a year and in 1261, six of his colleagues got over £1,400 of the royal money. Few Gascons could equal these totals.[6]

The role of this cluster of London patricians in the wine trade stands out in sharp contrast to the overall picture of a 'colonial' English economy largely under alien control. The trade, of course, was still young. The connexion with Gascony was close, English cloth went south; the wine trade would be one of the few in which the thirteenth-century English could be something more than clients of the aliens. And one may perhaps doubt how far the eminence of the few was matched by the industry of the many. Outside the wine trade, the leading

---

[1] *Pat. Rolls 1225–32*, p. 265; *C.R.1234–7*, p. 217; *C.R.1251–3*, p. 330; *C.Lib.R. 1226–40*, pp. 38, 285, 398, 481; *C.Lib.R. 1240–5*, pp. 20, 39, 40, 102, 118, 210; *C.Lib.R. 1245–51*, pp. 56, 113; *C.Lib.R. 1251–60*, pp. 204, 274, 328.

[2] *C.R. 1261–4*, p. 375; *C.R. 1268–72*, p. 64.

[3] See below.

[4] *C.P.R. 1281–92*, p. 168.

[5] *C.C.R. 1272–9*, pp. 87, 142; *C.R. 1279–88*, p. 127; *C.C.R. 1288–96*, p. 97; *C.P.R. 1272–81*, p. 126; *C.P.R. 1281–92*, p. 148; *Cal. E.M.C. Rolls*, pp. 38, 39; outline biographies of Waleys and Rokesle may be found in the Appendix.

[6] Lib. Roll 37, m.7; for comparison, see the sales by Gascons in *C.P.R. 1301–7*, pp. 128–496, *passim*.

F

Londoners cut little ice. Their contact with the Italian companies, the giants of European trade, seems to have been sporadic and fortuitous. Some mercers and pepperers, of course, bought their goods; indeed in later years the city spicers drew many of their recruits from the *Lombards*.[1] But the great companies remained in London rather than of it. William de Durham was in debt to the Betti in 1280 and Anketil de Auverne deposited £200 with the Riccardi in 1291, but London's thieves seem to have made more use of the Italians' facilities than its aldermen.[2] That their relations were closer with the lesser, more localized companies of Cahorsins and Jews is symptomatic.

Yet, minor figures though they were in the general economy, among their own people, they stood apart. Members of the Turri family were established in Genoa by the late twelfth century; some of the Eswys were trading as far afield as Leipzig in 1250, and these may not be the freakish examples they appear.[3] In the London context, there is some justification for the view that they, and the wine merchants in particular, were 'merchant princes'.[4] Silhouetted as they are in the meagre royal records, they have the air of a small and perhaps precocious élite, without roots in any integrated and fully developed commercial milieu. For as the city grew to maturity, royal merchants of their peculiar type tended to disappear.

Clearly, the key was the monarchy. The city's élite of wine merchants was dependent on royal favour. Their fate under Edward I suggests that they were utterly dependent. Edward's accession signalized an abrupt transfer of royal favour to

[1] See Chapter V.

[2] K.R. Acc. V. (Alien Merchants) E101/126/28, m.2; K.R.M.R. 40, m.8; *Cal. E.M.C. Rolls*, pp. 94, 200, 201; see also *Cal. E.M.C. Rolls*, pp. 109–29; A.R. 1187, m.9d; K.R. Acc V. (Sheriffs Accounts) E101/571/8(5) and *Cal. Letter-Bks., A, B, C, passim.*

[3] *C.R. 1247–51*, p. 289 (the family of the Adrien named descended from Adrien Eswy and ranked as a branch of the Eswy dynasty); R.L. Reynolds, 'Some English settlers in Genoa in the late twelfth century', *Economic History Review*, iv (1933).

[4] See M. M. Postan, 'The trade of medieval Europe: the north', *Cambridge Economic History of Europe*, ii, 240; all the men named there, save the Ludlows, were Londoners, but more important merchants, such as Gisors and Tailor, are omitted and that these dynasties 'merged imperceptibly' with the fourteenth-century oligarchs is doubtful, at least in London (see Chapter V and VI).

Gascons and Italians, and with equal abruptness, London patricians were displaced from the wine trade. This was the most important single economic factor in the disruption of the dynastic social order in London. At the same time the royal organization and concentration of the wool trade profoundly affected the composition of the patriciate.[1] Within the context of general trade expansion, it was the operation of the monarchy which fixed the pattern of the aldermanic economy.

The decisive feature of that economy before the Barons' Wars was the continuation of the close rapport with the Household market and system which aldermen had established in the reigns of Richard and John and during the minority of Henry III. The key mercantile posts were the royal chamberlainship of London in the wine trade and the wardenship of the Exchange. Before the coming of Edward to power, London goldsmiths and vintners virtually monopolized these posts. In the twenties and thirties, the chamberlainship was held by Bukerel, Joynier, Gervase le Cordwaner and Simon fitz Mary. John de Gisors held the office twice and was succeeded by Mathew Bukerel and John Blund.[2] The goldsmith Michael de St. Helena succeeded his alderman brother at the Mint in 1217 and married off his daughter to William de Gloucester, King's Goldsmith, Master of Exchange and father of a future alderman. William fitz Benedict followed; Andrew Bukerel bought control of the Exchange, Renger leased it. William fitz Richard held the office for many years in mid-century and as late as 1283 John fitz Peter of the fitz Ailwins was serving as keeper at Canterbury.[3]

Even if vague positions such as that of 'King's merchant' are ignored, four out of every ten aldermen held important offices in the royal administration.[4] The earlier generation specialized

---

[1] See Chapter V.

[2] *Pat. Rolls 1216–25*, p. 364; *Pat. Rolls 1225–32*, p. 226; *C.R. 1227–31*, p. 123; *C.R. 1231–4*, p. 386; *C.Lib.R. 1226–40*, p. 158; *C.P.R. 1232–47*, p. 167; *C.P.R. 1247–58*, pp. 180, 505; *C.R. 1254–6*, p. 368; *C.R. 1261–4*, p. 375; *C.Lib.R. 1251–60*, p. 335.

[3] L.T.R.M.R. 1, m.5, 6, 7; 4, m.3d, 4d; K.R.M.R. 41, m.2; Hust. Roll 2 (18), 14(36); *Pat. Rolls 1216–25*, pp. 138, 272; *C.P.R. 1258–66*, pp. 249, 513, 516; *C.R. 1264–8*, p. 206; see also the brief tenure of John de Gisors in 1262–3—*C.P.R. 1258–66*, pp. 197, 219, 227; *C.R. 1261–4*, pp. 198, 202.

[4] See table of interests in the Appendix.

in financial service.[1] Others served as keepers of the Jews.[2] Ralph de Ely and Richard de Hadestok joined the Exchequer staff, Northampton, Adam de Basing and Laurence de Frowyk were Wardrobe buyers. There was a wide range of contractual service. William fitz Richard, Roger le Duc, Stephen Bukerel, Henry de Cookham paid the wages of royal workmen, went surety for royal debts and sometimes repaid them. Roger Blund and others acted as confidential agents; John le Minur conducted the Wardrobe from London to Winchester at Christmas 1255.[3] With this official establishment went an entrenched position in the royal markets. Household supply became an increasingly important element in aldermanic enterprise and, in the wine trade, the Londoners were a vital and perhaps dominant supply group. Royal patronage was the highroad to success.

The most eminent of these royal merchants, for example, was John de Gisors. He was something of an outsider.[4] His father Peter was an important citizen, but his grandfather John had been an alien, probably of Norman origin, who was selling wine and buying land in London in the early years of the century. The family joined the international fraternity of the wine trade; two of Gisors' nephews were Gascons of Bordeaux. John himself was a pepperer, one of the group in closest touch with the aliens, but he handled the customary wide range of goods, from lead to wool, in constant traffic with Italians, Gascons, and Rouennais, and in frequent attendance at Boston and the fairs. He used his own ships, which brought merchandise from Scotland in 1242 and carried the queen and her retinue to Gascony ten years later. His first important success was in 1236. In that year he was buying heavily from Gascon importers and sold wine worth £100 to the Seneschal at Bordeaux. He

[1] See, for example, *Pat. Rolls 1216–25*, pp. 272, 512, 527, 528; *C.P.R. 1232–47*, pp. 209, 217, 218, 230; *C.Lib.R. 1226–40*, pp. 326, 327.

[2] *C.Lib.R. 1226–40*, pp. 196–226 and *passim*; *C.R. 1231–4*, pp. 246–415 and *passim*; *C.R. 1234–7*, pp. 78–396 and *passim*, for Joce fitz Peter as Keeper of the House of Converts; see also L.T.R.M.R. 3, m.2d; *C.P.R. 1258–66*, p. 577; *C.R.1247–51*, p. 260.

[3] See, for example, *C.Lib.R. 1226–40*, pp. 21, 103; *C.Lib.R. 1251–60*, p. 513; *C.Lib.R. 1240–5*, pp. 18, 207; *C.R. 1227–31*, pp. 383, 384; *C.R. 1231–4*, p. 564; *C.R. 1242–7*, pp. 32, 305; *C.P.R. 1232–47*, p. 244; *C.P.R. 1258–66*, pp. 293, 294, 456, 457, 569.

[4] An outline biography, with references, may be found in the Appendix.

and his partner were commissioned to buy spices and Lagny cloth for the Court and almost at once he was made royal chamberlain of London and king's butler. The all-important connexion with the Household had been established.

It developed into a personal relationship with Henry. As early as 1237 the king was taking pains to ensure the Londoner's safe possession of his manor of Great Baddow in Essex, and in the forties, Gisors was acting as Henry's personal agent. He found him a falcon in 1240, sold him a palfrey for his gift to the count of Toulouse five years later. He bought wheat for the Household and paid the wages of the king's men-at-arms. His wine flowed into the royal cellars. From 1240 Gisors was buying great properties in the Vintry and in 1243 was elected alderman of the ward. Two years later he was mayor and exempt from the prise of wine for life.

Installed as Protector of the House of Converts in 1250, he was reappointed chamberlain three years later, and his wine sales to the Household climbed over the £250 a year mark. The bishops of London and Carlisle, Philip Lovel and the earl of Pembroke were among his customers. His brother Peter joined him, and when John relinquished office in 1256, Peter succeeded, though at the king's request the alderman continued to assist his brother, occasionally transporting royal wine in his own carts. On resigning office, he went on a special mission for Henry to Amiens, was pardoned for monetary offences and finally exempted from tallage for life. Two years later, he was mayor again and in 1262 Henry made him Master of Exchange. It is not surprising that John de Gisors was the leader of the royalist faction in London during the Barons' Wars.

His sales to the Court continued to 1261, averaging £53 a year over twenty-four years. He married the sister of Arnold fitz Thedmar and kept adding to his Vintry estate. Outside the walls, he leased three manors in Essex, three in Kent and some property in Hertfordshire from the earl of Chester, Ralph de Tony, Philip de Columbariis and William de Valence, and while Peter installed his daughters as nuns at Kilburn and married off his sons into the Bukerels and Wilehales, John founded a civic dynasty of the first order. One of the great mayors himself, his son John and grandsons John, Anketil and Henry became merchants, rentiers, aldermen and mayors of considerable prestige. Though the thirteenth and fourteenth centuries were its golden age, this family remained prominent in London life for three hundred years, leaving Gisors Hall as its memorial.

It may be doubted whether Gisors or any other of London's patrician merchants would have made any showing in an English economy still overshadowed by alien enterprise without the vital prop of royal service and supply. It was the removal of that prop after the Barons' Wars which set in train the trans-formation of the aldermanic class. Before the Wars, service in the royal administration was a formative influence in patrician society. Office meant privilege, exemptions, wardships, lands. It opened up avenues for the promotion of trade and useful social relationships. It conferred status and a certain security. Thomas de Durham, for example, entered the service of Joan, Queen of Scots, in the thirties. After her death, he disposed of her goods at Boston Fair and managed her manor of Driffield in Yorkshire. He remained in the service, going on missions to Scotland and elsewhere. Land was his reward and on that land his son Jollan lived as a knight.[1]

Inevitably, these aldermanic groups and the coteries of law-yers, clerks and officials clustered at the administrative hub in Westminster became increasingly interpenetrated. There was a complementary movement, slow at first, but accelerating with the growth of the English community, from royal service into the patriciate. Richard de Ewell, for example, who became alderman of Ludgate-Newgate in 1258, acquired his alder-manry almost in passing. The son of a Surrey gentleman, he entered Wardrobe service and became a trusted royal agent, emerging in the reign of Edward I as a king's familiar, the recipient of lavish favours, and the owner of nine manors. His career as a London alderman was transient; his will contains merely a curt injunction to sell his city property.[2] The intrusion

---

[1] *C.Ch.R. 1226–57*, p. 250; *C.P.R. 1232–47*, pp. 183, 214, 235; *C.P.R. 1247–58*, p. 133; *C.R. 1237–42*, p. 128; *C.Lib.R. 1226–40*, p. 319.

[2] References to Ewell are too numerous for individual mention. See, in general, *C.R.*, *C.C.R.* and *C.P.R.* for the period 1247–96, and, in particular, *C.Ch.R. 1226–57*, p. 422; *C.P.R. 1281–92*, pp. 46, 417, 418; *C.P.R. 1247–58*, p. 221; K.R.M.R. 40, m.8; 42, m.14d, 18, 20d, 27; Cur. Reg. Roll 174, m.10, 11d, 20d; 175, m.27; A.R. 538, m.6d; *Cal. Inq. Misc.*, i, 272; *Ann. Lond.*, p. 74; *Cal. of Wills*, i, 100, 245, 249.

of such men in increasing numbers tended to disturb the rhythm of patrician life. Before the civil war they were few enough merely to strengthen the Westminster-Guildhall connexion. Inevitably, royal service, with its prestige, its training, its prizes, profoundly affected the temper of the aldermanic class. With the exception of Ralph Hardel, whose family tradition was distinctive, all the great wine merchants, for example, were ardent royalists during the troubles.[1]

Of basic importance to communal society in the first phase of self-government, therefore, was the fact that there was little fundamental change in the character of the royal connexion. A certain shift in emphasis may be detected. Aldermen of the earlier generation seem to enjoy higher status. Renger and Reyner de Bungheye served as justices. They and their friends were familiars of the Marshals, witnessed the deeds of archbishops. Gervase de Aldermanbury, in a deed of 1237, ranked fourth after the Chancellor, John fitz Geoffrey and Robert de Muscegros. Londoners attended at the deposition of Peter des Rivaux; the dower of Berengaria was settled by a committee which included the mayor, Thomas de Haverhill and William fitz Benedict.[2] Moreover, they seem more markedly a landed and official class; they include a large number of non-traders, and there is little of that substantial and regular sale of goods to the Household which characterized the later men.[3]

The change is in part illusory. Only after the loss of Normandy in 1204 did the royal household, the great courts, and the seat of administration find a permanent home in England. Only as Henry's reign got under way did the supplying of the Household, with its vast and insatiable demand, become a vital element in the city's economy. Moreover, Richard had been an absentee king; under John, the country was divided; for a considerable time after 1216 England was ruled by a council of regency. In conditions of this kind, London and Londoners tended to assume a political and social importance they did not otherwise enjoy. The shift in emphasis after the coming-of-age

[1] See Chapters VII and VIII.
[2] See, for example, *Pat. Rolls 1216–25*, p. 265; *C.P.R. 1232–47*, pp. 53, 281, 427; *C.R. 1234–7*, pp. 535, 561; *C.R. 1237–42*, p. 403; *C.R. 1242–7*, p. 253; *C.Lib.R. 1240–45*, p. 85.
[3] See tables in the Appendix.

of Henry is dutifully reflected in the royal records, the sole important source of information, and in those single-minded documents, aldermen gradually become more 'bourgeois' and less 'knightly'. The record changed more than the reality.

This is not to deny the increasing importance of trade within the complex pattern of aldermanic interests. The expansion bred new groups and families; by mid-century it was beginning to have its effect on the structure of the patriciate. But before the coming of Edward, the aldermanic class remained unchanged in its essentials. Victuallers and representatives of the industrial crafts, of the new Baltic and Spanish trades, were rare birds on the council. It was wine, cloth, wool, goldsmiths' work and spices, with their five or six patrician fraternities, which produced aldermen, still drawn almost exclusively from the old families. It was the strength of their inherited position at Court and on the land, coupled with the assimilative power of their 'baronial' traditions, which enabled the dynasties to ride the expansion.

Adam de Basing, for example, was typical of his fellows.[1] His family had been established in the patriciate since the mid-twelfth century; his father had been one of the 'knightly' landowners of the Minority. He himself married Desiderata, offspring of the union of the dynastic Viels and fitz Alulfs. His landed inheritance in Aldermanbury, with its Basing Lane and Basinghall Street, supplemented by the fitz Alulf selds, buttressed his commerce, and he adjusted himself easily to the demands of an expanding economy. He immersed himself in the Irish trade, handling corn and hides, and acting as surety for the executors of the archbishop of Tuam, but it was the royal trade which made him. He became an outstanding supplier of costly fabrics and luxury goods, larest, cloth of gold, samite copes and precious ware. It was he who provided rich vestments for the abbot of Westminster, the bishop of Besançon, and for a score of royal chapels. The silver dishes which the queen gave to Simon de Montfort in 1242, Lord Edward's tunics, were purchased from him. As payment in 1244, he was granted the entire wool clip of the bishopric of Winchester, which brought him in over £200, and over the twenty-three years from 1238 to

---

[1] An outline biography, with references, may be found in the Appendix.

1260 his annual sales to the Household averaged £79. In the late forties and early fifties he was making £250 a year. It was at that peak period, too, that he went on royal missions, got his aldermanry and bought the great Aldermanbury soke. His son was shaping to a brilliant career in the wool trade when he was cut down by sudden death, but his nephew Thomas and kinsman Robert were important figures in the Low Countries trade, and his grandchildren married into the Hadestoks, Bedyks and Frowyks, giving the latter a new lease of life. Their landed establishment and, more important, their position in the royal system carried the mercantile Basings through to the early fourteenth century, even as many of their dynastic cousins lost their footing as expansion mounted to a peak and royal support dwindled at the turn of the century.

The Basings displayed an unusual capacity for survival in the Edwardian world, but before 1263 many other old families were equally adaptable. Despite the intensifying social pressures exerted by a buoyant economy, the dynasties more than held their own, so that in London society the first seventy years of the thirteenth century were, in essence, a prolongation of the twelfth. The patriciate was never a caste. The motives and opportunities for dispersal, so effective in later years, were scarcely less attractive at this period. There was a constant pull towards the church, the law, the royal service. John Renger took the fitz Reiners out of the city; the main line of the fitz Ailwins married into the knighthood and the family patrimony was dispersed among Aguillons and Bardolfs. The sons of Peter fitz Alan and William fitz Richard were clerks and pleaders at Westminster. Patrician families were constantly disappearing. Fitz Alulfs vanish from sight. There were still Bucointes in London and Middlesex in 1300, but they had fallen from the patriciate a hundred years earlier.[1] Natural misfortunes and political accidents took their toll. Such disappearances, however, were few and of merely marginal importance.

No less marginal were the handful of thrusting newcomers who joined the élite.[2] Most of these were immigrants or of

[1] See W.A.M., St. Paul's, *passim*; Hust. Roll 1(36); W. Page, *op. cit.*, *passim*; Hust. Rolls and A.R., *passim*, and compare S. L. Thrupp, *The Merchant Class of Medieval London*, especially pp. 191–233.

[2] For this section, see the table on aldermanic origins in the Appendix.

recent immigrant antecedents. Only two of the aldermen elected before 1263 are known to have risen from established but non-dynastic London families; four others may have done so. The intensely self-conscious oligarchy of cousins preferred successful outsiders, turned to alien or English immigrant circles, each of which supplied eight or nine new aldermen in the period. It is extremely difficult to be precise about the origins of such men, but the degree of precision is unimportant, for new aldermen of immediate or recent immigrant antecedents before 1263 numbered less than a score. The overwhelming majority of the aldermen came from families which had been established in the patriciate in the twelfth century.

For the hallmark of the régime was its stability. There was no serious failure of fertility or shift of interest. This was a tenacious aristocracy, essentially urban in character, riveting on London a patrician régime whose solidity contrasts strangely with that of its successors. Before 1230, over 80 per cent of the aldermen were drawn from the established families. Only in the last ten years before the explosion of 1263 did their representation fall below 50 per cent, as the first fishmonger and the first skinner reached the council. Even so, among the 'outsiders' in that decade were Arnold fitz Thedmar, who became a spokesman for the dynasties, and Philip le Tailor, who married into them. Dynastic representation as a whole was overwhelming. In the period from 1240 to 1250, it was running at no less than 85 per cent.

The core of the class was a group belonging to the oldest families in the city. The fitz Ailwins, for example, originated in Ailwin Horne, a thegn of Edward the Confessor who held land in Hertfordshire. His grandson became portreeve of the city and other kinsmen, the church-founder Orgar, and Leofstan, one of the *cnihtenagild*, were prominent in London affairs around 1100. Henry fitz Ailwin, the first mayor, was a grandson of Leofstan, and his brother Alan carried on the city branch. Between 1191 and 1263 this family alone supplied out of its natural members at least ten aldermen.[1] The Viels, aldermen since the early twelfth century, supplied five, so did the Bukerels.

---

[1] For the early history of this family, see T. Stapleton, preface to *Lib. de Ant. Leg.*, and W. Page, *op. cit.*, 248–52.

Others dated from the mid-twelfth century, Blunds providing ten aldermen, Eswys five, fitz Alulfs, Bats, and Basings, three each.[1]

They were enmeshed in a web of marriage-relationships. An alderman's daughter could not be disparaged and there was dower to consider. Newcomers had to be assimilated. Towards the end of the century, as social mobility accelerated, the marriageable daughters of aldermanic families were acting as a stabilizing influence, preserving old standards of conduct and belief in a time of disconcerting changes. In earlier years, intermarriage was a powerful cohesive force, welding these families into an estate. Four of the oldest families, for example, the fitz Ailwins, Viels, Bukerels and fitz Alulfs were closely related by marriage, and by the same tie bound to other cousinhoods only slightly less venerable, Blunds, Eswys, Basings, Hadestoks, Hardels, Bats and Durhams. To these were linked the newer families of fitz Thedmar, William fitz Richard, Frowyk, Winton and Gisors.[2] This *lignage* alone, itself connected to other groupings, provided sixty-four of the ninety-five aldermen elected before 1263. Nearly 70 per cent of the aldermen who held office before the civil war belonged to no more than sixteen interlocking families. Left to themselves, London's aldermen would have created a régime similar to that of the Thirty-Nine of Ghent.[3]

In their own eyes, they were the commune. Their chronicles were aristocratic in temper. They maintained a traditional style. Lavish in their patronage of the Church, they founded hospitals, built choirs, endowed monasteries. They were the keepers of the law. Above all, they were the heirs of illustrious ancestors to whom the city, as a political community, owed its very existence. The aldermen had inherited a patrimony and a tradition. The peace of London depended on the way they administered their inheritance.

[1] See the genealogical tables in the Appendix and W. Page, *op. cit., passim.*
[2] See the genealogical tables in the Appendix.
[3] Compare with H. van Werveke, *Gand: esquisse d'histoire sociale* (Brussels, 1946).

CHAPTER IV

The Administration and its Officers

GOVERNMENT in the early years of the commune was a matter for practised amateurs of good family. The administrative resources at their disposal were by no means negligible. The corpus of city custom was already massive, Husting and wardmoot were mature tribunals. City clerks and the fiscal chamberlain of Guildhall were functioning before the twenties.[1] At this date, however, there is no trace of the complicated structure and large staffs of later years and there were no *clerks*, no professional civic administrators on the aldermanic council.

As the city grew, so did its administrative service. There was a tradition in the fourteenth century that Henry fitz Ailwin, the first mayor, gave comprehensive definition to procedure in all the *assizes* of London on the morrow of autonomy. The first building assize followed in a few years and, sometime in the twenties, the council promulgated twenty-five articles as the 'statutes of London'. Preceded by justificatory preambles and concluding with a sonorous exhortation to the Londoners to live in Christian amity and endow a city chaplain, these articles may well represent the council's first venture into new legislation.[2] A stream of regulations and ordinances followed over the years to culminate in the codification of city custom by Mayor Gregory de Rokesle between 1274 and 1280. Rokesle's *assizes*, amended after close scrutiny by royal officers who took over the city in 1285, remained the basis of all further legislative and administrative action.[3]

[1] Lib. Ordinationum, fo. 172b; Ancient Deeds B 4416; *Cat. Anc. Deeds*, i, 14 (A140).

[2] Lib. Ordinationum, fo. 169, 172b–4; *Lib. Albus*, pp. 319–22; *Lib. de Ant. Leg.*, pp. 206–11.

[3] For Rokesle's *assizes*, see Lib. Ordinationum, fo. 174b ff.; *Lib. Cust.*, pp. 282–3; *Cal. Letter-Bk. A*, 217–19; Edward's ordinances are found in Lib. Ordinationum, fo. 190b–202b, with copies in *Lib. Cust.* and *Lib. Albus*; see Chapter IX.

The first ordinance to be passed in the twenties established communal archives. By this date, Husting records were entered on rolls and there were other official collections, traces of which abound in the city chronicles. Most of them, however, were personal and private. The earliest legal compilation of the commune dates from John's reign and probably emanated from the Cornhill family.[1] Aldermen like fitz Thedmar created private archives. So did the sheriffs.[2] The council, addressing itself to this problem of dispersal, established a registry at Guildhall, and centralized all muniments. In future, full record was to be kept of all public business. Enrolment of freedoms and apprentices was ordered in the twenties, special Iter records in midcentury. By 1252, date of the earliest surviving Husting roll, wills and deeds already formed a separate class.[3]

It is from the reign of Edward I that most surviving city records date and this is surely no accident. The English state was growing to maturity and the structure of city government was shaped in response. Bartholomew de Castell, trained royal official and clerk to the Chancellor Burnell, was serving as alderman in this period.[4] It is tempting to see in him a civic Hubert Walter, but hardly necessary. The city was following the trend of the times, manifest even in such minutiae as the standardization of deeds under the Common Clerk Hugh Waltham.[5] From 1272 begins the dual series of Husting plea

[1] Addit. Ms. 14252 in M. Bateson, 'A London municipal collection of the reign of John', *English Historical Review*, xvii (1902), 480–511, 707–30. One cannot accept Miss Bateson's view that this was an official collection. The author describes Thames-side rents as 'our soke'; there were no Chamber rents here in the fourteenth century and 'our' can scarcely refer to the city, since the writer repeatedly describes city land as 'the king's soke'. The tone of the compilation is that of a *modo*; the writer is very interested in the Cornhill family, constructs its pedigree and includes a great deal of material on the civic justiciars of Henry II, the most important of whom was Gervase de Cornhill. The collection was compiled between 1206 and 1216; John de Cornhill was serving as alderman in this period (Beaven, i, 366).

[2] *Lib. de Ant. Leg.*, p. 253 and *passim; Lib. Albus*, pp. 44, 199–223; *Lib. Cust.*, p. 280.

[3] Lib. Ordinationum, fo. 172b, 173; Misc. Rolls AA, BB; Hust. Rolls; *Cal. of Wills*.

[4] Chanc. Misc. 3/21(18); Hust. Roll 16(125); 24(57); *C.R. 1264–8*, p. 262; *C.P.R. 1266–72*, pp. 394, 596, 651; *C.R. 1268–72*, p. 399; *Lib. de Ant. Leg.*, pp. 114–15.

[5] See, for example, the city deeds in St. Paul's A/17, many of which bear Waltham's signature.

rolls, what survives of the rolls of the mayor, sheriffs, and chamberlain. Under the rule of royal wardens between 1285 and 1298, duplicate court rolls were ordered and whole new series created. The administrative tradition of the city crystallized as the precedent letter-books were drawn up. Andrew Horn and Hugh Waltham compiled the magnificent London law-books, and carefully copied Brunetto Latini's treatise on town government into *Liber Custumarum*.[1] There was an abiding interest in the sheer craft of government. For government had become a craft. Systematic record gave backbone to the administration, called for trained staff. It bred professionalism.

Increasing complexity in the process of government, of course, was merely a reflection of its increasingly complex responsibilities. The communal conception of the good life called for the most minute regulation of all citizen activity. Foremost among all the ordinances were those regulating commerce and industry. The purpose was simple, the maintenance of the equalitarian oligarchy of citizens. The primary aim was to ensure an adequate food supply at reasonable prices, by controlling victuallers and suppressing middlemen. No less important was the citizens' trade monopoly. No alien merchant, save the privileged, was to stay more than forty days; he was to deal only with citizens, live in a licensed hostel, and operate through a sworn broker. Then there were the crafts to be scrutinized, measures tested, market-selds managed.[2]

The legislation which resulted was monumental in scale, a staggering display of civic ingenuity and resource. Rolls and law-books are full of edicts and prosecutions. The difficulties the system encountered were matched only by the zeal with which it was enforced, a zeal which entailed virtually continuous

[1] Misc. Roll CC is the only surviving sheriff's roll; extracts from others and from the chamberlains' records may be found in the Letter-Books and *Cal. E.M.C. Rolls*; the earlier Recognizance Rolls (Statute of Merchants) and most of the Husting plea rolls survive—see P. E. Jones and R. Smith, *A Guide to the Records in the Corporation of London Records Office* (London, 1951); for the duplication order, see Lib. Ordinationum, fo. 201; for Latini, see *Lib. Cust.*, pp. 16–25.

[2] These voluminous regulations bulk large in all city records; for some typical specimens, see M. Bateson, *op. cit.*, 496–502, 710–11, 724; *Lib. Albus*, pp. 228–9, 310, 323; *Lib. Cust.*, pp. 61–4, 164–6; Lib. Ordinationum, fo. 225–6; for their enforcement, see some examples in K.R. Acc. V. (Alien Merchants) E101/126/6, m.1; and *Cal. E.M.C. Rolls*, pp. 50–3, 58, 59, 72, 84, 161, 168 and *passim*.

administrative and judicial action, endless inquest, presentment and punishment. The basis of all action was informed public opinion, the good men of trade and ward, but every new provision called for new appointments and by the early fourteenth century, a staff of permanent and part-time supervisory officials had been called into existence. There were even traces of a class of professional brokers.[1]

Hardly less challenging was the problem of order. Police resources were inadequate and in a community of lusty spirits given to heavy drinking and the more hair-raising entertainments, breaches of the peace were commonplace. But not all offences were as quixotic as that of John le Furber of Cornhill who used church-towers as targets for crossbow practice.[2] There was a small but dangerous group of professional thugs, the *bellatores*, reinforced by a whole fraternity of wrongdoers, ranging from robber gangs of 'Roarers' to idle chaplains with a taste for mayhem and fraudulent bakers who roamed the streets after curfew, armed to the teeth, looking for trouble among the equally illicit dice-players in the taverns.[3] Murder was serious enough to wait on the Iters and the city relied in the main on the frankpledge system and the vigilance of wardmoots, countering serious resistance with the hue and cry.[4] Rokesle tightened up the regulations but the first sustained attack on the problem was made by Mayor Henry le Waleys in 1281–4, on royal orders, when the council tried to open a dossier on everyone living in the city.[5] Despite the furious controversy over jurisdiction which attended these edicts, they remained in force. They produced the first crop of criminal proceedings to appear in the letter-books in 1281 and were the warrant for similar prosecutions under the reforming mayor Richer de Refham in 1311. In 1324 Hamo de Chigwell petitioned for their

[1] On the general aspects of this system, see Unwin, *Gilds*, pp. 30 ff.; S. L. Thrupp, *A Short History of the Worshipful Company of Bakers of London* (London, 1933); H. Pirenne, *Histoire économique de l'occident mediéval*, pp. 310–30; L. F. Salzman, *English Trade in the Middle Ages* (Oxford, 1931), chapters 4–6.

[2] *Cal. E.M.C. Rolls*, p. 205.   [3] See *Cal. Letter-Bk. B*, 1–12, 256–80.

[4] See Misc. Roll AA, p. 52; A.R. 1187, m.9; *Cal. E.M.C. Rolls*, pp. 218–19, 211; the frankpledge system enforced group responsibility for individual conduct.

[5] *Lib. Cust.*, pp. 82–3, 213, 282–3, 292, 327–29; Lib. Ordinationum, fo. 197b–8; *Cal. Letter-Bk. A*, 120, 121, 208, 213, *B*, 13, 14, 241–44, *C*, 15–17, 84, 85; *Ann. Lond.*, p. 90.

renewal.[1] In 1327 the mayor was made *ex officio* justice of gaol delivery at Newgate and empowered to hang hand-having thieves. A series of multiple hangings followed.[2] The good men of the ward were still the basis of the police system, but with wider powers and responsibility and greater reliance on registration, a staff of enforcement officers came into being, from searchers in the wards to Guildhall clerks seconded to peace duties.

It was the pressure of this primary legislation, above all, which stimulated the development of the wards. There were twenty-four of them, the suburb outside Portsoken, vaguely de-limited by bars, falling within the jurisdiction of the nearest intramural ward. By the fourteenth century, the extramural appendages of Aldersgate, Bishopsgate, Cripplegate and Far-ringdon were being treated as separate entities.[3] The ward was the basis of the entire system and by the reign of Edward II had become a flexible instrument of government. It had its own staff headed by the beadle and his serjeants, supple-mented by numerous temporary officials. The moot, presided over by the alderman and directed by his clerk, registered free-men, examined victuallers and hostel-keepers, appointed scavengers, ale-conners and other officers, sealed measures. All proceedings were recorded. A long series of undifferentiated articles parallel to the general *assizes* was presented to it, in the manner of the royal Iter, and the answers of its juries were entered on an indenture, one copy going to the alderman, the other remaining with the ward, which must have had archives of its own.[4]

For action on the wardmoot verdicts, the city turned to its courts. Indeed, the practice of government was interpreted almost entirely in judicial terms, and in these functions, which by their nature called for a measure of skill or training, the

---

[1] *P. and M. Rolls*, i, 5; *Cal. Letter-Bk. D*, 1-14, 262-7.

[2] *Historical Charters*, ed. W. de G. Birch, p. 53; *Cal. Letter-Bk. E*, 276-80, 288-9; on the commission of the peace in London, see A. H. Thomas, *Cal. E.M.C. Rolls*, xi-xxix.

[3] *Cal. Letter-Bk. A*, 209; *Cal. Coroners Rolls*, p. 5 and n.1; see the tax returns in Ekwall, *Two Early London Subsidy Rolls* and Weinbaum, ii, 203-15; also the civic muster temp. Edward I in K.R. Acc. V. (Army and Navy) E101/13/39.

[4] *Lib. Albus*, pp. 36-9, 257-60.

advance in technique and efficiency was striking. The private franchises offered no real obstacle. They were certainly numerous. In 1275 there were said to be eighteen in one ward.[1] The immunists were often important men and many sokes remained active throughout the century—the appointment of fourteen soke-reeves was recorded in Husting between 1273 and 1313— but their constitutional importance was negligible.[2] There was a fierce struggle with Westminster Abbey, whose wide franchise clashed with that of the city itself, and a running fight with St. Martin-le-Grand over sanctuary rights, but most sokes were petty liberties whose only serious effect was to offer some hindrance to shrieval distraint for debt.[3] A royal justice decided in 1221 that, to be viable, a foreign soke must have regular records and a court of twelve freemen and this must have crippled many.[4] In an affray with bloodshed a soke could not shelter a man, and it was the alderman who took the fee for all conveyances, even in soke land. The Husting exercised appellate jurisdiction and even before the growing popularity of action by writ had undermined the franchisal courts, they were common rather than proprietary in character.[5] They fell into place naturally as units of local government and their chief importance lay in the training their management offered to aspiring city clerks.

The life of London centred on its public courts, whose pattern of jurisdiction had been fixed since the twelfth century. The city was recognized as a separate judicial entity. Many Londoners were entitled to plead in the Exchequer and Iters were heard at the Tower; pleas of error went before the king's

[1] For a general view of the sokes, see *Hundred Rolls*, i, 403-33; F. M. Stenton, *Norman London*, pp. 14-15; W. Page, *op. cit.*, 127-58; A.R. 546.

[2] For the appointments, see Hust. Roll (Common Pleas) 1, 3, 4, 9, 29, 33, 36, 38 and Hust. Roll (Land) 1; see also *Cal. E.M.C. Rolls*, pp. 81, 89-91, 122; *Cal. Letter-Bk. C*, 7; Misc. Roll CC, m.2.

[3] For Westminster, see *Hundred Rolls*, i, 403-10, *passim*; W.A.M., Domesday, fo. 22b, 61, 66b, 98b; A.R. 543, m.39; *C.P.R. 1258-66*, pp. 288, 588; *C.Ch.R. 1257-1300*, pp. 238, 241; see cartulary of St. Martin-le-Grand and Box 225 of its general records in the Muniment Room of Westminster Abbey; on the ordinary soke, see, for example, Misc. Roll AA, p. 49; M. Bateson, *op. cit.*, 487, 492-3.

[4] *Lib. Albus*, p. 116; foreign soke meant a private franchise within the city owned by a non-citizen.

[5] *Lib. Albus*, p. 66; Lib. Ordinationum, fo. 173b; M. Bateson, *op. cit.*, 487, 490-3, 709; A. H. Thomas, *P. and M. Rolls*, ii, xvi-xviii.

G

justices. Appeals, however, were heard at St. Martin for the citizens were exempt from pleading outside the walls, except for the most serious offences and for foreign tenements, and they regularly appointed wardens to conduct the trial of indicted fellow-citizens at Boston, Winchester and probably other fairs.[1] Within the walls, the king administered justice through the citizens' courts and by their law. Crown pleas at the Iter were presented by elected sheriffs and a coroner who was usually a city clerk. Licensed powers of summary jurisdiction were conferred on the council in increasing measure, and in 1327 the mayor was made *ex officio* justice of gaol delivery at Newgate and royal escheator in the city.[2] This very real autonomy the Londoners vigorously defended. They were as intransigent in their opposition to the court of the Steward and Marshal as to the ecclesiastical courts, with which they clashed over probate of wills, debt, contract, and the religious sanctions applied by illegal craft organizations.[3] The very vigilance of their defence tends to obscure the real nature of the problems they had to solve. For the remarkable development of their judicial system in this century was largely a reaction to external stimulus.

In the early years of autonomy, the central court of Husting heard all pleas except those of the Crown.[4] This simplicity could not be maintained in face of the legislative enterprise of the English monarchy. The multiplication of popular writ-actions set in train a remorseless increase in the volume and complexity of legal business. By 1244 it had forced a reorganization, common pleas being differentiated from pleas of land, with courts held in alternate weeks. Additional days had to be allotted to the former, and in 1260 writ-actions of dower and rent were transferred to it.[5] Other courts were available to receive delegated business. The shadowy chamberlain's

---

[1] *Cal. Letter-Bk. C,* 98–100, *D, E, passim.*

[2] For a general picture, see *Lib. Cust.,* pp. 169, 239–46; *Lib. Albus,* p. 13; Misc. Roll AA; and A. H. Thomas, introductions to *Cal. E.M.C. Rolls* and *P. and M. Rolls,* i.

[3] Chanc. Misc. 109/1(14); *Lib. Cust.,* pp. 111–12; *Cal. Letter-Bk. B,* 87, 90–1; *Cal. E.M.C. Rolls,* pp. 12, 28–9, 34, 111, 156.

[4] For a general view, see *Lib. Albus,* pp. 181–99.

[5] Misc. Roll AA, p. 8; *Lib. de Ant. Leg.,* p. 45.

court tended to specialize in apprenticeship and franchise cases; the sheriffs' jurisdiction was more general but minor.[1] Assumption of burdens shed by the Husting tended to enhance their status, but all important cases would still have to be decided by mayor and aldermen, and under pressure, an entirely new tribunal, the mayor's court, came into existence.

No doubt, it had existed in some form since the creation of the mayoralty, but its growth was stimulated by the direct intervention of the Crown. Delay in debt litigation was a perennial problem. In commercial London, it became a matter of urgency and at the Iter of 1221 the royal justices ordered that piepowder cases which could not wait for the Husting should go before a special daily court of the mayor, sheriffs and a few aldermen.[2] Large numbers of debt actions involving aliens passed immediately to its jurisdiction. Actions between citizens followed.[3] By mid-century, the Husting was delegating to it cases arising out of disobedience to city officers; actions by plaint were squeezed out into the mayor's court. Pleas of error from the sokes, sheriffs' and chamberlains' courts strengthened its position. As the Husting developed into the city's formal land court, the mayor's court became primarily a tribunal for personal actions, particularly in commercial relations.[4] Meeting daily and tackling those problems most characteristic of an urban community, it out-paced all others. The statutes and ceaseless judicial activity of the reign of Edward I sharpened the problem of external legal relations and led to the creation of an entirely new civic staff of law officers, whose headquarters was the mayor's court. Their skill and ambition spurred on its growth. With a jurisdiction which ultimately came to rival that of the Chancery and Common Pleas, the mayor's court of London represents the climax of urban autonomy in England. For

---

[1] See *Cal. E.M.C. Rolls*, pp. 46–8; *Lib. Albus*, pp. 199–223; *Lib. Cust.*, p. 280; H. A. Harben, *A Dictionary of London*, p. 166.

[2] *Lib. Albus*, p. 67; piepowder, i.e. *pieds poudreux*, 'dusty-feet'—a court for migrants; it became essentially a merchants' court.

[3] *Cal. E.M.C. Rolls*, pp. 69, 70, 101, 183; Misc. Roll CC, m. 26d; Lib. Ordinationum, fo. 173–3b.

[4] There is a masterly and heavily documented analysis of the development of the mayor's court and its relationships with other city tribunals in A. H. Thomas introduction to *Cal. E.M.C. Rolls*.

five centuries, the city was able to punish any citizen who carried an action within its cognizance into the courts of common law.[1]

Legal growth was not merely quantitative. Though based firmly on tradition, the London codes proved remarkably flexible. Compurgation, refined by royal ordinance, remained important, but the jury system made great inroads upon it. The courts turned more and more frequently to the panel of experts as its guide, until the jury became stock procedure, particularly in the mayor's.[2] From the twenties, ordinance after ordinance defined and redefined legal practice, the status of suitors, jurors, essoiners and attorneys. The influence of the royal courts was all-pervasive. The Husting, in its procedure, was a copy of them, and under the king's wardens, in 1285, city law and practice were brought increasingly into line with that of the royal system.[3] The whole process of law became more subtle and sophisticated. The consequences were perhaps inevitable. In 1280 the lawyers of London formed a craft gild.[4] A few years later, professionals entered the patriciate.

There was a parallel development, though not quite so clear-cut, in the field of general city management. The council's major achievement was the establishment of a civic water-supply. With the Thames polluted and the number of wells diminishing, population growth made the problem acute and, in 1237, the city bought out Gilbert de Sandford, took over his wells at Tyburn and built a reservoir there. By mid-century, water was being piped to a great conduit in Cheap.[5] The management of this public service became a model for all civic enterprise. Immediate control was vested in a marshal or

---

[1] A. H. Thomas, *Cal. E.M.C. Rolls*, xxiv–xxv, and 'Illustrations of the medieval municipal history of London from the Guildhall records', *Trans. Royal Hist. Soc.*, 4th. ser., iv (1921), 84–5; on the legal staff, see below.

[2] See the demands for a jury in *Cal. E.M.C. Rolls*, pp. 175, 173, and Misc. Roll CC, m.4; see also *C.Ch.R. 1257–1300*, p. 98; *Lib. de Ant. Leg.*, pp. 102–5; under compurgation, the innocence of the accused was established by the ritual swearing of oaths in support of his credibility by appropriate numbers of 'oath-helpers'.

[3] *Lib. Ordinationum*, fo. 173b, 190b–202b; Misc. Roll AA, p. 56; *Lib. Albus*, pp. 182, 189–90, 280–97; *Cal. Letter-Bk. A*, 206 and *passim*.

[4] *Lib. Cust.*, pp. 280–2; *Lib. Albus*, pp. 570–2.

[5] *Cal. Letter-Bk. A*, 14–15, *B*, 273, *C*, 202 and *passim*; S. L. Thrupp, *The Merchant Class of Medieval London*, p. 136, n. 107.

warden, often a neighbour of the conduit.[1] Specific revenues were assigned to it, including the annual fee of 50 marks paid by the Somme woad-merchants for their privileges and, after 1312, a fine levied from brewers and fishmongers.[2] The revenues were handled by a committee under the supervision of an alderman. In 1325, for example, the marshal was a councillor and warden of the ironmongers, while the funds were managed by a councillor and a clerk-controller appointed by Guildhall.[3] This association of representative citizens with chamber officials in its administrative committees was characteristic of the city, at least from the reign of Edward I onwards.

For it was during the mayoralties of Gregory de Rokesle and Henry le Waleys in the seventies and eighties that the council adopted a systematic policy in such matters. Public health provides an odd but intriguing illustration of the whole process. Sanitation was rudimentary and sporadic attempts to control butchers, tanners and other offenders met with little success. The prevalent habit of keeping pigs in the street was tolerated as a natural remedy.[4] In the late thirteenth century, a more rational approach was adopted. Responsibility for public health, hitherto diffused by craft regulation and special ordinance, was vested in the chamberlain, who took prompt action against the offending trades, banishing their obnoxious practices to the suburb and launching periodic drives on the markets. A regular corps of scavengers, four to a ward, was appointed and, in final symmetry, four men were sworn to take and kill any pig found in the streets.[5]

The number of this type of city official increased steadily. A

[1] Thomas de Conduit, marshal from 1285 to 1298, was a vintner of St. Mary Colechurch, the conduit parish—*Cal. Letter-Bk. A*, 54, 60, 89, 94, 95, 162, 176, 177, 215.

[2] *Lib. Albus*, p. 228; *Cal. Letter-Bk. D*, 299.

[3] For the appointment, see *Cal. Letter-Bk. E*, 204, 205; the marshal, Henry de Ware—*Cal. Letter-Bk. D*, 129, *E*, 220, 221, *F*, 239; Ekwall, *Two Early London Subsidy Rolls*, p. 297; the councillor, Geoffrey de Gedelston—*Cal. Letter-Bk. E*, 233, *F*, 110; Ekwall, *op. cit.*, 295; he lived near the conduit (*Cal. Letter-Bk. F*, 29). The controller was the clerk Benedict de Gildhalle.

[4] See, for example, St. Paul's A/12/1143; *Cal. Letter-Bk. A*, 173–4; *Lib. Albus*, pp. 323–24.

[5] *Cal. E.M.C. Rolls*, pp. 161–2; *Cal. Letter-Bk. A*, 183–4, *C*, 6. See E. L. Sabine's three articles on butchering, sanitation, and city cleaning in late medieval London in *Speculum*, viii (1933), ix (1934) and xii (1937).

small staff of master masons and carpenters, generally the leading members of their craft, was sworn to enforce the building
regulations. Rokesle ordered each wardmoot to elect four street
inspectors, who were reinforced in 1303 by a central civic staff
of four paviours, their expenses met by a levy on the house-
holders of the route under inspection.[1] In all fields, there was the
same tendency to create official services, to make them autonomous self-running accounting units, and increasingly to
strengthen them with professional administrators. It was a
city attorney who supervised pavement repair in Langbourn in
1312, a chamber clerk in Bishopsgate Without thirty years
later.[2]

The most striking illustration of the process was Henry le
Waleys's handling of the problem of the Bridge. The Bridge
was maintained by a trust invested in Bridge House, a chapel
founded in 1209, to which alms flowed in from all quarters.
The trust was managed by city officials, and the generosity of
Crown and public, together with the enterprise of its managers,
who imitated St. Paul's, for example, in making site-develop-
ment a condition of lease, built it into a great landed corporation.[3] After the Barons' Wars, however, Henry III granted the
Bridge to Queen Eleanor, and it reverted to the city in the reign
of Edward I in a shocking state of neglect.[4] Waleys responded
with an imaginative application of the system of rent allocation.
In 1282 and 1283 he carved two new civic estates out of the
city's public domain and earmarked their revenues for the
Bridge. Building a new hall, the Stocks, in the centre of the
city, he leased it to a protected group of fishmongers and butchers and created a new market. This bold action, which bruised
so many vested interests, proved a success. Wardens accounted
to the Bridge-wardens and the chamberlain, final concords

[1] *Cal. Letter-Bk. B*, 15, *C*, 86, 115, *D*, 14, *E*, 55–6, 118–19, 201; *Cal. E.M.C. Rolls*,
p. 178.

[2] *Cal. Letter-Bk. D*, 312; Ekwall, *op. cit.*, 231.

[3] On the Bridge, see, *inter alia*, *Cal. Letter-Bk. A*, 2, 157, 158, 216 and n. 3;
B, 216 and n.2, *C*, 61–2, *E*, 148, 149; *Lib. Albus*, p. 152; Misc. Roll AA, p. 75;
Lib. Cust., p. 95; *Pat. Rolls 1225–32*, p. 501; Hust. Rolls and *Cal. of Wills, passim*;
Bridge House Deeds form a separate class in the Corporation of London Records
Office.

[4] *C.P.R. 1266–72*, p. 459; *Lib. de Ant. Leg.*, pp. 141–2; *Hundred Rolls*, i, 408, 410;
Cal. Letter-Bk. C, 61–2.

being enrolled in the Husting.[1] The history of his second enterprise was more chequered. He secured a block of undeveloped
sites near St. Paul's, with the intention of raising houses. The
cathedral protested, Waleys tried to get hold of the property
himself and a confused squabble ensued, stilled only by an
Exchequer suit in 1293, when the houses, now rebuilt, reverted
to their original function.[2]

The Bridge trust, with its extensive endowment and elaborate
system of record and account, became in practice a separate
department of London government. A financial department,
moreover, and hence considered too important to be left to
specialized officials. The two wardens of Bridge, elective after
1311, were sometimes aldermen like Anketil de Gisors or chamberlains like Thomas Prentice. More frequently they were
councillors, often inhabitants of Bridge ward, fishmongers of
good family such as John Sterre and Edward Horn, or an ironmonger like John de Wymondham.[3] But within the service
there was an active and growing staff of officials—bailiffs, collectors, record-keepers, the ubiquitous renters. Here, professionals, such as the renter John atte Hall, a Guildhall clerk,
became more important, as trained clerks moved towards a
monopoly of the everyday administrative jobs.[4]

The hub of this staff was the city's financial administration,
which controlled all governmental operations. The one large
and regular item was the annual shrieval farm paid to the Crown,
fixed at £300, raised to £400 after the Barons' Wars, but restored to its original figure in 1327.[5] Court fees were one source
of revenue, but more important were local tolls, scavage on
imports, pesage dues, the harbour and market tolls at Billingsgate, Queenhithe, Smithfield and elsewhere.[6] Though the
farming of Middlesex was banned in 1283, it is difficult to say

---

[1] Hust. Roll 14(16); 50(90); *Cal. Letter-Bk. C*, 55, *D*, 282; *Cal. E.M.C. Rolls*, p.
234; *Lib. Cust.*, pp. 95, 96, 117–20, 275, 385–406.

[2] *C.P.R. 1281–92*, pp. 23, 24, 193, 194; K.R.M.R. 66, m.7; *Cal. Letter-Bk.* A,
213–14.

[3] *Cal. Letter-Bk. D*, 28, 275, *E*, 41, 42, 143–7, 296; Ekwall, *op. cit.*, 214, 216, 218,
324, 331; Beaven, i, 379, 380.

[4] *Cal. Letter-Bk. E*, 52 and *passim*.

[5] *Lib. de Ant. Leg.*, p. 124; *Ann. Lond.*, p. 80; *Hundred Rolls*, i, 403–12; *Historica.
Charters*, ed. W. de. G. Birch, p. 53.

[6] These tolls were listed for the king in 1265—see *Lib. Albus*, pp. 223–38.

whether the prohibition was effective.[1] Revenues were not auto-matically farmed. There was a fixed scale of fees for the bailiff of Bridge, for example.[2] But the practice seems to have been common. In 1295 Billingsgate was farmed for £20, four years later for £44.[3] This possibly explains the popularity of such posts among city clerks and serjeants, for professionals appeared everywhere. Middlesex in particular was their fief. The earliest Middlesex sheriff of the thirteenth century known by name, for example, was Martin, a Guildhall clerk. The first recognizable Common Clerk held the office in 1278, while the shrievalty of the chamber serjeant Roger de Appleby, from 1290 to 1305, became almost a permanent feature of the county landscape.[4]

For the staff required to administer the farm was large and tended to increase. So did that of the chamber, which managed the independent finances of the commune. Financial policy and administration in London appear relatively primitive when contrasted with those of the great European cities. In part, this is illusory, a product of the city's accounting methods. There was really no central budget. The only accounts of a general nature which survive are four accounts of the chamberlain, the chief financial officer, covering the period from 1326 to 1335.[5] These do not cover a fraction of total expenses, not even all the working expenditure, for the civic accounts were almost totally decentralized, many heavy items delegated to autonomous trusts and departments whose records have disappeared. The formal chamberlains' accounts hint at a wealth of resources at the commune's disposal, but the scope of its activity was severely restricted.

A prime cause, without doubt, was the strictly limited char-acter of the city's fiscal autonomy. At no time did London enjoy the freedom of Ghent or Bruges. The pressure of the royal system was inescapable. Tallage, levied eleven times between 1223 and 1253, became regular, falling on average once every

---

[1] *Select Excheq. Pleas*, pp. 118–19; *Cal. Letter-Bk. A*, 206; *Lib. Cust.*, p. 9.
[2] *Lib. Albus*, p. 236.   [3] *Cal. E.M.C. Rolls*, p. 4; *Cal. Letter-Bk. B*, 100–1.
[4] Ancient Deeds B 4416, 4264; *Cat. Anc. Deeds*, i, 14(A140); A.R. 1187, m.9d; A.R. 541a, m.29, 32d; Misc. Roll BB, m.3; W.A.M. 4486, 4512; K.R. Acc. V. (Sheriffs Accounts) E101/571/5, 6, 8 (nos. 9, 10); *Cal. E.M.C. Rolls*, p. 23; *Cal. Letter-Bk. A*, 76.
[5] Calendared in *Cal. Letter-Bk. E*, 216–17, 247–8, 270–1, 292.

three years.[1] Under the Edwards, subsidy was little less frequent, until taxation was standardized in 1334. Tallage was generally compounded for at 2,000 marks, though larger sums were sometimes paid. Under Edward I, assessments, apart from the Thirtieth of 1283, were never less than £1,200 and usually around £2,000. In the four years from 1294 to 1297 the city was assessed at nearly £7,350. The total subsidy assessment for the reign of Edward II was some £8,000, for Edward I, £16,000. By the charter of 1327, London was assessed at the lower county rate and its tax fell sharply, to be standardized in 1334 at little over £733.[2] Except, perhaps, for the war taxes of Edward I, the burden was not heavy, but in addition, there was a stream of extraordinary levies and pressure was intense and continuous, dominating the minds of aldermen.

In the chamberlains' accounts of the early fourteenth century, fully half the expenditure covered running expenses, most of which were the result of royal demands. The other half went on the salaries of civic officials, at least three-quarters of whom simply did not exist in the reign of Henry III. The provision of public services like the Bridge and the conduit was a product of the thirteenth century itself. In the early years of autonomy there could have been no financial policy in any real sense of the term. The demands of the monarchy governed London's life at all times, and for much of the thirteenth century, civic 'financial policy' must have been almost entirely a matter of fiscal relations with the Crown.

The poverty of communal property was a contributory factor. The first surviving register, dating from the early years of Edward II, lists a score of items.[3] They included a tract of Moorfields and St. Botulph's Wharf, but most were petty

---

[1] S. K. Mitchell, *Studies in Taxation under John and Henry III* (New Haven, 1914), pp. 10–343 and notes, *passim*; F. M. Powicke, *King Henry III and the Lord Edward*, pp. 308–9.

[2] Taxation totals are taken from three articles by J. F. Willard, 'The taxes upon movables in the reign of Edward I/Edward II/Edward III', *English Historical Review*, xxviii (1913), 517–21, xxix (1914), 317–21, xxx (1915), 67–73; and from J. H. Ramsay, 'Statistics of subsidy rolls of Edward II', *English Historical Review*, xxiv (1909), 317–19.

[3] *Cal. Letter-Bk. C*, 237–9—roster prepared when John de Bauquell was still alive, i.e. before 1308, referring to grants made earlier (the property held by Joanna Goldcorn was first granted her in 1291—*Cal. Letter Bk. B*, 55), and supplemented by notes added under Edward II.

serjeanties attached to the gates. When Roger de Clifford sold
his mansion near Guildhall to the city in 1280, the aldermen at
once prepared to sell or lease it. It passed, under royal pressure, to the Common Clerk John de Bauquell in whose family
it remained for two generations before reverting to the
commonalty to become famous in the cloth trade as Bakewell
(Bauquell) Hall.[1] The council was reluctant to build up a
powerful civic patrimony. There was no funded debt. The
nearest approach was aldermanic management of orphans'
property which was administered by the council as an invest-
ment trust.[2] They deliberately tried to lighten the burden of
staffs and salaries at the centre, to make all new services self-
supporting and self-sufficient, in the manner of conduit and
Bridge. Many ward officers' wages were paid by specific levies
on the wards themselves. The growing weight of public services
was constantly hived off to semi-independent institutions.
The chamber still exercised overall control, minutely scrutin-
izing all accounts, but those accounts were kept quite separate
and never appeared on the chamberlain's rolls, not even in
summary form.

   This attitude found forceful expression in the reform movement of 1311 which remodelled the civic constitution. The movement was itself largely a protest against the growing cost and
efficiency of government and the reformers tried to counteract
the trend by limiting staffs and setting up a controller and a
standing, watchdog committee of auditors over the chamberlain.
Further, they invented a new technique of control, as effective
as it was unpublicized. City officers were paid basic salaries,
supplemented, indeed doubled and trebled, by perquisites
drawn in the main from one source—the fees paid for enrolment
of deeds, wills and 'writings' in the chamber. This class of
revenue was now withdrawn from the chamberlain and vested
in the elected auditors. For the first time, the *probi* laid hands
on the innermost levers and, in the process, one more item disappeared from the chamberlain's accounts.[3]

---

[1] *C.P.R. 1272–81*, p. 381; *Cal. Letter-Bk. A*, 227, *C*, 12, 13 and n.1; *Cal. of Wills*,
i, 343; Hust. Roll 19(19) (20), 17(12), 22(55) (56); *Ann. Lond.*, p. 89.

[2] See, for example, *Cal. Letter-Bk. C*, 33, 34, 193–9, 200–2, 205–7, and *passim*.

[3] *Cal. Letter-Bk. D*, 79, 83, 88, 275, 276, 286–7; *E*, 12–14; and see Chapter X.
No explicit order for the appropriation of enrolment revenue can be found, but

The reforms of 1311, however, were merely an unusually vivid expression of an attitude of mind which was permanent and deep-rooted. No doubt, there was anxiety over the creation of an expensive central staff, but it went deeper than that. It was an ingrained outlook on government. London had no *rentes*, no audacious communal policies, because in the last resort, Londoners did not want them.

The chamberlains' accounts of 1326–35 are fairly uniform.[1] Easily the largest single item of revenue were the fees paid for the enrolment of freedom-admissions and apprenticeship-covenants, which averaged some £81 a year. Chamber rents of civic property brought in an average of £12 annually, while the enrolment-fees for debt recognizance had dwindled to a mere £4. Loans, arrears of former levies and other items appeared at irregular intervals. The main expenditure was on the salaries of civic officers which averaged some £50 a year. All other spending was irregular, though 'general expenses', covering repairs to buildings and a host of minor tasks, could be substantial and ran to an annual average of £34. Miscellaneous expenses, such as travelling grants to parliamentary representatives or the purchase of pens and parchment, fluctuated wildly. Taken as a whole, the working expenses of the city, as reflected in the chamberlains' accounts, ran to a little over £100 a year.

Ever present in the background, as inevitable as the weather and frequently as unpredictable, were the taxes of the royal government, supplemented by any number of irregular demands, some of them heavy. The Londoners paid 2,000 marks for confirmation of their charters in 1299, £300 in the cause of general goodwill in 1324.[2] A memorandum on city expenses in 1325 lists not only the fees of its officers, but annuities paid to a number of royal officials, presumably for services rendered or expected. Even the Exchequer doorkeeper got a pair of gloves.[3]

it may be deduced from a comparison between the chamberlains' accounts in *Cal. Letter-Bk. E*, 216–17, 247–8, 270–1, 292, with the position outlined by Carpenter in *Lib. Albus*, pp. 47–50, set in the context of the 1311 reforms. See, for example, auditor control over the chamberlain's personal clerk, its scope defined in *Lib. Albus*, p. 48, and in actual operation in 1328–30, Letter-Bk. E, fo. ccib-ccii (the calendar gives insufficient detail).

[1] Letter-Bk. E, fo. clxxiib–clxxiii, ccib–ccii, ccxxixb–ccxxx, ccxliiib–ccxliv.
[2] *C.C.R. 1296–1302*, p. 303; *Cal. Letter-Bk. C*, 107, *E*, 186–7.
[3] *Cal. Letter-Bk. D*, 313–15, *E*, 194–6.

This was a regular practice, oiling the wheels and easing the millstones. There were always old debts to be paid, new demands for special occasions.

Skilful improvisation solved many of these problems. Loans from the aldermen met the mayor's travelling expenses in 1298, but sometimes, as in 1297, the council had to order a general survey of the city's indebtedness and take special measures to clear it.[1] Royal grants of murage occasionally helped. Those of 1276 and 1279 helped to rebuild the wall after the construction of Blackfriars.[2] Small loans from citizens were frequent and from the late thirteenth century the city turned to the great Italian companies, borrowing from the Riccardi in 1274, the Pulci in 1292, the Frescobaldi in 1304. The money paid for the recovery of the franchise in 1299 was borrowed from the Spini, Mozzi, Cerchi Neri, Frescobaldi Bianchi, Pulci, Boncini and Amanati.[3]

Borrowing, however, was unpleasant. The aldermen preferred direct taxation. Civic levies were geared to the assessments for national taxation, made by juries of twelve in every ward. In May 1295, for example, to maintain three ships in the royal fleet, a levy of 2d. in the £1 on movables was ordered, to be raised according to the assessment for the recent Sixth.[4] Taxes on rents had been raised in John's reign for military purposes, and in 1266 to pay the great fine imposed on the city after the civil war. They seem to have been emergency measures. A tax on rents, 3 shillings in the £1, to the limit of £1,000, to supplement a levy of 500 marks on movables, was ordered in 1321, to compensate citizens troubled by the Iter of that year.[5] A tax on movables was the normal practice, the rate varying between 2d. and 1s. 6d. in the £1.[6]

Local taxation, possibly novel and certainly suspect, as the Hundred Rolls show, was an inflammable issue, one of the

---

[1] See, for example, *Cal. Letter-Bk. B*, 74–6, 237–9, *C*, 43–4, *D*, 214, *E*, 186.

[2] *C.P.R. 1272–81*, pp. 147–8, 258; *Cal. Letter-Bk. C*, 71–2; Weinbaum, ii, 146.

[3] K.R. Acc. V. (Alien Merchants) E101/126/5; *C.C.R. 1272–9*, p. 123; *C.C.R. 1296–1302*, p. 303; *Cal. Letter-Bk. A*, 208, *C*, 143.

[4] *Cal. Letter-Bk. C*, 21; see *Lib. de Ant. Leg.*, pp. 240–2.

[5] M. Bateson, *op. cit.*, 726–8; *Lib. de Ant. Leg.*, pp. 239, 240; *Cal. Letter-Bk. E*, 148.

[6] See, for example, *Cal. Letter-Bk. B*, 234–6, 236–40, *E*, 114–15; *Cal. E.M.C. Rolls*, p. 126.

causes of the revolt of 1263, but it became frequent and even regular, and the city developed an administrative staff to handle it. The way of the collector was sometimes hard. William de Aldgate was stabbed, Richard Leving had his head cracked on the pavement, and John Fuatard's finger was bitten by an irate matron.[1] But if courage was needed at street level, trained skill was at a premium everywhere. The financial system was complicated. There was an endless process of account and audit, and the continuous drafting and inspection of accounts, the formation and execution of policy, demanded the full-time service of professionals. It is possible that the policy of decentralization in the interests of economy defeated its own ends. For the number of professionals increased and from the chamber their influence radiated through all branches of administration. By the reign of Edward I, the effects are obvious. The aldermanic régime had created a civic bureaucracy.

The shrieval staff was certainly large, bailiffs, keepers, gaolers and their underlings supplementing the permanent central body of clerks and serjeants. In 1320, there were a dozen serjeants serving the sheriffs' courts. A decade or so later, their central staff of serjeants was limited to eight, while a salary sheet of the same period allowed them four clerks and four serjeants at fees ranging from £5 to £2 10s., with perquisites. In fact, their clerks alone numbered six, or even nine, and every clerk and serjeant had his own staff of subordinates.[2]

There was no rigid distinction between the staff of the sheriffs and that of the commune, in the chamber. John Juvenal, able member of a family of officials, served in both capacities, and, in 1304, bore the official title of 'serjeant of the chamber and the sheriffs'.[3] When Joce Botedieu quitted the shrieval for the chamber staff in the same year, however, his salary was increased by half.[4] For the chamber was the heart of the administration. There, the serjeants were headed by the three personal aides

---

[1] For the numerous assaults on these unhappy men, see, for example, *Cal. E.M.C. Rolls*, pp. 11, 31, 61–2, 126, 143–4 and *passim*.

[2] Misc. Roll CC; Lib. Ordinationum, fo. 157b; *Lib. Albus*, p. 45; *Lib. Cust.*, p. 98; *Cal. Letter-Bk. C*, 147, 178–9, *D, E, passim*.

[3] *Cal. E.M.C. Rolls*, pp. 25, 35, 153, 159, 174; *Cal. Letter-Bk. C*, 126.

[4] Lib. Ordinationum, fo. 157b; *Cal. Letter-Bk. D*, 313–15.

to the chamberlain and the mayor's *familia*—his crier, sword-bearer and at least two other serjeants. Here, too, was the hub of the clerical system. A large staff of clerks was needed in both chambers of Guildhall. Every alderman had his own clerk; so had the Common Clerk himself, the chamberlain, later the recorder. The mayor had his clerk, and after 1327, a second for escheats. These men seem to have been seconded from the chamber, for the 'Clerks of the Chamber' were an inner élite, with a special oath of secrecy. One clerk and one serjeant supervised the entire chamber staff and at the lowest rung of the official hierarchy, there are traces of a class of scriveners, the apprentices of the craft.[1]

By the early fourteenth century, these men were grouped under three superior officers drawing identical salaries of £10 a year, supplemented by valuable perquisites and liveries; the chamberlain, in control of finance and partly responsible for records, the Common Clerk, a civic chancellor, and the Common Serjeant-at-Law, general supervisor of the city's legal system.[2] The chamberlain's was an office of long standing. In marked contrast to his colleagues, he was rarely a professional. The typical chamberlain was a man like Hugh Motun the pepperer, who, perhaps Jewish in origin, was kinsman to merchants of Montpellier. Hugh, an importer of dyes, paints and spices from the Gascon ports, was an important leather merchant, marrying off his daughters to Simon Godard, the leading city pepperer, and to Hamo Box, the sheriff-corder. With his property spread over five parishes, he was a typical rank-and-file member of the mercantile patriciate, down to the punning humour of his seal, which bore the representation of a sheep.[3] His colleagues were similar. Financial administration was too serious to be left to financial officers. His fellow heads of the executive service, however, the Clerk and the Serjeant, were invariably professionals, and it is typical that their offices

---

[1] *Lib. Albus*, pp. 37, 47–50; Hust. Roll 36(85); Misc. Roll CC, m.26; for some transfers, see *Cal. Letter-Bk. B*, 184, 232 (marginal note), *C*, 147, 179, *E*, 5, 6, 20, 21; *Cal. E.M.C. Rolls*, pp. 38, 258, 259, and *passim*.

[2] *Cal. Letter-Bk. D*, 313–15; *Lib. Albus*, p. 47.

[3] St. Paul's A/20/302; *Cal. Letter-Bk. A*, 4, 6, 26, 27, 45, 69, 78, 81–6, 88, 94, 106–8, 160, 169–70, 210; *Cal. of Wills*, i, 24, 91, 236; for his seal, see W.A.M. 13988.

emerged, in their characteristic form at least, only in the reign of Edward I.

There must always have been a communal clerical officer of a sort, but Ralph Crepyn, described variously as 'Clerk of the Mayor and Sheriffs' and 'Clerk of London' in 1278–9, seems to be the first to merit the title of Common Clerk. The title itself was first used in 1284, when the famous John de Bauquell held office.[1] He was followed by Hugh Waltham, whose great Clerkship, endorsed by the reforming assemblies in 1311, ended only with his death in 1335.

In the same period, entirely new offices appeared, a controller in 1311, a bailiff of Southwark in 1327.[2] The most striking advance, however, was in the legal field. A few years after the legal profession in the city had been recognized as a craft by the council, a city prosecutor made his appearance. In May 1291 came the first recorded appointment of a Common Serjeant, with special responsibility for legal service to the commonalty, when Thomas Juvenal, of good civil service stock, was given the post. He was succeeded by a lawyer Thomas de Kent, and by Gregory de Norton, the son of a recorder, destined to follow in his father's legal footsteps.[3]

More striking was the development of the city's external legal relations. To maintain itself in the new Edwardian society, it was driven to enlist the service of the best lawyers in the country. In 1298, immediately after the city had recovered its franchise, it appointed, as attorneys at the Exchequer and Common Pleas, the Westminster lawyers William de Esthalle, William de Grantham and the eminent Gilbert de Toutheby. Appointments of London lawyers followed in 1303 and 1306, and when William de Burgh was sworn general attorney in 1311, he was ordered to assist the city's senior representatives, who were no lesser persons than Edmund Passelewe, Robert de Mablethorpe and Geoffrey de Hartpol, all three destined to become royal justices. By 1319 the city was retaining a dozen

[1] C.P.R. 1272–81, pp. 285, 339–40; C.C.R. 1272–9, p. 557; Cal. Letter-Bk. A, 161 and n.3.

[2] Cal. Letter-Bk. D, 275, E, 231, 274–5; Historical Charters, ed. W. de G. Birch, p. 53.

[3] Lib. Cust., pp. 280–2; Lib. Albus, pp. 570–2; Cal. Letter-Bk. A, 123, C, 11, 14, D, 14, 209, E, 20, 32.

attorneys, most of them distinguished practitioners, fixed stars in the Westminster firmament.[1]

The process reached its culmination with the appearance of the recorder. Alderman Geoffrey de Norton was appointed in 1298 to what was in fact a recordership, but the title was first used in 1304, when John de Wengrave was sworn to do justice to poor and rich, to defend the city's liberties, and to survey, set in order and record all pleas. His salary of £10 a year, with enrolment fees, was soon raised, for, always on the mayor's right hand, the recorder had to be 'unus de peritissimis et virtuosissimis apprenticiis legis totius regni'. Ability of the highest order cost dear when the city had to bid in the Westminster market and by mid-fourteenth century, his salary had rocketed to 100 marks. The men who filled the office, Norton the deputy mayor, Wengrave, one of the heaviest taxpayers in 1319, Hartpol and Robert de Swaleclive, royal justices, were some of the most distinguished lawyers of the realm.[2]

The focus of this pattern of expansion was clearly the monarchy. The city, in adopting it, was following a European trend, as manifest in Toulouse and Dijon as among the urban giants of Flanders and Italy. The closest parallel, even in terminology, was in Germany, where, from 1300, appear the familiar phenomena of *Stadtbucher*, fiscal *Kammerer*, clerical staff under the *Stadtschreiber*, and finally, the civic employment of professional jurists. London progressed, less by professionalizing its own patriciate, than by creating subordinate services and tapping the resources of the central government, but thanks to the precocious development of the English monarchy, the city was a century in advance of its German rivals, and even in numbers, its service stood at least equal to the twenty clerks of Cologne and the forty of Lübeck.[3]

[1] *Cal. Letter-Bk. B*, 215, 216, *C*, 26, 115, 116, *D*, 186, 187, 251, 253, 254, 313–15, *E*, 39; *Lib. Cust.*, p. 112; E. Foss, *The Judges of England* (London, 1851), iii, 264–5, 286–7, 459–60.

[2] *Cal. Letter-Bk. B*, 218–19, *C*, 132–3, *D*, 233, *E*, 11, 12, 242–43; *Lib. Albus*, pp. 24–5, 42–3; S. L. Thrupp, *op. cit.*, 86; H. Cohen, *A History of the English Bar and Attornatus to 1450* (London, 1929), p. 248.

[3] The most convenient general survey is *La Ville, première partie; Institutions administratives et judiciaires*, recueil de la Société Jean Bodin, vi (Brussels, 1954); see especially, J. Schneider, 'Les villes allemandes au moyen âge', *La Ville*, i, no. xvii. The London service should have numbered at least thirty-five clerks.

But it was not merely a matter of numbers. A new social interest had emerged in London society. The administration rapidly became its fief. Of the fourteen soke-reeves appointed between 1273 and 1313, seven were clerks. A city attorney was bailiff of Southwark.[1] Professionals tended to monopolize minor posts.[2] Ralph Pecok, the city prosecutor, held much of the communally owned Bethlehem Moor, and when the murage was farmed in 1332–4, most of it was leased to the clerk John Vincent.[3] In most of the thirty land transfers involving clerks enrolled between 1307 and 1318, the second party was a clerk or lawyer himself.[4] They went surety, attorney, executor for each other with remarkable regularity. Whole families, like the Walthams and Wengraves, specialized in administrative service; immigrants sponsored the admittance of neighbours' sons to the profession. The greater men, Waltham the clerk, Robert de Kelsey the lawyer, Wengrave the recorder, emerged as foci of social patronage, around whom threads of connexion and influence were woven into complicated patterns.[5]

Few were interested in trade, though some, like Ralph Pecok, kinsman to leathersellers, occasionally took a hand in the family business.[6] However, like their counterparts on the continent, they were active in finance and moneylending. Ralph Crepyn, the Common Clerk, debtor of Cahorsins and attorney to the Frescobaldi, was an important creditor of county knights, while his successor Bauquell got mortgages on aldermen themselves.[7] In all cases and at all levels, such business meant

---

[1] Hust. Roll (Common Pleas) 1, m.1; 3, m.3; 4, m.4; 9, m.2d, 7d; 29, m.22; 33, m.1d; 36, m.9; 38, m.2; Hust. Roll (Land) 1, m.9; *Cal. Letter-Bk. E*, 234–5.

[2] *Cal. Letter-Bk. C*, 43–4, 135, 179, 183, *D*, 241, *E*, 167, 196 and *passim*.

[3] *Cal. Letter-Bk. C*, 107–8, 161–3, 165, 237–9, *D*, 231, 235, 244–6, 253, *E*, 120–1, 193, 273–4; of the fourteen tenants named in the first list of chamber rents, eight were clerks and serjeants.

[4] Hust. Rolls 36–47, *passim*.

[5] For some examples, see Hust. Roll 31(25); 36(90); 37(109); 38(121); 40(59); Recog. Roll 7, m.5d; W.A.M. 25372; *C.P.R. 1301–7*, p. 383; *Cal. Letter-Bk. B*, 108, 190, 223, *C*, 144, 194, *D*, 57, *E*, 46, 58, 96, 226; the chamber clerk and alderman John de la Chambre held land in Hardingham in 1313; in 1334, a John de Hardingham was clerk to the sheriffs (*C.P.R. 1307–13*, p. 593; *C.P.R. 1333–7*, p. 260; *Cal. Letter-Bk. E*, 200).

[6] Recog. Roll 4, m.3; *Cal. Letter-Bk. A*, 140–2, 146–7, *B*, 87, 143.

[7] See K.R. Acc. V. (Alien Merchants) E101/126/27, m.3; Recog. Roll 1(88) (111) (162) (234); 2(152) (275); 4, m.2; 7, m.2, 3d, 4, and especially Roll 6, *passim*;

H

property. William de Wengrave, sheriff's clerk, an obscure kinsman of the recorder, got a stranglehold on Robert le Bret, a
goldsmith of respectable lineage, in 1309, and within three years
had relieved him of much of his inheritance.[1] He was typical,
and landed wealth, certainly, was characteristic of the group.
Great mansions fell to lawyers like Reginald Wolleward and
clerks like Thomas de Upton who, in 1320, bought his spacious
hall in Cornhill with its extensive stabling, from James de
Audley himself, cash down.[2] Even minor figures owned property in several parishes.[3] Tracing the clerks and lawyers
through the rolls, there is every time a quickening sense of
growth, often from very undistinguished beginnings.

The clerks illustrate this social mobility better than most, for
they were drawn from all social levels. The Juvenal family, for
example, had been patrician since the early years of Henry III,
and Henry de St. Osyth's father had been wine factor to an
alderman.[4] William de Londonstone, on the other hand, was
the son of a baker and the nephew of a locksmith.[5] Most spanned
the broad middle zone of society. The chamber clerk John de
Harrow was perhaps most typical, for his roots lay in the
mediocres. He was the grandson of an obscure immigrant. His
father was a mercer on a small scale with property in two
parishes. His brother William was a goldsmith, paying his half-
mark in tallage, marrying his daughters into respectable
families of saddlers and farriers, adding a little to his stock of
inherited property, but never one to be chosen as councillor
for his native Cripplegate. It was John who was the success of
the family, serving long years in the chamber, moving among

C.C.R. 1272–9, pp. 111, 113, 349, 557; *C.C.R. 1279–88*, pp. 361, 483, 528, 536;
Cal. Letter-Bk. A, 112, 115, 127, 133, *B*, 97, 178, 197, *C*, 172; *Cal. E.M.C. Rolls*,
p. 105.

[1] Recog. Roll 6, m.5; Hust. Roll 41(30).

[2] *Cal. Letter-Bk. E*, 114; *Cal. Coroners Rolls*, pp. 22–3.

[3] See the property of a beadle and a serjeant's assistant in Hust. Roll 15(54);
16(63); 26(30) (32); 27(41); *Cal. Letter-Bk. B*, 66; *Cal. of Wills*, i, 304.

[4] Hust. Roll (Land) 1, m.5; Hust. Roll (Common Pleas) 1, m.1; Hust. Roll
7(11); W.A.M. 4512, 4486, 13256, 13354; St. Paul's A/16/1227, 1228, A/17/1318;
Misc. Roll AA, p. 49; *Hundred Rolls*, i, 421; *Cart. S.M. Clerkenwell*, pp. 239–40;
Cal. E.M.C. Rolls, p. 101; *Cal. Coroners Rolls*, p. 15; *Cal. Letter-Bk. D*, 245; Ekwall,
op. cit., 342.

[5] Hust. Roll 40(8); *Cal. Letter-Bk. D*, 313–15; *A Calendar of the Feet of Fines for
London and Middlesex*, ed. W. J. Hardy and W. Page (London, 1892), p. 107.

the great merchants, making a few loans, doing a little business with the Gascons, acquiring properties in Castle Baynard and St. Paul's and ending his days, childless, in one of the great houses.[1]

The patriciate itself could not remain immune. The career of Hugh Waltham, whose distinguished Common Clerkship spanned the first quarter of the new century, was symptomatic. Hugh belonged to a family which had climbed to near-patrician status by the mid-thirteenth century. His uncle Alexander had actually held aldermanic office. But they were patricians with a difference. Alexander was a leader of the merchant-ironmongers, a new interest which was forcing its way into the patriciate. Moreover, he had been one of the irreconcilable leaders of the popular revolt of 1263 and had lived out the last twenty years of his life in exile.[2] Hugh's friends were the Oystergates, another rebel family, and Hugh Pourte, one of the new alderman-fishmongers, representative of the most powerful of the dissident crafts of 1263.

Unorthodox, then, in origin and affiliation, Waltham made the clerical service his stepping stone. Clerk to the sheriffs by 1290, within ten years he had earned himself a place in aldermanic society and secured himself among the new patricians by his marriage to Pourte's daughter Agnes.[3] After the alderman's death in 1308, much of his property, in three concentrated holdings, fell to the clerk and he launched out into eight years of intense activity in the victualling trades, financial transactions, and land purchase.[4] By 1311 he had become Common Clerk and in 1312, within a few months of the death of his first wife, he married Juliana, daughter of Alderman Nicholas Picot, who brought with her the great mansion in Cornhill, once the

---

[1] Hust. Roll 32(81); 36(88); 38(96); 45(34) (51) (203); Recog. Roll 5, m.3; 6, m.1d; St. Paul's A/24/1088; *Cal. Letter-Bk. A,* 46, *B,* 8, *C,* 10–11, 58, 213, 244, *D,* 237–8, *E,* 33, 34, 135; Ekwall, *op. cit.,* 154; *Cal. E.M.C. Rolls,* pp. 103, 174, 212; *Cal. of Wills,* i, 52, 84.

[2] *Cal. of Wills,* i, 399–400; *Cal. Letter-Bk. B,* 59; see Chapter VIII.

[3] *Cal. Letter-Bk. A,* 124, 150, *B,* 184, 226, *D,* 147, 168; *Cal. E.M.C. Rolls,* pp. 38, 221, 258–9.

[4] Hust. Roll 29(87); 32(63)(64); 37(16); *Cal. Letter-Bk. B,* 160; Ancient Deeds E 501, 509; *Cal. of Wills,* i, 399–400; for his commercial dealings, see Recog. Roll 9 and *Cal. Letter-Bks. A, B, D, E, passim;* for his land acquisitions, Hust. Roll 37–48 and *Cal. Letter-Bk. E, passim.*

home of Thomas fitz Thomas, the revolutionary mayor of 1263, where Waltham now established himself.[1]

A dozen years of careful, unspectacular acquisition followed, enlivened only by his election as parliamentary representative in 1319, until in the thirties Waltham, now ageing, embarked on a series of ambitious land purchase projects to secure endowments for his son and married daughter. In the twenty-five years before his death in 1335, he acquired nearly fifty properties.[2] He had seen his son Stephen, also a clerk, married into the aldermanic family of Box, his daughter Agnes into that of Lucas, social leaders in the fishmongers' fraternity. His brother John, formerly a chamber clerk, was vicar of Windsor, another, rector of St. Michael Bassishaw. A second daughter was a nun at patrician St. Helen's and, thanks to his efforts, the Walthams had their burial-vault in St. Peter Cornhill, their well-endowed chantries in St. Magnus and St. Mary Southwark.[3] The cadet turned clerk had restored the family fortunes.

If the rise of the clerks loosened the structure of dynastic control, the emergence of the lawyers was even more disturbing. Legal training was the key to the highest office. Of eleven professionals elected to aldermanries between 1280 and 1330, ten had had some legal training, seven were professional lawyers, five of these serving as royal justices and two spending their lives in the king's service and the common law courts.

The legal profession in the city took shape during Rokesle's mayoralty, and in 1280, after controversy over the standing of attorneys, civic ordinances were passed at the request of the leading practitioners. These enforced strict standards and entrusted supervision to a select group sworn to that purpose, the 'men who know their business'.[4] They are an elusive fraternity. All were Westminster-trained and few struck roots in the city. As far as one can tell, only one was a native Londoner,

---

[1] Hust. Roll 32(82); 33(96); *Cal. Letter-Bk. B*, 17, 24, *D*, 275, 304–5, *E*, 5, 6, 12, 21, 236; *Cal. E.M.C. Rolls*, p. 38, n. 2; *Lib. Cust.*, pp. 137 ff.; *Cal. of Wills*, i, 233–4.

[2] Hust. Roll 48–61, *passim*; *Cal. Letter-Bk. E*, 104–5, 235–6.

[3] Hust. Roll 64(51); Ancient Deeds E 501, 509; *Cal. Letter-Bk. C*, 172, *E*, 75, 76; *Cal. of Wills*, i, 399–400.

[4] *Lib. Cust.*, pp. 280–2; *Lib. Albus*, pp. 570–2; H. Cohen, *op. cit.*, 224–59.

Reginald Wolleward, the son of a clerk, and even he was kinsman to the keeper of the king's houses in Westminster.[1] Even those of them who became official city attorneys were Westminster men rather than Londoners.[2] Toutheby himself, king's serjeant, legal assistant at parliaments, and royal justice, was one.[3]

After the royal closure of London's own law schools in the early thirteenth century, the city had to draw its legal talent from outside, through the Westminster filter. Four of the six Common Serjeants of the period were immigrants, three of them former royal officials. Of the six recorders, one owed his promotion to royal patronage, while two were simply king's justices invited into the city for brief terms of service. Of the fourteen known civic attorneys at the central courts, only one was a native Londoner. All the others were Westminster men, five destined for the bench.[4] In marked contrast to Paris, London was unable to create a legal class with a corporate life of its own. The minds the city attracted to its service were minds shaped in the common law courts. They brought with them a crispness and rigour somewhat alien to civic tradition. Their impact on city society was the impact of Chief Justice Scrope on society at large—Scrope, a self-made Northerner, as so many of the London lawyers were, driving his way into the ranks of the aristocracy.[5]

The Scrope of the period in London was Robert de Kelsey. The lawyer's family were landowners in North Kelsey, Lincolnshire. His brother Richard inherited and Robert set out for the south. While a kinsman, Sir Robert de Kelsey, became a

---

[1] Misc. Roll CC, m.1; Hust. Roll 36(90); *Cal. Coroners Rolls*, pp. 22–3; Hust. Roll (Common Pleas) 9, m.7d; Lib. Roll 50, m.7.

[2] See, for example, the attorneys Grantham, Esthalle and Hertweyton in *C.C.R. 1296–1307*, *C.P.R. 1281–1307*, and *Cal. Letter-Bks.*, *passim*.

[3] *Cal. Letter-Bk. B*, 215, *C*, 185–7; E. Foss, *The Judges of England*, iii, 531–532.

[4] On the general situation, see H. Cohen, *op. cit.*; Serjeants: *Cal. Letter-Bk. D*, 14, 209, 262, 269, *E*, 6, 20, 32, 165–6, 270; Recorders: *Cal. Letter-Bk. A*, 175, *B*, 213, *D*, 251, *E*, 11, 12; *C.P.R. 1313–17*, pp. 414, 678, 690, 700 and *passim*; *C.P.R. 1321–4*, pp. 313, 361, and *passim*; E. Foss, *op. cit.*, 264–5; Attorneys: *Cal. Letter-Bk. C*, 115, 116, *D*, 251, 313–15 and *passim*; Ekwall, *op. cit.*, 144, 172, 180, 202, 244, 270, 297, 299, 327, 348 and *passim*; E. Foss, *op. cit.*, 264–532, *passim*.

[5] See E. L. G. Stones, 'Sir Geoffrey le Scrope, Chief Justice of the King's Bench', *English Historical Review*, lxix (1954), 1–17.

Chancery clerk and trod the path of royal patronage at Westminster, his namesake moved purposefully on London.[1] By 1298 he had bought a house, become a citizen and was practising in the city courts. A junior to Toutheby himself in 1300, when his professional conduct was impugned in a celebrated case, perhaps the earliest of its kind, he had become one of the sworn pleaders of the city by 1305. Marriage followed, into the Boteller family of mercers.[2] Recognizances for debt, for anything up to £150, began to weave their intricate and confusing tracery around him, with the customary consequences.[3] In 1301 he lent money to the mercer Robert de Bery. Ten years later, much of the mercer's property was his.[4] Enmeshed in a web of recognizances to the executors of Alderman William de Combemartin, he emerged with a sizable proportion of the Combemartin inheritance.[5] In six years, fifteen properties fell to him, many from the last, failing representatives of the house of fitz Ailwin.[6] By 1311 he was Common Serjeant. He served twice at a parliament and his salary was trebled. In 1315 he became alderman of Billingsgate and received a license to crenellate his house.[7]

He was still riding high when disaster struck, for in 1320 he was toppled from his perch and deposed from his aldermanry as a prime mover in an alleged plot to inflate tax-assessments to curry favour with the king.[8] For seven years his presence dwindled, but after the revolution of 1326 he returned to favour. A chosen companion of the aldermanic partisans of Isabella and Mortimer, he was six times city representative in

---

[1] *C.C.R. 1330–3*, p. 420; *Cal. Letter-Bk. E*, 168–9; for Sir Robert, see *C.P.R. 1313–1324*, *passim*.

[2] Hust. Roll 27(109); 37(70); *Cal. Letter-Bk. B*, 119, *C*, 147–8, 185–7; *Cal. o, Wills*, i, 511.

[3] Masses of recognizances and land transactions are recorded, particularly between 1309 and 1315; for a general view, see Hust. Roll 31–58, *passim*; *C.C.R. 1313–27*, *passim*; Recog. Roll 6 and 7, *passim*, and *Cal. Letter-Bk. B*.

[4] *Cal. Letter-Bk. B*, 109; Hust. Roll 30(150); 38(89)(90); St. Paul's A/22/1635.

[5] *C.C.R. 1313–18*, p. 540; *C.C.R 1323–7*, pp. 353–4; Hust. Roll 40(103); 47(34); 54(46)(64).

[6] Hust. Roll 37(88); 38(109); 57(53).

[7] *Cal. Letter-Bk. D*, 228, 257, 262, 269, 289, 291, 314, *E*, 30, 33; Beaven, i, 381; *C.P.R. 1313–17*, p. 292.

[8] *Cal. Letter-Bk. E*, 11, 12, 54, 94, 121, 124; Ekwall, *op. cit.*, 275; *Ann. Paul.*, p. 287; *French Chronicle*, p. 40.

1327 and 1328, serving as a keeper of the land of alien priories under Edward III.[1] Re-established in London, he took his friends among the aldermen and his kinsman in the Chancery north to Lincolnshire in 1331, to witness his reception of the family estate at Kelsey from his brother's widow. On his death four years later, he left his widow, his two younger boys and his eldest son, Sir Thomas, a clerk in service at Westminster, richly endowed with property in a dozen parishes.[2]

The administrative élite had penetrated the patriciate. The first of the civic administrators to reach aldermanic office was Ralph Crepyn, the Common Clerk, in 1280. From that date onward, a professional entered the council, on average, once every five years. They brought novelty and disturbance with them. Of the seven elected between 1280 and 1315, five were deposed. Crepyn's career ended in a scandal; his successor Bauquell was ejected as a king's man. The alleged plotters in the tax conspiracy of 1320 were the recorder Wengrave, the lawyer Kelsey and the clerk John de la Chambre.[3] Public opinion made such men the scapegoats for its own impotent dislike of the growing bureaucracy and for a long time London found it difficult to love its lawyers.

They were novel in other, less obvious, but more important respects. They represented a sharp breach with the dynastic tradition. Crepyn seems to have been connected with the aldermanic family of Gloucester, but he was an exception.[4] Hartpol and Swaleclive were royal justices, Norton the recorder, Kelsey and Chambre, ambitious immigrants. Bauquell's family were leather merchants, cordwainers and skinners of no social standing.[5] Those of them who built large city estates did so at the expense of the established.

Nor did they establish dynasties in turn. Only two of them

---

[1] *C.C.R. 1327–30*, p. 167; *C.C.R. 1330–3*, pp. 57, 384; *P. and M. Rolls*, i, 25, 30, 51, 60, 63, 70, 74; *Cal. Letter-Bk. E*, 168, 169, 222, 226.

[2] *C.C.R. 1330–3*, p. 420; *Cal. of Wills*, i, 412, 413.

[3] See Beaven, i, 379–85 and Chapters IX and X.

[4] Hust. Roll 27(46)(47)(48)(49); the Crepyns were sometimes called 'de Gloucester', and Ralph and his son served as aldermen of Cornhill in succession to two members of the Gloucester family (Beaven, i, 121).

[5] For some key references, see A.R. 543, m. 19, 30, 42; St. Paul's A /22 /10; *C.Lib.R. 1251–60*, pp. 29, 261; *Cal. Letter-Bk. A*, 127; *Cal. of Wills*, i, 390; E. Foss, *op. cit., passim*.

were followed in office by their sons. Crepyn's son Walter became an alderman, but it was with Middlesex that he was associated and his own sons sold the London property. By 1332 their great mansion in Cornhill had gone and the Crepyns broke contact with the city.[1] The recorder Geoffrey de Norton established himself more firmly than most, with his marriage to Idonia, daughter of Alderman Ralph Blund. His property, however, was concentrated in Middlesex—*atte Shire* was the family's nickname—and the London holdings were largely his wife's. His son Gregory followed as alderman and recorder, but added nothing to the patrimony. From his death in 1337 the story is one of sales, and the grandson, Thomas atte Shire, seems to have had little to do with the city.[2]

Most made even less of an impression. Wengrave and Waltham installed clusters of dependants in the administration, but they did not last. Bauquell's widow entered the wool trade in which her first husband had made his name. The clerk's son was a Westminster official and in mid-century the family was represented in London only by the rector of a city church.[3] Kelsey's eldest son moved to Westminster and his youngest was cut down by the plague.[4] Wengrave, the clerk John de Vintry, and the royal justices left nobody. The overall effect, in brief, was to install new men in the aldermanic class and to loosen the dynastic grip on city government.

The most lasting achievement which the patrician régime had to its credit, in London as elsewhere in Europe, was the coherent organization of city life. Yet in one sense, the aldermen, in their zeal to promote the city's welfare, pronounced sentence of death on their own exclusive fraternity. Throughout the century they were exposed to the pressures of growth. Not the least was that exerted by the professional class which the aldermen themselves had called into being. Its rise was not a revolutionary force as that of a new mercantile or industrial

---

[1] *C.C.R. 1318–23*, p. 700; *C.P.R. 1313–17*, pp. 49, 350, 461, 530; *C.P.R. 1317–21*, p. 348; *C.P.R. 1321–4*, pp. 124, 225; Hust. Roll 52(70); 58(16)(79); *Cal. Letter-Bk. E*, 168, 181, 269.

[2] Hust. Roll 29(2)(3); 51(12); A.R. 543, m. 19, 30, 42; *C.C.R. 1307–13*, pp. 563–4; *Cal. Letter-Bk. B*, 92, *E*, 20, 167, 242–3; *Cal. of Wills*, i, 277, 429, 549.

[3] Hust. Roll 37(20)(73)(74)(75); 60(13); 124(57); *Cal. Letter-Bk. D*, 253.

[4] See *Cal. of Wills*, i, 511, 518, 519; *P. and M. Rolls*, i, 259; Hust. Roll 56(160).

interest often was. Indeed, offering a career to a certain extent open to the talents, it acted as a safety-valve. Nevertheless, its coming signified change, for these men were new men, no less than their counterparts in the world of industry and trade.

CHAPTER V

The Mercantile Interests

'URBS illa puteus est inexhaustus', cried the frustrated Henry III in 1248, glowering at those Londoners, rich 'usque nauseam', who had just bought his jewels, and resolving on the spot to screw them down with tallages which would break a Jew. Such, at least, is Matthew Paris's interpretation of royal fiscal policy in mid-century.[1] Tax collectors certainly never lacked business in London and it was among merchants that they found most of it.

In the Fifteenth levied on foreign trade by King John, London paid the largest single sum, but was followed closely by Boston, outranked by Boston and Lincoln combined. If the tax be any guide, London was handling some 16 per cent of English foreign trade in 1203–5.[2] By the early fourteenth century, when the trade in wool, cloth and wine was at its peak, the city was taking a third of the wool, from a quarter to a third of the wine and a large proportion of the cloth. Its skinners dominated the English fur trade, its fishmongers, corders, and cornmongers formed important ship-owning interests in the Baltic commerce. Under the impact of the expansion, the composition of its patriciate, the structure of its government and the pattern of its social organization had been transformed.

Trade had entered the very bone structure of communal life. Royal confiscation of French merchants at the outbreak of war in 1294, for example, suddenly lifts the veil on a trade between London and Paris quite remarkable in its range and intensity, with humble painters and saddlers shuttling to and fro between the cities and handling an astonishing variety of everyday

[1] *M. Paris*, v, 22, 49, 50, 333, 334, 409.
[2] See the figures, derived from the Pipe Roll, printed by N. S. B. Gras, *The Early English Customs System*, Harvard Economic Studies, xviii (London, 1918), pp. 221–2.

wares, cutlery, washbowls, and pins.[1] Piracy cases heard at
Montreuil a few years later unmask London housewives as
exporters of English cloth.[2] And every city record points to a
mounting population, a swelling tide of immigrants. Mistery
after mistery was organizing itself to cope with the newcomers and with a rising pressure of numbers. Family after
family in old and new trades alike was climbing to aldermanic
rank; a butcher reached the council. There were many of the
hallmarks of a runaway boom.

By 1300 all the currents of European trade were flowing into
London harbour. Anything could be bought there, except,
possibly, the finest armour and the most expensive horses. The
old trades with Gascony and the Low Countries flourished;
the newer Spanish and, even more, the German trade developed
rapidly. The break came early in the new century. Famine,
dislocation in Flanders, the rise of craft régimes, the slackening
in the pace of growth and the impact of the plagues created a
novel European situation. In England, with the outbreak of the
French wars and the formation of Edward III's wool syndicates,
the economy was remodelled. Cloth, dispersed country-wide
by the fulling-mill, moved forward to displace wool as a basic
export, Gascons were ousted from the wine trade, and native
merchants, mobilized in the syndicates, suddenly emerged as a
power, focused increasingly on London. By the late fourteenth
century their companies were challenging the Hansards themselves.[3]

The process of growth was governed by the operation of the
monarchy. The wars of Edward I and his conscious intervention
in and manipulation of trade made the royal market and the
royal connexion an increasingly vital sector of the city economy,
and the planting of the Great Wardrobe in London under

[1] See. K.R. Acc. V. (Alien Merchants) E101 /126 /6, 7, 14, 28.
[2] See the records printed in G. P. Cuttino, *English Diplomatic Administration
1259–1339* (London, 1940), appendix 4, table 1, pp. 161–8.
[3] The literature on this subject is vast. See, in particular, E. M. Carus-Wilson,
Medieval Merchant Venturers: collected studies; Cambridge Economic History of Europe, ed.
M. M. Postan and E. E. Rich, ii; *Rapports du ixe. Congrès International des Sciences Historiques; Studies in English Trade in the Fifteenth Century,* ed. E. E. Power and M. M.
Postan; E. A. Kosminsky, 'Peut-on considérer le xiv. et le xv. siècles comme l'époque
de la décadence de l'économie européenne?', *Studi in Onore di Armando Sapori* (Milan,
1957).

Edward II, followed as it was by the permanent focusing of government agency in the south during the French wars, was an all-important factor in London's rise to capital status.[1] Crown business loomed large in the affairs of city merchants. Its direct demand alone could feed many impulses into the intricate network of trade relationships. The building of a galley in 1295, for example, gave employment and business to over 150 Londoners, while a small order for ornate harness and armour in 1341 provided three or four mercers with a year's income and teams of sempstresses and painters, over forty of them, with weeks of work.[2] Saddlers, cordwainers, farriers, operated virtually under contract to the Great Wardrobe, making up to £80 a year.[3] The Wardrobe hired a London mercer to supply the backdrops of Edward of Caernarvon's interludes and a London bookbinder to paste pictures into the Prince's French copy of *The Life of the Blessed Edward*. It sent a 'disher' to Scotland with 2,700 plates and 3,100 dishes, and an alderman to Wales with German engineers for the royal mines.[4] To the city goldsmiths, the regular royal market, with the aristocratic trade which went with it, was vital. Roger de Frowyk, one of the dynasts who became King's Goldsmith, made up to £450 a year from Household sales alone.[5] The Wardrobe became, in particular, a magnet for those provincial merchants whose thrusting entry into London society was a characteristic trend of the early fourteenth century.

For the migrations of the Household, with its massive war purveyance, accelerated the growth of an English merchant class, whole sectors of which were geared to the needs of the

[1] See T. F. Tout, *Chapters in the Administrative History of Medieval England* (Manchester, 1920–33), iv, 398–407, and *The Beginnings of a Modern Capital*, Raleigh Lecture, British Academy, 1923; *Finance and Trade under Edward III*, ed. G. Unwin; and see below.

[2] K.R. Acc. V. (Sheriffs Accounts) E101 /571 /1, 2, 3; K.R. Acc. V. (Wardrobe) E101 /384 /17.

[3] See, for example, Wardrobe Debentures E404 /481 /120, 266; E404 /497 /15, 32, 44, 46, 131; Wardrobe Books E101 /354 /5(1), fo. 3, (2), fo. 6, 30d; E101 /363 /18, fo. 7d; subsidiary documents in E101 /377 /10, no. 40, 54.

[4] For these instances, see the account book of the wardrobe of the Prince of Wales, 1302–3, E101 /363 /19, fo. 7d, 8, 12, 13; and Debentures E404 /482 /254.

[5] For a run of ten years (1313–23) in the Frowyk accounts, see Debentures E404 /481 /58, 67, 228, 265; 482 /356; 485 /385; and also the books E101 /354 /5(1), fo. 10d; 357 /15, fo. 22d; 369 /11, fo. 1d, 3d, 7d, 8, 9d, 167.

Crown. It always returned, bringing provincial traders and their goodwill, Yorkshiremen in particular, in its train. London's tentacles stretched deeper into England. Its victuallers and general merchants were entrenched among the large and affluent East Anglian and East Midlands trading populations, towards whom much of the city's commerce was directed. With the growing importance of the Hanse trade, the decline of the fairs and the dislocation of the urban cloth industry, much of the region's wealth and enterprise was funnelled into the city, and under Edward II, migrations of Norfolk and Lincolnshire merchants into London became socially significant. The Crown's attempt to mobilize and direct the merchants in the wool staples of 1294 and 1313 was a sharp stimulant to this slow process of fusion; so were Edward III's charters to the city and its wealthier crafts. The syndicates of the French wars were the culmination of a process which was turning the London patriciate into a mirror to the English merchant class.

The impact of the Crown was more immediate. With the accession of Edward I, aliens captured the royal ear and purse. The Italian companies, all established in London, became controllers of the financial service; they and the Gascons ousted Londoners from Household offices and markets, with decisive consequences for the city's dynasties of royal merchants. Further, in the interest of his creditors and the service of his own vision of the national good, Edward forced through a policy of free trade. After a head-on political collision, he annulled the city's liberties in 1285 and virtually abrogated the citizen trade monopoly.[1] As fitz Thedmar had ruefully remarked in mid-century, it was the influx of Italians and Southerners, with their lucrative cargoes, in particular, which posed the chief threat.[2] Only the Picards and the Germans were legally exempt[3] and the fierce hostility to Edward's policy came to centre on those Gascons who had toppled the dynasties from their perch. In 1288, 1292, and after the recovery of the franchise in 1298, the Londoners tried vainly to reimpose their regulations, but in 1303, at the price of the New Custom,

---

[1] These events are treated in some detail in Chapter IX.
[2] *Lib. de Ant. Leg.*, p. 118.
[3] *Lib. Cust.*, p. 71.

the Gascons, with other aliens, won exemption from prise
and complete freedom of trade, except in the bitterly contested last ditch of retail enterprise. It was the convulsive
city reaction to this policy which gave such strength to the
developing craft movement, and with the victory of the Ordainers in 1311 the Londoners reimposed their monopoly, to
the accompaniment of a violent campaign of expulsions, physical assault and sustained obstruction. The Gascons, however,
led by Arnold de Hispannia, recovered under Despenser, and
by 1335 the free trade policy had been reaffirmed. The Londoners, who had murdered Hispannia in the revolution of 1326,
would not yield and in 1337 recovered, at least nominally, the
full exercise of their commercial franchise.[1]

This confused and ambiguous battle was symptomatic, for
the monarchy's dependence on aliens set the tone for two generations. In these circumstances, the snug dynastic order lived
under perpetual threat. As the expansion mounted to a climax,
the city's commercial population outgrew the formal structure
of the commune; whole sectors of it organized themselves in
belligerent misteries. London was becoming the prime distributive centre of the realm and from the provinces came not
only its customers, but most of its apprentices and much of its
enterprise. Dynastic property, dynastic heiresses, dynastic wardships lay at the disposal of those newcomers who in increasing
number climbed to wealth and power. It was this interaction
between an expanding economy and an intrusive monarchy
which settled the fate of the aldermanic class.

Central to that economy was the wool trade. Before the civil
war, one in every eight London aldermen had entered it, but
as late as the last quarter of the thirteenth century, the city was
in no sense the hub of the traffic. In 1281-2 Boston's export of
10,000 sacks was double the city total and through the decade
1280-90, when national exports ranged from 24,000 to 31,000
sacks, London accounted for some 25 per cent of the total
against Boston's 37 per cent.[2] Londoners themselves accounted

[1] For a crisp general account of this struggle, see the essay by F. Sargent in
Finance and Trade under Edward III, ed. G. Unwin; *N. S. B. Gras, op. cit.*, chapter 2;
and M. K. James, 'The fluctuations of the Anglo-Gascon wine trade during the
fourteenth century', *Economic History Review*, 2nd. ser. iv (1951).

[2] All national figures for wool export, derived mainly from the Enrolled Customs

for still less. In 1297–8, the first year for which reasonably full particulars of city exports are available, Londoners supplied 5 of the 49 ships and 1,200 sacks of the city total of over 10,000.[1] In 1273 six in every seven wool exporters in the city were aliens or foreigns. Italians handled 24 per cent of England's wool, Northern French 16 per cent, Brabanters 11 per cent.[2] Such particulars as survive from the period 1297–1306 indicate that Londoners accounted for no more than 4 per cent of the total.[3]

The trade sustained a fairly numerous group of city middlemen. Inland centres like Dunstable, Winton and Burford recur constantly as city surnames, and Londoners like John Gamel's agent in Shropshire in 1298 or Walter le Fundur with his eight sacks of the Swansea clip at Bristol in 1313, were for ever riding up-country.[4] They had to compete with the Italian companies, the long-established traders of the Low Countries and with important provincial merchants such as the brilliant Ludlow family of Shropshire, at this time the greatest English merchants in the business. Rarely were they successful. Elias de Bristol, one of the more prominent Londoners, was operating in 1305 simply as a commission agent between the Bardi and the Ludlows.[5] In 1294 Italian companies had 250–350 sacks ready for export; three years later, of forty-three Londoners who exported, only three shipped out more than a hundred sacks, only four others, more than fifty.[6] And much of the wool these men handled was of mediocre quality, assessed at five to seven marks a sack.[7]

Accounts and subsidiary documents, have been supplied to me by the kindness of Dr. E. B. Fryde.

[1] K.R. Customs Acc. E122/68/6, 7.

[2] A. Schaube, 'Die Wollausfuhr Englands vom Jahre 1273', *Vierteljahrschrift für Sozial und Wirtschaftsgeschichte*, vi (1908).

[3] Particulars of customs, giving information on individuals, survive from the period for three complete years—1297–8, 1312–13, 1324–5, and for parts of four others—1303, 1306, 1322–3, 1332. See K. R. Customs Acc. E122/68/6, 7, 8, 9, 16, 17; E122/69/7, 12; E122/70/1, and the stray in E122/157/7. These accounts have been analysed and correlated with other sources, and the results incorporated in four tables (Group A), appended to this chapter, which should be read in conjunction with the text. For the London totals, see Table A.1.

[4] *Cal. E.M.C. Rolls*, pp. 17, 18; *P. and M. Rolls*, i, 52.

[5] *Cal. E.M.C. Rolls*, pp. 32, 33.

[6] K.R. Acc. V. (Alien Merchants) E101/126/7 and Table A.2.

[7] See the particulars in K.R. Customs Acc. E122/156/15 and Excheq. Misc. E163/5/17.

A small group, however, bought the best. William de Combe-martin, greatest of the city exporters, dealt in Lincolnshire wool, buying consignments at £500 a time from Bardney. The drapers, Stephen de Cornhill with his impressive roll of baronial custo-mers, and John Adrien who married into the Ludlows, traf-ficked with the earls of Warwick and Surrey and it was the high-priced wool of the Cotswolds and Flaxley Abbey that Gregory de Rokesle and Thomas de Basing shipped.[1] During the Flemish troubles of the early seventies, eight London merchants of this type accounted for a tenth of the wool nominally covered by export licences bought by Englishmen.[2]

Prominent among them was the dynasty of Basing. Adam's nephew Thomas, with his licences for 160 and 200 sacks, his purchase of ninety-two confiscated sacks at Newcastle in 1273, and his £227 export in the following year, was a celebrated London figure, sent by the king as royal proctor to Flanders in 1276, in company with the incomparable Nicholas de Ludlow, whose sales of silver to the Mint ran at an annual £900, to Thomas's £400.[3] The Londoner's kinsman Robert bought Lindsey and Kesteven wool; employed as factor in Antwerp the second heaviest citizen exporter of the nineties, and by the end of his life had added manors in Essex and property in fourteen London parishes to his ample patrimony. His daughter had married into a family of tenants-in-chief; he himself had been knighted; he had set up one son as a clerk and married off another to the daughter of a Kentish knight, whose marriage he had bought from Sir John de Lovetoft.[4] It was no doubt the sheep that paid for all.

They were reinforced by general royal merchants like Gre-gory de Rokesle and Elias Russel, and ebullient newcomers—

[1] Recog. Roll. 1(102); C.C.R. 1272–9, pp. 248, 255, 355; C.C.R. 1279–88, p. 527; C.C.R. 1302–7, p. 322; Cal. Letter-Bk. B, 38; Excheq. Misc. E163/5/17.

[2] C.P.R. 1266–72, pp. 595, 713; C.P.R. 1272–81, pp. 14–68, passim; C.Supp.C.R. in C.Chanc.R., pp. 2–11, passim.

[3] C.C.R. 1272–9, pp. 32, 33; C.P.R. 1281–92, p. 77; C.P.R. 1272–81, p. 187; K.R. Acc. V. (Mint) E101/288/6, m. 2, 3, 6, 7, and passim.

[4] Excheq. Misc. E163/5/17; K.R. Acc. V. (Mint) E101/288/29, m.1; Hust. Roll 9–18, passim; C.C.R. 1272–9, p. 123; C.C.R. 1279–88, p. 475; C.C.R. 1302–7, p. 340; C.P.R. 1281–92, pp. 410, 384, 334; C.P.R. 1301–7, pp. 323, 335, 539; Cal. Letter-Bk. A, 30, 150, B, 62, 78, 184, C, 18, 19, 191; Cal. of Wills, i, 35, 112, 135, 228, 229.

Reginald de Thunderle, the immigrant draper, with his circle of debtors ranging from merchants of Bruges and Cambrai through city tailors to Bartholomew de Badlesmere, and a cluster of newly important ship-owning fishmongers, men like Richard de Chigwell with his export licences or Thomas Cros, who shipped wool worth £672 to Bruges in 1298.[1] Individually, they were often weaker than their country cousins. Before the Anglo-Flemish tribunal of 1274, for example, the largest compensation claims for piracy losses by Londoners were those of £187 and £227 by the two Basings. Dunstable and Cork merchants were asking for £230; Nicholas de Ludlow claimed £1,928.[2] As a group, however, the Londoners formed an important interest among English merchants and stood out from the ruck of city middlemen and petty exporters as a minuscule élite.

Its importance was enormously enhanced by the development of royal policy. In 1294 Edward established the first recorded wool staple in Brabant. Laurence de Ludlow commanded the first wool fleet but his deputy was a London draper, and on the continent, Londoners predominated. Thunderle, Robert de Basing's man William Cosyn, and the corder John atte Gate were the most active agents, while at Antwerp from 1295 to 1298 chief control rested with the draper Elias Russel.[3] Their eminence presaged a more fundamental change. In the early nineties London's export totals climbed slowly towards Boston's. The Brabant staple accelerated the process. Of the £90,000 revenue from the special wool tax, London supplied over a third. Under the levy, total export shrank, but London's share of it increased precipitately—6,600 of 16,600 sacks in 1294–5, 8,300 of 20,600 in 1296–7. In the staple years of 1294–8 London's share of the English wool trade rose sharply from 25 to nearly 40 per cent.

[1] See, for example, K.R. Acc. V. (Alien Merchants) E101/126/27, m.1; K.R· Acc. V. (Butlerage) E101/77/5, m.1; Wardrobe book E101/354/5, fo. 11; Chanc· Misc. 109/1(44); *C.C.R. 1296–1302*, pp. 192, 475; *C.P.R. 1301–7*, pp. 312, 411, 412; G. P. Cuttino, *op. cit.*, 163–7; and Table A.4, where the leading city wool exporters are listed.

[2] Excheq. Misc. E163/5/17.

[3] For this staple, see, in particular, J. de Sturler, *Les relations politiques et les échanges commerciaux entre le duché de Brabant et l'Angleterre au moyen âge* (Paris, 1936), pp. 142–245 and notes; *C.C.R. 1296–1302*, pp. 555, 556.

I

Royal concentration and control strengthened the general trend. London's hold grew firmer, increasing numbers of its citizens were drawn into the trade; expansion became cumulative. In 1304–6, when exports were running as high as 40,000 sacks, 14–15,000 passed through the city annually. Boston was outstripped. The staple of 1313 was another fillip. By 1315 London was exporting 17,000 sacks, and the city maintained itself through the diminished exports of the twenties. In 1334–5, on the eve of the syndicate-staple enterprises of Edward III, London, with over 13,000 sacks, was handling some 44 per cent of England's wool trade, more than double Boston's, nearly treble Hull's percentages. In thirty years, royal policy, working in a context of secular trade expansion, had made the city the premier wool port of the kingdom.

Citizen enterprise increased at an even faster rate. Exports by Londoners through London rose from 1,200 sacks in 1297–8 to over 6,500 in 1312–13. This was one of the fabulous years, but there were nearly 4,000 sacks in 1324–5, 2,000–3,000 in a few months of 1322–3 and 1332. Surviving particulars are fragmentary and incomplete, but in general terms the Londoners' share of London exports between 1297 and 1332 rose from 13 to 38 per cent. Trebling their share of the city trade, they quadrupled their stake in the national. The proportion of England's wool export handled by Londoners rose in a single generation from 4 to 16 per cent.[1]

The pattern of growth runs clear through all the records. Exporting Londoners, 43 in 1297, were 172 in 1312, 122 twelve years later. Every roll has a high proportion of new names. No Londoner exported more than 200 sacks a year in the records of Edward I; in 1312–13 there were four who did so, with ten more over the 100 mark. The number of men handling over fifty sacks a year trebled, and among the ten to fifty sacks a year group there was a remarkable increase.[2]

The trade, never a closed shop, was flung wide open. Drapers and woolmongers naturally predominated, but men from the other patrician misteries, the rising crafts of the Baltic connexion and the city cloth industry took a hand. In 1297–8, nine crafts were represented among exporters; draper-woolmongers

[1] See Table A.1.   [2] See Table A.2.

accounted for a half to two thirds of them and practically monopolized the higher grades of export. In 1312–13 there were twenty-four crafts, in 1324–5 eighteen. Though still the largest single craft group and entrenched among the major exporters, draper-woolmongers dwindled to a quarter of the total. Men of the greater misteries, old and new, vintners, mercers, pepperers, fishmongers, cornmongers, jockeyed for a share of the heavier grades of export, while below the fifty sacks a year level, there was an inflow of men from all manner of middle class and artisan crafts, burellers, dyers, cordwainers, potters, tanners, chaplers. There were even two butchers.[1] With the rise of London in the wool trade and the intensification of effort by the patrician misteries, there was a surge of enterprise from below.

At the heart of the city trade were its Tower and Billingsgate families of woolmongers, the Turgys, Brothers, Uptons and Beauflours, solidly placed among the fifty sacks a year men, paying substantial taxes and serving on councils.[2] Above them formed a new élite. From the disjointed records of 1297–1332, forty-two leading figures emerge. They were a cohesive group. John de Oxford and Richard de Rothing, the vintners, were sons-in-law of the leading wool merchant William de Combemartin; Hakeneys, Fullers and Brayes, a complexity of interlocking clans.[3] Twenty-five of them traded regularly in partnership. They led in the community, too. Pulteney, Hakeney, Oxford, Prior and the others were some of the foremost English merchants. Twenty of them paid from £1 to 40 marks in the tax of 1292, 8 marks to £10 in that of 1332. Eighteen were councillors, no fewer than seventeen, aldermen, for under Edward I and II, some 40 per cent of the patriciate were committed to the wool trade.[4]

Of the Basings, however, there is no sign. William de Bydik

[1] See Table A.3.

[2] On individuals, see Table A.4; they may be traced in other city records, notably, Recog. Rolls, Hust. Rolls, *Cal. Letter-Bks.*, and *Cal. of Wills*; for rapid cross-reference, see Ekwall, *Two Early London Subsidy Rolls*.

[3] See, for example, *Cal. Inq. P.-M.*, viii, 101, 244; Hust. Roll 17(18); 55(3); Misc. Roll BB, m.6; *Cal. of Wills*, i, 113, 297, 298, 467, 468, 549, 550, 625, and *passim*; Ekwall, *op. cit.*, 220, 247, 284, 287, 312, 331, 337, 343, 344, 350.

[4] Ekwall, *op. cit.*; M. Curtis, 'The London lay subsidy of 1332', *Finance and Trade under Edward III*, ed. G. Unwin; *Cal. Letter-Bks.*, *passim*.

was related to them by marriage, but of all the forty-two, he is
the solitary merchant with dynastic antecedents.[1] The three
fishmongers, the two skinners, the corder and cornmonger
were men of the newly prominent trades of the late thirteenth
century, but even among the five pepperers, four vintners and
two mercers who reinforced the hard core of twenty-two draper-
woolmongers, new names and new families predominate. Most,
like Hakeney, Fuller and Prior, came of middle class London
stock,[2] but thirteen of them, and those the most important, were
immigrants. William de Combemartin himself, he who could
export 438 sacks in a single year and scorn all rivals except his
own nephew Henry, was a county immigrant. He paid the
queen's 1,000 mark debt to the Bellardi in 1305 and nine years
later was bracketed, as royal surety, with the king's celebrated
Genoese financier, Antonio di Passano. The whole family
flitted into and out of the patriciate in two generations.[3]
William Curteys came from Northamptonshire, Rothing from
Essex. Oxford, Pulteney, and Grantham were all newcomers.
William Cosyn's father was a foreigner with property in Ypres
and Douai; Henry Nasard himself an alien.[4] The dynasties
had been dislodged or sidetracked. The rapid growth of the
London wool trade in the late thirteenth and early fourteenth
century carried a new generation to the commanding heights
of city society.

Royal intervention in the wine trade was even more decisive.
Wine was London's own staple. In 1300-1, a bad year, the city

[1] N. G. Brett-James, 'John de Drokensford, Bishop of Bath and Wells', and
C. W. F. Goss, 'History of the parish of St. Mary the Virgin, Aldermanbury',
Trans. of the London and Middlesex Archaeological Society, n.s. ix (1944-7), 119-21; x
(1951), 295, 296.

[2] St. Paul's A/1/117; *Cal. of Wills*, i, 408; *Cal. Letter-Bk. E*, 76, 77, 185, 186, 233;
Ekwall, *op. cit.*, 344.

[3] *C.C.R. 1302-7*, p. 328; *C.P.R. 1301-7*, pp. 341, 372; *C.P.R. 1313-17*, pp. 157,
197, 205, 218, 231, 368 and *passim*; *C.P.R. 1317-21*, p. 473; *C.C.R. 1323-7*, pp. 353,
354; *C.C.R. 1330-3*, p. 152; *C.C.R. 1333-7*, p. 663; *C.C.R. 1337-9*, p. 433; *C.C.R.
1341-3*, pp. 51, 53; Hust. Roll 31-58, *passim*; *Cal. of Wills*, i, 276; see Table A.4.

[4] For Curteys, see J. J. Stocken, 'The Briklesworths of London and Northampton', *The London and Middlesex Notebook*, ed. W. P. W. Phillimore (London, 1892),
pp. 210, 211; on the Cosyns, see Hust. Roll 14(84); 15(19); *C.C.R. 1302-7*, p. 483;
C.P.R. 1301-7, p. 312; *Cal. Letter-Bk. B*, 154, 187, *C*, 68, 99, 100, 247; *Feet of Fines
for the County of Essex*, ed. R. Kirk (Colchester, 1899), ii, 99-232; *Cal. of Wills*, i, 479,
480; Pulteney appears in the *D.N.B.* Outline biographies of the others are given
below.

handled 3,600 tuns of the national import of 14,800, twice as much as Boston, Bristol and Sandwich, three times as much as Southampton. Seven years later, when exports from Gascony were at a peak of 97,000–102,000 tuns a year, aliens alone brought nearly 5,500 and 7,300 tuns to the city in two consecutive years, and London must normally have handled a quarter and more of an average national import of some 20,000 tuns annually. There were slumps in 1310–12 and 1315–1317, but by the early twenties Londoners themselves were shipping in from a third to a half of city imports which were running from 5,500 to over 8,000 tuns a year. They were thus well placed to deal with the shift in control which followed the dislocation of the war of 1324–7. In 1327 they won exemption from the prise, and after a generation of struggle, the Gascons began to pull out in large numbers. By 1330, Englishmen were importing as much in one year as Gascons formerly in two. They largely took the trade over, as native shipments climbed from fifty-eight in 1327–8 to the large totals of the late thirties when fleets of over 300 sailed in. Londoners, with their exemption, evade record, but the royal butler, in 1330, put their imports at 3,600 tuns at least, in forty-three ships, over a third of the total. By 1350 they were handling half the English trade.[1] These figures, taken in conjunction with the bitter struggle over the citizen trade monopoly, suggest an almost classic instance of the emancipation of a native mercantile interest from alien tutelage.

In the process, however, the structure of the city trade had been radically altered. Early in the reign of Edward I, the patrician merchants who had dominated the royal market under his father were abruptly displaced. Though Henry le Waleys and Gregory de Rokesle maintained themselves for a while, the London dynasties dwindle away rapidly. They never reappear. It was Gascons who served as butlers and from them the Household bought its wine, a practice which survived even the decline in Gascon numbers after 1327. There were some purchases from

---

[1] All national totals and all assessments of the general trend of the wine trade are taken, unless otherwise stated, from the text and tables of M. K. James. 'The fluctuations of the Anglo-Gascon wine trade during the fourteenth century'. *Economic History Review*, 2nd. ser. iv (1951).

Londoners, the wars especially, with their bulk demands for cheaper wines, bringing them in. In 1311, for example, William de Hallingbury was paid £177 for wine and victuals at Berwick; a year later the royal goldsmith included twenty tuns with the grain he sent to Perth. But Londoners no longer scintillate in the records. Typical was a Wardrobe debenture of February 1311, acknowledging a debt of over £3,524 to a group of vintners. Only three were Londoners.[1]

The butler's regular purchases, of course, fluctuated with the movements of the Household, but at all times the Londoners' totals were low. In the winter of 1326–7, for example, when Court and baronage were concentrated in London and the city was making the pace in the overthrow of Edward II, 1,018 tuns Gascon were bought there between 15 October 1326 and 20 April 1327. Little over a hundred tuns were bought from Londoners, fourteen of them, one a naturalized Gascon. The largest payment to a citizen was one of £93 for twenty-six tuns to Richard de Rothing, who in 1321–3, was importing 140–180 tuns a year.[2] In 1329–31 Londoners at London supplied 7 of 349 and 2 of 98 tuns Gascon.[3] They were rather better placed in the small market in Rhenish wine, but merchants of southern France, some Germans and, above all, Gascons outnumbered them well into the thirties.[4] John de Oxford, who imported nearly six hundred tuns in 1322–3, sold two tuns here, seven tuns there.[5] John de Gisors III, grandson of the great royal wine merchant of Henry III's time, was making £10–12 a year providing cellarage for wine bought from Gascons; indeed there is little evidence that the grandson sold any wine at all.[6]

The notables of the previous century, mercers and pepperers most of them, had been an élite dependent on the royal market.

[1] Wardrobe Debentures E404/482/431, 485/75, 365.

[2] K.R. Acc. V. (Butlerage) E101/78/2; K.R. Customs Acc. E122/69/9.

[3] K.R. Acc. V. (Butlerage) E101/78/5, 8.

[4] Accounts of the royal butler are rather scrappy. The most useful are K.R. Acc. V. (Butlerage) E101/77/1 (with a draft in C47/3/21), 77/5, 7, 10, 11, 13 and E101/624/1, for a roll of wine debts 29–30 Edward I, with a good run of accounts from 19 Edward II to 10 Edward III in E101/78/1, 2, 3, 4, 5, 8, 10a, 11, 12; E101/613/5 (for 8–9 Edward III) and E101/78/16.

[5] K.R. Acc. V. (Butlerage) E101/613/5; C.C.R. 1333–7, pp. 617, 627; K.R. Customs Acc. E122/69/9.

[6] K.R. Acc. V. (Butlerage) E101/78/2, 4, 5, 8, 10a, 11, 12, 16.

With the change under Edward I, they were eclipsed. The London wine trade became markedly less patrician in character. Before 1263 twenty of the ninety-five known aldermen had been vintners, twenty-nine of them had been interested in the trade. Between 1265 and 1307 only eight of the hundred aldermen were vintners, only nineteen of them were involved in the trade.[1] During the following thirty years, though there was some recovery in numbers, the wine trade remained the weakest of the aldermanic interests, overshadowed even by the newly important commerce in Baltic produce. The older trades in wool, cloth, mercery and spices flourished, the newer trades, based on the German connexion, grew. The wine trade itself was relatively less important and there was a transference of aldermanic enterprise, but the royal wine market had been the prop of the old patrician economy, and its loss threatened the whole structure of dynastic power. Under Edward II, the city wine trade which operated outside the royal sector grew in strength, and by 1337 had created a small élite. But it was a new élite, which in terms of aldermanic society, represented a second wave of enterprise, a fresh start.

A type figure of the transitional period was William Trente, for the most important 'Londoner' in the trade under Edward I came from Bergerac. Together with his brother Gerard Dorgoyl, Trente hailed from Puyguilhem[2] and in the eighties and nineties was busy selling to the Household, exporting corn, importing salt for the Scottish wars. He built up a clientele of knights, even sold shoes to a visiting Gascon nobleman on one occasion.[3] After several years of royal service, including the purchase of wine at Cologne in 1296, he became king's butler in 1302 and keeper of the exchanges under Edward II.[4] Establishment in London came late. In 1300 he and his brother were

[1] See the tables on interests and designations in the Appendix.

[2] *C.C.R. 1279–88*, p. 549; *C.C.R. 1288–96*, p. 359; K.R. Acc. V. (Alien Merchants) E101/126/6, m.2d; *Cal. Letter-Bk. B*, 68, *C*, 65, 242.

[3] K.R. Acc. V. (Butlerage) E101/75/5, 77/7, 10; Wardrobe book E101/354/5 fo. 3; *C.C.R. 1302–7*, pp. 369, 374, 370; *C.P.R. 1301–7*, p. 500; Recog. Roll 5, 6, 7, 8 9, *passim*; *Cal. Letter-Bks. A, B, C, passim*.

[4] *C.P.R. 1301–7*, pp. 3, 74, 77, 78, 328; *C.C.R. 1288–96*, p. 359; K.R. Acc. V. (Butlerage) E101/77/11, 13; *Cal. Letter-Bk. C*, 116; *Lib. Cust.*, p. 243; T. F. Tout, *The Place of the Reign of Edward II in English History*, 2nd ed. rev. H. Johnstone (Manchester, 1936), appendix D 3.

warned for breaking the anti-alien regulations and five years
later Gerard, travelling abroad and leaving Bernard de la
Rochelle in charge of his 'wines and wife', was still counted a
foreigner.[1] His wife, however, was a London woman and so
was William's—Joanna de Blithe, a widow with a son by a
former marriage.[2] Trente himself was soon buying city property, in one transaction of symbolic appropriateness acquiring
the Hardels' wine-wharf for 640 marks.[3] In 1305, like many of
his compatriots, he became a citizen. Within a year he was
serving on councils and in 1309 became alderman of Bread
Street. His brother took up the franchise and his sister settled and
married.[4] This powerful clan sponsored many city vintners of
the twenties. Joanna's son took his step-father's name and followed him into the trade; James Beauflour was quick to snap
up the wardship of Trente's nephew. Gerard's apprentice
Richard de Essex emerged in the twenties as one of the leading
dozen of city vintners.[5]

Essex's apprenticeship was symptomatic. Ralph de Honilane,
who inherited property worth less than £20 a year, launched
into the trade as a factor of Gonsalin Bonet of Bordeaux. Deals
with the abbot of Westminster, the earl of Arundel, Bartholomew de Badlesmere, knights and ecclesiastics followed. In
1298 Honilane became an alderman and a settlement with
Bonet in 1302 cleared off debts of 200 marks. Shortly afterwards,
however, Bonet died and in 1306 Honilane went bankrupt. He
never regained his aldermanry, but he re-established his fortunes and several members of his family were active vintners
under Edward II, one serving as warden of the craft in 1328.[6]

It was in the shadow of the aliens that the city trade developed. Forty-three Londoners were amerced for selling wine
against the assize in 1276. Vintners predominated but the patrician misteries and wholesale victuallers, with their shipping,

[1] *Cal. E.M.C. Rolls*, p. 168; *Cal. Letter-Bk. C*, 65, 242.
[2] Hust. Roll 47(91)(94)(116)(117); *Cal. of Wills*, i, 267; *Cal. Letter-Bk. B*, 185.
[3] St. Paul's A/15/1411; Ancient Deeds E 326.
[4] *Cal. Letter-Bk. C*, 143; *Cal. of Wills*, i, 267.
[5] *Cal. Letter-Bk. D*, 143, *E*, 82.
[6] For Honilane, see St. Paul's A/17/1314; W.A.M. 5422, 28045, 29006, 29016;
Recog. Roll 2(99), 5, m.2; Hust. Roll 2–14, *passim*; *Cal. Letter-Bk. A*, 79, *B*, 115, 137,
203, 211, *C*, 189, 245–8; *Cal. E.M.C. Rolls*, p. 241; *Cal. of Wills*, i, 42, 186, 189, 257,
260.

made a mark.[1] In truth, however, wine functioned in the city almost as currency and there was a continuous process of direct purchase from importers by all manner of people, from syndicates of cordwainers to housewives.[2] The city's wine assize of 1330–1 included rates for areas within a radius of fifty-four miles and in fact its recognizance rolls between 1285 and 1317 record wholesale purchases by men, taverners and 'merchants' of Stony Stratford to knights and churchmen, from almost every corner of England. The Midlands and the Home Counties were most heavily represented, but there were several from the far north and even a taverner from Beaumaris in Anglesey. William de Hallingbury, who bought constantly from the Gascons, did a regular trade with the taverners of Caterham and Dartford; a handful of small merchants in Warwickshire came regularly to a London vintner called Leamington.[3]

Within the city, the tied house was common. The retail trade was profitable and even the leading importers kept a firm hold on it. William Barache, an importer of Gascon descent, controlled a chain of taverns, and mercers and skinners joined the vintners in setting up houses.[4] Many taverner families, however, Scots, Farnhams, and Colchesters, made a niche for themselves, regularly buying and distributing consignments of over £20 and getting a hold on the retail trade and small-scale wholesaling in Middlesex.[5] One of them, Thomas de Conduit, was making heavier purchases from the aliens at Boston and London in the eighties. His son, Geoffrey, climbed to an aldermanry on a trade which embraced knights and barons buying at £100 a time, and set his apprentice, Reginald de Rothing, on the road which led him, as Reginald de Conduit, to the mayoralty and headship of Edward III's wool syndicate.[6]

---

[1] Misc. Roll BB, m. 3 and *passim*.   [2] *Cal. Letter-Bks.*, *passim*.

[3] Recog. Rolls 1–9 cover the period; those for 1309–11 are particularly full. For Hallingbury and Leamington, see especially Recog. Roll 6, 7, 8, 9, and *Cal. Letter-Bk. B*, 48, 51, 202, 253, 254, 255.

[4] See, for example, K.R. Customs Acc. E122/193/4 (a stray); Lib. Roll 60, m.3; C.C.R. 1272–9, p. 49; *Cal. Letter-Bk. A*, 41, 43, 44, 52, 55, 69, 71, 83, 84, 96–9; Select Excheq. Pleas, p. 103.   [5] *Cal. Letter-Bk. A*, *passim*.

[6] *Thomas*: *Cal. Letter-Bk. A*, 54, 60, 89; *Geoffrey*: Recog. Roll 2–7, *passim*; K.R. Customs Acc. E122/68/6, 7; A.R. 543, m.14; Misc. Roll BB, m.1; *Cal. Letter-Bk. B*, 17, 41, 159, 197, *C*, 22, 38, 177, 178, *D*, 146.

These vintners, with their complex system of agencies and partnerships, were a substantial group in city society. Suffolks, Herefords, John de Cheshunt, prince of the Pui, the diminished Hardels, sat solid on the councils.[1] The chance survival of an arbitration award between two of them in 1305 illustrates the nature of their enterprise.[2] The men involved were William le Barber of Fleet, a vintner of some standing,[3] and John de Chigwell, a fishmonger intimately connected, probably by service, with the merchant family whose surname he bore. His agent was a man from Henley, the grain centre, and John was evidently committed to that complex traffic in grain, fish and Baltic products which flowed between London, Henley, Yarmouth and the Low Countries and which buttressed the power of the Chigwell family. In May 1304 they drew up an indenture of partnership. Each was to contribute £40 towards a *societas* which was to last for one year and conduct a venture to embattled Scotland.

Chigwell's £40 were potential rather than actual, residing in ten tuns of woad bought at Amiens by his Henley agent and at that moment en route through St. Valery, or so John optimistically asserted. But if he could not supply the woad, he certainly provided the ship, for it was he who did all the travelling. 'Us must put our good in aventure', as the son of another vintner wrote later, and Barber bought ten tuns at £2 6s. 8d., eight at £2 13s. 4d., threw in £15 of oats, £9 of salt, paid the 2 marks wages of John's mariners and sent the enterprise north. At Berwick and Stirling, royal officers took two tuns and some oats, but Barber's men, Thomas de Barrow and John le Gourder, sold the salt for £11 11s. and disposed of the rest for something over £70. This they promptly invested in the purchase of hides, woolfells and wool from John Comyn and Walter of Bedwyn, which Chigwell shipped south to sell at St. Omer. Barber claimed an ultimate profit on the year of £36 and more, but Simon of Henley and his woad never appeared and the partnership dissolved in a welter of conflicting claims over allowances and what proportion of what was or was not *extra societatem*.

[1] For some examples, see *Cal. Letter-Bk. A*, 36, 57, 66, 68, 94, 95.
[2] See K.R. Acc. V. E101 /506 /1, for litigation over this partnership.
[3] *Cal. Letter-Bk. B* ,48, 155, 162, 192, 193, 222, *E*, 58, 104, 119.

Barber's man Thomas de Barrow reappears six years later when he took up the franchise as a factor of William de Boddele, one of the leading importers and a partner of Hamo de Chigwell.[1] The Chigwell-Barber connexion was of earlier date. Barber's father John had been a leader of the popular revolt of 1263. His neighbour in Fleet and a fellow rebel was Simon de Pourtepoll, the weaver, whose daughter married Richard de Chigwell, a leader among those fishmongers who supplied so many recruits to the revolt, and the founder of the family fortunes.[2] The Heyruns were another rebel family which sent some of its members into the wine trade after the civil war. Mary, the mother of one, married two vintners in succession, one a warden of the craft, another an immigrant from Ipswich, Robert le Chaucer, whose son John followed in the business, and whose grandson Geoffrey, of course, trafficked in an even headier commodity.[3] It was from these hidden reaches of London society and from immigrants that the city's wine trade drew its men after the eclipse of the dynasties.

Their progress may be traced even in the distorting mirror of the recognizance rolls. No trade seems to have been so vulnerable to political pressure. As soon as the throne passes to Edward II, English names begin to displace Gascon and with the victory of the Ordainers, a favourable tide sets in.[4] A handful of royal gauge accounts which survive from 1318–23 chronicle a city interest on the eve of spectacular mid-century success.[5] In these years, London's imports ran from 5,500 to over 8,000 tuns a year, with 50–70 shipments out of national totals ranging from 130 to 206. In 1322–3, indeed, London may well have taken a half of the national, two-thirds of the aliens' imports. Of this

[1] *Cal. Letter-Bk. D*, 54; K.R. Customs Acc. E122/69/9.

[2] St. Paul's A/2/611, 613, A/12/1128, 1130, A/17/406; *Cal. Letter-Bk. B*, 17, 116, *C*, 56, 60; *Cal. of Wills*, i, 48; *Lib. de Ant. Leg.*, pp. 119–20.

[3] Misc. Roll BB, m.1; *Cal. of Wills*, i, 27; *C.C.R. 1272–9*, pp. 2, 137; V. B. and L. J. Redstone, 'The Heyrons of London: a study in the social origins of Geoffrey Chaucer', *Speculum*, xii (1937); *The Works of Geoffrey Chaucer*, ed. F. N. Robinson, 2nd. (New Cambridge) edn. (Cambridge, Mass., 1957).

[4] Based on a numerical analysis of wine transactions recorded in Recog. Rolls 1–9.

[5] The gauge account, the only detailed record of import by individuals, may be found in K.R. Customs Acc. E122/69/9, and has been subjected to the same type of analysis as the wool customs. See Tables B.1–4, at the end of the chapter, which should be read in conjunction with the text.

city trade, Londoners themselves, with totals running from 2,300 to 3,700 tuns a year, handled from 34 to 47 per cent.[1]

The numbers involved, some sixty men a year, were half those of the wool trade. In the peak year, 1321–22, thirty-eight Londoners accounted for 3,700 of the total of 8,000 tuns, a *per capita* import more than double the normal rate of 40 tuns a year. Much of the shipping, seventeen vessels in 1321–2, they supplied themselves. Conduit had his own ship, *la Katerine*, which in 1325 carried nearly 1,500 quarters of salt from Colette in Poitou.[2] William Prodhomme the fishmonger and his craft colleagues of the Pyk family tended to specialize in the carrying trade and in 1318–19, the year he became mayor and won for the London commonalty its great charter, Hamo de Chigwell stowed his wine, with that of two other fishmongers, alongside Hugh Despenser's forty-three tuns in the hold of the *Margaret de Bread Street*, a Billingsgate craft.[3] It was their command of shipping which no doubt accounts for the remarkable number of fishmongers and, to a lesser extent, of cornmongers in the trade, for these were ship-owning crafts and their joint interest in the grain which Gascony demanded drew them into wine more consistently than into wool.

The general craft structure of the wine and wool trades differed considerably.[4] In the former, there were really only two large groups, vintners and fishmongers. Vintners were well ahead with a third of the total of 132 importers over the four years; sometimes they numbered over a half. Only at the lower forty to seventy tuns a year level were they seriously challenged by the usual cluster of wealthy misteries, only below the forty tun mark did they dwindle to a minority, and that never less than a quarter of the total. Yet the range of twenty-five crafts represented was every whit as broad as in the wool trade. Qualitatively, it was broader, for, as taxpayers, the wine importers ranged from the absolute maximum to the absolute minimum. The score of leading wine merchants show little of that concentration in the upper tax brackets characteristic of

---

[1] See Table B.1.   [2] *P. and M. Rolls*, i, 8, 9.

[3] K.R. Customs Acc. E 122/69/9, m.1d and *passim*, and see M. K. James, 'The medieval wine dealer', *The Entrepreneur*, papers of the annual conference of the Economic History Society (Cambridge, 1957), pp. 5–13.

[4] See Table B.3.

the forty leading woolmen.[1] In short, there was a much more clear-cut division between a majority of petty merchants and a handful of greater men. Among the majority, there was a constantly shifting pattern, rapid changes of personnel, with few men importing more than fifty tuns over a run of consecutive years. Above them were a small group who imported regularly on a business-like scale. Few even of these would qualify as London merchants of the first degree by their wine trade alone, but at the top were two or three outstanding figures. John de Oxford handled 10–17 per cent of the Londoners' total imports; between them, Oxford, Reginald de Conduit and Richard de Rothing, practically a quarter of the citizen trade.[2]

In the twenties, all three emerged in the front rank of city merchants. Oxford, with his imports at times nearing the 600 tun mark—over £2,500 at current butlerage prices—must have been one of the greatest. Rothing, with his exports climbing steadily, ranked ninth among the woolmen of 1298–1332. Oxford was no mean wool-exporter either and both, marrying daughters of William de Combemartin, were assessed at the highest figure in the Fifteenth of 1332. It was Oxford who took the lead in loans to hard-pressed abbeys and priories from the late twenties which drew the chief city merchants into financial transactions on a scale not hitherto recorded. Alongside the Wardrobe drapers, the handful of mercers, pepperers and corders, the three great men of the wine trade, leading wardens of the craft in 1328, took their place in the inner commercial élite of the city and in that national syndicate of Edward III of which Conduit was the head.[3]

All three were immigrants. Richard and Reginald (de Conduit) Rothing were kinsmen, appearing together as witnesses in 1313. Both were admitted to the freedom in 1311 and both got off to a good start. Reginald was apprenticed to Alderman Geoffrey de Conduit, probably the most eminent Londoner in the trade at that date. Richard, apprenticed to Thomas de Rothing, was admitted free, at the request of Sir John de Sandale. His sister Margaret had married the Exchequer official

---

[1] See Table B.4 and Ekwall, *op. cit.*   [2] See Tables B.2 and 4.
[3] *Cal. Letter-Bk. E*, 232; *Cal. Inq. P.-M.*, viii, 101, 244; Hust. Roll 55(3); Ekwall, *op. cit.*, M. Curtis, *op. cit.*, and *C.C.R. 1337–41, passim*.

Augustine de Uxbridge, none other than a son of Henry le Waleys himself.[1] Oxford, more of an outsider, climbed even more rapidly. An immigrant from Oxford, he rose to the head of every tax roll and subscription list, but made no attempt to build up an estate in the fashion of his colleagues. In his will, bequests of money, totalling nearly £1,000, completely over-shadow legacies in real estate. The creditor of twenty-one religious houses, he was a great man for annuities, but sold city property as quickly as he bought it.[2] His acquisitions, however, included the last strongholds of the Eswy patrimony and the central property of the Hardels.[3] For all three climbed over the ruins of dynasties. None founded a dynasty himself. The wine trade had been the mainstay of the old aldermanic class and the careers of these three men are perhaps the most vivid instance of change.

While the wine trade went through its travails, that in cloth, on the other hand, went from strength to strength. From the sixties there was a sharp reversal and the number of aldermen in cloth rose to double and even treble the number in wine. Over the whole period from 1216 to 1340 drapers were easily the strongest single trade group among aldermen, and if those men designated simply as woolmongers are counted with them, as well they might be, they were twice as numerous as any other group. In the early fourteenth century, political disruption in the Low Countries and the shift to cloth-production at home were having their effect. Imports fell from their peak in the first decade, and in the thirties fell more sharply still. Of thirty-three drapers who became aldermen in the fourteenth century, twenty served before 1350, when there were twice as many draper mayors and sheriffs.[4]

---

[1] Recog. Roll 8, m.1; *Cal. Letter-Bk. D*, 131, 146–7; Hust. Roll 41(4)(7); 50(70); *C.C.R. 1307–13*, p. 58; *C.C.R. 1318–23*, p 375.

[2] The key references for Oxford are: *Cal. of Wills*, i, 460–1, 699; *Cal. Inq. P.-M.*, viii, 244; *C.C.R. 1341–3*, p. 461; *C.C.R. 1349–54*, p. 527; see also Hust. Rolls 51–9, *passim*; *C.P.R. 1324–7*, p. 201; *C.C.R. 1333–7*, pp. 617, 627; *Cal. Letter-Bk. E*, 232, 261, 300; for his role in the syndicate, see especially *C.C.R. 1337–46*; his financial transactions are considered below.

[3] Hust. Roll 51(35–8)(56)(135); *P. and M. Rolls*, i, 176; *C.C.R. 1349–54*, p. 465.

[4] See tables of interests and designations in the Appendix; Beaven, *passim*; and for a general picture, E. M. Carus-Wilson, 'Trends in the export of English woollens

But if these were the last years of a great commercial tradition, it certainly did not end with a whimper. Alien imports
in the ten years after 1300 were at the peak level of 12,000
cloths a year and English wool exports were running at their
maximum. The Italian companies were dominant, though
Flemings were still numerous in the 1280's.[1] In the nineties,
men of Brabant were multiplying in London, the cloth of Malines
and Louvain displacing that of rival cities and fetching a
better price at the Great Wardrobe.[2] The Picards with their
vital woad, Dutch, men of Artois proliferated; the power of the
Hanse built up in London and the east coast. In 1304 Utrecht
and Dordrecht ships filled the Pool and two years later, the
piracy cases heard at Montreuil give a brief glimpse of the
narrow seas crowded with shuttling craft, Londoners from
alderman-fishmongers to mercers' widows shipping out wool
and English cloth to Antwerp, drawing back cargo after cargo
of Brabant russets and Hansard goods.[3]

It seems probable that Londoners increased their stake in the
trade. At the Iter of 1276 not far short of two hundred men
were amerced for selling cloth against the assize in London.
Ninety-three were Low Countries merchants, Flemings still
numerous. Second, at fifty-two, were the Londoners, three-
quarters of the aldermanic council among them. The city
sheriff Stephen de Cornhill ranked with the queen's personal
Italian; three aldermen paid as much as the redoubtable John
Boinebroke himself.[4] Londoners were established among the
élite, at least at the distributive stage. Royal confiscations in
1274 and 1294 and the multitudinous debt recognizances reveal
dozens of aldermen and councillors buying in bulk from Andrew
Brotherlamb of Ypres, Henry Schauff of Malines and many of
their fellows, selling to Robert de Montfort, the countess
of Pembroke, and Hugh Despenser, trading in partnership

in the fourteenth century', *Economic History Review*, 2nd. ser. iii (1950), together
with the introduction and other essays in *Medieval Merchant Venturers*.

[1] See, for example, Misc. Roll BB; *C.C.R. 1272–9*, p. 338.

[2] See the accounts of the Great Wardrobe listed below.

[3] See writs ordering withernam on Flemish goods in 1304–6, one on a ship
freighted by a 'multitude of poor weavers of Flanders', in Chanc. Misc. 109/1(53)
(55)(56); G. P. Cuttino, *op. cit.*, 161–8; *Cal. E.M.C. Rolls*, pp. 162, 221; *Cal. Letter-
Bk. C*, 124.

[4] Misc. Roll BB, m.5.

with Brabanters and Douaisians.[1] The big men of the 1294 staple were all drapers; so were most of those Londoners who reported the seizure of their wool in Brabant between 1300 and 1317. Under Edward II, Londoners handled a third to over a half of the cloth purchases of the Great Wardrobe, and if its activities were concentrated in the city, as during the revolutionary winter of 1326–7, they swept the board.[2] Solidly ensconced in its councils were a whole class of men like Ralph de Upton, whose purchases from the aliens and sales to Bartholomew Burghersh and his friends in the 1330's provided him with sustenance not only material but spiritual—lucrative properties in nine parishes for death-bed bequests and the cost of a vicarious pilgrimage to Santiago for a peaceful mind with which to make them.[3]

In sharp contrast to the wine trade, the dynasties held their own well into the reign of Edward I. Towering over the city trade in the seventies was Stephen de Cornhill of distinguished pedigree. His business embraced Kentish tailors, Lincolnshire knights, abbots of Westminster and a particularly close involvement with the Beauchamp earls of Warwick. Between 1275 and 1281 he drew from cloth and wool deals an annual £114 to supplement his inherited rent-roll of £70 a year.[4] The Basings flourished, and closely allied with them were the Abyndons, Stephen and Simon. They were an Abingdon family, settled in the city from the late thirteenth century, which may have

[1] K.R. Acc. V. (Alien Merchants) E101/126/27, m.1–4, 127/2, 3; Recog. Rolls, especially 7 and 8, passim; Misc. Roll BB, m.3, 5; C.C.R. 1272–9, p. 44; Cal. Letter-Bk. A, 3, 7, 12, 23, 40; E. B. Fryde, 'The deposits of Hugh Despenser the Younger with Italian bankers', Economic History Review, 2nd. ser. iii (1951).

[2] Particulars of account of Great Wardrobe purchases, giving information on individuals, survive in usable form for six years, viz, 1300–1, 1315–16 (incomplete), 1323–4, 1324–5, 1325–6, and 1326–7 (which really covers only that winter); see K.R. Acc. V. (Wardrobe), Great Wardrobe Purchases, particulars, E101/359/18, 376/30, 379/12, 380/14, 381/9, 382/2; overall totals and totals under the four Wardrobe categories of drapery, furs, mercery and spices have been tabulated in Tables C.1–3 at the end of the chapter.

[3] Recog. Rolls, passim; C.C.R. 1330–3, p. 418; C.C.R. 1333–7, p. 564; C.C.R. 1341–3, p. 261; C.C.R. 1346–9, pp. 206, 449; Cal. E.M.C. Rolls, pp. 9, 10, 66; Cal. Letter-Bk. E, 239, 260, 284; Cal. of Wills, i, 453–4.

[4] Recog. Roll 1(101)(128)(155)(160); C.C.R. 1272–9, pp. 235–578, passim; C.C.R. 1279–88, pp. 46–538, passim; Ancient Deeds D 4257, 5285, 4641, 5689, 4635, 4625, 6467, 4616, 7096; W.A.M. 28044; Cal. Letter-Bks. A, B, C, passim; M. M. Postan, 'Credit in medieval trade', Economic History Review, i (1928), 248.

been related to the London dynasty. Indeed, they may have been kinsfolk of the Abingdons of the Exchequer. Stephen, a travelling merchant (he was robbed at Lens in 1310), became royal butler, leased the Stannaries and was involved in the political intrigues of Edward II, falling victim to Arundel under Despenser. His daughters married knights from wool-growing Shropshire and the Abyndon-Basing group, at the turn of the century, was acting as a central interest in the patriciate, towards which successful immigrants gravitated.[1]

Those immigrants, however, were many and in the cloth trade, no less than in wool, the dynasties were soon overshadowed. Many of the rank-and-file drapers were of solid London stock, but in the reign of Edward I in particular, aliens multiplied. The patrician family of Cosyn, which was selling Poperinghe cloth in bulk to the Court in the sixties, descended from a Malinois; Arras, Bethune, Betteville, Armentiers were aldermanic surnames in the nineties. Indeed, the most important city draper in the early fourteenth century was Henry Nasard, certainly an alien and possibly one of the Nazarts of Arras.[2] He bought wool at 700 marks from a Cotswolds knight, witnessed agreements at Shrewsbury with Stephen de Abyndon, and went surety for men of Ypres.[3] He specialized as a Wardrobe merchant, particularly during the Scots wars. In 1307-9 he was paid £735 for loans at Berwick towards the Scots garrisons and £300 for cloth supplied at London. Two years later, royal debts to him totalled £640, for cloth sold at London and Boston, Scottish purveyance, the queen's Christmas liveries, and a loan towards the maintenance of Perth. Regular payments of £500-600 followed and between 1312 and 1317 frequent assignments on customs and subsidies were made him as 'king's merchant'. In 1315 it was his personal agent, Richard Box, who took to Berwick Nasard's

---

[1] The Abyndons throng in the royal records; see, in particular, C.C.R. 1323-33, passim; C.P.R. 1313-27, passim; C.C.R. 1307-13, p. 245; Cal. Letter-Bk. C, 53, D, 26, 46, E, 17, 24, 70, 165, 166, 243; Hust. Rolls and Recog. Rolls, passim; Cal. of Wills, i, 413, 414, 416, 417, 677.

[2] Cal. Letter-Bk. D, 217-18; Wardrobe Debentures E404/482/17; C.C.R. 1307-13, p. 131; J. Lestocquoy, Les villes de Flandre et d'Italie sous le gouvernement des patriciens, p. 139.

[3] Recog. Roll 7, m.5d; C.C.R. 1313-18, p. 621; C.C.R. 1318-23, pp. 181-513, passim; Cal. Letter-Bk. D, 46; see Table A.4.

K

forty-two coloured and fifty-seven rayed cloths, together with the Riccardi's twenty-eight, and the Londoner Simon de Swanland's fifty-one, purchased by royal agents at Westminster Fair.[1] Not until 1309 did the draper become a London freeman. A £5 tax assessment and an aldermanry followed, but he resigned the latter within eighteen months, because he was busy in the north. He married a London woman, but his only property in the city was a house in All Hallows the Less, bought from the Armentiers in 1315.[2]

His meteoric career illustrates the importance of the royal market, particularly in a warlike age. By the reign of Edward II, the important drapers in London were the Wardrobe men. Of six wardens of the craft named in 1328, five were men who appeared regularly on the rolls of the Great Wardrobe.[3] In a scatter of Great Wardrobe particulars which survive, particularly from the period 1323-7, a group of Londoners emerge as merchants of distinction.[4] In 1300-1, for example, most Wardrobe business was in the north, but a dozen city drapers supplied a third of the cloth, with much higher proportions of the spicery and furs. In 1325-6, on the other hand, the Bardi got most of the business and Taldo Valori swept triumphantly through all four Wardrobe categories, reducing the nine London drapers to a quarter share and supplying, that year, even the burels of Candlewick Street.[5] The year 1323-4 was perhaps a more normal period. Of £327 paid out, £221 was spent at London on twelve occasions between December and July. Simon Slepe of Louvain, two other aliens and two provincial merchants were involved, but the lion's share of £171 went to twelve Londoners. Taking the year as a whole, nine London drapers supplied all the scarlet, 80 per cent of the 'coloured' cloth, 62 per cent of the cloth dyed in grain and 23 per cent of the rayed. Two city mercers handled the worsted, Ivo de Winton, a

[1] Wardrobe Debentures E404/481/101, 327; 482/432; 483/32, 34, 134, 136, 271; 485/73; book of debts, E101/357/15, fo. 13; C.C.R. 1313-18, pp. 409, 549; C.C.R. 1318-23, pp. 281, 663; C.P.R. 1307-13, pp. 207, 515, 523, 524; C.P.R. 1313-17, pp. 214, 340, 341, 615; C.P.R. 1317-21, p. 154.
[2] Hust Roll 44(1); C.C.R. 1327-30, pp. 47, 50; Cal. Letter-Bk. B, 209, D, 28, 217, 218, 316, E, 138, 172, 194; Ekwall, op. cit., 217.
[3] Cal. Letter-Bk. E, 232.
[4] See Tables C.1-3.
[5] K.R. Acc. V. (Wardrobe) E101/359/18, 381/9.

bureller, the Candlewick. Simon de Swanland was well ahead of everyone else, with £110, followed by his friend Henry Darcy.[1]

The most striking account, however, is that for 20 Edward II, which actually covers only the few months from September 1326 to January 1327—the crisis parliament of Edward's deposition, with the city filled with the trains of the barons. Wardrobe cloth responded far more readily than butlerage wine. A couple of small deals in worsted in August–September were followed by heavy purchases of good quality cloth at London through to the new year. There were five non-Londoners, Slepe and a colleague of Louvain, James le Scutler of Bruges, Henry Schauff of Malines, with John Brasse of Boston supplying some of the worsted, but of £1,000 paid out, £766 went to ten Londoners. Swanland, with scarlets, Louvain, Malines, Ghent and rayed cloths of mixed origin, got over £354; Darcy, nearly £200. Eight London drapers handled nearly all the scarlet, 65 per cent of the grain, 166 'diverse' cloths of Malines, Louvain, Brussels, Ghent—97 per cent of the total—and scores of rayed cloths. Winton again supplied the Candlewick, John Dalling, a mercer of Norfolk origin, some of the worsted. Swanland alone supplied a third of the total, he and Darcy together a half.[2] With the sudden clarity of a flare, this account shows what resources city drapers could command.

Wardrobe purchases, of course, are no adequate indication of a man's trade, but what is certain is that this handful of men were the leaders of London commerce, members of that inner ring which was to sponsor the city's contribution to the syndicates of Edward III. By the reign of Edward II, there were no dynasts among them. Swanland and Darcy were immigrants from the north. The Swanlands, in fact, were a whole Yorkshire clan planted in London, four brothers, three of them drapers, and the fourth a clerk with a living in York diocese. The soil proved fruitful, for they were kinsmen of no less a person than William Melton, archbishop of York from 1317 to 1340, the shrewd and pious Yorkshireman, himself a franklin, who left behind him a knightly family safely ensconced in Yorkshire

---

[1] Calculated from K.R. Acc. V. (Wardrobe) E101/379/12.
[2] Calculated from K.R. Acc. V. (Wardrobe) E101/382/2.

county society.[1] When Simon de Swanland appeared in London about 1310, he was already a king's merchant armed with his exemptions.[2] In 1317 he was commissioned to make unusually heavy provision of cloth for the king, relieved of subsidy on 2,000 cloths for the purpose; two years later he and Thomas de Abyndon were exporting wool in royal service.[3] He was certainly one of the leading woolmen, having cargoes worth 2,000 marks in the four ships commissioned by Prior, Combemartin, Beauflour and himself which were pirated by Calais men in 1315.[4] Between 1314 and 1327 his Wardrobe sales ranged from £100 to £500 a year; from the first year of Edward III, he regularly supplied the cloth for the Christmas liveries, at up to £400 a time.[5] Manors, a commission of array in Middlesex, and a knighthood followed in due course.[6] As early as 1310 he was buying property in London, but he never became a city magnate.[7] Dealing constantly with the Bardi and Peruzzi on behalf of his influential kinsman, he managed to survive both the Despensers and the financial chaos of the syndicates and, in the forties, extensive family settlements among the bewilderingly prolific Swanlands bespeak the planting out of offspring among the county gentry and the partitioning of gains. These would have been considerable. In the Twelfth of 1319 Swanland ranked with his fellow-northerner Kelsey at £20, third highest on the roll.[8]

He found time to help a neighbour, for Henry Darcy was born at Toothill, Rastrick, in the West Riding, with a brother

[1] See, for example, *C.C.R. 1327–30*, pp. 406, 561; *C.C.R. 1346–9*, p. 45; *C.C.R. 1349–54*, p. 396; *C.P.R. 1313–17*, p. 593; *P. and M. Rolls*, i, 214–15; *Cal. Letter-Bk. E*, 190; Hust. Roll 63(166)(167); L. H. Butler, 'Archbishop Melton, his neighbours and his kinsmen, 1317–40', *Journal of Ecclesiastical History*, ii (1951).

[2] Hust. Roll 38(118); *C.P.R. 1307–13*, p. 235.

[3] *C.C.R. 1313–18*, p. 496; *C.P.R. 1317–21*, p. 390.   [4] *C.C.R. 1313–18*, p. 315.

[5] In addition to the Great Wardrobe particulars, see Debentures E404/481/123, 482/432, 483/258, 497/1, 4, 43, 186, 197; K.R. Acc. V. (Wardrobe) E101/377/10, no. 9; *C.C.R. 1313–18*, pp. 170, 171; *C.C.R. 1327–30*, p. 192.

[6] *C.P.R. 1307–17*, *C.C.R. 1313–46*, *passim*, for multitudinous references of this character; for his honours, see, in particular, *C.P.R. 1307–13*, p. 235; *C.P.R. 1313–17*, p. 519; *C.C.R. 1313–18*, p. 496; *C.C.R. 1327–30*, p. 140; *C.C.R. 1339–41*, pp. 118, 233, 274; *C.C.R. 1343–6*, p. 477.

[7] Hust. Roll 38(118)(122); 63(166)(167); *Cal. Letter-Bk. D*, 228, *E*, 94, 232, 271; *P. and M. Rolls*, i, 66, 74, 88.

[8] Ekwall, *op. cit.*, 217 and *C.C.R. 1349–60*, *passim*.

Hugh a tenant in nearby Fixby. He came to London in 1306 as apprentice to Philip le Tailor's son-in-law. Free in 1310, he joined the wool-exporters and in six years had attached himself to Swanland. By the thirties he was a full-blooded royal merchant, heavily committed to purveyance with the syndicate men. In 1321, he married the grand-daughter of a Frowyk and by 1330, he was an alderman. His purchases of city land began late and never amounted to much, but he had come a long way from the franklins of the West Riding.[1]

Their careers mirror that remarkable inflow of Yorkshiremen and northerners in general into the civil service characteristic of the early fourteenth century, a product, no doubt, of the northward shift in the focus of government during the Scots wars. One civic recognizance in 1316 recorded a bond for £198 executed by Joce de Spalding, an immigrant from that town, then a London draper. Swanland and Darcy were his witnesses. His creditors were two Lincoln mercers, who in a few years were London citizens themselves.[2] The path was already well-worn which took the celebrated de la Pole family a few years later from Hull to glory, or at least the peerage.

The great John Pulteney himself, another draper, had a background not unlike Darcy's. It is paradoxical that it should be the drapers' trade, in which the older families held on longest, which illustrates the process so vividly. For these were the new men, who emerge as soon as the dazzle of the aliens begins to fade late in the reign of Edward I, men with an extremely sharp nose for government business, adapting themselves to every switch and tremor in royal policy. Rising from citizen families, but more often entering from the mercantile and small landowning classes of the provinces, they were swarming into the old trades, rising with the new, turning the old dynastic order into a memory.

The impact of immigrant enterprise was even more notable in the other traditional trades of the patriciate, those of the mercers and pepperers. In the decade 1317–27, for example, when political upheavals caused an unprecedented number of

---

[1] *C.C.R. 1323–7*, p. 56; *C.C.R. 1327–30*, p. 575; *C.C.R. 1330–3*, p. 166; *C.C.R. 1337–1339, passim*; *C.C.R. 1313–18*, p. 329; Recog. Roll 9, m.1; Hust. Roll 59(146)(147); 60(25)(31)(91)(92); 61(94); *Cal. Letter-Bk. D*, 119; Ekwall, *op. cit.*, 218.

[2] Recog. Roll 9, m.1; *Cal. Letter-Bk. E, F, passim.*

aldermanic vacancies, no fewer than eight mercers and five
pepperers reached the council, completely overshadowing the
four new aldermen from the traditionally dominant drapers.[1]
The majority of them, the mercers in particular, were immigrants from the English provinces. Neither of these trades, it is
true, was strongly represented at the Wardrobe. The *mercery*
section of the Great Wardrobe accounts was an incredible rag-
bag, and city mercers appear selling the most surprising commodities, from twill sacks to wash bowls. Generally, they handled
the usual gold cloth and velvet and practically all the Aylsham,
worsted and English cloth, but in the surviving particulars of
Edward II's reign, no London mercer got more than £80 a
year.[2] In the oddly diffuse spice accounts, most London pepperers display themselves after the fashion of John le Callere,
who for 1s. 4d. in 1326 supplied 8 lb. of soap for the use of the
doubtless apprehensive king's ward John Jermyn.[3] Even in
1300–1, when twenty-one Londoners supplied 67 per cent of
spicery worth £1,600, it was Elias Russel the draper and his
fellows who took the lion's share, supplying wax. At the end of
Edward II's reign, when Londoners handled most of the purchases, it was the relatively obscure men who appeared, drawing
small sums. This was at a time when the Riccardi got 60 per
cent of the £780 mercery account in 1301, when Passano was
getting £500 for his spices and Anthony Bache of Genoa £1,750
for his.[4] Clearly, it was the Italians who controlled the royal
market.

The Wardrobe accounts, however, are no measure of these
men. Andrew Aubrey and John Hamond, pepperers who could
import £2,000 of merchandise in a year, hardly appear;
neither does Adam de Sarum, the Salisbury immigrant and
financier who was Hamond's master.[5] Among the three leading

[1] See table of designations in the Appendix.

[2] Calculated from the Great Wardrobe particulars used as base for Tables
C.1–3 and cited above.

[3] K.R. Acc. V. (Wardrobe) E101 /381 /9.

[4] K.R. Acc. V. (Wardrobe) E101 /359 /18, 376 /30; for the Italians, see Debentures E404 /485 /352, 353; 497 /17, 299, for example.

[5] For Sarum, see *C.C.R. 1330–3*, p. 232; *C.C.R. 1323–33, passim; Cal. of Wills*, i, 361,
362, 515–17; Hust. Roll 58(113); *P. and M. Rolls*, i, 9; Debenture E404 /497 /148;
on Hamond and Aubrey, see S. L. Thrupp, 'The Grocers of London', *Studies in
English Trade in the Fifteenth Century*, ed. E. E. Power and M. M. Postan, p. 250.

Wardrobe mercers, each of whom made little more than £50 annually from sales to the Household, Hamo Godchep and Hugh de Garton were assessed at £10 in 1319, while Simon Fraunceys paid 10 marks in 1332, and in 1340 contributed £300 to a city loan, ranking with Oxford as the heaviest contributor on the roll.[1] When merchants of French allegiance had their goods confiscated in 1294, it was the city mercers and pepperers who figured as their chief customers. The Paris branch of the Bellardi, for example, importing spices and mercery, was owed £1,000 by forty-one city debtors, twenty-one of them mercers, ten, pepperers. Thomas Bonbaron and Raoulino Bek of Paris had sold their goods to the value of over £400 to twenty-two mercers and six pepperers. The pepperers were more markedly the clientele of the southern companies, the Berauds and Andreus of Montpellier and Cahors, groups of six to ten city pepperers purchasing from them at £100 a time. Nearly all the Italians and French were lodging with city pepperers, and individual transactions could be large. William de Garton had bought spices to the value of £140 when the confiscations occurred; the mercer Richer de Refham, using three factors, was nearing the £300 mark; there were a score of men over the £50 level.[2]

Their standing in the luxury import trade was one source of strength. The Lucca goldcloths, velvet, laces, jewellery, and smallware luxuries of the mercers commanded a restricted but lucrative market everywhere, and in composition and range of activity, it is the mercers who seem the most English of the London trades. It was to them even more than to the vintners that the 'merchants' of Steeple Bumstead and Stony Stratford came.[3] In 1316 Hugh de Garton was making a whole series of sales under £20 to people from every county in England, and frequent transactions, ranging over £200, testify to an intense two-way traffic with men from Yorkshire to the Home Counties.[4] More than any other group, the mercers were rooted in the mercantile society of provincial England.

[1] P. and M. Rolls, i, 120–1; Ekwall, op. cit., 245, 261, 300.

[2] Calculated from K.R. Acc. V. (Alien Merchants) E101/126/6, 7, 14.

[3] Recog. Rolls 1–9, where mercers' recognizances are second only to the vintners' in number and greatly outweigh them in value.

[4] See, in particular, Recog. Roll 9, m.1d, 3, 3d.

One key, perhaps, was the trade in English cloth. By 1330 its centre of gravity had shifted to the settlements clustering around the rural fulling mills, and Kendal, the West Riding, and East Anglia were already shaping to a brilliant future when, in mid-century, cloth moved to displace wool as the 'great industry' of England. London had been an important centre of production of the cheaper cloth. Its burel of Candlewick Street ranked with the russets of Colchester and the kerseys of Essex and Suffolk. The woad merchants of Amiens, Nesle and Corbie bought exemption from the city's trade regulations with a contribution to the farm of the conduit, an indication of the importance of their trade to the burellers and dyers who controlled the quasi-capitalist structure of the London industry. That industry, it is true, was hit by the changes of the late thirteenth century. In 1298 and 1310 there was trouble over the fulling mills at Stratford and Enfield; short time and strikes were common; by the early fourteenth century, the number of looms was said to have fallen from 380 to 80. London remained, however, a natural outlet for Colchester, the kerseys of Essex and the important production of the Stour district during the age of expansion.[1]

The drapers had occasionally sold burel and some of their scarlets may have been English, but in the main they were wholeheartedly committed to the import trade.[2] Much of the cheaper cloth escaped the customs, leaving historians blind. Not until 1347 were denizen cloth-exporters customed and even then the early returns throw only a fitful light. In the period 1348–53, for example, it was Bristol which ran off with the cloths of assize, Yarmouth with worsteds, the trade in each case controlled by Englishmen. London offered a striking contrast—low figures and the predominance of Germans and Frenchmen. Of sixteen Londoners who paid custom in those seven years, however, the largest single group were nine mercers. In 1352–3, a typical year at this time, the sole citizen

[1] See E. M. Carus-Wilson's seminal articles on 'The English cloth industry in the late twelfth and early thirteenth centuries', 'An industrial revolution of the thirteenth century', and 'Trends in the export of English woollens in the fourteenth Century', reprinted in *Medieval Merchant Venturers*; see also *Lib. Cust.*, pp. 64–6, 68, 69, 121–31, 416–25 and Chapter VI.

[2] See the roll of debts in Chanc. Misc. 3/29.

contribution among fifteen busy Hansards was 250 worsteds shipped out by three mercers, two of them of Norfolk origin.[1]

At Montreuil in 1306 several Londoners claimed compensation for piracy losses and English cloth figured prominently among their cargoes. Seven obscure citizens laded blue robes for Antwerp; one woman exported cloth in partnership with a Malinois. Cecilia atte More shipped ninety-eight English cloths to Antwerp in three vessels, and she was the widow of a mercer.[2] In 1277 the lady Almois de Périgord, widow of a lord of Quercy, was buying burel from those *mercadiers* of Villeneuve who were some of the London mercers' closest foreign associates.[3] There are other oblique correlations. In the mid-fourteenth century, mercer families like the Wychinghams, Horshams, Lacers and Godcheps, were handling worsted, serge, tunics and friezes. Dyers were prominent among the customers of mercers in constant commerce with the merchants of Toulouse. The mercer John de Depham shipped in woad, his colleague John de Causton traded in Picardy.[4] Mercers were active in the wine trade when Gascony was England's best customer for cloth. Immigrants from the cloth centres entered mercery far more regularly than any other trade. Even the fulling-mill sites appear. The Enfield family were mercers; Strubby in Lincolnshire provided some, so did Leeds; Wellingborough produced a crop. The Worsted family were almost hereditary mercers.[5]

The evidence is necessarily scanty and speculative, but the accounts of the Great Wardrobe strengthen it. Aylsham linen and English *tela* appear under *mercery*, worsted and wadmol now under *mercery*, now under *drapery*, but with the exception of

---

[1] Calculated from a short series of returns of particulars on the custom on exported cloth made by John de Wesenham and Henry Picard. That for 1350–1 is in its logical place in K.R. Customs Acc. E122/158/15; the remainder are in K.R. Acc. V. E101/457/19, 20, 22, 23, a reference I owe to Dr. E. B. Fryde.

[2] G. P. Cuttino, *op. cit.*, 161–7.

[3] L.d'Alauzier, 'Achats d'étoffes d'une dame du Quercy au xiiie. siècle', *Annales du Midi*, lxx (1958), note and document, 87–9.

[4] See, for example, Recog. Roll 8, m.2; 9, m.2 and *passim*; *Cal. of Wills*, i, 506–7; *C.C.R. 1313–18*, p. 220; *C.C.R. 1323–7*, p. 531; *C.C.R. 1354–60*, p. 136; *Cal. Letter-Bk. E*, 76; Ekwall, *The Population of Medieval London*, pp. 50, 66, 88.

[5] For these examples, see Ekwall, *The Population of Medieval London*, pp. 89, 90, 159, 160, 188 and 1–92 in general.

Candlewick, a preserve of the burellers, whenever English cloth appears by name, it is almost invariably a London mercer who is handling it. Apart from Aylsham, it was the more plebeian cloth they handled; it was nearly 'all worsted for the honour of Norfolk'.[1]

As well it might be, for one of the most striking and clearly defined social phenomena of the period was the remarkably large number of Norfolk men among the London mercers. From 1280 to about 1350 at least one hundred city mercers were men of immediate or recent Norfolk origin; at least fifty-nine of them were immigrants in their own lifetime.[2] This is a movement abundantly documented in letter-book and recognizance roll. John de Dalling's apprentices came from Norwich; Aylshams and Sechfords were apprentices to Caustons; Hardinghams made bequests to Hedersetes, Horshams to the Franciscans at Walsingham—the relationship was close and continuous.[3] The one clearly marked immigration trend was a flow into London from the rich, commercialized provinces of the old Danelaw, East Anglia, the east Midlands, east Lincolnshire and southern Yorkshire. Possibly displacement in the old cloth towns and the decline of the fairs were contributory factors. London's trade was already oriented towards these provinces; the connexion was already close, with the Husting closing for Boston Fair and the city fishmongers colonizing Yarmouth. East Anglia in the great years of English cloth was second only to the west itself and it specialized moreover in 'kerseys and suchlike stuffs'. Certainly, the Norfolk-mercer link stands out even in the overall pattern of eastern counties migration. Working through the London mercers from 1300 to 1340 is like thumbing a Norfolk directory.

[1] See, in particular, K.R. Acc. V.(Wardrobe) E101/379/12, 380/14, 381/9, 382/2.

[2] The basic source is Professor Ekwall's painstaking *Studies on the Population of Medieval London*, an excellent reference work. His conclusions on immigration are sometimes a shade dogmatic, since place-name evidence is frequently misleading, but on the Norfolk trend, which can be verified, particularly by some information from Hust. Rolls, the evidence is incontrovertible. See Ekwall, *op. cit.*, especially 1–206 and xxxi–lxxi; Hust. Rolls, *passim*.

[3] See, for example, *Cal. Letter-Bk. D*, 131, 158, 63; Recog. Roll 3 (Dalling); *Cal. Letter-Bk. D*, 155, 272; Ekwall, *op. cit.*, 36 (Aylsham and Sechford); *Cal. of Wills*, i, 506, 507, 667, 694, 695 (Hardingham and Horsham); instances could be multiplied.

By 1290 the inflow was being reflected in the aldermanic council. Between 1290 and 1349 twenty-one mercers were elected to aldermanries.[1] Two were from Yorkshire, a third of citizen stock.[2] Three Hauteyns and a Picot held office in the nineties. It cannot be proved that they were Norfolk men, though all took Norfolk apprentices and were more heavily involved with that county than with any other.[3] Even if they be totally excluded, there remain fourteen men, two-thirds of the total, all with Norfolk background. Six of them were probably immigrants, seven others the first generation descendants of immigrants.[4] Of nine wardens of the craft listed in 1328, six were Norfolk men; of the three wardens of the closely linked haberdashers in the same year, Geoffrey de Causton was the grandson of an immigrant, Andrew Sechford the son, Roger Madour an immigrant himself, all from Norfolk.[5] It was in the same period that the London dialect changed from East Saxon to East Midland.[6]

If the places of origin of these men are plotted, the pattern which results is logical enough to astonish. The largest cluster was around Aylsham, the second around Worstead. There were smaller concentrations near Lynn and the Wash.[7] The Wardrobe men, it is true, fall outside this pattern. Hamo Godchep came from a rooted London family,[8] but the two leading

---

[1] Beaven, i, 377–87.   [2] Outline biographies of these men are given below.

[3] See, for example, *C.C.R. 1323–7*, p. 633; *C.C.R. 1346–9*, p. 289; *Cal. Letter-Bk. C*, 203–4; *D*, 45, 126, 132, 158; *Recog. Rolls, passim*.

[4] See them under the appropriate place-name in Ekwall, *op. cit.*, under Norfolk; men with the surnames Callere and Lacer were also Norfolk men—see *Cal. Letter-Bk. C*, 188, *D*, 58, 132, *E*, 242 and Hust. Rolls, *passim*; the Paris family seems to have originated in Necton, Norfolk—see *Year Books of Edward II*, i (Selden Society, 1903), 11–13.

[5] *Cal. Letter-Bk. E*, 232, 233; correlated with Ekwall, *op. cit.*, under appropriate place-name, and *Two Early London Subsidy Rolls*; on the Madour (madder) family see *Cal. Letter-Bk. D*, 141, 158, 189 ff.; they seem to be from Fakenham, Norfolk, though some or all of them may have come from the Suffolk village of the same name.

[6] Ekwall, *The Population of Medieval London*, xiv–xxxi, where the author develops a suggestion made in his introduction to *Two Early London Subsidy Rolls*; and see the references cited there.

[7] Calculated from the evidence in Ekwall, *The Population of Medieval London*, xxxi–lxxi, 1–206.

[8] Hust. Roll 45–55, *passim*; *Cal. Letter-Bk. C*, 204, *D*, 231, 274, *E*, 85, 86, 282–3; Recog. Roll 9, m.1, 3d, 5d; *Cal. of Wills*, i, 251, 581, 582; Great Wardrobe particulars.

figures were once again Yorkshiremen. Hugh de Garton was an immigrant from the East Riding and took his apprentice from Maltby in Lincolnshire. He ended his life a landowner in Norfolk, Essex and six city parishes, leaving 200 marks to his widow and £300 to be invested in trade for his children.[1] He was overshadowed by his compatriot, Simon Fraunceys, who came from Pontefract, bringing many of his kinsfolk with him. Fraunceys, who exported wool through Hull and imported herring from Flanders to Newcastle, sold spices as well as mercery and was heavily involved in the syndicates of Edward III, paying his forced loan on 800 sacks in 1351. He emerged with property in four counties and a city estate substantial enough to buttress the fortunes of a second generation of mercers.[2] The Wardrobe market, however, was far less important among mercers than among drapers and the leading figures in the city trade were the Norfolk men. John de Causton, for example, was a brilliant figure. He handled Picard wheat, Irish grain, Malines cloth; he traded at St. Omer and stocked Ghent fabrics in his shop at Boston. He exported wool from London and Yarmouth, lead from Boston.[3] His factor sold mercery worth £172 to the Court in 1341 and it was Causton who supplied much of the velvet and Aylsham for thirteen sets of ornate armour ordered in the same year.[4] His first wife was the daughter of a Norfolk pepperer and Causton himself made bequests to the fraternity of St. Anne. The bequests were munificent, for on his death in 1353, the mercer had property in Norfolk, Middlesex and nine city parishes, including one of the city landmarks, the tenement near the Tower called the Cardinal's Hat.[5]

The London mercers, drawing their recruits in large numbers

---

[1] Recog. Roll 6, m. 12, 13; 7, m.3; 8, m.2d; 9, m.1d; *Cal. Letter-Bk. B*, 18, *D*, 217, *E*, 189, *F*, 80; *C.C.R. 1318–23*, p. 233; *C.C.R. 1323–7*, pp. 192, 323, 337; *Cal. Inq. P.-M.*, vii, 97; Hust. Roll 46(164); 53(43); *Cal. of Wills*, i, 688.

[2] *C.C.R. 1327–30*, pp. 250, 251; *C.C.R. 1349–54*, pp. 348, 468, 476, 483; *C.C.R. 1354–60*, p. 465; *Cal. Letter-Bk. D*, 150, *E*, 224; *P. and M. Rolls*, i, 48; Hust. Roll 56(141); 57(156); 58(2); 59(70)(83); 62(96).

[3] *C.C.R. 1313–18*, p. 220; *C.C.R. 1321–24*, pp. 454, 455; *C.C.R. 1327–30*, pp. 83, 85, 86; *C.C.R. 1330–3*, pp. 89, 94, 96, 97; *C.C.R. 1338–41*, pp. 132, 133, 186; Ekwall, *The Population of Medieval London*, pp. 44, 45.

[4] Wardrobe Debentures E404/497/38; K.R. Acc. V. (Wardrobe) E101/384/17.

[5] Hust. Roll 39(29); *Cal. Letter-Bk. C*, 169, *E*, 209, 212; *C.C.R. 1323–7*, p. 192; *Cal. of Wills*, i, 672, 673.

from Norfolk and English provincial society, with their stake
in the English cloth trade, their ventures in wool and wine,
their intimate contact with Italian and French companies and
European marts, were geared, perhaps more effectively than
most, to the very rhythm of English commerce. As England's
trade and England's merchant class grew, they grew with them.
Before 1263 they had ranked fourth among the aldermanic
misteries, with seven office-holders; by 1307 they were third,
with a tenth of the aldermen. Between 1307 and 1337, thanks in
part to their forceful entry into city politics under Edward II,
they doubled their representation, climbed to first place alongside the drapers, and in the late fourteenth century, they supplied more aldermen, sheriffs and mayors than any other craft.[1]
In the thirties and forties, it is the mercers who catch the eye—
Roger de Horsham, bequeathing the debts owed him by the
notorious Paul de Monte Florum to the friars at Thetford and
Walsingham, and leaving his widow all his jewellery, 'except
1,800 Oriental pearls and the ring with the large diamond',[2]
or the wealthy Richard le Lacer, creditor in recognizances for
£1,000 to city merchants, county knights, and the prior of St.
John Jerusalem, with their inevitable by-products, the manors
in Kent and Essex, the gardens at Greenwich and, every
Christmas, an annuity from the Order of St. John, with a set of
their livery, skin-lined for his wife, fur-lined for himself.[3] In
March 1327, when London won its most lavish charter and
when some of its important misteries assumed a position of
national leadership, it was a mercer, Geoffrey le Lacer, kinsman
to the fur-lined Richard, who set out with goods worth £1,050 on
a venture to Bologna.[4] In the powerful 'community of the
mercers' of early fourteenth-century London, one can already
trace the outlines of their great company and of the Merchant
Venturers of the late Middle Ages.

Their colleagues of the Mediterranean connexion, the pepperers, were a far more restricted élite. Here, aliens were

[1] See tables of designations in the Appendix and Beaven, i and ii.
[2] *Cal. of Wills*, i, 506–7.
[3] For his debts: *C.C.R. 1339–41*, p. 120; *C.C.R. 1341–3*, p. 657; *C.C.R. 1346–9*,
pp. 157, 276, 366; *C.C.R. 1354–60*, p. 136; his lands: *C.C.R. 1333–7*, p. 87; *C.C.R.
1339–41*, p. 328; *C.C.R. 1341–3*, p. 277; his livery: *C.C.R. 1339–41*, p. 649.
[4] *C.C.R. 1327–30*, p. 41.

numerous. The outstanding alderman-pepperer of the early
fourteenth century was himself a Cahorsin. William Servat came
to England at the head of a company of Cahorsin merchants,
trading in wool and spices and making loans in the manner that
the Berauds had made traditional.[1] His purveyance accounts
were weighty—in 1311–13 he got £518 for cloth and £600 for
wine.[2] Entering the royal service, he continued to move in a
circle almost exclusively Cahorsin and Italian, progressing
through a blizzard of assignments and recognizances. Between
1312 and 1318, when Passano's money was keeping the government afloat, the years of Pope Clement's loan and the 'time
of the obligation' in Gascony, Servat was handling huge sums.[3]
Typical of many was an order of June 1315, when the customs
of four ports were assigned him in part payment of a debt of
over £2,073, covering £1,000 paid to Passano, £600 for wine,
£311 advanced to a royal agent, and over £100 spent on the
garrison of Dundee and on the provision of a ship to take Queen
Isabella to France.[4]

By 1292 he was a citizen, paying £2 in tax in Cordwainer,
where he ran a large 'inn' for his compatriots. In 1301, he decided
to settle, and sent Peter Andreu of Montpellier home to collect
his twelve-year-old son and bring him (with ginger and cinam-
mon worth £445) to London.[5] Eight years later he was alderman of Walbrook, serving conscientiously until his death in
1319. He passed through the patriciate like a comet. He had
few houses, and by 1317 they had passed to Passano.[6] Nor were
his progeny notable. It may be significant that, in 1309, he

[1] For Servat as a Cahorsin, see *C.P.R. 1272–81*, p. 37; *C.P.R. 1292–1301*, pp. 557,
558; *Cal. Letter-Bk. A*, 31, 37; for one of his transactions, see *C.C.R. 1288–96*, pp.
192–5; *C.P.R. 1281–92*, pp. 352, 383.

[2] For some of these purveyance accounts, see Wardrobe Debentures E404/482/159,
483/317, 485/9; K.R. Acc. V. (Wardrobe) E101/357/15, fo. 11d, 359/18, 369/11,
fo. 56d, 354/5, *passim*; *C.P.R. 1307–17, passim*.

[3] See, in particular, *C.C.R. 1307–23, passim*; for some instances, see *C.P.R.
1301–7*, pp. 111, 454, 538; *C.P.R. 1307–13*, pp. 187, 270, 274; Debentures
E404/485/426.

[4] *C.P.R. 1313–17*, pp. 305–6.

[5] Ekwall, *Two Early London Subsidy Rolls*, p. 177; *C.P.R. 1292–1301*, pp. 73, 76;
C.C.R. 1302–7, pp. 8, 9, 48, 49.

[6] *C.C.R. 1318–23*, p. 2; *C.P.R. 1317–21*, pp. 42, 53; see also the litigation over his
property, with its valuable evidence of his commercial and financial business in
Misc. Roll CC, m.26.

sponsored the admission to citizenship of an oatmonger, for after the death of this man, one of the foremost merchant-financiers of the realm, the only Servat found in the London records is Thomas, an undistinguished cornmonger.[1]

Less flamboyant immigrants built more solidly. The French-man, William de Bethune, an intimate of the Rustigazzi and merchants of Montpellier, built up an estate in Essex, Kent and eight city parishes to bequeath to his son.[2] The Italian, Thomas Romeyn, an associate of the Berauds and the Bellardi, became spicer and creditor of the abbot of Westminster, and at the end of his life was assuming an extremely aristocratic posture, with his Hauteyn wife, his daughters in Holywell nunnery, his tax assessment of £5, his tenements in eleven parishes and his manors in Edmonton, Enfield, Erith, Clapham, Stockwell and Southwark.[3]

Men like these, with a knot of immigrant merchants from Languedoc as their core, were the pivot of the trade at the turn of the century. Around them the next generation formed. Alderman Richard de Bethune, mayor of the staple in 1326, for example, was William's son, a dabbler in high politics, and interested, like his brother Thomas, in every trade, from spices and wool to the management of his tavern in St. Pancras 'Where le Bere Toumbeth'.[4] More typical were the immigrants from the counties who attached themselves to alien masters. John de Burford, an immigrant from Burford, whence he drew his wool and his apprentices, was an associate of Romeyn's. By 1292 he was paying £3 in tax, in the same ward as Servat and the Italian. Five years later, he was selling spices worth £222 to the Wardrobe.[5] Shipping out west of England wool, 229

---

[1] *Cal. Letter-Bk. D*, 38; Hust. Roll 60(69); 69(38); Recog. Roll 9, m.4.; on Servat, see also F. Ahrens, 'Wilhelm Servat von Cahors zu London', *Vierteljahrschrift für Sozial und Wirtschaftsgeschichte*, xi (1913).

[2] See Recog. Roll 1(29) and *passim*; Misc. Roll BB, m.5; *Feet of Fines for the County of Essex*, iii, 58; *Cal. Letter-Bk. A, B, C, passim*; *Cal. of Wills*, i, 170, 171, 445.

[3] W.A.M. 25372, 28045, 28046, 28817, 28842, 28925, 29048; Recog. Roll 2(196); K.R. Acc. V. (Alien Merchants) E101/126/6, m. 1, 2; Hust. Roll 11–32, *passim*; *C.P.R. 1301–7*, p. 73; *Cal. Inq. P.-M.*, iv, 60; Weinbaum, ii, 2, 13.

[4] *C.C.R. 1323–7*, pp. 378, 384, 505; *C.C.R. 1327–30*; p. 523; *C.P.R. 1324–7*, p. 92; *Cal. Letter-Bk. C*, 199; *Cal. of Wills*, i, 352, 445.

[5] Recog. Roll 6, m.5d, 9d; *Cal. Letter-Bk. D*, 157; *C.C.R. 1313–18*, p. 600; Ekwall, *op. cit.*, 178; Debentures E404/482/247, 483/22; K.R. Acc. V. (Wardrobe) E101/354/5, fo. 17d; W.A.M. 5752.

sacks of it in 1312–13, he served almost continuously as London warden at Boston Fair and dealt heavily with the Bellardi.[1] He married Romeyn's daughter, acquired a block of the Italian's property, and inherited his role as a supplier of Westminster.[2] He may have inherited his goodwill, too, for from 1313 the number and value of his recognizances increased sharply, concentrated among Cotswolds knights and Northamptonshire pepperers, from whom he acquired two manors and much other property.[3] Almost the last act of Burford's life was to put down the earnest money, in 1322, on the spice cargoes of the great Italian dromonds anchored that year in the Pool.[4] His widow, Roesia, who, with her mother, qualified for an inquisition post-mortem, carried on his business in spite of illness. She inherited the rest of the Romeyn property in 1326 and three years later passed it on to her nine-year-old son James, then under the wardship of her brother-in-law Thomas Bethune and John Pulteney. Declared of age in 1342, James de Burford lived on those estates as a county gentleman.[5]

It is notable that the leading pepperers, Burford, Bethune, Sarum and John de Grantham, all became aldermen within a few years of each other in 1321–5, to head a powerful interest among the oligarchs. They were the backbone of Mortimer's party in the city, and the leading advocates of the Bruges staple.[6] They had always been an élite. The insatiable medieval hunger for spices had seen to that. In every epoch, the great men, Bukerels, Gisors, Frowyks, had been pepperers. Their fraternity, organized since the twelfth century, was in the ascendant among the distributive dealers in avoirdupoids at the King's Beam, and acted as an important stabilizing influence in the late thirteenth century, as the dynasties began to

---

[1] See Table A.4 and Recog. Roll 7, m.5d, 8; *C.P.R. 1307–13*, p. 388; *Cal. Letter-Bk. C*, 98–101.

[2] *Cal. Inq. P.-M.*, vi, 426, vii, 165–6; W.A.M. 24372; *C.P.R. 1321–4*, pp. 11, 12; Hust. Roll 41(92).

[3] Recog. Roll 6–9, *passim*; *C.C.R. 1313–18*, pp. 475 and 101–624, *passim*; W.A.M. 4266, 14285.

[4] *C.C.R. 1318–23*, p. 460; his will is in W.A.M. 25372.

[5] *Cal. Inq. P.-M.*, vi, 426, vii, 165–6; *C.P.R. 1321–4*, p. 207; *C.C.R. 1323–7*, pp. 336, 525, 659; *C.C.R. 1327–30*; p. 458; *C.C.R. 1330–3*, p. 234; *C.C.R. 1341–3*, pp. 550, 551; *P. and M. Rolls*, i, 3; *Cal. of Wills*, i, 352.

[6] Beaven, i, 382–3; see Chapters X and XI.

give way to alien immigrants and the growing number of provincial newcomers.[1] Their strength increased steadily. Smaller than most misteries, they were still fifth or sixth among the aldermanic crafts in 1300. With the influx of provincial talent in the early fourteenth century, they rose to be second, even in number, to the mercers and drapers, and by the mid-fourteenth century, few could equal them as individual merchants. John de Grantham, for example, one of their leading figures, was massively propertied in London and St. Omer, as active exporting wool as importing salt. He was a key man in a small but powerful group of city merchants who launched into the speculative series of loan transactions with English priories which characterized the leading patricians of the twenties. An immigrant from Lincolnshire, he served as apprentice to a Wardrobe pepperer of Lancashire origin, married his master's widow, and fell into place naturally as a leader of London's men in the syndicates.[2]

Towards the end of his life, came the upheaval of the French war, the syndicates, the crumbling of some strongholds of the aliens and the emergence of English merchants from their shadow. Goldsmiths, skinners, fishmongers, tried to extend their control beyond the walls. The era of the English companies was beginning. The pepperers themselves took the lead in the new enterprises. A select group of twenty-one Sopers Lane spicers called in their junior colleagues, the apothecaries, and made contact with the corders. These were a new mercantile group thrown up by the expansion, men of the Baltic connexion, with whom the pepperers shared, in particular, the trade in wax. In a fusion of established élite and successful newcomers, they joined forces in an attempt to impose their standards and their control on a whole sector of English trade. In 1345, the year they buried John de Grantham, they founded that institution so characteristic of the late medieval city, the Grocers' Company of London.[3]

[1] Unwin, *Gilds*, p. 50; S. L. Thrupp, 'The Grocers of London', *Studies in English Trade in the Fifteenth Century*, ed. E. E. Power and M. M. Postan.

[2] Hust. Roll 44–57, *passim*; *P. and M. Rolls*, i, 4, 120, 121; *Cal. Letter-Bk. D*, 165, 259; *C.C.R. 1318–23*, pp. 234–5; *C.C.R. 1323–7*, pp. 115–16; *C.C.R. 1333–7*, p. 60; *C.C.R. 1337–9*, pp. 148, 177; *C.P.R. 1324–7*, pp. 74, 143; *C.C.R. 1337–46*, *passim*; Ekwall, *The Population of Medieval London*, pp. 167–8; Ekwall, *Two Early London Subsidy Rolls*, p. 265; *Cal. of Wills*, i, 475–6; see Table A.4.

[3] S. L. Thrupp, *op. cit.*, 248 ff.

L

The founding of the Grocers' Company symbolizes a new phase in London's history. In two generations, the climate and structure of the patriciate had been transformed. The importance of the monarchy as a directive factor in this transformation needs little elaboration. It is possible, without undue distortion, to interpret the transition in terms of the royal connexion. Under Edward I, royal policy eased the path of the new men, fishmongers, skinners, and corders, rising from established citizen families, but it was the aliens and their associates and official merchants who dominated the scene. Typical of a whole generation were the seven men whom Edward II summoned to warrant a recognizance in 1314, as chief merchants of the kingdom. Antonio di Passano headed the list, followed by his fellow-Italian John Vanne. Third was William de Doncaster, the king's Chester merchant. There were four Londoners— William de Combemartin, the immigrant woolmonger, John de Burford, the immigrant who linked his fortunes to those of the Italians, William Trente the Londoner from the Agenais and William Servat the Londoner from Cahors.[1] It is from the same period, however, that a new élite takes shape in the records, an élite drawn largely from the ranks of English provincial society—Swanland, Darcy, Garton, Grantham, Oxford, Rothing, Pulteney, Pole.

It was an élite which ventured into new fields. From 1324 onwards, a group of city merchants constantly re-appear in the Close Rolls as creditors of abbeys and priories and sometimes knights, all over England, on a scale hitherto quite without precedent for Londoners.[2] The leading London figure was John de Oxford, recognizances in his favour from a score of religious houses reaching the nominal total of over £8,000 in the period from 1324 to 1344. His vintner colleague Richard de Rothing ran him a close second. John de Grantham, John Pulteney and John de Preston the corder were also heavily involved; Henry de Combemartin, Adam de Sarum and the cornmonger Walter Neel occasionally participated. Some of the recognizances may

---

[1] *C.P.R. 1313–17*, pp. 157, 197, 205, 218 and *passim*.
[2] For these recognizances, see *C.C.R. 1323–7*, pp. 310–656; *C.C.R. 1327–30*, pp. 386–578; *C.C.R. 1330–3*, pp. 146–541; *C.C.R. 1333–7*, p. 669; *C.C.R. 1337–9*, pp. 102–40; *C.C.R. 1339–41*, pp. 120, 228, 616; *C.C.R. 1341–3*, pp. 106–498; *C.C.R. 1342–1346*, p. 363; *C.C.R. 1346–9*, pp. 152, 163.

represent transactions in wine and grain, but most were loans. A recognizance to Oxford by the Order of St. John Jerusalem, the heaviest debtor, specifically stated in 1327 that £320 had been received from the Londoner at the time of the 'making of presents' for the Order's affairs. The priory was one of Despenser's victims and all the houses were heavily taxed in the period. Among the lay debtors was William de la Zuche, who had married Despenser's widow and was in trouble over jewellery which Despenser had acquired. Merchants of Florence and Chieri appeared as creditors along with citizens. Evidently, a group of Londoners had committed themselves to the tricky business of loan finance, responding to the opportunities offered by royal policy, loans leading into a mesh of contractual relationships culminating in the annuities which the prior of St. John granted to the wives and children of Oxford and Rothing in the thirties and forties.[1]

The Londoners were a closely-knit group. Oxford and Rothing were the leading vintners and both had married cousins of Combemartin. Preston's son married Oxford's daughter; Pulteney was a familiar and Neel was Pulteney's kinsman. They were also novel, for never before had Londoners played the role of Cahorsins. These men, with the Wardrobe drapers and a few others, were the hard core of London's contingent in the syndicates of Edward III. Their emergence at this date marks a stage in the evolution of the English merchant class. The process of fusion and concentration in the city had only begun, but it is evident that it was well under way before the outbreak of the great war. From the late thirteenth century, the London patriciate, under political pressure, took on a new form and adapted itself to the changing pattern of English commerce. By the 1320's it was assuming characteristic shape, with its Norfolk mercers, its Yorkshire drapers, its Wardrobe men and staplers, its ceaseless ebb and flow of aldermanic families.

The dynasties belonged to a different world. Their discomfiture completed by political defeat, they dwindled to nothing with remarkable speed. For it was not simply a matter of a new breed of merchant in the established trades. Among the

[1] *C.C.R. 1338–41*, p. 271; *C.C.R. 1341–3*, pp. 109–10; *C.C.R. 1346–9*, p. 504; see Oxford's bequests to priories in *Cal. of Wills*, i, 460–1.

money-lenders of the 1320's were Preston the corder and Neel the cornmonger. Fishmongers were prominent in the wine trade and bid fair in the early fourteenth century to become the most powerful single interest in the city. Skinners had won hegemony over the fur trade. A whole cluster of trades had by 1300 achieved a social and political eminence which was quite novel. The formation of the Grocers' Company was itself part of a general process of absorption and readjustment. For these were products of a newer commerce. They were products, also, of the general intensification of commercial life which affected every sector of the city's population and every aspect of its society. They brought with them new forms of organization and a new outlook. A new mercantile patriciate meant a new social order.

TABLES
Group A: London and the Wool Trade

TABLE A. 1: Wool export through London, 1297–1332 *(to nearest sack)*

Export	1297–8	Mar.–Sept. 1303	June–Nov. 1306	1312–13	Mich. 1322– Easter 1323	1324–5	Feb.–Oct. 1332
Total	10,030	6,362	9,292	16,058	5,930	12,828	8,770
By Londoners	1,218	819	1,174	6,515	2,228	3,936	3,780
Londoners' Percentage	12%	14%	13%	41%	38%	31%	43%

Sources: K.R. Customs Acc. E122/68/6, 7, 8, 9, 16, 17; 69/7, 12; 70/1; 157/7

TABLE A. 2: Classification of Londoners as Wool-exporters, 1297–1332

Grade	1297–8	Mar.–Sept. 1303	June–Nov. 1306	1312–13	Mich. 1322– Easter 1323	1324–5	Feb.–Oct. 1332
I. Over 200 sacks	—	—	—	4	—	2	1
II. 100–200 sacks	3	1	1	10	1	3	4
III. 50–100 sacks	4	2	6	19	7	13	12
IV. 25–50 sacks	10	5	10	34	8	17	16
V. 10–25 sacks	10	19	23	66	10	50	16
VI. Under 10 sacks	16	22	8	39	5	37	11
Totals	43	49	48	172	31	122	60

TABLE A. 3: Trade-designations of Wool-exporters

Craft	1297–8	1312–13	1324–5
Woolmongers	14	29	19
Drapers	11	18	12
Fishmongers	4	12	8
Vintners	2	4	9
Skinners	2	9	2
Mercers	—	6	5
Goldsmiths	2	5	2
Cornmongers	—	3	6
Corders	2	4	2
Burellers	—	6	1
Cordwainers	—	5	3
Pepperers	—	2	3
Tailors	—	2	3
Dyers	2	2	—
Girdlers	—	2	1
Chaucers	—	3	—
Butchers	—	2	—
Potters	—	1	1
Tanners	—	1	2
Clerks	1	—	—
Leathersellers	—	1	—
Chaplers	—	1	—
Chaloners	—	1	—
Hosiers	—	1	—
Armourers	—	1	—
Saddlers	—	—	1
Curriers	—	—	1
Unknown	3	51	41
Total	43	172	122
Total No. of Trades	9	24	18

TABLE A. 4: Londoners in the wool export records, 1297–1332
(*wool to nearest sack*)

Name	1297–8	1303	1306	1312–13	1322–3	1324–5	1332
1. William de Combemartin	138	128	137	438	—	—	—
2. Henry de Combemartin	—	—	—	—	51	234	186
3. William le Fuller	34	54	57	324	—	—	—
4. William Curteys	—	—	—	107	84	84	63
5. John de Burford	—	—	73	229	—	—	—
6. Thomas atte Mire	—	—	—	—	96	205	—
7. Henry Norman	—	—	—	184	24	—	86
8. John de Grantham	—	—	—	—	164	125	—
9. Richard de Rothing	—	—	—	—	15	75	164
10. John Prior	—	15	8	228	—	—	—
11. John Baret	—	—	—	29	59	128	32
12. John Beauflour	110	96	21	—	—	—	—
13. John Pulteney	—	—	—	—	—	—	217
14. Roger Chantecler	—	—	—	—	—	57	150
15. Richard de Hakeney	—	—	—	40	9	85	69
16. Richard de Bethune	—	—	—	—	86	30	86
17. William Cosyn	113	14	71	—	—	—	—
18. Vincent de Storteford	—	44	56	76	—	—	—
19. Thomas Vigerous	—	—	—	—	6	110	55
20. Robert le Callere	—	—	35	131	—	—	—
21. Simon Turgys	—	—	30	—	49	44	31
22. Henry Nasard	—	—	2	131	16	—	—
23. Walter le Fundur	—	—	—	147	—	—	—
24. Maurice Turgys	—	—	—	59	58	24	2
25. John le Fuller	—	—	—	39	43	59	—
26. John de Oxford	—	—	—	—	16	83	41
27. Ivo Perceval	—	—	—	115	20	—	—
28. Wymond Brother	—	19	13	58	29	13	—
29. Peter de Bosenho	99	32	—	—	—	—	—
30. William de Hakeney	9	6	14	99	—	—	—
31. William le Hunte	—	—	—	—	47	55	25
32. John Codington	—	—	—	126	—	—	—
33. Hugh de Nettlestede	—	—	—	21	16	43	38
34. Thomas de Burford	—	—	—	—	59	58	—
35. William de Grantham	—	—	—	—	—	—	116
36. Thomas Beauflour	—	—	63	29	23	—	—
37. William de Bydik	—	—	—	113	—	—	—
38. Roger de Havering	—	—	—	92	—	—	15
39. Thomas de Abyndon	—	—	—	106	—	—	—
40. John Turgys	58	22	—	—	—	—	21
41. William de Hockele	—	—	—	100	—	—	—
42. Robert de Mordon	—	—	—	—	—	4	96

Group B: Londoners and the Wine Trade

TABLE B. 1: Wine imports at London, 1318–23 (*to nearest tun*)

Wine Imported	1318–19	1319–20	1321–2	1322–3
Into London	5,499	5,872	8,005	8,077
By Londoners	2,341	2,276	3,771	2,780
Londoners' Percentage	43%	39%	47%	34%

TABLE B. 2: Classification of Londoners' wine imports, 1318–23

Grade	1318–19	1319–20	1321–2	1322–3
I. Over 200 tuns	1	2	3	1
II. 100–200 tuns	1	2	8	5
III. 70–100 tuns	4	4	2	5
IV. 40–70 tuns	15	14	14	14
V. Under 40 tuns	39	35	11	36
Total	60	57	38	61
Per Capita Imports	39	40	99	46

Source: K.R. Customs Acc. E122/69/9

TABLE B. 3: Trade-designations of Wine-importers, 1318–23

Craft	1318–19	1319–20	1321–2	1322–3	Total
Vintners	25	25	21	25	46
Fishmongers	13	9	5	11	24
Mercers	3	4	1	5	8
Woolmongers	5	3	1	1	8
Cornmongers	3	5	2	—	8
Skinners	1	2	1	1	5
Pepperers	2	2	—	2	3
Drapers	3	—	—	—	3
Dyers	1	2	1	2	2
Corders	—	—	1	1	2
Burellers	—	—	—	2	2
Armourers	—	—	—	2	2
Pursers	2	—	—	1	2
Wine-drawers	—	1	1	1	1
Ironmongers	—	—	—	1	1
Hosiers	—	—	—	1	1
Tailors	—	—	1	—	1
Girdlers	—	1	—	—	1
Potters	—	—	1	—	1
Tapicers	1	—	—	—	1
Glovers	—	1	—	—	1
Cutlers	1	—	—	—	1
Brewers	—	—	1	—	1
Shearmen	—	1	—	—	1
Saddlers	—	—	—	1	1
Unknown	—	1	1	4	5
No. of Crafts	12	12	12	15	25

Total Number of Individuals = 132   Total Number of Crafts = 25

TABLE B. 4: Londoners in the wine import records, 1318–23
(*wine to nearest tun*)

Name	1318–19	1319–20	1321–2	1322–3
1. John de Oxford	282	211	574	517
2. Reginald de Conduit	134	216	334	94
3. Thomas de Hameldon	71	112	202	84
4. Richard de Rothing	57	74	184	143
5. William de Boddele	92	110	129	57
6. Alexander de Watford	66	84	114	107
7. Stephen de Bercote	62	49	135	105
8. Walter de Bread St.	18	42	165	59
9. Richard de Essex	12	37	76	97
10. Alan de Chigwell	23	43	57	83
11. William Bernard	—	—	—	187
12. William Prodhomme	40	24	69	25
13. Adam de Exeter	57	12	106	22
14. Richard Baynard	35	—	119	28
15. Bartholomew de Honilane	48	5	56	48
16. Adam Burgoyne	14	27	—	107
17. Henry le Palmer	57	21	—	55
18. Thomas Flory	—	—	126	—
19. Roger de Suthcote	61	64	—	—
20. William le Gaugeour	—	—	64	53
21. Hamo de Chigwell	55	47	10	—
22. Geoffrey Beaufleur	57	53	—	—
23. John le Palmer	—	50	56	—
24. Robert de Conduit	33	—	42	28
25. Reginald le Piper	57	45	—	—

Group C: London and the Great Wardrobe

TABLE C. 1: Great Wardrobe Purchases: Totals

Purchases	1300–1	1315–16	1323–4	1324–5	1325–6	1326–7
	£ s. d.	£ s. d.	£ s. d.	£ s. d.	£ s. d.	£ s. d.
Total	3,942 10 3	731 14 0½	886 13 3	445 13 10	948 11 9½	2,371 2 9¾
From Londoners	1,947 7 0½	334 18 6	528 1 4½	311 7 7	274 13 7½	2,026 9 8¼
Londoners' Percentage	49%	46%	60%	69%	29%	85%

TABLE C. 2: Londoners' Percentage of Purchases: By Categories

Drapery	= 39	100	52	41	28	75
Furs	85	100	73	100	25	99·6
Mercery	15	1 minus	91	90	37	79
Spices	67	52	45	100	—	100
Overall	49	46	60	69	29	85

Source: K.R. Acc. V. (Wardrobe) E101/359/18, 376/30, 379/12, 380/14, 381/9, 382/2.

TABLE C. 3: Great Wardrobe Purchases: By Categories

Drapery

	1300–1	1315–16	1323–4	1324–5	1325–6	1326–7
	£ s. d.	£ s. d.	£ s. d.	£ s. d.	£ s. d.	£ s.
Total	1,253 14 5	65 1 0	327 9 4	212 15 2	556 3 7	1,017 12
From Londoners	490 14 2	65 1 0	170 18 10	86 4 6	153 8 8	765 18
Londoners' Percentage	39%	100%	52%	41%	28%	75%

Furs

	1300–1	1315–16	1323–4	1324–5	1325–6	1326–7
	£ s. d.	£ s. d.	£ s. d.	£ s. d.	£ s. d.	£ s.
Total	315 7 8	121 2 2	82 19 8	109 1 0	206 4 4	910 15
From Londoners	267 9 4	121 2 2	60 6 4	109 1 0	51 19 4	906 18
Londoners' Percentage	85%	100%	73%	100%	25%	99% pl

Mercery

	1300–1	1315–16	1323–4	1324–5	1325–6	1326–7
	£ s. d.	£ s. d.	£ s. d.	£ s. d.	£ s. d.	£ s.
Total	781 16 4	265 13 1½	175 17 3½	81 6 8½	186 3 10½	424 4
From Londoners	115 6 3½	2 12 0	160 8 9½	71 11 1½	69 5 7½	335 2
Londoners' Percentage	15%	Less than 1%	91%	90%	37%	79%

Spices

	1300–1	1315–16	1323–4	1324–5	1325–6	1326–7
	£ s. d.	£ s. d.	£ s. d.	£ s. d.	£ s. d.	£ s.
Total	1,591 11 10	279 17 9	300 6 11½	42 10 11½	None	18 10 1
From Londoners	1,073 17 3	146 3 4	136 8 5	42 10 11½	Listed	18 10 1
Londoners' Percentage	67%	52%	45%	100%	—	100%

CHAPTER VI

The Rise of the Crafts

IN 1295 the king had a galley built in London. It took twenty weeks and cost over £400, and apart from some timber supplied by magnates and a couple of general merchants, all the material was provided by men of three city crafts heavily dependent on the German trade, the ironmongers, fishmongers and corders.[1] At the same time, men of all three trades were making their first appearance on the aldermanic council, to sit in unwonted equality among mercers and drapers.

The corders, for example, were busy on the galley, selling German rope, twistlines, Bayonne cords, canvas and pitch, Almaine boards, even the streamer for the mainmast. These, with wax, were the commodities they handled, and they handled them so successfully that in 1345 the pepperers themselves were happy to take them into partnership. For by this time, their Baltic trade was weighty and significant. By 1307 one in every seven aldermen was handling Hanseatic goods.[2] The Rokesle family itself went over *en bloc*. The first generation of Rokesles, led by the great mayor Gregory, had been traditional wine and wool merchants. The second were all corders.[3] One of them, John Vivian, bought the town of Dartford with his profits.[4] The respectability of the trade had been established in 1285, when Thomas Box, first of the corders to do so, reached the aldermanic council. A typical figure, he held much property in Yarmouth and Lynn; it was inherited by his corder

---

[1] K.R. Acc. V. (Sheriffs Accounts) E101 /571 /1, 2, 3.

[2] See the table of interests in the Appendix.

[3] Beaven, i, 376 ff.; for Gregory, see Chapter IX and the outline biography in the Appendix.

[4] On Vivien, see *C.P.R. 1307–13*, p. 506; *C.C.R. 1313–18*, pp. 606, 608, 612, 613, 615; *C.C.R. 1318–23*, p. 329; *C.P.R. 1321–4*, p. 8; *C.C.R. 1349–54*, p. 204; *Cal. of Wills*, i, 10, 99, 291, 380, 539; Ekwall, *Two Early London Subsidy Rolls*, p. 218.

kinsman Hamo, owner of a wharf, workshops, dyehouses and tenements in eleven parishes, a £4 taxpayer in 1292, a sheriff in London and a pilgrim in Rome.[1]

The corders of the early fourteenth century were thus a mixed group, humble citizens mingling with landed Rokesles. John Vivian's apprentice was the son of the town-crier of Westminster and most of them sprang from rooted London families. John de Preston was the greatest of them. Paying 5 marks in the tax of 1319, and associating with Lübeck merchants, he sold canvas to the Wardrobe, dabbled in mercery and wool. In the twenties, he was a colleague of Swanland and Darcy and a friend of Oxford, whom he followed into his credit deals.[2] His aldermanry in 1321 capped a career of intensive estate-building. The whole of fitz Thedmar's property passed into his hands and he died in very proper manner, bequeathing rents to the chapel he had built in All Hallows Haywharf.[3] His grandfather, however, had been a rebel in 1263, one of the dissident girdlers' craft. It was John's father who had gone into ropery, working closely with the corder branch of their fellow-rebels, the Heyruns, as clients of the Rokesles.[4] The corder's son, who married Oxford's daughter, followed in the trade, but the craft-livery he bequeathed in 1352, along with his armour and his psalter, would have been a new one, for in 1345 the corders disappeared into the Grocers' Company, a Rokesle serving as the last of their aldermen.[5]

Their brief glory illustrates at once the strength of the Baltic trade and the adjustments in patrician society it compelled. For by 1300 the Hansard had created a new axis for London's commerce. The Steelyard of Hamburg and Lübeck replaced

[1] Hust. Roll 16–33, *passim*; K.R. Acc. V. E101 /571 /3, m.20; *C.P.R. 1281–92*, pp. 270, 383; *Cal. Letter-Bk. A*, 201, 202, *B*, 62; Ekwall, *op. cit.*, 164; *Cal. of Wills*, i, 135, 380; Cur. Reg. Roll 185, m. 12d; 186, m.27d; 191, m. 6d; 193, m.16.

[2] K.R. Acc. V. (Wardrobe) E101 /380 /14; *C.C.R. 1323–7*, p. 342; *C.C.R. 1339–41*, p. 60; *Cal. Letter-Bk. E*, 60, 137, 231; *P. and M. Rolls*, i, 90, 175; *Cal. of Wills*, i, 435–6, 669–70.

[3] Hust. Roll 44–63, *passim*; *Cal. Letter-Bk. E*, 78, 85; *P. and M. Rolls*, i, 183; *Cal. of Wills*, i, 435–6.

[4] St. Paul's A /22 /1630, 1631, 1634; Hust. Roll 17(24); *Cal. Letter-Bk. A*, 56, 58, 118, 119; Ekwall, *op. cit.*, 163, 217, 218.

[5] *Cal. of Wills*, i, 669–70; see alderman John de Rokesle in 1343, Beaven, i, 386 (in Hust. Rolls and other records, the name is Rokesle, not Rokele, as Beaven gives it).

the old Cologne guildhall; taking over responsibility for Bishopsgate, the chartered men of the Hanse bought an immunity in London that few could rival.[1] Their basic and bulky trade in fish, timber, furs and sylvan products exerted a growing pressure on the craft and commercial structure of the city. German grain had saved it from famine in 1258, German wax and furs bulked larger in its Wardrobe business.[2] Londoners took men of Rostock and Lübeck as partners, brought back their ships from Antwerp laded with Hanse goods. From the eighties, Germans were buying land and shipping cloth in increasing number. Corders, potters, leathersellers, ironmongers, figure constantly in the recognizance rolls, taking up heavy consignments from the Isplingrodes of Dortmund and their colleagues; practically every city merchant of consequence had some dealings with the Germans.[3] A whole galaxy of city interests drew nourishment from the trade.

The best documented case is that of the skinner in the fur trade.[4] With soaring demand, abundant supply and an increasingly complex process of distribution, the skinners emerged as a specialized craft from the general ruck of the skin trades. Baltic furs were flooding the market, and there was little to stop them. In the eighties, the drive of the merchants had created the skinners' gild, with a hierarchy of craft-organizations forming in dependence on it, and by the reign of Edward II, they had captured the Household market and the lion's share of the English trade.

The Wardrobe bought almost all its furs, sometimes in massive purchases, from Londoners. They supplied 85 per cent of the total in 1300–1.[5] A single skinner, Robert Persone, supplied

---

[1] *C.P.R. 1258–66*, p. 77; *C.P.R. 1266–72*, pp. 5, 20, 23; *Lib. Albus*, pp. 485–8; *P. and M. Rolls*, i, 151–2; *Cal. E.M.C. Rolls*, pp. 140, 182, 183.

[2] *Lib. de Ant. Leg.*, p. 37; *M. Paris*, v, 693, 694, 702, 710–12; and see Lib. Roll 48, m.4; *C. Lib. R. 1251–60*, pp. 58, 99, 186, 190, for examples.

[3] See Recog. Roll 7, 8, 9 in particular; G. P. Cuttino, *op. cit.*, 161–7; Misc. Roll AA, p. 47; St. Paul's A/15/204, 284; *P. and M. Rolls*, i, 9, 10; *C.P.R. 1272–81*, p. 430; *C.C.R. 1327–30*, p. 74; *Cal. E.M.C. Rolls*, pp. 140, 141, 181, 182, 183; *Cal. Letter-Bk. A*, 46, 52, 53, 84, 88, *C*, 41; *Lib. Cust.*, pp, 112, 113, 196, 197.

[4] I am greatly indebted to Dr. Elspeth M. Veale, both for her valuable study, 'The London Fur Trade in the later Middle Ages with particular reference to the Skinners' Company' (Ph.D. thesis, typescript, London, 1953) and for her personal kindness in discussing with me the many problems which bristle in this field.

[5] Calculated from K.R. Acc. V. (Wardrobe) E101/359/18; see Tables C.1–3.

all the fur in 1315–16 and 1324–5.[1] In the winter of 1326–7, £910 was spent on furs, practically all of it in twenty-five skinners' shops in the city.[2] Assessed at £2 in 1292, Persone, whose hold on the Wardrobe market survived even the incursion of the Bardi, was paying twenty-five marks in 1319 as the third highest taxpayer in London. In his last years, the Wardrobe was giving him debentures for £600 at a time.[3] He was succeeded by a group of his friends. William de Cave, a regular recipient of £100–300 a year, got £1,239 for five years' purchase in 1335, £1,014 ten years later. The King's Skinner was almost invariably a Londoner, with reason, and in 1327 a royal charter gave the Londoners rights of search throughout the kingdom.[4]

Political recognition followed. In 1293, under the rule of royal wardens, two skinners reached the council. Adam de Hallingbury, a typical product of the transitional period, called himself a currier and tawyer in early days, before settling down, after three marriages, as a merchant skinner, paying thirty shillings in tax in 1292 and buying corn for the royal army, as his aldermanic colleague John de Dunstable bought horses, exported wool and traded with Calais.[5] Their successors were men of the stamp of Peter de Bosenho, sixth among the wool exporters of 1298–1306, or Thomas Sely, a founder member of the gild, who traded in German timber and Irish goods and who built chapels in Honey Lane and Milk Street, to be followed in office in 1319 by his son Robert, an owner of beerhouses and John Cotun, an owner of manors.[6] The skinners never touched the heights, but they were firmly, if rather narrowly, rooted

---

[1] K.R. Acc. V. (Wardrobe) E101/376/30, 380/14.

[2] K.R. Acc. V. (Wardrobe) E101/382/2, and m.3–6 in particular.

[3] See Great Wardrobe particulars listed above and Debentures E404/483/44, 45, 46; 497/142; K.R. Acc. V. E101/376/7; *C.C.R. 1307–13*, p. 47; *C.C.R. 1296–1302*, p. 556; *C.C.R. 1318–23*, p. 46; *C.C.R. 1327–30*, p. 29; *C.C.R. 1333–7*, p. 6; *C.P.R. 1317–21*, p. 7; Ekwall, *op. cit.*, 173, 217.

[4] See Debentures E404/497/21, 29, 30, 31, 39, 105, 192, 200, 428, 450; K.R. Acc. V. E101/384/6, 16; 385/1; 386/5; E. M. Veale, 'The London Fur Trade', pp. 108 ff., 511 ff.

[5] K.R. Acc. V. (Army and Navy) E101/5/13, 13/39; *Cal. Letter-Bk. A*, 27, *C*, 112; *C.P.R. 1266–72*, p. 85; *C.P.R. 1301–7*, p. 358; Ekwall, *op. cit.*, 153, 172; *Cal. of Wills*, i, 168, 190, 264.

[6] Hust. Roll 14(164)(170); 35(90); 39(15); Chanc. Misc. 3/7(47); W.A.M. 31757; K.R. Acc. V. (Army and Navy) E101/13/39, m.2; *C.C.R. 1288–96*, pp. 260, 454; *C.C.R. 1296–1302*, p. 275; *C.P.R. 1307–13*, p. 472; *C.P.R. 1317–21*, p. 417;

in the upper middle class. Between 1290 and 1365 eleven of them served as aldermen and two as mayors, and in 1363 they equalled mercers and fishmongers in their contribution of £40 towards a city loan.[1] A new interest had emerged in the upper reaches of London society, born of the Baltic trade.

They were overshadowed by the victuallers, for it was in this period that the victualling interest in London, which was to be such a storm centre of city politics, assumed characteristic form. The city had always been a high-price grain centre, Gascony and the Low Countries were clamouring for foodstuffs, and population and commercial pressure was mounting. Despite the obsessive suspicion of the city authorities, the rise of a class of wholesalers could hardly be checked. Londoners shipped grain and fish in bulk, swarming along the east coast, where Lynn was a focus of Midland production and the Germans, with their Baltic and Rhineland grain, were a power.[2] In these years before the plagues, the correlation between food prices and the city's rate of growth evidently afforded the victuallers a measure of differential advantage. It is difficult otherwise to account for that remarkable occasion in 1336 when the *probi* of Aldersgate elected as their alderman the first butcher to hold office before the nineteenth century and probably the only practising butcher ever to do so.[3] It was in the years after 1280 that the fishmongers established their characteristic hegemony; in this period, and this period only, was *cornmonger* sufficient designation for a newly-elected alderman.[4]

In 1300 at least thirty-eight men were operating in the wholesale grain trade in London. The cornmongers, or bladers as they called themselves (much to the confusion of a York cutler who

C.P.R. *1324–7*, p. 56; C.C.R. *1327–30*, p. 115; *P. and M. Rolls*, i, 69, 70; *Cal. of Wills*, i, 228, 704; Ekwall, *op. cit.*, 157, 228; S. L. Thrupp, *The Merchant Class of Medieval London*, p. 365.

[1] *Cal. Letter-Bk. G*, 172; Beaven, i and ii, and see the comparison with other crafts in E. M. Veale, *op. cit.*, 101, 178, 179.

[2] Royal accounts teem with victualling purchases; see, for example, Debentures E404/481, 482, 483; K.R. Acc. V. (Wardrobe and Sheriffs Accounts); *C. Lib. R. 1251–60, passim*; see also N. S. B. Gras, *The Evolution of the English Corn Market* (Cambridge, Mass., 1926) especially chapters 2 and 3.

[3] *Cal. Letter-Bk. D*, 83, *E*, 109, 233; *P. and M. Rolls*, i, 141; *Cal. of Wills*, i, 455 456; Ekwall, *op. cit.*, 327; the butcher, Nicholas Crane, figures as a wholesale victualler in *C.C.R. 1318–43, passim*.

[4] See Beaven, i and ii, for the paucity of *cornmongers* in earlier and later periods.

M

tried to join them in 1382), were the core, a handful of the city's substantial families, Wades, Gubbs and Scots. One was from Yarmouth, another from Winchelsea. The eastern influence was strong. The Husbonds were as much men of Lynn as of London, and Adam Lutekyn, indeed, was the son of a German.[1] The victualling of the 1302 parliament was largely shared between a handful of Germans and nineteen city bladers. They served the Household. In 1295 it was two alderman-cornmongers, John Wade and John de Canterbury, who made the heavy purchases of grain for the army in Gascony, buying from nine city bladers and three fishmongers. In 1322–3, when £2,700 was spent on grain for the Scottish war, £1,600 was paid out in London, nine citizens supplying most of it, Robert de Ely the fishmonger and Walter Neel the cornmonger accounting for over £1,100 between them.[2]

In the early years of the fourteenth century the number of aldermen in the grain trade nearly trebled.[3] Most of the city bakeshops were tied houses. Of fifty-three bakers inspected in 1303, only seven owned their bakehouses; most were held under lease from the wholesalers, who, together with the fishmongers, held a commanding interest in half the twenty-eight mills near the city.[4] In that same year, the cornmongers, led by Roger le Palmer and Roger Husbond, secured the abolition of haulage dues at their market in Queenhithe, despite pleas of ancient usage; several years later, Walter Neel, John Husbond and several of their colleagues were trying to get rid of the shipping tolls at Henley, the inland centre.[5]

They could not hope, of course, to monopolize the business. Londoners of many trades thronged the sea-route from the city and Yarmouth to Berwick.[6] But the small group of bladers took

[1] The list in *Cal. E.M.C. Rolls*, pp. 63, 64, correlated with *Cal. Letter-Bks.*, *passim*, and, in particular, K.R. Acc. V. (Sheriffs Accounts) E101/571/3; Debentures E404/483/191; Misc. Roll BB; *Cal. Letter-Bk. D*, 84; Ekwall, *op. cit.*, 198, 329; for the confused cutler, see *Cal. Letter-Bk. H*, 206.

[2] The victualling of parliament is recorded in B.M. Addit. Charter 26587, printed in Weinbaum, ii, 260–70; royal purveyance in K.R. Acc. V. (Army and Navy) E101/5/13, 14; 16/18, 19.   [3] See table of interests in the Appendix.

[4] *Cal. E.M.C. Rolls*, pp. 152, 155; *Cal. Letter-Bk. A*, 2.

[5] *Cal. E.M.C. Rolls*, pp. 150, 151, 155; *P. and M. Rolls*, i, 62, 63, 87.

[6] For some examples, see Debentures E404/481–485, *passim*; *P. and M. Rolls*, i, 89, 90; *C.C.R. 1327–30*, p. 218.

the lead. In 1328 they were one of the twenty-five recognized gilds, with nine elected wardens,[1] and their leading man, Roger le Palmer, was a prominent political figure. Palmer, who owned granaries at Henley, bakehouses in London and land in Berkshire, was a great victualler of Scottish garrisons. It was he who stocked Stirling in 1312. In the following year, he supplied the Christmas grain for the Household and he shared the custody of the Templars' lands with the king's Cahorsin Servat. He was the right-hand man of the fishmonger, Hamo de Chigwell, a colleague at Henley, during the reform struggle under Edward II.[2] Four of his colleagues reached the council during the generation after 1290, the last of them, Walter Neel, being a kinsman of John Pulteney himself.

Their season of power was brilliant but brief. By the 1360's their craft had dwindled. One of them who tried to transfer to the stockfishmongers in 1398 showed a grasp of realities.[3] For the power of the fishmongers proved all too permanent. It was they above all who shared the grain trade. Of the thirty-eight corndealers in 1300, twelve were fishmongers, and the Wardrobe accounts teem with grain and victual purchases from the rooted Bridge and Billingsgate families. Three of the London shippers who were protesting at Henley in 1328 were fishmongers; two of them were Chigwells.

The Chigwells were equally prominent at Yarmouth. From an early date the London fishmongers had moved out to 'embrace' the Yarmouth fisheries and tap the Skaania trade. Of thirty-three of them who served as councillors between 1285 and 1307, twenty at least owned property in Lynn, Ipswich, Boston and, in particular, Yarmouth.[4] At the height of the quarrel between Great and Little Yarmouth in 1327, thirteen Londoners established there wrote to the mayor Hamo de Chigwell (himself heavily involved) to complain that their

---

[1] *Cal. Letter-Bk. E*, 233; 'beaders' is obviously 'bladers'.

[2] Debentures E404/482/22; K.R. Acc. V. (Army and Navy) E101/5/13; *C.P.R. 1307–13*, p. 411; *C.P.R. 1313–17*, p. 41; *C.P.R. 1317–21*, p. 590; *C.C.R. 1313–18*, p. 578; *Cal. E.M.C. Rolls*, p. 103; *Cal. Letter-Bk. B, C, D, E, passim*; Ekwall, *op. cit.*, 270, 273; *Cal. of Wills*, i, 177, 363; see Chapter X.

[3] *Cal. Letter-Bk. H*, 443; N. S. B. Gras, *op. cit.*, 167 ff.

[4] Individuals from *Cal. Letter-Bk. C*, in particular, correlated with *Cal. of Wills*, i; for some examples of fishmonger enterprise, see *P. and M. Rolls*, i, 26, 28, 65, 86, and *passim*.

colleague, Robert de Ely, was helping the Great Yarmouth men. They all belonged to the leading families of the London trade, Lambyns, Pikemans, Prodhommes, and Hansards. Their curing sheds were in Little Yarmouth and the quarrel was paralysing their business. Twelve Londoners were plundered off-shore by Yarmouth seamen a little later. Eight were fishmongers and four cornmongers.[1] The complex trade in English corn, Dutch and Hansard herring and Baltic goods, that trade which was so important to them in the late fourteenth century, was no less vital to this earlier generation.[2] It drew them into the buoyant commerce of the Hanse.

A contributory factor was their command of shipping. To the leading fishmongers and cornmongers, a ship was virtually a necessity, and the Londoners at both Yarmouth and Henley were ship-owners. In 1302 the fishmonger Robert Turk was ordering Buckinghamshire grain by the shipload and the family of the cornmonger Alan Gille had been in the shipping business since the 1270's, buying or leasing craft from Antwerp men.[3] It is difficult to fix numbers and trace final ownership, but probably two-thirds of the ships named in city court records between 1300 and 1340 belonged to men of the two chief victualling crafts.[4] The fishmongers Pyk, Hansard and Prodhomme became carriers in the wool, and even more markedly, in the wine trade, where their craft-colleagues were so numerous.[5] In March 1306, when two merchants challenged the jury in a case against a Brightlingsea shipmaster, the men they accused of being 'of the affinity' of the mariner were two fishmongers, Alexander Pyk and Thomas Cros and two cornmongers, Adam Lutekyn, son of a German, and Adam Ballard, son of a Winchelsea man.[6]

When the king's galley was built in 1295, the master of the

---

[1] P. and M. Rolls, i, 34–8, 51, 172.

[2] See N. J. M. Kerling, Commercial Relations of Holland and Zeeland with England from the late Thirteenth Century to the close of the Middle Ages (Leiden, 1954), pp. 108 ff., 136 ff. in particular.

[3] Cal. E.M.C. Rolls, p. 123; for the Gilles hiring foreign nefs, see K.R. Acc. V. (Alien Merchants) E101 /127 /3.

[4] Impression derived from study of Cal. E.M.C. Rolls and P. and M. Rolls, i.

[5] See the particulars of wool customs and wine gauge cited earlier and M. K. James, 'The medieval wine dealer', The Entrepreneur, p. 10.

[6] Cal. E.M.C. Rolls, pp. 243–5.

project was Arnold de Bayonne, but four of his five most highly-paid assistants were city fishmongers and cornmongers. Of sixty-one men named as shipwrights, at least fifteen were fishmongers and five cornmongers. No less striking was the importance of fishmongers as suppliers of the enterprise, handling German timber, rope and canvas. One is at once reminded of Thomas Lucas. This man, a Londoner, had bought stockfish worth £30 and much timber from the German, Arnold Grele, at Lynn, and had then fled by night without paying. Hotly pursued by the irate Arnold, he had trailed through Boston, Lincoln and Hull back to London, where he was finally imprisoned in the Tower. Whereupon, the Londoners of his craft begged the royal warden to keep him there. He had ruined their credit. The men of Almaine now demanded full payment in cash, whereas previously they had been able to buy from the Germans, on credit or for 1d. earnest money, goods to the value of £500–800 at a time. This case, heard before the warden in 1292, has often been cited as an illustration of the Law Merchant in action. More interesting is the fact that Lucas was a fishmonger.[1]

By the late thirteenth century, his trade, with its old craft autonomy and new Baltic wealth, was flourishing. Of a thousand councillors known by name from the reigns of Edward I and II, no fewer than 200 were fishmongers. They were perhaps the strongest single mercantile interest, in terms of numbers and local political power, in the city. Their wards, certainly, were strongholds of the middle class. Their leading men were active in the wine and wool trades and establishing themselves in the patriciate. The fishmongers, a political cipher in the years before the civil war, were entering into an inheritance of power which they were to keep throughout the later Middle Ages. The London sheriff who won such glory at the battle of Sluys was a living symbol of the change. He was a fishmonger, he was a ship-owner, and his surname was Hansard.[2]

It was under the royal wardens that his craft penetrated the aldermanic class. Adam de Fulham was elected in 1291. A man

[1] Chanc. Misc. 109/1 (48) (48a)(49).

[2] R. R. Sharpe, *London and the Kingdom* (London, 1894), i, 182; on the general strength of fishmongers among councillors and in the community, see Ekwall, *op. cit.*, under Bridge and Billingsgate, and *Cal. Letter-Bk. A–E, passim.*

of Bridge Street, where he owned a large wharf, he was the leading fishmonger of his day, supplying the Household at £200 a year, and chalking up debts which totalled £950 in 1305. With property in seven parishes, he exported wool, sold German timber and financed lesser colleagues.[1] He was followed by a number of important merchants in swift succession, Thomas Cros the wool exporter, Hugh Pourte, who averaged a wool export of sixty sacks a year and bought land in Boston,[2] above all, by Richard de Chigwell, who overshadowed them all. Owner of ships, quays, mills, with a large staff of agents, Chigwell handled Hanseatic timber, cloth, wool, wine and massive quantities of grain. Selling to the Court and a wide circle of lesser customers, he added property in Kent and Essex to his holdings in ten city parishes and at £6, was the third highest taxpayer in 1292. His son Robert may have served as clerk to Queen Philippa. Certainly his name was one to conjure with. Hamo, the most prominent mayor of Edward II's reign, borrowed it after serving as Richard's factor.[3]

In the wake of these men, dozens of their colleagues climbed to the council. It was a Chigwell who introduced the mayoral barge for Westminster installations. Between 1342 and 1350 a fishmonger reached the council every year. Twenty-three of them served as aldermen between 1290 and 1365; six of them were mayors. In the fourteenth century as a whole, no fewer than forty of them held aldermanic office. By Edward III's reign, the power of the fishmongers was a prop of the civic establishment and a *bête noire* to a new generation of dissidents.[4]

[1] Recog. Roll 1 and 2, *passim*; Hust. Roll 7–31, *passim*; K.R. Acc. V. (Sheriffs Accounts) E101 /571 /3, m.1; (Butlerage) E101 /77 /5, m.12; (Mint) E101 /288 /29, m.6; Wardrobe book E101 /354 /5, fo. 8; Chanc. Misc. 3 /21 (9); Ancient Deeds E 501; *C.P.R. 1266–72*, p. 595; *C.P.R. 1281–92*, p. 377; *C.P.R. 1301–7*, pp. 297, 298; *Cal. of Wills*, i, 77–521, *passim*.

[2] St. Paul's A /23 /25, 1717, 1728, 1729; Ancient Deeds E 500; Hust. Roll 29–37, *passim*; *C.P.R. 1301–7*, pp. 262, 349; *Cal. of Wills*, i, 192–6, 399–400; Ekwall, *op. cit.*, 145; G. P. Cuttino, *op. cit.*, 163–7.

[3] K.R. Acc. V. (Sheriffs Accounts) E101 /571 /3, m.1; (Butlerage) E101 /77 /1; A.R. 543, m.7; Recog. Roll 2 (53); Hust. Roll 2–32, *passim*; St. Paul's A /12 /1128, A /18 /155; W.A.M., Domesday, fo. 494b, 496; *C.P.R. 1266–92*, and *C.C.R. 1272–1307*, *passim*; *Cal. Inq. P.-M.*, iii, 494–5; *Cal. Letter-Bk. A, B, C, passim*; *Cal. E.M.C. Rolls*, pp. 2, 3; Ekwall, *op. cit.*, 149; *Cal. of Wills*, i, 48, 155, 183, 308, 329, 383.

[4] See Beaven, i and ii; *Ann. Paul.*, p. 298; R. Bird, *The Turbulent London of Richard II*.

Nothing would have seemed less likely in 1263. So many fishmongers joined the popular insurrection of that year that a radical mayor could be denounced as their hireling. They were not alone. Many of the newer trades which peopled the aldermanic council after 1300 had been dissidents and outsiders in mid-century, the skinners, ironmongers and corders among them.[1] Their appearance alongside the traditional misteries signalled a revolutionary change. It was more than a question of personnel. These were men of the newer Baltic and Spanish commerce. Theirs were victualling and industrial trades, hitherto excluded from the charmed circle. The aldermen among their leaders, in contrast to the traditional merchants, were neither dynasts nor county immigrants. For the most part, they came from long-established London families. In terms of social structure, therefore, their penetration of the patriciate was even more disruptive than the entry of provincial merchants.

For it was, in essence, simply the most dramatic symptom of a general intensification of commercial activity, a surge of enterprise from below. These men climbed to aldermanries from those families, groups and interests among the mercantile middle classes, which had been most affected by the expansion. Among such groups, there was a stirring of ambition, and those ambitions they tried increasingly to realize through organization. For, as merchant skinners and leathersellers took their seats on the council, lesser colleagues were shaping the skinners' and cordwainers' gilds. The establishment of these men in the patriciate ran parallel to, indeed, was sometimes synonymous with the establishment of the craft as a characteristic institution of London society.

In London, 'the crafts' burst into view at the insurrection of 1263, when numbers of them won recognition from the revolutionary commune. In the second popular outbreak of 1272, they were the power behind the radical mayor Walter Hervey, who conferred civic charters on the most important of them, charters which were promptly annulled when the aldermanic régime was restored.[2] The wording of the aldermanic ban in 1274 was virtually identical with that of Article 152 of the patrician register of Cahors in 1260, or of the proclamation

[1] See Chapter VIII.   [2] See Chapters VIII and IX.

against misteries issued by the *Confrérie des Damoiseaux* at Tournai twenty years later.[1] For the conflict which convulsed London was European in scope. Towards the end of the century, the Low Countries, Italy and Germany plunged into civil struggle as, between 1250 and 1400, 'the crafts' of scores of cities overthrew, penetrated or attacked the older patriciate. In many places, it meant civil war, sometimes accompanied by revolutionary chiliastic movements of the utmost violence, as sectors of the urban population of northern Europe followed the Brethren of the Free Spirit into socio-religious conflict of a Taborite ferocity. It was a mountainous labouring which ultimately, and somewhat paradoxically, produced in so many cities that craft régime with its mathematical distribution of power and its indomitably petty-bourgeois spirit, which has so often been taken as the norm of medieval urban society.[2]

To cross the Channel is to enter a more temperate zone. The royal power in England kept urban passions straitly confined. John, it is true, between weavers and patricians, was available to the highest bidder, but for London, the intervention of Edward I, which deflected the conflict from its normal European course, proved decisive. For this reason, there was little bloodshed. Fishmongers died in arms at Lewes and thirteen mistery-men were hanged after a craft riot in 1267, but the social fabric was never in serious danger.[3] Nevertheless the struggle was real and the consequences profound. For precisely the same elements of conflict were present.

The city had no gild merchant to do battle with the insurgent crafts, but the cluster of patrician misteries, with the Pui, perhaps, as focus, fulfilled the same function. A handful of mercantile misteries, the drapers, pepperers, goldsmiths, mercers and vintners, maintained control over the city's commercial and industrial life and dominated the aldermanic council

---

[1] *Lib. de Ant. Leg.*, pp. 164–6; F. Lot, *Recherches sur les cités*, iii, 216–17; L. Verriest, *Les luttes sociales et le contrat d'apprentissage à Tournai jusqu'en 1424*, pp. 8, 9.

[2] From a great corpus of writings, one may select as good general introductions H. Pirenne, *Les villes et les institutions urbaines*, i, 226–45, ii, 27–38; *Histoire économique*, pp. 575–87; M. V. Clarke, *The Medieval City State* (London, 1936); E. Coornaert, 'Les ghildes médiévales', *Revue Historique*, cxcix (1948); G. de Vergottini, *Arti e popolo nella prima metà del secolo xiii* (Milan, 1943); N. Cohn, *The Search for the Millennium* (London, 1957).

[3] See Chapters VIII, IX and X.

throughout the early, dynastic phase of the commune. And, until 1327, when crafts began to buy royal charters, the aldermanic court remained the source of all craft authority. This was inevitable in a society where minute government regulation was normal, where sneezing could be denounced as a form of fraudulent advertisement.[1] Whatever the social reality, the crafts remained, in legal terms, instruments of city government and in earlier days, their subjugation was real. The enormous bulk of detailed trade regulation required some form of trade organization to make it effective; technical necessity and voluntary association apart, the demands of market supervision alone would have created those specialized trade quarters and artisan groupings as characteristic of London as any other medieval city, its Cordwainer Street, Milk Street, Budge Row and all the others.

The very name applied to the city crafts mirrors their origin. A craft was an *officium*, a term of the same emotive colouring as the contemporary German *Amt*, signifying function and official, controlled status. Most important trades and industries must have been organized in some form as members of the body politic. The bakers and fishmongers certainly were in pre-communal days. At the Feast of St. Edward in 1251, fitz Thedmar records, citizens offered tapers, 'de quolibet officio unum cereum quadratum'.[2] At Dinant, the distinction is clear. It was the bakers, artisans, and the usual clutter of small-town trades who formed *officia*, administered by a seigneurial *ministerialis*; the *batteurs* of the more massive and more recent export industry of pottery, on the other hand, were a mistery, belligerent and self-assertive, wresting autonomy from the authorities.[3]

That it would have to be wrested followed from the patriciate's concern for its power and professions. Self-governing combinations would threaten the whole structure of control. In the victualling trades, especially, 'covins' were as suspect as commodity stocking or alien-citizen partnerships. The patricians were general, wholesale merchants; new organizations would arise primarily in industry and victualling and might

---

[1] H. Pirenne, *Les villes et les institutions urbaines*, i, 201.
[2] *Lib. de Ant. Leg.*, p. 18.   [3] H. Pirenne, *Les villes et les institutions urbaines*, ii, 28–9.

disturb the flow of trade. To fitz Thedmar, the popular craft charters were 'abominations' which ruined foreign commerce. In any event, the crafts would be political rivals. It was a question of power and interest, of ambitious new men, perhaps personally obnoxious to the propertied and pedigreed. If John of Gaunt's clerk could call Brembre and Philpot 'Nichol' and 'Jankyn', how could such as they suffer delegation of their authority to 'ribalds with blue nails'?[1]

They were not invariably hostile. Even in the noisy sixties, lorimers and chaplers were quietly granted ordinances; in 1299 an illegal confederacy of smiths was condoned because its provisions seemed reasonable.[2] These, however, were poor or inoffensive crafts. A body of entrepreneurs in the leather trades, middlemen fishmongers, rebellious weavers on piecework, en-countered a very different response. The merchant's outlook governed all. It was those trades which produced a mercantile element which ran into or provoked trouble and the point of transition was frequently in that zone where the quality and quantity of their mercantile enterprise ceased to be regarded as a potential threat and acquired enough strength to make respectability inescapable. Even so, political action was often necessary, and in the far more open patriciate of 1300 the *arrivistes* were applying identical criteria to misteries even lower down the social scale. In 1298 and 1300, for example, the council, half of them representatives of newly emancipated industrial and victualling misteries, had no hesitation in break-ing attempts at organization among coopers and spurriers.[3]

In both these cases, the abortive crafts had centred them-selves on a church, had imposed oaths and applied ecclesiastical sanctions, including excommunication, to recalcitrants. This was a general practice and one reason for the commune's hostility to the claims of ecclesiastical courts. For it was the fraternity, usually focused on a church, which provided the instrument for transforming the passive *officium* into the aggres-sive mistery. All the misteries seem to have crystallized around

[1] *Lib. de Ant. Leg.*, p. 56; A. H. Thomas, 'Illustrations of the medieval municipal history of London from the Guildhall records', *Trans. Royal Hist. Soc.*, 4th ser. iv (1921); S. L. Thrupp, *The Merchant Class of Medieval London*, p. 259.

[2] *Cal. E.M.C. Rolls*, pp. 33–4 and see below.

[3] *Cal. E.M.C. Rolls*, pp. 1–2, 16, 52.

one or more. On the pursuit of these elusive and sometimes weird associations, historians have expended much labour to little purpose.[1] There can have been no age which did not know the ritual and colourful joys characteristic of, say, the Freemasons; to stigmatize obsession with funeral rites as peculiarly medieval is clearly an error.[2] Indeed, it is probably a mistake to attempt any detailed classification. Fraternities, multitudinous in every age, are inevitably chameleons. Certainly, in thirteenth-century London, there were scores of them among all manner of people, sometimes vaguely demarcated, sometimes overlapping.

Even the clergy had their rather ominous 'Secret Confederation of London Rectors'. One of its primary purposes was to ensure a good funeral, for all members were to attend and say thirty masses for the deceased. Another was to ensure at least one good congregation a year, for all were to attend on the saint's day of a member's church. With these went regulations to protect the secrecy of the gild and its members' professional interests—solidarity in life and death.[3] Benefits and socioreligious motives loom large in all the gilds, but what distinguished them, of course, were precisely the provisions for solidarity in everyday life, which normally meant the regulation of a calling. No doubt, in some cases, the motives were primarily economic from the start, but in most, social, religious and economic motives were inextricably intermingled. It is difficult to believe that men in the same line of trade, bunched together in Bridge Street or Budge Row, would not form some kind of association. The skinners' fraternity seems to have had its origin in the ordinary church gild of a Walbrook parish, where skinners happened to be a majority of the parishioners.

---

[1] For a useful summary of gild theory, which has produced a voluminous literature, see J. Kulischer, *Allgemeine Wirtschaftsgeschichte* (Berlin, 1928), i, 181–92; E. Coornaert, *Les corporations en France avant 1789* (Paris, 1941); G. Mickwitz, *Die Kartellfonktion der Zunfte und ihre Bedeutung bei Entstehung des Zunftwesens* (Helsinki, 1936); E. Meyer, 'English craft-gilds and borough governments of the later Middle Ages', *University of Colorado Studies*, xvi, xvii (1928–30); I owe most to the late Professor Unwin; see Unwin, *Gilds*, pp. 1–126, and *Industrial Organisation in the Sixteenth and Seventeenth Centuries* (London, 1904).

[2] See the recent study of such phenomena in E. J. Hobsbawm, *Primitive Rebels* (Manchester, 1959).

[3] Unwin, *Gilds*, pp. 100–2.

When they shaped their company, they took their fraternity with them, to function in fluctuating, but organic relationship with the mistery.[1] London was honeycombed with gilds, not least among its *officia*, some embryonic misteries from the beginning, others simply groups of like-minded men clustered around a collective chantry. On this situation, the force of the trade expansion expended itself. Whether a mistery would emerge, what form it would take, what position it would hold, depended entirely on the strength of the economic drive and the political reaction.

In the early days of the commune, few crafts had emerged from the shadowy undergrowth of *officia*. In the country at large, only the cloth industry could sustain organizations on any scale, though association among victuallers, leather and skin traders was sensitive to the weight of demand.[2] In London, there were humble gilds of cloth-workers and butchers among the adulterine associations amerced in 1180, though neither was important in the thirteenth century. Some tailors had a land-owning fraternity in that century, which had probably come into existence much earlier, while the saddlers' fraternity of St. Martin-le-Grand was flourishing before 1200.[3] Even earlier in the pre-communal period, bakers, weavers and fishmongers had formed misteries.

The victualling gilds emerged from the structure of control itself. Overall surveillance tended to be delegated to regular hallmoots run by a bailiff, where tolls were paid. By 1155 the bakers had bought the farm of the tolls, assumed the authority of the bailiff and appeared in the Pipe Roll as an organized gild, paying £6 a year. Subject as they were to the 'regularized lynch law' of the assize of bread, they never developed into a full-blooded mistery; by 1382 their hallmoots had fossilized into Holy Moots and bakers were protesting against compulsory attendance.[4] The fishmongers' hallmoots were much more

---

[1] E. M. Veale, *op. cit.*, 170–206; the skinners' fraternity, to which two pepperers belonged, was notable for the number of its *honorary* members.

[2] See E. M. Carus-Wilson, 'The English cloth industry in the late twelfth and early thirteenth centuries', *Economic History Review*, xiv (1944), reprinted in *Medieval Merchant Venturers*.

[3] The best account of these is Unwin, *Gilds*, chapter 3, 4, 5 and 8.

[4] *Lib. Albus*, pp. 356–8; Addit. Ms. 14252 in M. Bateson, *op. cit.*, 710–11, 724; *Cal. Letter-Bk. H*, 207; Unwin, *Gilds*, pp. 30–1, 36–7.

powerful. Held twice a year, they imposed a fine of 21*d*. on absentees. In addition, there was a weekly court to settle disputes in the market, which could meet daily to deal with foreign fishmongers. In fact, the fishmongers' court seems to have been the earliest piepowder court on record in London. By Henry III's reign, they were paying two marks a year to their bailiff, who could claim Husting cases for the hallmoot in Bridge Street. Fines went to the sheriff—an indication of origin—and at the Iter of 1321, when they survived a sustained attack, the fishmongers claimed that the system had operated from 'time immemorial'.[1]

Primary jurisdiction over a trade was a hallmark of craft autonomy and the fishmongers' court became a model. Their wardens were virtually soke-reeves. Indeed, in the sheriff's court in 1320, the weavers' warden was specifically said to have claimed 'his soke'.[2] Their case was the most striking of all. The earliest craft to appear in the record, their authority derived from the Crown itself. The gild appears in the Pipe Roll of 1130, paying sixteen marks into the Exchequer, leading a number of provincial weavers' and fullers' gilds. Confirmed by later monarchs, the gild exercised a trade monopoly, and despite civic hostility and economic subjection, it retained its legal rights throughout the period, with its weekly court, four elected bailiffs, with power to claim cases from the Husting, a gild clerk and serjeant and an annual ceremony at St. Nicholas Acon on St. Edmund's Day.[3]

All these gilds had won autonomy in pre-communal days. Once the commune was established, they were attacked. As soon as the aldermen had consolidated their power, they offered John sixty marks and a farm of twenty marks a year to abolish the weavers' gild, which he did in 1202. The weavers countered, raised their farm to twenty marks and a running fight ensued. In 1221 the embattled weavers deposited their charter in the Exchequer for safety; in 1247 they bought a confirmation from Henry III; five years later a royal writ spoke of unwonted

[1] *Lib. Albus*, pp. 373 ff.; *Lib. Cust.*, pp. 385–406; Unwin, *Gilds*, pp. 37–42.
[2] Misc. Roll CC, m.2, a confirmation of Unwin's speculation, characteristically perceptive, in *Gilds*, p. 44.
[3] *Lib. Cust.*, pp. 121–31; Unwin, *Gilds*, pp. 44–6; F. Consitt, *The London Weavers' Company* (Oxford, 1933); E. M. Carus-Wilson, *Medieval Merchant Venturers*.

customs and demands overwhelming them. The struggle
emerged into the light in 1300–1, when a violent quarrel between the weavers and the cloth entrepreneurs, the burellers,
led to civic intervention against the former. At the Iter of 1321
the weavers were still fighting a rearguard action against civic
opinion.[1]

It was as a comment on the 1300 case that Horn or Waltham
copied into *Liber Custumarum* the ferocious regulations of Winchester, Marlborough, Oxford and Beverly, which excluded
weavers from the franchise and from trade and denied them
legal rights against burgesses, who included their controlling
employers, the dyers and drapers. These laws first appear in
John's reign, in a private London collection, which probably
emanated from the Cornhill family.[2] They are said to be derived
from London custom. There are certainly some similarities. In
Oxford, if a weaver's widow wished to continue in the trade, she
could marry no-one but a weaver, while in London, if she married a non-weaver, she was compelled to give up her loom to
one of the weavers' gild. On the other hand, the postulate of a
London origin rests only on a statement at the tail of the Winchester and Beverly ordinances, and when the codes were
copied into *Liber Custumarum*, someone went to the trouble of
erasing *Wyntonie* from the title.[3] The statement itself almost
certainly refers only to the last clause of the two codes, the provision that a weaver entering the franchise must foreswear his
craft. It is entirely credible that a new communal council,
confronted with a trade immunity, would make such a provision, but whatever the economic similarities, neither this
nor any other of the legal disabilities in fact appears in the
London records.

Early ordinances are vague and ambiguous, and even the
settlement of 1300–1 is inconclusive. It distinguished, for
example, between weavers' court procedure for foreigns and
for men of the mistery who 'soit de la citee', and in the *quo*

---

[1] *Cal. Letter-Bk. C*, 55, 56, 60; *Lib. Cust.*, pp. 48, 121–31, 416–25; M. Bateson, *op.
cit.*, 509; *C.R. 1251–3*, pp. 206–7.

[2] M. Bateson, *op. cit.*, 509; *Lib. Cust.*, pp. 130–1.

[3] Compare M. Bateson, *op. cit.*, 509 and *Lib. Cust.*, p. 131 with *Lib. Cust.*, pp. 124,
125; and see *Lib. Cust.*, pp. 60, 130, notes 1 and 3 and H. T. Riley, editor's introduction.

warranto proceedings in 1321 the jury asserted that weavers were free to buy and sell all things pertaining to their trade, 'sicut alii liberi civitatis'. Even this was qualified by an 'a tempore praedicto' which may refer to a series of ordinances made in execution of the settlement of 1300. For in the October of 1300 the gild paid twenty marks to have a letter 'under the names of' its wardens sealed with the commonalty seal. As Sharpe points out, this equals the farm paid by the weavers for their charter.[1] Moreover, while it is impossible to identify weavers among the taxpayers of 1292, they can be found among those of 1319 and 1332.[2] If the weavers did renounce or modify their charter in 1300, however, the renunciation must have been shortlived, for in 1303, the year of *Carta Mercatoria*, they bought an *inspeximus* in the old terms from Edward I.[3] The legal status of the weavers remains something of a mystery. Their leader, Simon de Pourtepoll, held much suburban property and married his daughter to a Chigwell,[4] but the weavers as a whole were the great absentees of political life. On orthodox and dissidents alike they seem to have left no impression.

About their economic status, however, there can be no doubt. They were piecework employees of the burellers who supplied the material, exercised a measure of control over looms, and dominated the mixed commissions appointed to settle disputes. The troubles in the early fourteenth century arose from the depressed state of the urban trade. The weavers had resorted to go-slow and restrictive practices, cut the number of looms by four-fifths, and met any awkward bureller with a strike. The reaction merely emphasized their subjection. There was no comparison between the two groups. The six burellers appointed to administer the decrees of 1300 were all councillors, land-owners and merchants; of the six weavers, three bore the sur-names of burellers and were probably their servants. In 1319 burellers' taxation ranged from 16s. 8d. to £2, weavers', below 3s. In 1332 one weaver appeared above the 5s level, but others,

---

[1] Lib. Ordinationum, fo. 173b; *Lib. Cust.*, pp. 123, 124, 416–25; *Cal. Letter-Bk. C*, 55–6, 60 and n. 3.   [2] See Ekwall, *op. cit.*, and M. Curtis, *op. cit.*

[3] *Lib. Cust.*, pp. 418–19; an *inspeximus* was a king's confirmation of a charter of one of his predecessors.

[4] St. Paul's A/2/611, 613, A/12/1128, 1130, A/17/406; *Cal. Letter-Bk. B*, 17, 116, *C*, 56, 60; *Cal. of Wills*, i, 48.

with fullers and shearmen, were much lower, most probably paid no tax at all.[1] The dyers, who shared control with the burellers and covered much the same range of taxation, in 1298 imposed their will on fullers in a quarrel over fulling at the mills outside.[2] Their leaders on that occasion, William Bernard and Adam Absolon, were important merchants, Bernard a wine importer, Absolon, a lessor of dye-houses, both propertied men.[3] Dyers were prominent in the cloth, wine, and wool trades, and of eighteen identified between 1278 and 1290 sixteen served as councillors. The next generation produced an alderman.[4]

Nor was their entrepreneurial supremacy of recent date. As early as John's reign, the private collection which listed the laws of Winchester was informing its readers that the levying of debt from goods 'commended' to a debtor was forbidden in market selds and in the houses of dyers, fullers and dubbers, 'where much is commended'.[5] It was the rebellion of weavers which caused trouble. In their control of marketing and raw materials, their web of outwork contracts, piecework rates, supervision over looms, the bureller and dyer entrepreneurs of London differed only in degree from the celebrated Douaisian John Boinebroke himself.[6]

The existence of equalitarian, small-master crafts of 'classical' type required a pattern of supply and demand which simply did not exist in any city of importance.[7] Technical exigencies, a

---

[1] Ekwall, op. cit., 168–75, 205–11, 237–42; M. Curtis, op. cit., passim; Lib. Cust., p. 122; Cal. Letter-Bks. A–D, passim.

[2] See Lib. Cust., pp. 127–9; Cal. Letter-Bk. C, 51, 52; Ekwall, op. cit., particularly 205–42.

[3] Cal. Letter-Bk. B, 8, 235, C, 51, 52; Ekwall, op. cit., 149; see Table B.4 of Chapter V.

[4] For the councillors, see Cal. Letter-Bk. A–D, passim; the alderman was Walter de Pappesworth, see Cal. Letter-Bk. D, 79, E, 94; C.C.R. 1313–18, p. 466; C.C.R. 1323–7, p. 531; Beaven, i, 383; Cal. of Wills, i, 326.

[5] M. Bateson, op. cit., 490–1; Miss Bateson's suggestion that this clause was a measure of protection for fullers is surely off target. The protection is for those who 'commended' the goods, and is some indication of entrepreneurial control. 'Commending' here is surely analogous to the commenda of continental finance and partnership—see M. M. Postan, 'Partnership in English medieval commerce', Studi in Onore di Armando Sapori, and 'Credit in medieval trade', Economic History Review, i, (1928).

[6] See G. Espinas, Sire Jehan Boinebroke, patricien et drapier douaisien (Lille, 1933).

[7] For a good, brief summary of the issues, see S. L. Thrupp, 'Medieval gilds reconsidered', Journal of Economic History, ii (1942).

wide and varied hinterland, dependence on imported supplies, and the sheer volume of demand led to specialization and differentiation, the emergence of mercantile and entrepreneurial elements, and the creation of hierarchies of function within and between crafts. The bureller-weaver relationship in London was not something freakish. On the contrary, it was the norm, to which most other industries approximated to a greater or lesser degree. It is no accident that the great majority of craft ordinances in the thirteenth century regulated the affairs not of one mistery but of several. The significance of the trade expansion was that it operated upon a structure which was, in actuality or in potential, hierarchical. The boom severely tested the supremacy of some crafts, but established that of others. It was this interaction which shaped the craft movement.

The trade of the saddlers, last of the misteries whose existence is attested in pre-communal days, exemplifies the process. The basic labour was done by joiners (fusters) who cut the wooden quarters and fashioned the saddle-trees. Lorimers in iron and copper worked the often ornate bits and bridles; painters supplied the decoration. The saddlers were the merchants, handling imported leather and linen and selling the finished product. They bought heavily from Spaniards and city middlemen and sold to the Household.[1] Roger de Linton, in 1303, got £50 for saddles blazoned with the coats of arms of France, England and St. George; under Edward III, William Pikerel, who also supplied Despenser, made up to £150 a year from more prosaic material.[2] The saddlers' ordinances refer interminably to their customers among the 'grands seigneurs'. They were the men of capital operating at the point of sale and the other trades fell into dependence upon them. The generality of saddlers, grouped in Foster and Gutter Lanes hard by St. Martin's, the fraternity church, paid upward of 6s. 8d. in the tax of 1319. Nearby, in Cripplegate Without, among leatherdressers and smiths, clustered the painters, lorimers and joiners, paying, those who did

---

[1] Cal. Letter-Bk. A, 10–145; Recog. Roll 1, passim.

[2] See Wardrobe Debentures E404/497/10, 15, 32, 44, 46, 131; Account book, E101/369/11, fo. 7d; E. B. Fryde, 'The deposits of Hugh Despenser the Younger with Italian bankers', Economic History Review, 2nd. ser. iii (1951), appendix.

N

pay, around 3s., 2s., and 10d. respectively.[1] The saddlers were a
mistery under their alderman and four echevins by the end of
the twelfth century, and though they had difficulty in maintaining their status among the greater misteries in later years,
they were one of the few crafts to achieve both a royal charter
and incorporation before the end of the fourteenth century.[2]

Long before that date, however, they had run into the same
kind of trouble as the burellers. In 1261 the lorimers won recognition with one of the earliest sets of craft ordinances to be
recorded.[3] They began in a manner which was to become traditional. Action was necessary because standards were being
debased. To avoid 'deceit', there was to be no night work, no
work in cast iron, no re-dubbing of old bits. No-one was to work
on Saturday afternoons or certain feast days or filch another's
apprentice. All apprentices were to pay a premium of 30s. and
serve ten years. Further, no stranger was to operate a forge
until he had joined the mistery, paid 6s. 8d. to the commune,
2s. to the craft poor-box and put himself in frankpledge. Four
wardens were to be elected and sworn before the mayor to
present offenders to civic justice.

The lorimers were a small, closely-knit group with established traditions, following a craft which demanded equipment
and skill. Aristocratic, not to say archaic in tone—in return
for recognition they presented the mayor with a good bridle
every Easter—they were trying to cope with the problems of
expansion. Evidently there had been an influx of new men into
lorimery, ignorant of or ignoring traditional work rhythms,
claiming their share of an expanding market, setting up all
kinds of pressures in the labour structure of the trade. In a
response which was typical, the lorimers organized themselves
to deal with it, to impose procedures, standards and control,
the *Zunftzwang* of the Germans. The sole duty of their wardens,
originally, was the initiation of newcomers. From one point
of view, the craft was simply an input-valve.

In lorimery, the problem was not too serious, but all trades

---

[1] Ekwall, *op. cit.*, 283–88, 321–7.
[2] Unwin, *Gilds*, pp. 53–4 and see the St. Martin's archives in Westminster Abbey
Muniment Room.
[3] *Lib. Cust.*, pp. 78, 79.

faced the challenge of growth. How were standards to be maintained, the citizen monopoly enforced, and customs honoured, with all sorts of men taking up the trade, working on 'commended' material in chambers and all manner of nooks and crannies? Trade after trade was compelled to move from the instinctive solidarity of tradition to formal organization, ordinance-registers, powers of search, and in trades where a large labour force was demanded, where there were considerable numbers of permanent journeymen and where competittion from the unestablished was easy and effective, the stresses could become violent, particularly since it was in such trades that growth entailed increasing specialization and a drive towards an entrepreneurial structure of control.

For, in saddlery, the joiners were hard on the heels of the lorimers. They were less skilled, but they were essential. It was easier for new men to enter, easier to break away from both joiner traditions and saddler hegemony. In the popular revolt of 1263 the joiners were to the fore; from Hervey they won a charter, only to see it annulled in 1274.[1] Their more skilled colleagues were luckier, for in 1283 the painters secured their ordinances, similar to the lorimers' in tone, regulating their three grades of craftsmen, serving-man, piece-worker and master who 'kept house by himself'.[2] At the turn of the century, trade was at its peak, and in 1308 the joiners at last got their charter, and got it moreover at the instigation of the saddlers themselves, for under severe competitive strain, the angry saddlers took the joiners before the mayor and tried to use them against their rivals.

Enormous frauds were being committed in saddlery, but the fault, said the saddlers, lay not in themselves, but in the joiners, so six wardens were to be elected, with powers of search, to make sure that the 'points of joinery' were kept as they should be. Every joiner was to work in the traditional manner and was to have an identification mark; no painter was to paint saddles 'made outside' until they had been certified by the joiner wardens. Runaway joiner apprentices and others were glueing together saddles in the woods, selling them to painters and 'false saddlers' outside the gild, so no joiner was to work

[1] *Lib. de Ant. Leg.*, pp. 164–6; *Hundred Rolls*, i, 404.   [2] Lib .Horn, fo. 341b.

in the woods and all false work was to be burned. For themselves, the joiners ordered that no-one was to take an apprentice unless he were a freeman, poach another's, work at night or forestall timber.[1] When allowance has been made for hyperbole, the pattern of expansion is clear.

The client status of the joiners is apparent. Of their six wardens, who all lived in Cripplegate, three paid tax in 1319, none more than 1s. 8d. Four of them were joiners' sons, one belonged to a family of cordwainers. The apprentice of one was a runaway bondman of Ashridge Abbey.[2] In a list of wardens in 1328, three of them reappeared, with a son of one of the originals and two Cripplegate men of tanner background and low assessment.[3] The four wardens of the painters in 1328, also Cripplegate inhabitants, paid decidedly higher taxation,[4] but the saddlers' wardens were wealthier and more numerous. There were fifteen of them, ten living in Farringdon. Twelve paid tax in 1319, most 6s. 8d., Ralph Blithe as much as £1.[5] Two of them paid low sums, and it is noteworthy that one of these was the son of a painter, while the other had actually begun life as a joiner. The son of one of the original joiner wardens also became a saddler.[6]

Social mobility found more violent expression, for in the early fourteenth century, as the political drive of the crafts got under way, the dependent misteries, now more firmly in control of their own trades, turned against their entrepreneurs. In 1320, the saddlers had the lorimers' ordinances burned in Cheap and, seven years later, at the height of the political crisis, fighting broke out in the streets. The wordy warfare which accompanied it struck a familiar note. The saddlers had started it, claimed the allied crafts, by trying to monopolize all their business, even though they already owed over £300. The allies,

---

[1] Lib. Cust., pp. 80, 81.

[2] Ekwall, op. cit., 154, 159, 192, 285, 288; for the bondman, see Cal. Letter-Bk. A, 170.

[3] Cal. Letter-Bk. D, 71, 142, E, 129, 234; Ekwall, op. cit., 285.

[4] Cal. Letter-Bk. E, 234; Ekwall, op. cit., 285, 287.

[5] Cal. Letter-Bk. E, 232; Ekwall, op. cit., 269, 290, 323, 324, 325, 327.

[6] Richard de Gravele, as Richard Buckskin, began as a joiner—Cal. Letter-Bk. D, 150; Purtreor was the son of a painter—Hust. Roll 12, m.4; Ekwall, op. cit., 161; John Danyel, saddler (Cal. Letter-Bk. E, 4; Ekwall, op. cit., 279) was the son of Richard Danyel, warden of the joiners in 1308—Misc. Roll CC, m.5; Lib. Cust., p. 81.

retorted the saddlers, threatened a general strike if one of their members were molested by a saddler; the lorimers would admit no newcomer unless he swore to conceal their misdeeds; painters and joiners juggled prices to make themselves kings of the land. Painters, lorimers and joiners were equals and commoners, came the rejoinder, they had a perfect right to swear newcomers to their ordinances. They were freemen and taxpayers, and their crafts had been recognized by the mayor.[1]

Here was the thirteenth-century movement in microcosm, crafts forming in response to competition, climbing to power over their trades, and rebelling against a craft which had assumed analogous power in a wider field a century earlier. In this instance, it was the dependent crafts which were the political rebels; in others, the rise of an entrepreneurial group was itself the disturbing force. In all cases, it was the drive towards mercantile enterprise and entrepreneurial formation, under the spur of expansion, which was the controlling factor. The act of craft formation itself was frequently not merely related to the emergence of a mercantile hierarchy; it was an integral element of it.

This was certainly true of the leather and fur trades. These were an important sector of the city economy and embraced a great variety of interlocking interests, preparatory curriers and tawyers who scraped and oiled skins, cofferers in cowhide, workers in bazen, cordwainers who made footwear from the best Cordovan leather, chaucers who repaired shoes, skinners, chaloners for bed-linen, chaplers for caps. Some trades, such as tannery, required heavy if cheap equipment, and all demanded a great deal of semi-skilled and unskilled labour. The doctrine that no-one should work at a trade unless he had been apprenticed, common among luxury and purely mercantile crafts, found no echo here.[2] Many were never apprenticed; there were large numbers of permanent journeymen. The cordwainers allowed a master to have eight workers in his own establishment and it was in these trades that the outwork system spread.[3] Trade competition from lower strata of the craft and from allied

[1] Unwin, *Gilds*, pp. 85–7; Riley, *Memorials*, pp. 156–62.
[2] On this point, see E. M. Veale, *op. cit.*, 147 ff.
[3] Lib. Horn, fo. 339b.

crafts not easy to demarcate was a perennial problem and it was the impact of an expanding market upon this particular sector of social life which generated much of the power behind the craft movement of the thirteenth century.

The key function, as always, was the merchant's and a particular impulse was the growth of the Spanish trade. In the seventies and eighties, some forty merchants were importing Spanish products into the city. The seven members of the Peres family from Burgos and Bilbao, the Mundenards from the Ebro, the Martins of San Sebastian, with their colleagues, and a handful of Cahorsins, men of Montpellier and Genoa, appear in the letter-books of Edward I's reign as frequently as the Gascons. City chaplers were dealing heavily in Spanish wool and yarn, city weavers regulating its use. Quantities of iron, oil, fats, and skins were fed into the markets and above all, there was the famous Cordovan leather.[1]

Groups of wholesalers appeared from the London crafts. There were a few general merchants like Hugh Motun, small groups of saddlers buying large consignments, a couple of distributive chaplers and a few skinners buying hides at £70 a time, but the most striking feature were the wholesale purchases made by small syndicates of cordwainers. In August 1276, for example, the Spaniard John de la Founs sold leather worth £132 to sixteen cordwainers, in two groups of nine and seven men, each buying £66.[2] A few weeks later, five of the larger group bought £78 of leather from two Gascons, and over ten years or so, thirty to forty cordwainers can be traced, constantly re-grouping themselves to buy up whole cargoes.[3] Between February and November 1278, ten of them accounted for leather worth over £600.[4]

At the same time, individuals who commanded greater capital were emerging as distributive merchants. Walter le Waleys, the cordwainer who owned a stall at St. Ives, was buying at £50 a time;[5] his colleague Richard de Morton,

---

[1] See, in particular, *Cal. Letter-Bk. A*, 8–79, *C*, 123, 124, 192; Recog. Roll 1. For background, see C. Verlinden, 'The rise of Spanish trade in the Middle Ages' (which, curiously, omits all mention of leather) and M. K. James, 'A London merchant of the fourteenth century', *Economic History Review*, x (1940) and 2nd ser. viii (1955–6).   [2] *Cal. Letter-Bk. A*, 8.   [3] *Cal. Letter-Bk. A*, 8–26.
[4] *Cal. Letter-Bk. A*, 17–25.   [5] *Cal. Letter-Bk. A*, 27 and *passim*.

brother to an attorney and involved in the Irish skin trade, was
buying heavily from the Spaniards between 1278 and 1285,
and a whole circle of cordwainers was dependent upon him.[1]
Such men were not necessarily cordwainers. The Braye family
of wholesalers were curriers, from whose humble ranks sprang
one of the most notable leather merchants, Ralph Poyntel, who
bought from the aliens and sold, in lots of from 15s. to £8, to
curriers, tawyers, cordwainers and saddlers.[2] His best customer
was John Tilly, who had his own clientele among Middlesex
tanners, and served as propertied leader of the kissers, another
preparatory craft. In 1286 he and Poyntel joined forces to set
up Ralph le Seur, a leather worker, in a shop which he was
to manage for three years at an annual salary of one mark. Both
paid a mark in the tax of 1292.[3] They were not giants, but men
like them were becoming important in city society.

At this time, skinners and cordwainers like Hallingbury and
Daniel le Chiltre, who often oiled and prepared their own skins,
could be described as curriers and tawyers from time to time,[4]
and there was little rigid demarcation, but under the pressure
of trade competition, the leather industry crystallized out into
craft organizations. The first to feel the need were the cordwainers. In 1263 they were in the vanguard of the popular
movement, and from Hervey they got their first charter. Demarcation on a hierarchical pattern was their prime concern. Two
grades of shoemakers were recognized, the cordwainers proper,
the Cordovan aristocrats, whose apprentices were to pay a
premium of 40s., and the inferior workers in bazen, whose
premiums were 20s. The latter could not touch cordwain,
though cordwainers could use bazen. Both were entitled to use
cowhide if they wished, but cofferers were not to meddle in any
kind of superior leather. Cordwainer apprentices were to be an
aristocracy within an aristocracy, for while the masters tried

---

[1] Recog. Roll 1(86); *Cal. Letter-Bk. A*, 17, 20, 21, 29, 49, 58, 68, 179, 192, 229;
Hust. Roll 18(8); *Cal. E.M.C. Rolls*, pp. 93, 130, 142, 143, 259 and *passim*; *Cal. of
Wills*, i, 138.

[2] *Cal. Letter-Bk. A*, 26, 27, 28, 29, 35, 41, 47, 48, 84, 109, 111, 117.

[3] A.R. 543, m.7d, 14; Ancient Deeds D 5349; K.R. Acc. V. (Army and Navy)
E101/13/39, m.3; *Cal. Letter-Bk. A*, 41, 97, 134, 150, 156; *Cal. E.M.C. Rolls*, p. 61;
Ekwall, *op. cit.*, 157, 179, 189.

[4] See, for example, *Cal. E.M.C. Rolls*, pp. 4, 5, 76; *Cal. Letter-Bk. A*, 27.

to ban the putting out of work to servants in their own homes, each was allowed to employ eight *serjeantz overours* in his shed. On no account were shoes to be sold outside the regular market in Cheap and there was to be no hawking within twenty leagues.[1]

The difficulties which beset cordwainers were those of the skinners, merchant tailors and fishmongers. No groups were so hostile to pedlars and *eveschepings*, the second-hand night markets. The cordwainers' troubles began within their own craft. Numbers could be so large. At a price enquiry in 1300, their fifty-seven craft masters were surpassed only by the fishmongers' fifty-eight. They were the first to encounter journeymen's organizations and one combination in 1350, which covered only a few masters, numbered sixty men.[2] During the citizenship drive of 1309–12, only one of the new cordwainers was an ex-apprentice, twenty-six were redemptioners. The ratio among skinners was 1:30, but cordwainers, with a bigger, cheaper market, felt the pinch more acutely.[3] Their solution envisaged strict demarcation, with master cordwainers at the apex of control.

They had a fight on their hands. It needed a revolution to put the charter through and, in 1274, it was suppressed, amid street riots. The rule of royal wardens once more brought a softening of attitude; skinners and fishmongers were reaching the council. In 1298 the cordwainers were again acting collectively, swearing in seven men to search for shoes of mixed leather. They presented thirty men, one of whom turned out to be unfree—typical of the trade's troubles. In 1303 their journeymen, frequently a source of illegal competition, rebelled against a wage-cut. The masters not only defeated them, but, within a month, secured a 'renewal' of their old charter. New clauses were added. No master was to trade unless he were free and no journeymen were to make *congregaciouns*. Four wardens were sworn, one of them a sinner of 1298.[4]

---

[1] See Lib. Horn, fo. 339b; *Hundred Rolls*, i, 404.

[2] *Cal. E.M.C. Rolls*, pp. 61–3; *P. and M. Rolls*, i, 231–2; for *eveschepings*, see, for example, *Lib. Cust.*, pp. 426 ff.

[3] The admissions are in *Cal. Letter-Bk. D*, 35–179; see also A. H. Thomas, *P. and M. Rolls*, ii, l-liii.

[4] *Cal. E.M.C. Rolls*, pp. 4, 5, 148, 149; for the renewed ordinances, see *Lib. Cust.*, pp. 83, 84.

This pre-occupation with citizenship was characteristic of the current craft mobilization in defence of the franchise. One of the leaders of the journeymen in 1303, for example, was William de Waltham. In 1310, among a bloc of cordwainers, he took up the franchise, paying a mark. In 1319 his tax was 1s. 8d., by 1332 it was 13s. 4d., and in 1328 he was a warden of the gild.[1] This extension of the mistery inevitably entailed a measure of control over lesser crafts. In 1300, price increases had been blamed on the curriers, over whom cordwainers assumed rights of search. The curriers were beginning to draw apart as a craft. In 1309 fourteen of them established a market of their own in the Shambles, and by 1349 there was a curriers' seld in St. Michael le Quern. In the same year, when the labour troubles of the plague era afflicted the trade, master cordwainers were given powers of search over journeymen cordwainers, curriers and tanners, their traditional unholy trinity of rivals.[2]

Those curriers who had joined the leathersellers were more fortunate. In 1300 the leathersellers were treated as a separate group, dominated by the Poyntel family. Fourteen years later, brokers were appointed for a joint 'craft' of cordwainers and leathersellers and a Poyntel again headed the list. By the mid-fourteenth century the leathersellers were an organized mistery; in 1319 their leader John Poyntel, who paid £5 tax in that year, reached an aldermanry, and it was an historical accident that they did not eventually take their place among the Greater Misteries.[3] The cordwainers were lesser men. Their wardens, the Ashbournes, Bristols and Reddings who staffed the assemblies, never became aldermen. Their taxation in 1319 ranged from 1s. to 10s. with a few men going higher. But they were solidly entrenched, and in the late fourteenth century hovered uneasily between Greater and Lesser Mistery status, before settling into the latter. Curriers, cofferers, tanners and the rest were much lower down the scale.[4] The leather trades, in short,

---

[1] *Cal. E.M.C. Rolls*, p. 148; *Cal. Letter-Bk. D*, 55, *E*, 233; Ekwall, *op. cit.*, 307.
[2] *Cal. E.M.C. Rolls*, pp. 61–3; *Cal. Letter-Bk. C*, 173; *P. and M. Rolls*, i, 231 ff.
[3] *Cal. E.M.C. Rolls*, p. 64; *Cal. Letter-Bk. C*, 127; for John Poyntel, see *Cal. Letter-Bk. C*, 127, 247, 248, *D*, 28, 153, *E*, 88, 89, 94, 134, 243; *Cal. of Wills*, i, 379, 380, 426, 540; on the leathersellers, see Unwin, *Gilds*, pp. 55, 87, 88, 160, 166–8.
[4] Ekwall, *op. cit.*, *passim*; *Cal. Letter-Bk. E*, 232–4 and *passim*; *Cal. E.M.C. Rolls*, *passim*.

provide an almost classic example of the mercantile expansion creating misteries and ranging them in a hierarchy of status, based on the principle of mercantile and entrepreneurial control, which required political changes of the first order for its establishment.

The skinners, on a higher plane, went through a similar process. The trade, organized in small units based on the merchant-shopkeeper, demanded a great deal of selective and technical skill and the labour force was large and varied. With mounting demand and a rising Baltic trade, the numbers of dependent workers out in chambers swelled, and control of this labour and its standards was a prime motive in the formation of the skinners' gild.[1] Apprentices were never more than a select minority. Of thirty-one skinners admitted to the franchise in a bunch early in the reign of Edward II, only one had been apprenticed. Ten paid less than 10s. and only four of these made any mark in the profession. More typical was William Bonenfaunt, a serving-man admitted in 1312. He paid 10d. with the lowest range of taxpayers in 1319 and died, poverty-stricken, in a hired apartment.[2] From men of this type, dependent trades, and semi-skilled foreigns, competition had threatened the masters' hold on the vital retail trade. The skinners took the lead in the attack on the *eveschepings*; in January 1304 a confederacy of journeymen skinners provoked violence within the trade and, in that same month, a currier was prosecuted, and judged by a jury of skinners, on the charge that he 'was a dealer in skins . . . and peltry against the ordinance and right of that trade'.[3] Fluidity was a thing of the past.

The cause, of course, lay in the emergence of the skinners' gild. Persone and Cave had carried the craft to control of the Wardrobe market and much of the English trade. As early as the mid-thirteenth century, the king was dealing with a skinners' *societas* who were renting halls at Westminster. Five of them were leaders of the 1263 revolt.[4] Their core was the group

---

[1] For a general picture, see E. M. Veale, *op. cit.*, 115 ff.; see Wardrobe agents touring the skinners' shops in the winter of 1326-7 in K.R. Acc. V. (Wardrobe) E101/382/2, m.3-6.

[2] E. M. Veale, *op. cit.*, 129-50.

[3] *Cal. E.M.C. Rolls*, pp. 61, 154, 156; *Lib. Cust.*, pp. 426-8; *P. and M. Rolls*, i, 1-3.

[4] Chanc. Misc. 3/29, m. 2, 3; W.A.M., Domesday, fo. 87, 343; see Chapter VIII.

established in Walbrook and concentrated in their local parish gild. By 1278 they were jointly hiring a solar, and in 1288, under the royal warden, they got their ordinances, when nineteen skinners, led by three councillors and a future alderman, laid down rules for the trade and helped to pass the first recorded piece of sumptuary legislation in London's history, regulating the wearing of furred headgear.[1] Within a few years, their bigger men were on the aldermanic council.

By this time, the curriers had been ruthlessly subjected. In October 1300 the skinners charged ten curriers with a conspiracy to raise prices. Despite a spirited and somewhat pert resistance by the curriers, the case ended in an agreement, by which their price for a thousand of greywork, raised from 5s. to 6s., was reduced to 4s., and other costs graded to fit. If a currier broke the agreement, his punishment would be decided by an impartial tribunal consisting of one currier and three skinners.[2] The burellers must have been envious. By 1327 the skinners were reaching further, for in that year they were one of the first four crafts to win a royal charter, which ordered the suppression of rival markets and gave them, in theory at least, rights of search through the kingdom.[3]

Their chartered colleagues in 1327 were the tailors, who faced similar problems and whose fraternity had long been powerful; the goldsmiths, represented by the middle class entrepreneurs who tried to vest all authority in their leopard's-head seal and canalize all trade through their shops in Goldsmiths' Row and Exchange; and the girdlers. The latter were another of the new crafts of the century. They, too, had been active in the 1263 revolt and had won their first charter from Hervey. By 1300, they had reduced the *batours*, or coppersmiths, to subjection. In that year, the *batours* formed their own rebel fraternity, but the girdlers were no longer outsiders. The aldermen broke the *batours'* gild and the girdlers' charter of 1327 bestowed recognition on an established supremacy, not unlike that of the cordwainers, saddlers, skinners, and burellers.[4]

[1] *Cal. of Wills*, i, 38; Lib. Horn, fo. 267; *Cal. Letter-Bk. A*, 220; E. M. Veale, *op. cit.*, 170-7.
[2] *Cal. E.M.C. Rolls*, pp. 61, 92, 93.
[3] *C.P.R. 1327-30*, pp. 29, 34, 40, 42.
[4] *Cal. E.M.C. Rolls*, p. 65; see Chapter VIII.

Evidence for this and other trades is very scarce, but the same pattern constantly reappears. The potters, who included brass-workers and bellfounders, and employed a large labour force, produced a class of large-scale contractors and importing merchants in constant commerce with the Germans and the merchants of Dinant.[1] Distributive merchants, like Walter le Potter, employed several apprentices and ran a workshop. In 1277 Walter set up a cauldron-maker with a capital of £5. Men of this type had been rebels in 1263. In the seventies Walter reached the council, and in 1316 the craft received formal recognition as a mistery, with eight wardens, four of them founders, four, 'dealers in the said trade'.[2] The ironmongers followed the same route, giving leaders to the popular movement in the sixties and aldermen to the council in the nineties. By 1300 they were a strong mercantile craft, putting out work to nailers and smiths, trying to exercise control over the Wealden smiths, whose products they bought up almost in their entirety. In 1301 they got elected wardens and control of the iron-measures, and emerged as a full-blooded mistery.[3] The first cutler to reach an aldermanry did so at the end of the century, a merchant who traded with Parisians. In the fourteenth century, the cutlers were an entrepreneurial gild, employing the blade-makers and sheathers.[4] Even the poor chaplers and chaloners, the obscure paternoster-makers, produced a small class of merchant-entrepreneurs, who exercised control through the medium of a craft.[5]

[1] See, for example, K.R. Acc. V. (Army and Navy) E101/13/39, m.1; Hust. Roll 13(64)(102); 29(36); *Cal. Letter-Bk. A*, 105, 106, 109, 110, 158, 173, *B*, 12, 54, 129, 238; Riley, *Memorials*, p. 100; *Cal. E.M.C. Rolls*, p. 140; Ekwall, *op. cit.*, 242–8, 249–54.

[2] *Cal. Letter-Bk. A*, 15; *Cal. of Wills*, i, 196; *Cal. E.M.C. Rolls*, p. 176; Riley, *Memorials*, p. 118; G. Unwin, 'London tradesmen and their creditors', *Finance and Trade under Edward III*, ed. G. Unwin, pp. 115, 116 and n.1.

[3] See, for example, *Cart. S.M. Clerkenwell*, pp. 140–1; *Cal. Letter-Bk. A*, 79, *C*, 88, 89; *Lib. Cust.*, p. 85; Riley, *Memorials*, pp. 78–85; Unwin, *Gilds*, pp. 68, 77, 138 and *passim*.

[4] The cutler was Solomon de Laufare, from one of the dissident families of 1263; see K.R. Acc. V. (Alien Merchants) E101/126/26, m.4; Hust. Roll 4(9); 13(39); 25(34); 27(11); 36(17)(101); *Cal. Letter-Bk. B*, 60; *Cal. of Wills*, i, 227; Unwin, *Gilds*, p. 73.

[5] See, for example, Recog. Roll 1(13)–1(220); *Cal. Letter-Bk. A*, 10–82, *passim*; *Lib. Cust.*, pp. 102–4; *Cal. Letter-Bk. D*, 271–3; for entrepreneurial trends even among humble trades such as that of the paternoster-makers, see *Cal. E.M.C. Rolls*,

The central purpose was to maintain or establish positions of superiority in an expanding economy, and, in the main, the ordinances of these crafts were directed against competition from below. Even the 'Secret Confederation of London Rectors' was designed to protect its members from the intolerable oppression of their curates.[1] In those trades which produced aldermen, such as the skinners', the new patricians rarely took the lead. The gilds were middle class in character. None was more so than the fishmongers'. Well-organized from an early date, they prospered in the Baltic trade, but were subject to intense and suspicious surveillance. It is not surprising that they were the backbone of the popular movement.[2] They recovered swiftly from the debacle of 1274 and, in 1280, reorganized their gild. In that year, they laid down a minimum of seven years for apprentices, appointed four men to keep an eye on new entrants and operated, with a strong sense of equality between gildsmen, under thirteen wardens.[3] The core of the trade were the distributors in Bridge Street and Old Fish Street, who monopolized wholesale purchase from ships at the wharves. Under the mayor Henry le Waleys, they had to make way for men of the new Stocks market he established. This may not have been easy, for at the end of the century, newcomers were finding it difficult to enter the trade. In 1290 the king amerced ninety London fishmongers, returning to the attack fifteen years later. In 1300 nearly sixty of them were subjected to close scrutiny by the council, which repeatedly ordered the men of the markets to allow the Stocks merchants to trade with them in equality, under threat of punishment.[4] It was difficult to act against them. By this time, large numbers were paying tax with the upper middle class and their leaders were getting a foothold on the aldermanic council.[5] Not until the Iter of 1321 was their position seriously threatened.

pp. 208, 251, 253; *Cal. Coroners Rolls*, pp. 27–30; see also D. Knoop and G. P. Jones, *The Medieval Mason* (Manchester, 1933), and G. Unwin, *Industrial Organisation in the Sixteenth and Seventeenth Centuries*, chapter 1.

[1] Unwin, *Gilds*, p. 100.
[2] See Chapter VIII.
[3] Lib. Ordinationum, fo. 225–6b.
[4] *Cal. E.M.C. Rolls*, pp. 63, 228, 229, 233; *Lib. Cust.*, p. 120; *C.P.R. 1281–92*, p. 377.
[5] See Ekwall, *op. cit.*, under Bridge and Billingsgate.

At the Iter, three wholesale shippers, all of them sons of founder-members of the Stocks, combined with pedlars and other non-gildsmen to attack the central group, accusing them of banning retail trade on the wharves in order to raise prices by a third. The twenty-four men they accused, led by Hamo de Chigwell and Andrew Horn, were all members of the trade's leading families, Fulhams, Lambyns, Sterres and Elys. It became clear that it was the hallmoot which had enforced the decree, after Chigwell had reached the mayoralty in 1319, and royal justices submitted the court to a testy attack. Chigwell, in defence, pointed to the danger of fraud, and claimed that the plaintiffs' real motive was profit. Selling wholesale, they made 2d. a thousand herring, retail, 8d. to a shilling. A jury pronounced in favour of the middlemen and the suspension of the Iter saved the hallmoot. The fishmongers' hegemony survived, to become a central issue in the days of John de Northampton.[1]

The motives of these middlemen fishmongers were very similar to those of the cordwainers, girdlers, skinners, indeed of most of the crafts which rose to prominence in the late thirteenth century. When the patriciate annulled the craft charters in 1274, they claimed that the ordinances benefited only the wealthier men of the trades, and ordered that everyone was to follow his calling, under civic regulation, as he saw fit, free from all intermediary controls.[2] The relevance of this proclamation to the ambitions of the major crafts is obvious.

Their achievement required the breaking of the aldermanic régime. In the insurrection of 1263, and during Hervey's mayoralty, it was these newer crafts of the rising middle class who made the pace. Far stronger than any others, they accounted for a good half of the rebel leadership.[3] Clearly, they were the hard core of the movement throughout the century. Most of them were intimately dependent on the German and Spanish commerce, and, from one point of view, the rise of the London crafts was simply a function of the growth of these newer trades in the thirteenth century. Taking a broader canvas, they were a reaction to the cumulative growth of population and

---

[1] For this classic case, see *Lib. Cust.*, pp. 385–406.
[2] *Lib. de Ant. Leg.*, pp. 164–6.
[3] See the analysis in Chapter VIII.

commercial enterprise which thrust new interests into prominence and carried new families into the patriciate. The crafts
took shape in an effort to canalize this enterprise, particularly
in those trades where the boom stimulated the formation of an
entrepreneurial structure of control. There were other aspects.
Some trades organized themselves to break this mould; humbler
men were stirred to action; the patrician misteries themselves
began to approximate to the stock pattern. But it was the fishmonger, the skinner, the cordwainer, the ironmonger and the
girdler who were the characteristic figures.

Their first effort, associated with sedition, failed. It was the
reign of Edward I which decided their fate. In 1285, in political
conflict with the dynasties, he suspended the city's liberties,
and for thirteen years, London was ruled by royal wardens.
The old families were displaced, as the king looked for his
officers outside their select circle. The men of aldermanic cali-
bre he found were precisely the new rich of the Baltic and
Spanish connexion. It was now that the newer trades, along
with the clerks, became a power, and, in exact parallel to the
lawyers, as the merchants took their seats, lesser colleagues consolidated their organizations, whose growth was stimulated by
the wardens' use of the trades as police units.[1]

But if Edward tolerated the crafts on the one hand, he stung
them into activity on the other. His free trade policy, imposed
on the city in 1285 and on the country in *Carta Mercatoria* of
1303, did not directly threaten the citizen monopoly of the retail trade, but it made much easier traffic between aliens and
non-citizens, with its consequent repercussions on the retail
trade. In fact, it aggravated the very irritant which had brought
crafts into existence in the first place, at a time when the inflow
of newcomers was at its maximum. The crafts' answer was the
Zunftzwang, an extension of control to bring every trader, at
least, within the orbit of citizenship and craft-membership.
From this date, the franchise became an obsession. Every craft
wrote into its ordinances the provision that no man should follow the trade unless he were free, while at the same time, they
tried to establish mistery control over citizenship admissions.

[1] This process is examined in some detail in Chapter IX; for the police use of the
trades, see, for example, *Cal. Letter-Bk. B*, 241, *C*, 84, 85.

When Edward's shadow lifted, the crafts moved into political action. The patriciate had been transformed, a new generation had come to power, and they easily recovered the charters they had lost amid violent controversy in the seventies. The impulse was communicated to less articulate regions and the city court rolls of the last years of Edward I record a ferment of craft formation among the humblest inhabitants.[1] Even fruiterers caught the infection of the times, and Edward II's reign opened with a constitutional onslaught on aldermanic power by the commons, with the crafts in the van.[2] Central to the campaign was a massive drive for citizenship rights in 1309–12, in which over 900 new citizens were enrolled in three years.

The situation then was fluid. Among mercers, goldsmiths, and corders, citizens by apprenticeship greatly outnumbered those by redemption; these were clearly well-established crafts in control of their trades. Fishmongers, girdlers, chaucers, butchers and tanners struck a fair balance, but among cordwainers, skinners, bakers and cooks, there were twenty-six, thirty, forty-three and thirty-six redemptioners to only one apprentice, and some trades recorded no apprenticeships at all. In these trades, mistery control was penetrating into sectors of the population hitherto untouched, corralling men who could no longer be ignored. Even among ex-apprentices, over a hundred were enrolled very late; a score of them had been working as foreigns for years. The organized misteries were behind the whole movement. This is clear not only from the tenor of contemporary reform edicts, but from the striking manner in which men of the trades were taking up the franchise in groups. Between 26 November and 10 December 1309, twenty-two skinners were admitted; in the next fortnight, twelve chandlers. In February 1311, thirty-five bakers became citizens.

Most of these were redemptioners. Apprentices, on the other hand, concentrated in the mercantile and entrepreneurial misteries, were qualifying for city leadership. No term was for less than seven years, sixty-six signed for eight years, forty-two

---

[1] *Cal. E.M.C. Rolls*, pp. 1, 2, 16, 18, 19, 25, 33, 34, 49, 52, 67; *Cal. Letter-Bk. C*, 7, 165 and n. 3; *C.P.R. 1281–92*, p. 519.

[2] See Chapter X; for the fruiterers, see *Cal. E.M.C. Rolls*, pp. 98, 157, 158.

for ten, one for sixteen. Apprenticeship was virtually synony-mous with adoption, and most of the youngsters were immi-grants, drawn mainly from the Home Counties and the east Midlands. The gilds they fed were the leaders of the movement, a leadership vividly reflected in the tax rolls of the period, where, with one or two individual exceptions, the gilds are spaced out in a hierarchy of wealth corresponding more or less exactly to their mercantile status.[1]

In the constitutional reforms which ensued, the power of these crafts won political recognition. After ten years of struggle, with the craft momentarily replacing the ward as electoral unit on one occasion, the reformers were led to victory by the fishmonger, Hamo de Chigwell, who enshrined their ordinances in the great royal charter of 1319. For the crafts, the key clause in the new constitution was an order that no stranger was to be admitted to the franchise unless he were vouched for by six men of the trade he wished to pursue, or by the commonalty, if he were uncommitted.[2] The crafts anchored themselves in the constitution and during the late Middle Ages citizenship and craft-membership became virtually synonymous.

Numbers alone multiplied rapidly. At the beginning of the reform movement in 1310–11, cappers, potters, tanners and ironmongers won recognition and, thereafter, the stream became a torrent, craft after craft registering its ordinances, each with the vital franchise clause. In 1328 an incomplete register of wardens listed twenty-five crafts; in 1377 fifty-one misteries were required to elect delegates to the Common Council; in 1422, 111 of them were leasing Brewers' Hall. The pageantry of the gilds, increasingly evident from the 1290's onward, had created the Lord Mayor's Show, had given the city its char-acteristic tone and colour.[3]

It was not merely a matter of numbers. In the early four-teenth century, the expansion gave way to a more confused and

[1] For the admissions, see *Cal. Letter-Bk. D*, 35–179; they have been treated by A. H. Thomas, *P. and M. Rolls*, ii, xxxii–xxxiv, xxxv–xxxvi, l–liii, and G. Unwin, review of *Cal. E.M.C. Rolls, History*, n.s.x, (1925–6).

[2] Letter-Book E, fo. 109–11b; *Lib. Cust.*, pp. 255–73; see Chapter X.

[3] *Cal. Letter-Bk. D*, 240, 271, E, 232–4; Riley, *Memorials*, pp. 78, 85; Unwin, *Gilds*, pp. 88 ff.

fragmentary period, and from 1327 there is evidence of some realignment in London. In that year, the skinners, goldsmiths, girdlers and tailors bought their royal charters. By the end of the century, they had been followed by the drapers, tailors, fishmongers and saddlers. Pepperers and corders formed their grocers' company; there are suggestions of new beginnings among the mercers and skinners.[1] This was the age of the syndicates and the livery companies, when London was recruiting its patriciate from the merchants of England.

But if the companies were new, they were constructed on an old model. The government of their wardens was a compound of mistery power, civic authority and, in some cases, royal warrant. It mirrored the entire history of the craft movement. New companies were but old crafts writ large; their power derived from and was rooted in the events of the early fourteenth century.[2] The constitutional bond, if anything, grew stronger with time. Eventually, it was to make craft and company membership almost meaningless as an economic category, but it was the pivot around which social life revolved. It was this which led Unwin, speaking of the early fourteenth century, to say: 'It was in fact the victory, not of one class over another, but of a new form of social and political organization over an old one and one of the main causes of the victory was that the ruling class had gradually transferred itself from the old form to the new one.'[3]

This generalization requires one important modification. The ruling class which 'transferred itself' was in fact a new ruling class. The dynasties had to lose power before the fusion could take place. For, as the history of the skinners and fishmongers in particular demonstrates, the transformation of the patriciate and the rise of the crafts were simply two aspects of the same fundamental change. In 1351, when the crafts were called on to elect the Common Council, thirteen of them ranked as chief misteries.[4] On the one hand, there were the mercers, drapers,

---

[1] *C.P.R. 1327–30*, pp. 29, 34, 40, 42; Unwin, *Gilds*, pp. 77 ff.
[2] See the detailed study of one company in S. L. Thrupp, 'The Grocers of London', *Studies in English Trade in the Fifteenth Century*, ed. E. E. Power and M. M. Postan.
[3] Unwin, *Gilds*, p. 75.
[4] *Cal. Letter-Bk. F*, 237, 238.

goldsmiths, woolmongers and vintners. Grocers embraced pepperers and corders. On the other, there were the fishmongers,
skinners, cordwainers, ironmongers, together with the tailors,
saddlers and butchers. Cordwainers and saddlers did not ultimately find a place among the Twelve Great Livery Companies,
being replaced by the wholly mercantile haberdashers and
salters,[1] but from a long-term point of view, this oligarchy represents on a larger scale the amalgamation which the Grocers'
Company embodies on the lesser. It marks the resolution of that
social conflict which first disturbed the city in 1263.

The craft movement, as time passed, embraced many of the
lesser trades. Its victory, even more effectively than the opening
of the patriciate, altered the texture of public life. Its essence,
however, lay in the rise of mercantile and entrepreneurial gilds
from the victualling and industrial trades of the Baltic and
Spanish commerce to join the new men and the new interests
coming to the fore in the traditional misteries of the patriciate.
It meant the destruction of one oligarchy and its replacement
by another.

That destruction was a political operation. It can be placed,
with reasonable accuracy, in the period from 1285 to 1298,
when the city's liberties were in suspension. But the conflict of
those years derived from the struggles of an earlier generation.
The root of all the changes lay in the revolt of 1263 and the disruption of the commune.

[1] Unwin, *Gilds*, pp. 82, 83.

CHAPTER VII

The Disruption of the Commune 1216–63

Wel semed ech of hem a fair burgeys,
To sitten in a yeldhalle on a deys.
Everich, for the wisdom that he can,
Was shaply for to been an alderman.
For catel hadde they y-nogh, and rente.

FOR Chaucer's gildsmen, of course, membership of one of the more 'solempne and greet' fraternities was a highroad to the patriciate. That road, however, had only recently been opened. Chaucer's father, the Thames Street vintner, had seen it happen. For gildsmen, as Chaucer knew them, were the product of a social revolution. This was no less true of some of their companions on the Canterbury Road—the Sergeant of Law, to whom everything was fee simple, or even the merchant 'hye on horse', loud on his winnings, silent on his debts, for he was one of the newer kind, much occupied with Middelburgh. In their persons they illustrate the long-term processes at work in the thirteenth century, the steady growth of a class of professional legists and clerks, the multiplication of powerful new mercantile interests, the surge of enterprise from below which fashioned the craft movement. These forces, operating in a context of expanding population and broadening mercantile activity, could not be contained within the confines of the little patrician commune which fitz Ailwin and the twelfth-century dynasties had created.

That commune was essentially an oligarchical conception. Even in the more liberal atmosphere of the early fourteenth century, the ideal which captivated the chronicler Andrew Horn and which he expounded to his colleagues, was that of Brunetto Latini's *Trésor*, the rule of an enlightened oligarchy, nursing its wealth and jurisdiction, striking a careful balance between the

social orders, rooted in exclusive enjoyment of power.[1] Brute
realities buttressed it. It took a man of substance to face the
terrors of Iter and Exchequer, to shoulder the burdens of public
life. In 1309 a wealthy skinner was prepared to renounce the
franchise to evade shrieval service. Between the Iters of 1244
and 1276, the pecuniary qualifications for pledges increased by
at least a third. The political commonalty were the 'wiser and
wealthier men' of the wards.[2]

This close identification of political and economic criteria,
with its overtone of moral judgment, coloured by older ideas of
patriarchy and lordship, bred a hierarchical mentality. By the
end of the thirteenth century, the council was passing its first
sumptuary legislation. Only 'dames' and not 'women' were
to wear hoods furred with budge, and 'the disreputable women,
nurses, brewsters and other servants' were rebuked for their
sartorial impertinence.[3] Public life was the monopoly of 'les
plus sufficeauntz'.[4] Even the popular movements of protest
were governed by the same outlook, swift to classify society
and to assign to each class its uniform. For when their claims
were not grounded in vague ideas of justice or utility, or in a
narrow concept of legal equality, they were based on a reassertion of the commons' importance within the hierarchical
framework. They, too, were sufficient.

'The city ought always to be governed by the aid of men engaged in trade and handicrafts', proclaimed the rebellious
crafts in 1312, and went on to propose measures to remedy
the ignorance of city custom among the young—a worthy display of civic responsibility, and possibly a deliberate one. For
it was precisely on these grounds, an alleged lack of responsible
understanding, that their claims were contemptuously dismissed by the patricians. They were 'mochel smale people that
konne non skyl of governaunce', as the followers of John de
Northampton were called a century later. 'Fools and ribalds
of the lower classes,' fitz Thedmar called them, 'servile sons of
diverse mothers, caring nothing for the welfare of the city.'[5]

[1] *Lib. Cust.*, pp. 16–25; see Chapter XII.
[2] Misc. Roll AA, p. 56; Weinbaum, ii, 136; *Cal. Letter-Bk, C*, 11, 180.
[3] *Cal. Letter-Bk, A*, 220.   [4] See, for example, *Lib. Albus*, pp. 182, 189, 190.
[5] See *Lib. de Ant. Leg.*, pp. 32, 77, 86, 99, 148–50; *Cal. Letter-Bk. E*, 12–14; S. L.
Thrupp, *The Merchant Class of Medieval London*, p. 16.

For the reality of aldermanic rule bore little resemblance to the communal ideal of Latini's *Trésor*. The operation of the oligarchy bruised many interests in an expanding economy. There was an erosion of confidence, a progressive disaffection. Official records and aldermanic chronicles are mute on the subject; rarely do we glimpse the affronted 'smale people' behind the assurance of fitz Thedmar. But in mid-century the storm broke. In 1258 Henry III struck at the patriciate, with an enquiry into fiscal abuses as his weapon. In 1263, during the Barons' Wars, the populace rose in incoherent insurrection. In 1275 Edward's great inquest loosened the tongues of the Hundred juries. The plaints of juries and the acts of rebels uncover the roots of disaffection.

'Thomas de Basing took a tallage of £15 from his ward,' protested several juries in 1275, 'no-one knows by what warrant or for what purpose.' Nor was this an isolated instance. The Hundred Rolls and the ward depositions of 1258 are one sustained chorus of charges of fraud. Mayors and sheriffs, on their own initiative, had levied tallages, exempted the greater and distrained the lesser citizens. Places of collection had been altered, no true account was rendered, no-one knew what happened to the money.[1]

A particular grievance was the purchase of exemption from royal taxation by patricians. The royal records yield twenty-two instances of the purchase or grant of such exemption between 1253 and 1271, fixing the recipient's tax at a nominal half-mark, or acquitting him altogether. Ecclesiastics were prominent, the abbot of Merton in 1256, the prior of Holy Trinity and the abbot of Waltham ten years later, but most were aldermen, Richard de Ewell, Adam de Basing, John de Gisors in the years before 1258, Philip le Tailor, Thomas de Basing, fitz Thedmar himself in the sixties.[2]

The purchase of privilege sharpened an already widespread suspicion of aldermanic conduct in local taxation. In 1258 the commons asserted that aldermen had dismissed tallagers before

[1] *Hundred Rolls*, i, 416 and 403–33, *passim*.
[2] For these grants, see K.R.M.R. 31, m.6; 40, m.3, 12; 42, m.9, 9d, 23; *Pat. Rolls, 1216–25*, pp. 151, 160; *C.P.R. 1247–72, passim*; *C.R. 1227–68, passim*; *C.C.R. 1302–7*, p. 202; *The Records of Merton Priory*, ed. A. Heales, p. 131; *Lib. de Ant. Leg.*, pp. 240–242; *Hundred Rolls*, i, 403–12.

the rolls had been sealed, had tampered with the assessments and even pocketed some of the proceeds. The accused vehemently denied the charges, but in the sultry crisis atmosphere of 1258 refused to face the verdict of ward-juries.[1] Some of the mud stuck. The accusations no doubt were false, but popular suspicion proved ineradicable. The crux was aldermanic irresponsibility. Thomas de Basing did not deign to explain his £15. and the novel popular claim that no local tallage should be levied without the consent of the commons was resisted. In 1258 the council admitted that the practice of submitting tallage rolls to public inspection had died out ten years before.[2] With aldermen known to be buying exemption, anger and resentment spread like a forest fire.

Differential taxation, more than any other single factor, was the cause of that disillusionment which rotted many of the communes of Europe in the thirteenth century. In France, it drove many lesser citizens to demand the abolition of their communes. Matters were never so desperate in London, but in 1258 the *populares* were prepared, indeed eager, to surrender the city's liberties to see their superiors punished. Under the control of an aldermanic estate enjoying the maximum of power with the minimum of responsibility, taxation was the chief dissolvent of communal unity.

And those who would be most incensed at real or imagined fiscal discrimination were also those most affected by more tangible expressions of the oligarchical mentality. Early in the fifties, the wealthy royal merchant Adam de Basing, uncle of the Thomas remembered for his £15 tallage, having completed his new mansion on the east side of Aldermanbury, decided to annex it to his old hall opposite and build a palace worthy of his line. His solution had at least the virtue of simplicity. He built across the street. No doubt he left a passageway for traffic, but in effect he blocked one of the main highways of north-west London. The *probi* broke into protest and Adam and his son were involved in litigation for years. But the houses still stood—until 1263, when they fell with the régime which had tolerated them.[3]

[1] *Lib. de Ant. Leg.*, pp. 31–7.   [2] *Lib. de Ant. Leg.*, pp. 33–4.
[3] *Hundred Rolls*, i, 403–33; Weinbaum, ii, 132; W. Page, *op. cit.*, 142.

All encroachments on public land were technically pur-prestures and figured among the articles of the Iter. Most were minor, and after 'perambulation' by the justices, were either destroyed or allowed to stand on payment of a fine to the king. In 1276, for example, sixty-one persons paid £32 7s. in such fines. Some, however, were on a larger scale. In that same year, the sheriff Stephen de Cornhill paid £2, two Jews £5 each. Reme-dial action in such cases was frequently difficult. The Templars' bridge over the Fleet stopped the passage of craft. They were ordered to remove it in 1221; the order was repeated in 1244. Thirty years later, the Hundred juries were still complaining, loudly but in vain.[1]

Enclosure on a considerable scale went on throughout the century, particularly in its third quarter. In 1252 St. Paul's se-cured royal licence to close Dicers' Lane and set up gates, and other ecclesiastical bodies followed suit. Holy Trinity closed the road from the city wall; the Dominicans were particularly active. Aldermen and their friends, like Geoffrey Batecock who enclosed Catte Lane in Tower ward in 1251, were no less prominent, and by 1276 much of the road around the city wall as well as lanes and streets in the centre had been enclosed by Thomas de Basing, Anketil de Auverne, Henry le Waleys and others of the council. In the fifties and sixties at least twenty public ways were stopped and the process reached a rude climax in 1285, when the Folkmoot site itself was swallowed up by St. Paul's.[2]

All classes were inconvenienced and by no means all the enclosures were backed by royal warrant. The active participation of aldermen was resented. The growing pressure of lay and ecclesiastical magnates on the pattern of civic ownership, in a context of rising rents and increasing demand for land, pro-voked a serious crisis. And, as in taxation, what was more dis-turbing, perhaps, was not the physical hurt itself, but the appa-rent arrogance and indifference with which it was inflicted. The lesser *proudhomme* who owned his house and a couple of shops and paid his half-mark in tallage, was not only protesting

---

[1] See Misc. Rolls AA, BB; Weinbaum, ii, 146.
[2] For these enclosures, see Misc. Roll AA, pp. 76–83; Weinbaum, ii, 138 ff.; *C.P.R. 1247–81, passim*; St. Paul's A/70/1756.

against aldermanic evasion of tax and closure of his public ways. He was rebelling against humiliation as much as anything else.

His anger found vent in a barrage of complaints.[1] There were sweeping accusations of wholesale corruption. Sheriffs like Mathew Bukerel and Gregory de Rokesle had levied illegal charges and juggled with the king's debts; aldermen like Henry de Coventry had influenced court judgments in their favour. Moreover, mayors like William fitz Richard and John de Gisors had been selling the franchise to aliens for years. This last voiced the anger of the crafts, anxious to maintain the value of apprenticeship, and here perhaps is the crux of the situation. The developing mercantile misteries were becoming restive at aldermanic restriction. Society was outgrowing its political framework, but the aldermanic régime, far from responding to the challenge, became more rigid. The balance was not adjusted. The men of the crafts, the rising traders, new men, successful and increasingly self-confident, found no sure place for themselves in aldermanic society, smarted under real or imagined insult and contempt. Inevitably they groped for a political solution.

'Whereas the commune ought to elect the mayor and sheriffs,' protested Langbourn ward in 1275, 'the aldermen meet and of their own will and no-one else's, elect their own friends.'[2] The voiceless unenfranchised had no stake in the régime, and many of the lesser citizens found their aspirations blocked by a political stone wall. In the decade 1240–50, nine out of ten of the new aldermen were men of the old dynasties, the rest wealthy immigrants. The discontented found no constitutional outlet. Many must have shared the feelings of Thomas de Flete, the frustrated fripperer who stood at the roadside and neighed like a horse whenever the aldermen rode by.[3]

There were more potent methods of protest. Yet, in all the Hundred Rolls of 1275, Langbourn's is the only political complaint. Not until the mayoralty of Walter Hervey in 1272 did the popular movement show signs of efficient organization; not before the reign of Edward II was it a party in any sense of the

---

[1] *Hundred Rolls*, i, 403–33.   [2] *Hundred Rolls*, i, 414, 418.
[3] *Cal. E.M.C. Rolls*, p. 261.

word. The rising of 1263 was its school; it learned by insurrection. And that insurrection itself was in large measure a by-product of national controversy. All the grievances of the commons add up to exasperation, not revolt. The political impulse came from above.

London politics were patrician politics and the politics of the patriciate were largely personal. Current political attitudes, centring on support of or opposition to the power of the monarchy, tended to become identified with rival groups, but the contact between internal and external faction was often fortuitous. Public life in the city was patterned by family feuds and alliances, often traditional in character, a kaleidoscopic interplay of interest, opinion and emotion. London never knew the bitterness of St. Quentin or Bordeaux or some of the great Flemish and Italian cities, but it was no stranger to patrician feud. Even in the twelfth century, when its political life seems monolithic, fitz Reiners and Cornhills wore different national colours under John. And in the early thirteenth century, its public life was governed by the guerilla which Simon fitz Mary and his friends waged against their opponents, moderate and extreme, on the aldermanic council.

Simon fitz Mary, a great landowner and founder of Bethlehem Hospital, was one of the dynasts, and for twenty years his clashes with Bukerels, Bats and Tovys enlivened fitz Thedmar's chronicle.[1] They began, apparently, in 1228, when Ralph Eswy II was killed. His sons accused the Juvenals and Lamberts of murder. Fitz Mary supported them, stood surety when they took out a royal writ, and was heavily involved with the sheriff Stephen Bukerel and the mayor Roger le Duc. Nothing came of the accusation, but five years later, when fitz Mary succeeded Gerard Bat as sheriff, he ran into trouble. The mayor he served was the formidable Andrew Bukerel, Stephen's kinsman, and in 1234 Bukerel, backed by the council, charged fitz Mary with waste and negligence and deprived him of the issues of the shrievalty.[2] So began fifteen years of strife. Within three years, fitz Mary had reached the council as alderman of Walbrook,

---

[1] For fitz Mary, see St. Paul's A/14/1704, A/17/214, A/25/1070; Ancient Deeds D 3160; *C.Ch.R. 1226–57*, p. 307; *C.Ch.R. 1257–1300*, p. 38.
[2] *Lib. de Ant. Leg.*, pp. 7, 8; *C.R. 1227–31*, p. 92; Misc. Roll AA, p. 40.

in company with his friend Ralph Eswy III and Robert de Cornhill, later a prominent city royalist. Hitherto the quarrel had been local, a ripple on the surface of London life. In 1239, however, it acquired a new dimension. At the Michaelmas elections, while the mayor Richard Renger was supervising the choice of sheriffs, fitz Mary thrust his way forward and demanded office, waving before the startled eyes of his colleagues special royal letters which, in defiance of the city's charters, ordered his appointment.[1] Henry III was taking a hand.

Fitz Mary's action brought the council face to face with the problem which dominated London's political life, its relations with the Crown. The quarrel of 1239 was the first of a series which in twenty years brought king and city to open war. In a sense this was in the nature of things. Defence of its liberties and the liberties of the land against over-mighty kings was the 'good old cause' of medieval London, the instinctive reaction, almost an automatic reflex, of the city people. This it was which had ranged them with the barons of Magna Carta, which was to make them allies of Montfort in 1263, of Bohun and Bigod in 1297, and which led them under Edward II to 'canonize' that unlikely saint Thomas of Lancaster.

Among patricians, this enthusiasm was never pushed to extremes. The commune had become conservative. The *lignages* had won most of the liberties they could hope to win. They were now the men in possession and their policy was basically defensive. Moreover they were more closely bound to the Court than their predecessors had been. Royal service gave them office, royal purveyance wealth. Indeed, the early years of Henry III witnessed the growth of a king's party in the city which was to become a powerful force under his son.

But there was a point beyond which they would not go. Their liberties were the touchstone, those liberties which they would defend against king and *populares* alike. Inevitably, there was a certain ambivalence in their attitude to the Crown. Almost in the same breath fitz Thedmar asserts the patriciate's loyalty to the king during the Barons' Wars and denounces the popular mayor for not wringing fresh liberties from the prostrate Henry in 1264. They fought Henry as they had fought John. The new

[1] *Lib. de Ant. Leg.*, pp. 7, 8; *C.R. 1237-42*, p. 254.

concepts of Montfort and the Dominicans were alien, and when they were confronted with a stark choice between a revolutionary Montfort and an unfettered king, they floundered. In 1258 the 'barons' of London were more feudal than the barons themselves and their vacillation led straight to disaster.

Before the crisis in mid-century, however, their duty seemed clear enough. They had to defend their liberties and the threat came from the Crown. From the late thirties, Henry resumed the Angevin drive. He tried to reassert his authority over the sheriffs, gave his favourite church at Westminster rights in London which undermined the power of the council. There was his tallage, resented more for its implication of servile status than for its monetary burden. The Londoners were proud, quick to take offence. Their acclamation was part of the Coronation service, they advised on finance and trade. They were people of importance and resented Henry's personal government. The Sicilian business, Henry's war of pin-pricks against the city, were offensive and ludicrous. They were resisted.

From the thirties, royal pressure on the city mounted, reaching its climax under Edward I and ceasing only with the paralysis of the monarchy under Edward II. In response, patrician opinion fluctuated between and crystallized around two minority factions, one composed of men who, like fitz Mary, were prepared to act as royal agents or, like John de Gisors, lent their support to royal policy; the other, stronger and more representative, of men who almost instinctively reverted to the traditional posture of radical opposition to the Crown. In the background, ever present, was the accumulating discontent of important groups among the citizens, and, in the countryside, the mounting hostility of knights and barons to the royal government. Caught in this multiple play of forces, the majority of the aldermen and their friends, those people whose views fitz Thedmar so faithfully reflects—careful, moderate men, proud, class-conscious and sensitive, quick to see the need for reform in national affairs, slow to recognize any fault in their own—were pulled this way and that by more assertive factions until in the turmoil of the Montfortian movement they were swept from power.

Their travail began in 1239. There had been few problems for the previous generation. Fawkes de Breauté's arbitrary execution of Alderman Constantine fitz Alulf after a street riot in 1222 was an incident as isolated as it was ugly and the only awkward moment came in 1226, when Henry asked for a tallage *per capita* instead of the usual 2,000 marks composition. The Londoners agreed and ultimately paid over 4,000 marks, but they exacted a promise that the 'aid' would not be made into a precedent.[1] The greater patricians, closely associated with the Marshals, were prominent during the Minority and in the early thirties, and in 1234, Andrew Bukerel and Gerard Bat, having deposed fitz Mary from his shrievalty, accompanied Renger and Joynier to assist at the surrender of the Tower by the disgraced Peter des Rivaux.[2] There was no strain and the crises of 1237 and 1238 left the city largely unaffected. It was then, however, that Henry embarked on his new course. He decided to reestablish control over the city sheriffs. The resentful fitz Mary was at hand. In 1239 internal faction fused with external pressure and London entered a harsher political era.

When fitz Mary presented his letters at Michaelmas, letters which would undo the tradition of a century, the aldermen promptly rejected them, chose their own sheriffs and elected Gerard Bat to the mayoralty. Henry immediately suspended the city's liberties and kept Bat waiting three months for admission. In the following October, when Bat was presented for a second time, the king lost his temper and dismissed the mayor on the spot.[3] The pattern had been set. Henry's sporadic exercise of a temper more childish than terrible had, within ten years, swung the council behind its radical faction. In the immediate aftermath of the quarrel, it is true, Ralph Eswy and his brother reached the council, in company with the king's favourite John de Gisors, but in the autumn of 1243 a group of young patricians, evidently enraged at fitz Mary's activities, broke into violence against his person and property. Their leaders were Mathew Bukerel, kinsman of the Andrew who had deprived fitz Mary of the shrievalty, Peter fitz Roger, son of the

---

[1] *Lib. de Ant. Leg.*, p. 5; *M. Paris*, iii, 121; *Pat. Rolls 1225–32*, p. 104; S. K. Mitchell, *Taxation in Medieval England*, ed. S. Painter (London, 1951), pp. 323–4.

[2] *Pat. Rolls 1216–25*, pp. 272, 512, 527–8; *Pat. Rolls 1225–32*, p. 482; *C.P.R. 1232–1247*, pp. 53, 209, 217, 218, 230, 281; *C.R. 1234–7*, pp. 535, 561.

[3] *Lib. de Ant. Leg.*, pp. 7, 8; *C.R.1237–42*, p. 254.

man who had been mayor when Ralph Eswy II was killed, and
Peter and Robert de Basing. The formidable Adam de Basing
was elected sheriff that autumn. The raids may have been a
partisan attack on a rival candidate.[1]

Electioneering more robust followed in two years. In 1244
Michael Tovy, a wealthy landowning goldsmith, had been
chosen mayor, Nicholas Bat, nephew of the unfortunate Gerard,
sheriff. At Michaelmas 1245 Tovy tried to have Bat re-elected
for a second term. This was contrary to an ordinance passed in
1230, and the council, fitz Mary in the van, opposed it. The
frustrated Tovy unleashed the populace. The *populares* were
summoned to Guildhall and they carried Bat's election. This
was an unheard-of innovation and the startled aldermen turned
to the king. Henry took the city into his hands, deposed both
Bat and Tovy and appointed John de Gisors as mayor. In the
following year, when Gisors was re-elected, fitz Mary at last
returned to the shrievalty.[2]

His triumph was shortlived. For the king now intervened yet
again, this time in favour of Margery, widow of Alderman John
Viel, who, annoyed at a recent alteration in the Husting law of
dower, had appealed to him for help. This was too much. City
opinion hardened. In October, Tovy and Bat returned to office,
and when the royal justice Henry of Bath came to London over
the Viel case in August 1248, they refused to hear him. Henry
immediately suspended the liberties and in October summoned
the mayor and aldermen to answer for their defiance. In the
same month, he ordered the closure of all city shops for the new
fair he had established at Westminster. The Abbey's claims,
which made great inroads on the council's jurisdiction, were
already a sore point. Now, in the same cause, the Londoners,
'non coacti sed quasi coacti', were forced to take their wares to
Westminster in the pouring rain. The rain did not last but the
fair did. So did the citizens' anger.

At Westminster, the king pressed for recognition of the
Abbey's rights. Nothing was more calculated to unite the city
factions. Fitz Mary was left isolated. Through three days of
argument the aldermen stood firm. They re-elected Tovy as

---

[1] Misc. Roll AA, p. 40; Beaven, i, 372.
[2] *Lib. de Ant. Leg.*, pp. 6, 10, 11, 12; Beaven, i, 372.

mayor, and in March 1249, weary of virtually continuous royal interference, turned on fitz Mary and deposed him from his aldermanry. He disappeared from public life. To replace him they chose Alexander de Waltham (le Ferrun), one of the rising merchant-ironmongers. Fifteen years later, his colleagues were to cherish an implacable hatred of Waltham, the very embodiment of an intransigent city Montfortian. In 1249, however, he seemed the man for the job.

For in 1250 the king returned to the attack, repeatedly demanding confirmation of Westminster's liberties. The Londoners made their final refusal on 18 May. Henry took the city into his hands and summoned the aldermen to answer him. But on 24 May they issued a defiant declaration of independence. They refused to attend at Westminster. They were 'barons' and as 'barons' should plead outside the walls only before their 'peers', the earls and barons of England. This startling claim threw Henry into a fury. The city's autonomy hung by a thread. But Simon de Montfort and Richard of Cornwall hurriedly intervened. Anxious to avoid a serious crisis, they persuaded the king to let the matter drop.

These three years were crucial. Henry's heavy-handed intervention had defeated its own ends. Between 1247 and 1250, because of an unprecedented number of vacancies, no fewer than fourteen new aldermen were elected in less than four years. Bat himself was chosen, so were William Viel, an opponent of Margery, several friends of Ralph Hardel, son of the mayor who had sealed Magna Carta, Waltham, Thomas de Wymbourn and Thomas fitz Thomas, the future rebels of 1263. At least ten of the new men proved themselves ready to resist the king; three were to be capable of resistance in arms. A new generation came to power and its first political experience was a dramatic struggle with the monarchy. The radical faction captured the council.[1]

Five years later they made another stand. There had been no ease, no relaxation. Henry seized every chance to harass and exploit the stubborn patriciate. Its liberties were suspended frequently on the flimsiest pretexts and large sums demanded

---

[1] For these three years, see *Lib. de Ant. Leg.*, pp. 14-17; *M. Paris*, v, 28, 29, 128; *C.P.R. 1247-58*, p. 65; Beaven, i, 372-3.

for their restoration. Between 1239 and 1257 the city was taken into the king's hands at least ten times.[1] And in 1254 Ralph Hardel was elected mayor. His father had been the mayor of Magna Carta, he himself one of the council which had made the classic claim to equality with the peers of England. The Exchequer had haggled over his admission and when Henry demanded a tallage of 3,000 marks in January 1255, he refused, offering instead the usual 2,000 marks, but offering it as an aid. The king sent Philip Lovel to London to raise the money *per capita*. This was a breach of the pledge of 1226 and the citizens boycotted the tallagers. Henry resumed negotiations. This time, Hardel took the offensive. London would not pay the arbitrary 3,000 marks, because by right it owed not tallage but aid.

This claim caused consternation. The liberties were at once suspended and the king ordered the Exchequer to treat the matter as one of the utmost gravity. For since 1237 the voluntary nature of the aid had been reaffirmed. As opposed to the obligatory tallage, the aid was a firmly established freewill grant. No doubt, it was the unusual sum demanded and the breach of the 1226 pledge which stirred the Londoners to action, but what they were claiming was the right to decide whether they would pay or not. Once more they were seeking parity with their 'peers'.

The king's right seemed unassailable. London was part of the ancient demesne and he could tallage his demesne at will. This conception of the demesne, however, was of recent origin, and when the Exchequer rolls were searched, it was found that before 1204 London's contributions were not in fact called tallages. A list which the Exchequer prepared for the Londoners made several significant omissions. The tallage of 1226 was not listed for obvious reasons. An omitted tax of 1230 was actually recorded as an *auxilium*, and 'aid' had also been paid in 1236 and 1253. Until the reaction of 1237 the distinction between aid and tallage had become increasingly blurred and the Londoners were able to use arguments which jarred the Council severely.

However, on 6 February, the Exchequer announced that since John's reign, London had paid six tallages but never an aid, and the citizens' nerve was not equal to the strain. They capitulated and paid the 3,000 marks.[1] But it had been a political demonstration of the first order. Barely three years before the Oxford Parliament, the Londoners, in revolt against the servile implication of tallage, had made a constitutional challenge to personal monarchy. And as the country moved towards crisis the council rallied to Hardel, re-electing the vintner year after year. On his second election, Henry suspended the liberties and exacted a 400 mark fine, ostensibly for refusal to pay Queen's Gold. He had Hardel's sheriffs imprisoned for alleged negligence and, even after their release had been bought for £300, insisted on their dismissal. One of them joined the Montfortians ten years later.[2] Hardel and his friends were marked men. But the struggles of the fifties, fought with the old weapons, had reached deadlock. The king needed a new instrument. In 1258 he found it. The aldermen had forgotten the 'fools and ribalds of the lower classes'.

Late in January 1258 the king announced that a petition from London citizens, accusing aldermen of fraud and peculation, had been 'found' in the Wardrobe. A commission of enquiry was appointed under John Mansel. The scheme may have originated in Mansel's fertile brain. No petition of the *populares* had received such prompt attention before. The aldermen tried to organize a boycott, but Mansel turned their flank. He summoned a Folkmoot. No moot had been called for years except as a formality. In the mass-meeting of lesser citizens, the king had found his weapon.

At the moot, the Londoners, aldermen excluded, were ordered to elect ward juries of inquest. The aldermen countered with the assertion that it was contrary to the franchise for such juries to take an oath. The disturbed jurors responded. They refused to swear and maintained their refusal for a week. But meanwhile excitement was mounting, and Mansel called another Folkmoot, this time an angry one. It listened to a powerful manifesto from the king. He demanded freedom to act against those who had

---

[1] For this controversy, see *C.R. 1254–6*, pp. 2, 157–8, 159–60; *C.P.R. 1247–58*, p. 142; *Lib. de Ant. Leg.*, pp. 19–21; *M. Paris*, v, 484, 493, 520; *Dunstable*, p. 195; S. K. Mitchell, *op. cit.*, 324–30; R. S. Hoyt, *The Royal Demesne in English Constitutional History 1066–1272* (New York, 1950).

[2] *Lib. de Ant. Leg.*, pp. 20, 22, 23, 91; *C.R. 1254–6*, p. 237.

P

aggrieved his 'faithful commons', promised to maintain the city's liberty. It carried the day. To fitz Thedmar's horror, the commons swept aside the cherished liberty and gave their assent to the oath. For a week the juries testified at Guildhall until twelve wards had made their depositions. On their evidence, the mayor Ralph Hardel and five aldermen were charged with fraud and oppression.

They angrily denied the accusations and demanded the right to clear themselves in the traditional manner, by the oath of twelve compurgators. Henry insisted that they stand by the verdicts of the remaining wards and added fitz Thedmar and the sheriff Henry Walemund to the list of accused. It had become a test of endurance. Hardel and Nicholas Bat gave way and threw themselves on the king's mercy. But the others held firm. The king had his answer. Once more the great bell of St. Paul's tolled, once more people flocked to the Folkmoot. Should the aldermen be allowed to clear themselves in the traditional manner, asked Mansel. 'No! No!', roared the crowd, and the aldermen, appalled at its virulence, surrendered.

At one stroke all were deposed. A general election returned most of them and the sheriff Thomas fitz Thomas was publicly exonerated and confirmed in office. The seven accused were in mercy. Fitz Thedmar was ultimately acquitted, but the others were so heavily amerced that in March some of them tried to sell their houses, perhaps to quit the city. It was nearly two years before they were restored to favour. By that time, only three were left. Walemund had fled to France, Nicholas Bat and John Tolosan were dead. So was Ralph Hardel, of a broken heart, said Matthew Paris.[1]

For the radical wing of the council had been shattered. Who were the victims?—Hardel, leader in the struggle of 1255, Nicholas Bat and Mathew Bukerel, enemies of fitz Mary and Westminster, Nicholas fitz Joce, sheriff when fitz Mary was deposed and Westminster rebutted, John Tolosan, sheriff when the city had proclaimed its defiance in 1250, John le Minur, colleague of Bukerel and ally of Hardel in 1256. A few weeks after

---

[1] For this enquiry, see *Lib. de Ant. Leg.*, pp. 31-7, 43; *M. Paris*, v, 663, 675; *C.R. 1256-9*, p. 298; *C.P.R. 1247-58*, p. 614; for the refusal of juries to swear, see F. M. Stenton, *Norman London*, p. 23.

their condemnation, young men from the Hadestok and Montpellier families tried to kill Mansel's men in London.[1] The friends of Hardel and Bukerel took a sharper revenge in 1263.

In the council their influence was eclipsed. During the crucial early years of the baronial movement, the city's leaders were all royalists—William fitz Richard, a Court draper, Philip le Tailor, Household vintner and enemy of the *mediocres*, John Adrien and Robert de Cornhill, ready to act as royal bailiffs in the future as they had been in the past, and above all, John de Gisors, the royal vintner, butler and familiar of the king.[2] On the very eve of the victory of the barons, the king had crippled the opposition in the city and through all the enterprise and exhilaration of the eighteen months of baronial rule, the aldermen of London moved with a dreadful caution. For the exasperation of the *populares* had at last found outlet. They had heard the Folkmoot in full cry. The angry spring of 1258 shook the aldermanic régime to its foundations.

With time the breach might have been healed, but there was no time, for in April the king's own power collapsed, and in June the great Oxford Parliament launched the country into the experiment of baronial reform. For eighteen months the power of the Crown was put into commission and the magnates wrestled with the 'reform of the state of the realm', reform which penetrated from the royal household into shire and vill, thrusting through barriers of liberty and privilege. For the first time, the ideas of baronial reformers, all the amalgam of hope and bitterness which the Oxford *Provisions* came to represent, captured the imagination of the inarticulate, and when the baronial movement stumbled into disunity and the power of the king revived, Simon de Montfort, 'Saint Simon', carried half England with him in his war against the 'perjured traitors' who had betrayed the cause. There had never been anything quite like it before.[3]

London was at the heart of the movement. It was at the Temple that the barons laboured 'ferociously', that the arguments were fought out. Day after day, the friars preached the

[1] A.R. 1187, m. 24d.   [2] Beaven, i, 372, 373.
[3] The most useful accounts of the reform movement are R. F. Treharne, *The Baronial Plan of Reform 1258–63* (Manchester, 1932) and F. M. Powicke, *King Henry III and the Lord Edward*, 2 vols. (Oxford, 1947).

new order; time after time, the bell of St. Paul's summoned Londoners to hear the latest ordinance, the latest sentence of excommunication against enemies of the *Provisions*. The current of reform breached the wall of citizen immunity. Political songs echoed in the streets, new ideas rang in people's heads. In a community which had just passed through its most serious internal crisis for a generation, they were sure of response. Two years of baronial reform and reaction were sufficient to reduce the tangled maze of city politics to the harsh simplicities of civil war.

The first challenge came in July, when on the 23rd, Montfort, the Earl Marshal and others of the baronial council came to the city and demanded that the Londoners affix their seal to the form of the oath to the *Provisions*. Fitz Thedmar at this date was not hostile to the reformers, but after the experiences of February, the aldermen were unsure. They asked for time to consult the king. The barons not only refused, they resorted to the very weapon which Henry had used with such effect. Once more a mass-meeting of *populares* was turned against the patricians. At Guildhall, they overruled the aldermen and set the common seal to the oath, 'saving the liberties of London'.[1]

The challenge of July was nothing to that of December. After a quiet summer, the council installed John de Gisors in the mayoralty, with his supporters John Adrien and Robert de Cornhill as sheriffs, and it was under their leadership that the city had to face the most provocative and characteristic expression of the baronial movement in its earlier days, the eyre of the Justiciar Hugh Bigod. The eyre, undertaken in fulfilment of the pledge to set right all grievances, had sent ripples of alarm and excitement running through county society. Bigod's zeal, his disregard of entrenched privilege, above all his tolerance of the widespread use of the simple oral *querela* which cut through established procedure, disturbed the conservative and conventional, but opened the paths of justice to the poor and ignorant, and met with an eager response. Already in July young Michael Tovy, son of the embattled mayor of the forties, had gone before the Justiciar at Waltham with a *querela* against two Londoners over a holding in Stepney. The case was settled on

[1] *Lib. de Ant. Leg.*, pp. 38, 39; *M. Paris*, v, 704.

the spot, Tovy retaining the land and winning damages, a verdict which must have reinforced parental example.[1] By winter, Bigod was taking the Surrey pleas at Southwark, doling out heavy penalties which fitz Thedmar noted with alarm. A plaint challenged the levying of tolls by city sheriffs beyond Stone Gate on the Bridge. Solely as a favour, since they were not compelled to plead outside the walls, the Londoners took their charters to St. Saviour's, but Bigod, ignoring the charters, settled the case by a jury of twelve Surrey knights. Though the issue was settled in London's favour, the affront was alarming.[2] Worse was to come. For around 17 December, Bigod moved to Guildhall.

The outburst which ensued was remarkable, even for Bigod's first eyre, a measure of the social strain which the tumult and famine of this memorable year had left in their wake. Aldermanic authority was flouted, time-honoured procedures scrapped. Bigod held an assize of bread and imposed novel penalties, ignoring the pained protests of the sheriffs. Scores of citizens flocked to the court, complaining against the aldermanic ban on the retaining of attorneys by plaintiffs in land pleas, and the Justiciar, brushing aside the indignant aldermen, promptly referred the matter to the Council. All but four of the cases heard were *querelae*. Land pleas themselves were not immune, neither were the great families. William Viel's widow sued her husband's patrician executors in *querela* after *querela*; a disputed marriage settlement between Rengers, Hadestoks and Bukerels was settled on the spot by the same means. The Husting was set aside, and the aldermen, with their acute sense of property, were compelled to submit to a procedure which seemed no procedure at all but a licensed orgy of recrimination and irresponsibility. Fitz Thedmar's chronicle suddenly becomes shrill. Bigod was determining pleas, 'without reasonable summons, allowing no essoins, observing no due procedure'; he was pandering to the populace, scorning those who wore the robes of justice.[3]

The chronicler had personal cause for complaint, for one of the *querelae* was directed against himself. Robert le Cordwaner

---

[1] A.R. 1187, m. 3.   [2] *Lib. de Ant. Leg.*, pp. 39, 40.
[3] See A.R. 1187, m. 8–10; *Lib. de Ant. Leg.*, pp. 40, 41.

had him haled before the Justiciar to answer a charge of trespass. Fitz Thedmar had destroyed the plaintiff's house in 1245, and Robert demanded compensation. The outraged alderman replied in the authentic voice of a landed citizen and patrician. Robert had harboured a gang of landless 'ribalds' who were not in scot and lot; fitz Thedmar had acted as an alderman, had ordered the removal of doors and windows with the authority of the council. There was no case to answer, he maintained, and a jury upheld him.[1]

This lurid *querela*, more than any other, illumines the state of London opinion in 1258. For thirteen years Robert had nursed his grievance, and it was when Bigod crossed the Bridge that he thought his hour had struck. To men with more reputable ambitions, the *Provisions* were an even clearer call. But what were the *Provisions* to fitz Thedmar but humiliation and the end of all legality? The reforming barons were becoming more of a terror than the king had been. The coming of Bigod marked a crucial, probably decisive stage in the polarization of civic opinion. The new men of the trades, those angry over tallage and purpresture or eager for political power, the unenfranchised, the displaced patricians hostile to Henry and all his ways, all who were discontented, found a banner and a cause. A great body of London opinion rallied to the *Provisions* and to the personality of Montfort who became their embodiment. The bruised and bewildered aldermen, on the other hand, recoiled sharply. In this new political world, the world of petitioning 'bachelors' and protesting *mediocres*, the passionate world of Montfort and Edward, the patriciate found no sure place. Some must have rallied to the old order at once, the others could only stumble from crisis to crisis, desperate for peace.

Early in 1260 crisis was upon them. After a quiet year, with the momentous Provisions of Westminster as climax, Henry left for France, and in his absence, baronial unity, already weakened by controversy over the scope of reform, dissolved into a welter of suspicion. Bitterness supplanted the hope of 1258. Tempers were already harsh in London. In February 1260 a gang of youths chased some Italian clerics through the streets and murdered them in the heart of the city in broad daylight. It was

[1] A.R. 1187, m. 9.

the first of those irrational outbreaks of passion and xeno-phobia which marred these years of increasing tension.[1]

In April the crisis in baronial ranks reached breaking point. Lord Edward and Earl Simon, bent on holding their forbidden parliament, moved on London; so did Gloucester and their rivals. Edward's advance guard rode in, took over the bishop of London's hall and broke into his wine cellars. Gloucester's serjeants tried to requisition the whole of Cornhill. The alder-men, panic-stricken, appealed to Richard of Cornwall and Hugh Bigod. They acted swiftly. Gloucester and his opponents were ordered to the suburb, the gates and walls were manned, all citizens over fifteen issued with arms. From St. Omer, Henry ordered the fortification of the Tower. London wore the livery of siege. Late in April Henry crossed with his army of mer-cenaries, overrode the city's neutrality and ordered the admit-tance of Gloucester and other royalists. A compromise was patched up but the atmosphere had suddenly become violent.[2]

And in February 1261, the campaign against the *Provisions* began. Henry installed himself in the Tower, fortified the city and concentrated his forces there. From this base, he sallied out to secure the Cinque Ports and proclaim the papal bull of absolution from his oath to the *Provisions*. There he sat out the storm, as rival sheriffs disputed in the counties and Simon de Montfort tried to call a parliament of knights. Secure in his fortress, Henry foiled every counter-move and held his ground until the winter, when, with the second defection of Gloucester, resistance collapsed. The king's power was again a reality.[3]

London, with its resources, its fortress, its command of interior lines of communication, had been the fulcrum of Henry's scheme, and the full force of royal power had been concentrated in the city. Under the leadership of the mayor William fitz Richard, the aldermen gravitated instinctively towards the centre. They were given occasion to do so. Twice in the summer of 1261, in jurisdictional quarrels, first with the town of Northampton and then with the royal court of the Marshalsea, the king

[1] *Flores*, ii, 444-5; *Dunstable*, p. 214.

[2] *Lib. de Ant. Leg.*, pp. 44, 45; *Ann. Lond.*, pp. 54, 55; *C.R. 1259-61*, pp. 35, 253, 254, 257, 258, 282, 283, 287.

[3] *Lib. de Ant. Leg.*, pp. 46-9; *Ann. Lond.*, pp. 57, 58; *C.R. 1259-61*, pp. 365-471, *passim*; *C.P.R. 1258-66*, p. 155; R. F. Treharne, *op. cit.*, 250-73.

decided the issue in London's favour, handling its franchises and susceptibilities with unwonted tenderness.[1] The royalist faction grew in strength. It was in 1258, after the depositions, that Richard de Ewell became alderman, a Wardrobe buyer and recipient of the queen's bounty. Two years later he was followed by Bartholomew de Castell, a royal clerk of Edward's retinue, and John de Northampton the skinner, whose contracts for furs with the Household were running at £240 a year between 1250 and 1260. Philip le Tailor, whose sales to the Court reached their peak in 1261–3, entered the council in the same year, joining his friend John de Gisors who was made Master of Exchange at the height of Henry's power in 1262. These were some of the greatest men in the city; they had influence.[2]

It was in the October of 1261, however, that Thomas fitz Thomas became mayor. A draper, well-endowed with city property, he came of respectable family, one established in the patriciate since the twenties. He was nephew to no less a person than William fitz Richard himself, the mayor who had replaced Hardel, who had hesitated to set the seal to the *Provisions*. Fitz Thomas's sheriffs were Philip le Tailor and Richard de Walbrook, king's men. Evidently the draper was wholly acceptable to his colleagues in this, the king's year. Yet he stands out from those colleagues. He had entered the council in the crisis years of 1248–50, in company with Nicholas Bat, Tolosan, fitz Joce, le Minur, the victims of 1258, at the same time as Alexander le Ferrun. He had served as sheriff to Ralph Hardel in 1257–8, with Mathew Bukerel and Michael Tovy's son as companions.[3] Of all the mayors and sheriffs of the years between 1258 and 1263, he alone bore the stigmata of association with the struggles of the early fifties. At the fiscal enquiry of 1258 he had emerged with great credit. Certainly from 1263 to 1270 his name struck fire in the city, but that lay in the future.

[1] *Lib. de Ant. Leg.*, pp. 46–9; *C.R. 1259–61*, pp. 188, 189, 452, 457, 458.

[2] For the elections, see Beaven, i, 374; the careers of Ewell, Northampton, Tailor and Gisors, were outlined in Chapter III. For Castell, see Chanc. Misc. 3/21(18); *C.R. 1264–8*, p. 262; *C.R. 1268–72*, p. 399; *C.P.R. 1266–72*, pp. 394, 596, 651; *Lib. de Ant. Leg.*, pp. 114–15; for Gisors' appointment in 1262, see *C.P.R. 1258–66*, pp. 197, 219, 227, 249; *C.R. 1261–4*, pp. 198, 202.

[3] St. Paul's A/8/1052, A/17/102, 539, 542, A/34/692, A/71/1818; Ancient Deeds E16; Hust. Roll 3(4); *Lib. de Ant. Leg.*, p. 49; Beaven, i, 373, 374. Fitz Thomas was not installed by the popular movement, as is sometimes asserted.

In October 1261 his election passed without comment at Westminster or Guildhall.

There seemed little need for comment. By 1262 the king was able to order the arrest of all who preached the *Provisions* and to depart for France in good heart. Appearances, however, were fatally deceptive. In the counties there was anger and a sense of betrayal. There were ominous stirrings all over England. It was not only in the shires that men were angry. 'Covins' and plots were reported among the London *mediocres*, the guard at the Tower was doubled, the roads to Essex were patrolled. In November, when a Jew knifed a Christian in Candlewick Street, savage anti-Semitic riots broke out which raged through a whole day and night. Thomas fitz Thomas, entering his second mayoral term, had to repel the rioters by armed force.[1]

In the autumn, disease decimated the Household at Paris and the king was reported dead. At once Llywelyn of Wales broke loose in the Marches and the home government lost grip. Roger Leyburn led the younger Marchers into a rebellious faction and the defence of the west collapsed under Welsh attack and English disunity. Disaffection found a focus and the supporters of the *Provisions* rallied. Henry crossed hurriedly from France at the beginning of 1263 to find the government tottering.

In London, the atmosphere again became tense. Once more city loyalties were to be subjected to the acid test. Once more the aldermen hesitated and drew back, this time from the king. At the end of February, when the Constable of the Tower tried to take a prise of corn from Thomas de Basing's ship before it reached Queenhithe, he stirred up a hornet's nest. Basing, no lover of Montfort or the commons, was ready enough now to appeal to one of Bigod's decisions of 1258. Others were prepared to go further. When the royal justice admitted he was ignorant of the rights of the Tower, fitz Thomas ordered the sheriffs to resist the Constable, by armed force if necessary.[2] It was symptomatic. Everywhere there was unrest, and in March, Henry demanded oaths of fealty from his subjects. On the 11th and 12th fitz Thomas and the aldermen were required to swear.

---

[1] *Lib. de Ant. Leg.*, pp. 50, 51; *C.R. 1261–4*, pp. 73, 138, 139; on the general atmosphere, see R. F. Treharne, *op. cit.*, 280 ff. and F. M. Powicke, *op. cit.*, 432 ff.

[2] *Lib. de Ant. Leg.*, pp. 51, 52.

On the 18th every citizen over twelve took the oath in his ward-moot before his alderman.[1] Henry had need of it. For at the end of April, Simon de Montfort landed in England.

Dissidents flocked to his banner and faction grew into a national movement.[2] The stunned king saw his system crumble. At the end of May, the earl and his followers sent their ulti-matum. The *Provisions* were to be restored, their opponents treated as public enemies. Henry, who had already summoned the feudal host, refused. Over half the country, the Mont-fortians broke into open revolt and stormed the manors of their enemies. The Marches were cleared and Earl Simon led his army in a drive for the Channel ports.

The shock of his advance dislocated royal resistance. The king and queen shut themselves up in the Tower. Panic swept the city.[3] Henry tried to raise a loan from the Londoners but the frightened patricians would have nothing to do with it. Edward, riding through to Windsor and desperate for funds, raided the New Temple. Public order collapsed. Earl Simon, from Kent, turned his army towards London and launched an imperious proclamation at the citizens. Did they adhere to the *Provisions* or not? The desperate aldermen sought out Henry and begged him to surrender. It was too late. Even as they made their way to the Tower, people were pouring into the streets with weapons in their hands.

[1] *Lib. de Ant. Leg.*, p. 53.
[2] On the rising, see R. F. Treharne, *op. cit.*, 299 ff.
[3] On events in London, see *Lib. de Ant. Leg.*, p. 54; *Flores*, ii, 481; *Dunstable*, p. 222; *Gerv. Cant.*, ii, 221–3; *C.P.R. 1258–66*, p. 279.

CHAPTER VIII

The Crisis of 1263-70

EDWARD launched his desperate raid on the Temple on 26 June. Within hours, John de Grey's mansion nearby was in flames, John himself scrambling through a window into the Fleet with a mob of Londoners at his heels. Angry crowds flooded the streets. Richard de Ewell's houses were wrecked, Simon Passelew's pillaged. Armed bands burst into the homes of Cahorsins, hunted down royalists and, loud for the *Provisions*, raged through the city in incoherent insurrection.

Within three days of the first outbreak, Mansel had fled to France and London was under blockade. For as the *populares* took possession of the streets, leaders emerged from the shadowland of their 'covins and confederacies'. The names of fifty men and more were marked down by their impotent enemies as, under their leadership, popular exasperation was channelled to coherent purpose. Demonstration after demonstration filled the July days until revolt grew to revolution and government was driven from the streets.[1]

To the embattled aldermen the restoration of authority became a condition of survival. They sent delegates to Montfort, sealed an alliance with the earl. Henry himself announced his capitulation on the 16th. His queen, bred to the harsher climate of Poitou, promptly set out up the Thames to join Edward in the royalist stronghold at Windsor. At once the streets were alive with hostile crowds. Eleanor ran a gauntlet of stones, curses and jeering mobs to the Bridge. She got no further. They drove her back to the shelter of St. Paul's. Three days later

---

[1] For the rising, see *Lib. de Ant. Leg.*, pp. 54 ff.; *Dunstable*, pp. 222–3; *Gerv. Cant.*, ii, 221–2; *C.R. 1261–4*, p. 307; *C.R. 1264–8*, p. 428; *C.P.R. 1258–66*, pp. 264, 279; for the list of rebel leaders, see *Lib. de Ant. Leg.*, pp. 119–21.

they were out again to greet Montfort on his victorious entry. Within a week Edward had surrendered, and as the peace was proclaimed at Guildhall, the aldermen made a desperate effort to regain control. They mobilized their supporters, sent out mounted patrols to clear the streets.[1] They were too late. For in the brief struggle for power which ensued, the old radical faction in the patriciate suddenly re-entered the political scene, with decisive effect. Prominent among them was Stephen Bukerel. With his properties in Aldermanbury and Cheap and his dynastic antecedents, Buke-rel was a patrician to his fingertips, but he was the son of that Stephen and the nephew of that Andrew who had been such bitter opponents of fitz Mary, a kinsman of the Mathew Bukerel deposed in 1258. Juliana, widow of Ralph Hardel, was his friend.[2] With him were Michael Tovy, goldsmith and land-owner, son of the radical mayor of the forties,[3] the rentier Richard de Coudres, executor of Nicholas Bat,[4] and Alexander le Ferrun, the ironmonger who succeeded fitz Mary as alder-man of Walbrook.[5] Around them formed a small but powerful faction—a cluster of former sheriffs, Osbert de Suffolk, Alex-ander's son-in-law, Stephen de Oystergate his friend, William Gratefig the pepperer;[6] more shadowy figures like the gold-smith Thomas de Wymbourn who acted as alderman of Port-soken for Holy Trinity,[7] and new men of the stamp of John le Chapler, one of the rising merchants and entrepreneurs of the hat trade, an intruder from the suburb where his properties

[1] *Lib. de Ant. Leg.*, pp. 54–7; *French Chronicle*, pp. 3–5; *Flores*, ii, 482; *Dunstable*, pp. 223–4; R. F. Treharne, *op. cit.*, 308.

[2] A.R. 1207, m. 9d; *C.R. 1268–72*, p. 102; *C.R. 1264–8*, p. 132; *C.P.R. 1258–66*, p. 483; *Hundred Rolls*, i, 430; *Cal. of Wills*, i, 36, 49–50.

[3] St. Paul's A/18/134, 1418; A.R. 50, m. 3d; *C.P.R. 1258–66*, pp. 417, 517; *C.R. 1264–8*, p. 132; *Cal. Inq. Misc.*, i, 253; Lib. Roll 48, m. 8; *C. Lib. R. 1251–60*, pp. 192, 193; W.A.M., Domesday, fo. 480–1, 487–8; *Cal. of Wills*, i, 19.

[4] Hust. Roll 2(81); Misc. Roll AA, pp. 15–76, *passim*; St. Paul's A/7/890, A/66/79; W.A.M. 287; Ancient Deeds E 16; *Cal. of Wills*, i, 4, 129.

[5] Hust. Roll 2(124); 3(11); *C. Lib. R. 1251–60*, pp. 55, 111; *C.C.R. 1272–9*, pp. 26, 50–1; *C.P.R. 1281–92*, p. 151; Cur. Reg. Roll 191, m. 6d; *Cal. Letter-Bk. B*, 59, 202; *Cal. of Wills*, i, 31.

[6] Hust. Roll 2(62); 4(108); 6(10); 19(22); 22(28); 29(30); *Cal. of Wills*, i, 56, 208, 283, 412; Chanc. Misc. 3/7(41); *C. Lib. R. 1226–40*, p. 256; *C. Lib. R. 1245–51*, p. 319; Ancient Deeds E 220.

[7] Hust. Roll 1(12)(33); 2(37); 8(26); *C.R. 1264–8*, p. 337; *C. Lib. R. 1251–60*, p. 274; Beaven, i, 373.

lined the Fleet, thrusting his way into the patriciate and the rebel leadership;[1] all of them directly or indirectly heirs to the radical group of the forties and fifties.

A new personality emerged as their ally. Master Thomas Puleston was a stranger to London politics, if not to city life. His was a Shropshire family which gave generations of service in the royal administration.[2] Master Thomas himself first appeared in the records in 1256 as a collector of the Sicilian Tenth; by 1261 he was Henry's personal proctor at the Court of France, by 1263, a royal justice.[3] His kinsmen Roger and Richard had just begun their own careers in the administration. A trained jurist and royal clerk, he was a person of some consequence in Montfort's party. Nor was his role in London affairs fortuitous. In 1259 he had married Helen, niece to Michael Tovy the elder, a marriage which brought him into intimate contact with radical circles in the patriciate. Indeed, Puleston probably supplied in his person the link between the city movement and the entourage of the earl himself.[4]

But the aldermen's discomfiture was turned to rout when the mayor himself went over to the rebels. For when the crisis broke, Thomas fitz Thomas threw off the inhibitions of office and reverted to his role of the fifties. He proclaimed himself leader of the *populares*, committed the power and prestige of the mayoralty to their cause. With the mayor, Puleston and the dissident patricians at their head, the commons swept to victory. Their scurrying bands were organized into a militia and the mounted patrols were driven from the streets. Aldermanic resistance collapsed and the commune disintegrated.[5]

---

[1] Recog. Roll 1(147)(225); K.R. Acc. V. (Alien Merchants) E101/126/6, m.1; Chanc. Misc. 109/1(84); Hust. Roll 34(103); St. Paul's A/66/79; *C.R. 1259-61*, p. 452; *Cal. of Wills*, i, 45, 46, 69, 150, 151, 303, 328.

[2] See my forthcoming article, 'The English Pulestons; pre-history of a Welsh gentry family', *Journal of the National Library of Wales*. The Pulestons were planted in North Wales after the Edwardian Conquest, to emerge in the fifteenth century as Welsh gentry.

[3] *C.P.R. 1247-58*, pp. 461, 552, 605-6; *C.P.R. 1258-66*, pp. 189, 198-99, 235; *C.R. 1256-9*, p. 465; *C.R. 1261-4*, pp. 91, 280. Puleston (Piwelesdon and variants) was a hamlet on the Shropshire-Staffordshire boundary—*Feudal Aids*, iv, 220, a reference I owe to Professor R. F. Treharne.

[4] *C.P.R. 1247-58*, pp. 477, 521; *C.P.R. 1258-66*, pp. 397, 416, 460, 462; Hust. Roll 2(88); *Cal. of Wills*, i, 32.

[5] *Lib. de Ant. Leg.*, p. 57.

Power passed to the sworn confederacy of the commons, the rebel *societas* of the royal clerks. Under fitz Thomas and Puleston, they organized themselves into a militia of sworn leagues bound together by the hundred and the thousand under oath. They shut down the Husting, swept away the closed committees of the old régime, treated aldermen as if they did not exist. Their instrument was the rejuvenated Folkmoot. The mayor constituted himself its spokesman and executive officer, submitted every issue to it. Daily, craft after craft, released from the aldermanic strait-jacket, came before the moot and had its ordinances ratified and proclaimed by the mayor. Hundreds of foreigns as well as lesser citizens flocked to the assembly and for the first time made their will effective. In response to that will, Puleston and Bukerel, with Tovy as ardent lieutenant, led out the militia, to Aldermanbury where they left the Basings' new mansion in ruins, to Catte Lane where they tore down Batecok's gates, to the enclosed road to Holy Trinity which they reopened by force. 'Like so many justices itinerant', they scoured the city, breaking open all enclosures.[1]

It was as allies of Montfort that they had triumphed, and the new Council indicated that any reasonable request would get a sympathetic hearing. The answer was prompt. On 26 August, Gilbert de Preston was commissioned to enquire into the liberties claimed by Westminster Abbey. In October he delivered his judgment. The abbot's claims were totally disallowed and he was compelled to renounce his royal charter. So Tovy and Hardel were avenged, the king humiliated, and Pope Clement IV driven to such rage that he penned a thunderous rebuke to the bishop of London, proclaiming to the world that the state of England was 'in a boiling whirlpool of universal disruption'.[2]

Disruption was indeed near that autumn. In October, Edward and the king broke off negotiations, moved to Windsor and gathered their supporters. Montfort took over the Tower and it was in a community bracing itself for war that the commons, brushing aside aldermanic resistance, re-elected fitz

---

[1] *Lib. de Ant. Leg.*, pp. 55–6; Weinbaum, ii, 132–52, *passim*.
[2] W.A.M., Domesday, fo. 22b; *C.Ch.R. 1257–1300*, pp. 238, 241; *C.P.R. 1258–66*, p. 288; *Lib. de Ant. Leg.*, pp. 56–8.

Thomas as mayor by mass acclamation, swearing him in on the spot, in defiance of the Exchequer. Henry refused to admit him and put the city under blockade, as the rival parties patched up a truce and submitted the dispute to the arbitration of Louis of France.[1]

At the end of November the truce broke down as Henry suddenly marched on the Channel ports. Rejected at Dover, he turned on London and on 8 December called on the citizens to expel Montfort without delay. As the earl's troops moved through the city into Southwark, the displaced patricians made a desperate attempt to rally conservative opinion, but at a tumultuous Folkmoot they were shouted down. Puleston and the mayor mobilized the militia in Montfort's cause. The despairing royalists resorted to violence. John de Gisors rallied a small group of his friends, his brother's partner Stephen de Chelmsford, Richard Picard, another Court vintner, and Augustine de Hadestok, a patrician magnate and ship-owner connected to Chelmsford by marriage.[2] They made secret contact with the royal army and, on the 11th, suddenly shut the gates behind Montfort's small force in Southwark, barred them with chains and hid the keys. At their signal, Edward from Merton and Henry from Croydon closed in. The trapped Montfortians took the Cross. But when the news broke in London, the *populares* surged out in angry crowds, battered open their own gates and carried the embattled band in triumph into the city. As the baffled king withdrew, the militia rooted out the four plotters and their accomplices. They were in peril of their lives until Montfort took them into custody.[3]

It was, then, an excited London, irrevocably committed to Montfort, which received Louis' Mise of Amiens in January 1264, and which, together with the Cinque Ports and nearly all the middle order of people in England, in the memorable words

[1] *Lib. de Ant. Leg.*, pp. 58, 59; *Flores*, ii, 484; *Dunstable*, pp. 224, 225; *C.P.R. 1258–66*, p. 295; *C.R. 1261–4*, pp. 316, 321, 327.

[2] For these men, see *Lib. de Ant. Leg.*, p. 62; *Wykes*, pp. 150–1; Hust. Roll 2(65) (143); 4(57); 14(117d); *C.P.R. 1247–58*, pp. 472, 521; *C.R. 1261–4*, p. 344; *C.Lib.R. 1251–60*, pp. 302, 518; Lib. Roll 37, m. 7, 11, 14; Excheq. Plea Roll 1E, m. 19d; Misc. Roll AA, p. 33; *Cal. of Wills*, i, 130.

[3] For the incident, see *Ann. Lond.*, p. 60; *Flores*, ii, 485; *Dunstable*, p. 226; *Chron. Duob. Bell.*, p. 508; *Wykes*, p. 138; *Royal and Other Historical Letters Illustrative of the Reign of Henry III*, ed. W. W. Shirley (London 1866), ii, 250–1.

of fitz Thedmar, wholly rejected it. Sporadic warfare broke out
in the west. There were riots in the city, wholesale arrests of
royalists. The Londoners renewed their sworn *societas*, armed
the militia, elected Puleston Constable and Bukerel Marshal of
the city host. And as March came in, the former Justiciar Despenser led them out against their enemies.[1]

They devastated Richard of Cornwall's mansion at Westminster, his manor in Isleworth. They circled London, ravaging
the lands of William de Valence and Philip Basset. Tovy,
Bukerel and Puleston led a force to Peter of Savoy's lands at
Cheshunt and left them a desert. They moved on to Merton
and destroyed Walter de Merton's property there, while Bukerel
and Bartholomew le Tailor, a kinsman of Nicholas Bat, raided
his manor of Finsbury. Raid followed raid. One, on James de
Audley's lands at Tottenham, was guided to the target by the
local vicar. Bukerel made himself a specialist in the art, con-
centrating on John Renger, son of the former mayor Richard
Renger, now an Exchequer official. Retribution was swift, and
scores of Londoners, including the royalist magnates, lost their
lands in a general confiscation.[2]

Almost at once Northampton fell. Defeat and the fear of renewed patrician treachery, coming hard on the excitement of
the great raids, worked harshly on the fevered minds of the
populace and in the week before Palm Sunday they vented their
frustration on the traditional scape-goats. In savage anti-
Semitic riots, over 500 Jews were killed and robbed. Fitz Thomas
and Despenser fought hard to restore order, rescuing the survivors and lodging them in the Tower. To the Tower, too, fled
the Italians and the Cahorsins, hurriedly collecting their money
from the abbeys and priories around London.[3]

The outbreak spent itself. Reason returned. Nothing could
compensate the royalists for the loss of London, which gave
Montfort a superb base and strategic centre. From it, in April,
the baronial army moved out and, after heavy fighting in which

---

[1] *Lib. de Ant. Leg.*, p. 61.

[2] For these raids and confiscations, see Cur. Reg. Rolls 175, 177, 178, 181, 182,
184, 184a, 185, 186; A.R. 1207; *C.R. 1261-4*, pp. 375, 376; *Chron. Duob. Bell.*, p.
514; *Wykes*, pp. 140, 141.

[3] *Lib. de Ant. Leg.*, p. 62; *Flores*, ii, 489; *Dunstable*, p. 230; *Wykes*, pp. 142-3; Cur.
Reg. Roll 175, m. 27d.

the Londoners distinguished themselves, took Rochester and stormed the outer bailey of the castle. Henry's army was drawn south, fitz Thomas reported activity among the royalist fifth column in the city. Montfort returned to London, took hostages from the disaffected, and with renewed confidence the baronial army marched out to encounter its enemy at Lewes. Final negotiations failed on the eve of 14 May.

The Londoners, drilled all night long in the Weald, provided the bulk of Montfort's infantry. They held the left, under Henry of Hastings and Geoffrey de Lucy. Bukerel was there, Michael Tovy busy on Earl Simon's staff 'as if chief of his familiars', according to the comment of an enemy in later years. Puleston served as second-in-command to the division directly under the earl himself, and before morning, all took the white cross of the Crusade. Behind them, down the hill, Hadestok, Picard, Chelmsford and another of the plotters of December, brought as hostages, lay in Earl Simon's standard-chariot.[1] On this same night, back in London, one of their colleagues, the draper Richard de Ware, tried to destroy Cheapside by fire. Many houses in Milk Street and Bread Street were burned before the incendiary draper was restrained.[2]

Nothing, however, could restrain the Lord Edward on the morning of the 14th when, as the surprised royalists rushed to arms, he spotted on the hill 'illi rustici Londonienses' who had insulted his mother. He led his cavalry in a furious onslaught. The city militia broke before the armoured knights and reeled down the valley. William Gratefig and Stephen de Oystergate were killed, scores of their fellows cut down or drowned in the Ouse. A troop circled the hill and butchered the unfortunate royalists in Simon's chariot. Far back towards London they pressed the pursuit. But in Lewes Simon launched his well-timed charge and the royalists were routed. Edward returned to find the king a prisoner, the battle lost.[3] Montfort bought his victory with the Londoners' blood. But victory it was and the army returned to a London secure in its new régime.

[1] *Chron. Duob. Bell.*, p. 525; *Wykes*, pp. 150-1; for the reference to Tovy, see A.R. 59, m. 19d.
[2] *Ann. Lond.*, p. 63; *Flores*, ii, 498; *French Chronicle*, p. 5 and n. 2; Weinbaum, ii, 132; fitz Thedmar does not mention the incident.
[3] *Chron. Duob. Bell.*, p. 527; *Flores*, ii, 496; *Lib. de Ant. Leg.*, p. 65.

Q

That new régime was an amateur affair. The *populares* concentrated exclusively on the mayoralty. Their sworn leagues and the moot displaced the *congregatio* and installed a popular mayor, but that was all. Even the shrieval elections escaped attention. Of the four sheriffs elected under the Montfortians, two were aldermen who had succeeded the deposed radicals of 1258, a third later served with the royal army at Kenilworth and the fourth was Gregory de Rokesle, named by fitz Thedmar as one of the foremost royalists in the city.[1] Nor did they make any attempt to replace the ward by the craft, as in later years. The mayor was 'keeping' Castle Baynard in 1264, in the absence of its alderman, but in that same year Michael Tovy was elected to Ludgate-Newgate, and the old system was retained in its essentials. Even the closure of the Husting proved but temporary. By the end of 1264, though the number of deeds enrolled was less than normal, the court was functioning again.[2]

Some property changed hands. Bartholomew le Tailor snatched houses in Thames Street which his kinsman Nicholas Bat had bequeathed to a hospital; a Jew was dispossessed; Holy Trinity, Westminster and St. Thomas Acon suffered depredation. Michael Tovy himself, prominent in the raids, was implacably pursued as a 'robber' after the wars, but there is no evidence to warrant the charge, unless his enrolled purchase, at twenty marks, of shops in Friday Street from the royalist Hadestoks in 1265 masks a more brutal transaction.[3] Stephen Bukerel, it is true, scorned a mask. He retained the lands he took from John Renger and two other royalists, and even blocked Foster Lane with a purpresture.[4] But in the circumstances, this did not amount to much. There were no proscriptions. The Husting roll for 1264-5, with its eighteen deeds, is resolutely normal. Indeed it was in this very year that the patrician champion Philip le Tailor finally entrenched himself

[1] *Lib. de Ant. Leg.*, pp. 69, 70, 114-15; Cur. Reg. Roll 175, m. 26d; 177, m.1; 181, m.2d.

[2] St. Paul's A/4/691; *Lib. de Ant. Leg.*, pp. 61, 70; Hust. Roll 2, 3.

[3] Cur. Reg. Roll 178, m.4; 189, m.23d; K.R.M.R. 41, m.2d.; *C.R. 1264-8*, pp. 96, 189, 238-9, 402; *Cal. Inq. Misc.*, i, 120; *Hundred Rolls*, i, 403; St. Paul's A/18/1436; *French Chronicle*, p. 14; *Cal. of Wills*, i, 4.

[4] *Cal. Inq. Misc.*, i, 104, 208, 247; *Hundred Rolls*, i, 427, 430, 433.

with his marriage to Sabine fitz Alan and her lucrative marriage-portion.[1]

The thoroughness and sophistication of later movements were absent and the overall impression is of political immaturity. Clearly, the national crisis had been a forcing-house. It was the success of the national Montfortian movement which thrust the ill-prepared *populares* of London into power before their formless discontent had crystallized into a coherent programme. They knew what they wanted to stop; beyond that, they were groping in the dark. What they did, however, was significant. This was the first successful displacement of aldermanic power, and the ambitions which found clumsy expression in 1263 became the permanent aspirations of the popular movement. They broke the bonds of oligarchy. The alliance of mayor and plebs was an expedient sufficient, for the time, to establish popular control over government. In response to the popular will, they reversed the craft and tenurial policy of the patriciate and extended the frontiers of the commune to find room for those newer social interests which the aldermen had ignored or suppressed.

It is this which makes the ordinances granted to the crafts so important, which links 1263 to the reform movements of the fourteenth century. Fitz Thedmar tells us nothing of the crafts involved except to imply that they were numerous. During Walter Hervey's mayoralty six years later, a renewed expression of the spirit of 1263, charters were granted to the cordwainers, girdlers, wool-packers and joiners, favour shown to the fishmongers and bakers.[2] These were no doubt among the beneficiaries of 1263. Cordwainers and girdlers were middle class misteries which had risen to a position of mercantile dominance over other crafts in the trade; the general tenor of Hervey's charters would have favoured especially the strong group of distributive merchants among the fishmongers as well as such rising crafts as the corders and skinners; the wool-packers were a skilled semi-mercantile body. No doubt, in older misteries, subordinate but expanding trades such as the joiners were organizing, and the impulse moved even humbler occupations, but to judge from the crafts named by chroniclers and from the

---

[1] Hust. Roll 3(18); see also Hust. Roll 3(1)(4)(11)(12).
[2] *Lib. de Ant. Leg.*, pp. 55, 56, 159, 162, 163, 164-6, 169, 170; *Hundred Rolls*, i, 404.

pattern of later events, the driving force behind the movement came from those crafts in which mercantile expansion and competition had produced groups of traders and entrepreneurs thrusting towards control of the trade and eager to clothe control in institutional form.[1]

What we know of the personnel of the rebel movement bears out this supposition. The handful of patrician leaders is, of course, a group apart. Alexander le Ferrun, it is true, was a merchant-ironmonger, one of a new group which was to penetrate the patriciate at the end of the century,[2] and John le Chapler, with his Spanish imports and ring of dependent craftsmen, was a leader of the small mercantile élite of his trade.[3] Oystergate was a fishmonger closely associated with the families of Fulham and Pourte, from whom sprang the first of the fishmongers to reach aldermanic status.[4] But most of the popular leaders of aldermanic rank belonged to the traditional misteries of the patriciate; they were drapers, goldsmiths, vintners and pepperers. In marked contrast to the hard core of city royalists, none of them was a royal merchant of the first order, in constant commercial intercourse with the Household, but this was equally true of many of their less elevated opponents, and their motives are more probably to be found in the pattern of political and personal conflict set by the struggles of the forties and fifties.

It is otherwise with the rebel *mediocres*. Fifty-four of them were listed by royalists during the troubles, and the records of judicial proceedings against Londoners after the restoration yield the names of a further eighty-three persons.[5] One is immediately struck by the preponderance of rising mercantile misteries of the type favoured by Hervey. Among the eighty-three people active enough in raid and sortie to be remembered, no fewer than nineteen were fishmongers, eleven cordwainers, five

---

[1] The growth of the crafts was discussed in Chapter VI.

[2] Hust. Roll 2(124); 3(11); *C. Lib. R. 1251–60*, pp. 55, 111; Cur. Reg. Roll 191, m.6d; *Cal. Letter-Bk. B*, 59, 202; *Cal. of Wills*, i, 31.

[3] Recog. Rolls 1 and 2, *passim*; St. Paul's A/66/79; W.A.M., Domesday, fo. 480; Hust. Roll 2(89); Hust. Roll (Land) 1, m.17; K.R. Acc. V. (Alien Merchants) E101/126/6, m.1; *Cal. of Wills*, i, 45, 46, 211, 303, and *passim*.

[4] Hust. Roll 4(108); 6(10); 19(22); Ancient Deeds E 500; *C. Lib. R. 1226–40*, p. 256; *C.R. 1234–7*, pp. 232, 485; *Cal. of Wills*, i, 412.

[5] See *Lib. de Ant. Leg.*, pp. 119–20 and Cur. Reg. Rolls 175–86; A.R. 1207.

girdlers. These three crafts given charters by Hervey accounted for thirty-five of the eighty-three. The six goldsmiths were mostly artisans, but the middle class tailors had four representatives, the rising mercantile communities of the corders and potters, three each. Individuals were drawn from a galaxy of gilds, but no less than 52 per cent of the active rebels belonged to rising middle class crafts of quasi-mercantile character. 'Patrician' misteries, generally represented by their humbler members, accounted for 16 per cent, the lesser crafts, a mere 7 per cent. Middle class representation as a whole is overwhelming —nearly 70 per cent. In the leadership the position is complicated by the adherence of dissident aldermen and outsiders like the Pulestons, but once more, the new crafts of the rising middle class predominate, the eight fishmongers, three ironmongers, two skinners, chapler and cutler comprising nearly a third of the total.[1]

An attempt, necessarily rather impressionistic, to classify these men by status strengthens the argument.[2] At the head of the fishmongers stood John de Stepney, a landowner of substance with his own ship and staff of agents, a man important enough to marry Thomas fitz Thomas's widow in later years. His colleagues were a solidly middle class group, a cluster of names from the Bridge Street and Fish Street middlemen who controlled the trade, Sowels, Scots, the Heyrun family with its four rebels, Greylonds and Albyns, councillors and property-owners. William May the skinner was a merchant of substance, selling £205 of silver to the Mint in 1263, exporting wool later in life, his son, who married into the aldermanic Cornwaleys family, a founder-member of the skinners' gild. The only weaver among the rebels, Simon Pourtepoll, owned much property in the suburb and married his daughter to Richard de Chigwell, greatest of the new alderman-fishmongers at the end of the century.

The men of the older misteries were more varied. Among the goldsmiths, for example, four men are merely names and of

[1] Based on data on named rebels derived in the main from Hust. Rolls; Recog. Rolls; *Cal. of Wills, Cal. Letter-Bks.* and Ekwall, *Two Early London Subsidy Rolls.*
[2] Brief biographical notes on these rebel leaders will be found in the Appendix, under the title *Communa Mediocris Populi.*

Richard le Orbatur we know nothing except that he held two shops in Cheap. But John Eliland came from a family which had once been patrician, while Walter de Watford was probably a patrician himself, with his land in Kent, his aldermanic factor, his wool-export of thirty sacks in 1273 and his silk deals in 1276. But among all groups, indications of status abound. The Laufares produced an alderman in the next generation, Suffolks and Poyntels were great men in wine and leather, Alexander le Potter owned shops in Bury and Winchester, and two Heyruns were chirographers of the Jews. Prestons, Albyns, Watfords, Baynards, Enfields, witnessed each others' deeds, went surety for each other. Richard de Coudres, William May and William de Basing lived next door to each other in the same street. Kinship, marriage, craft-comradeship and friendship gave cohesion to a movement which was singularly homogeneous. For most of the rebels were drawn from a common social environment. Men whom fitz Thedmar would call *inferiores* were no more than a fifth of all known rebels, though numbers of them were active in the leadership. The upper middle class group was over-represented, with one in every ten known rebels belonging to it, but by far the greatest number were solidly middle class citizens. Two-thirds of all known rebels, they easily outnumber every other social group. The 'communa mediocris populi' assumes recognizable human shape.

The revolt of 1263 was evidently a revolt of middle class citizens eager for political power commensurate with their social importance and impatient at the blocking of their ambitions by the constricting oligarchy of a few great families. They were led by a cohesive group of wealthy merchants and entrepreneurs of the rising trades nourished by the commercial expansion, for the heart of the movement lay in the crafts of fishmongers, cordwainers, corders, girdlers, skinners, ironmongers, potters, which were developing their mercantile associations as instruments of control. It was to such spirits as these that exclusion from power, purprestures and the suppression of misteries would be peculiarly obnoxious. Supported by lesser citizens whom their example stirred to action and by the scarcely political resentment of the foreigns, they were led and marshalled by the dissident patricians with a trusted mayor at their head. It was these men who seized power, resurrected the Folkmoot, liberated the crafts, freed the public ways and, with distracted minds and unpractised hands, tried to rebuild the commune. ⸗

Their commune owed its existence to Montfort. Its survival depended on his, and throughout the fifteen harassed months of his administration, the city leaders stood high in his counsels. In March 1265 Thomas Puleston was witness to a grant to the elected Chancellor when the king himself folded the writ. His kinsman Richard served as deputy-castellan of Bridgnorth in the troubled west, Bukerel and Tovy as escorts to royalist knights coming in for parley. The mayor fitz Thomas was an important functionary of the régime, duly rewarded with gifts and a lucrative wardship.[1] Within the city his reward was an intense popular loyalty destined to survive the worst rigours of defeat. In these years he won his place in civic tradition, standing to London as Giano della Bella to Florence or as Henri de Dinant had stood to Liège only ten years before. His rule was mild, a faithful reflection of his leader's endless and futile quest for reconciliation. William, the son of Augustine de Hadestok, the royalist plotter who met his death at Lewes, was quickly and easily admitted to the seisin of his father's manor at Walthamstow, and even John de Gisors found the government remarkably solicitous.[2] Through all the tension of the summer of 1264, as London levies moved to the threatened coast from a city laid under interdict, the leadership held to its policy of moderation and compromise, until in March 1265 it seemed to come to fruition. The famous parliament in which burgesses first took their seats marked the zenith of Earl Simon's power. The peace was proclaimed at a brilliant ceremony in Westminster Hall and at the swearing of fealty Thomas fitz Thomas felt confident enough to lecture the king on his duties in the minatory accents of an Aragonese noble.[3]

But the Montfortians fed on illusion. Already in February

---

[1] *C.P.R. 1258-66*, pp. 322, 341, 353, 397, 416, 419, 420; *C.R. 1264-8*, p. 46.

[2] *C.R. 1261-4*, pp. 344, 402; *C.R. 1264-8*, pp. 38, 89, 90; *C.P.R. 1258-66*, pp. 322, 431.

[3] *Lib. de Ant. Leg.*, pp. 72, 73 and marginal note. Fitz Thedmar believed that every borough sent four representatives to this parliament, in the manner of the Cinque Ports—an indication of the probable number of London members.

Derby had been arrested, and in April the quarrel between Gloucester and Montfort flared into open violence. On 28 May Edward broke loose. Marchers and royalists rose in arms and the Protectorate collapsed. The Court moved out to Hereford and the desperate manoeuvres in the west began.

In London, the texture of public life deteriorated rapidly. The militia mobilized, marched into Southwark and seized the lands of John le Moyne. Stephen de Cornhill, the draper of good patrician stock, gathered his men and galloped out to join the royalist army. Fitz Thomas at once threatened death for any breach of the peace within a radius of twenty-five miles. Bukerel rode to Dunmow and ejected Alderman John Norman. Fitz Thedmar's chronicle becomes pure melodrama as he unmasks an alleged plot to massacre the city royalists. At the end of June the Chancery stopped enrolling writs and the curtain of silence came down on the trapped army writhing in the Marches. At last, on 6 August, news of Evesham reached the city.[1]

For the popular leaders it spelt utter disaster. Bandit raids and wholesale confiscation disfigured the counties as Edward and the king proclaimed the disinheritance of their enemies and massed at Windsor for the siege of London. Simon's death and the sweep of resurgent royal power took the heart out of fitz Thomas and his friends. Alexander le Ferrun and a few others were for resistance to the end, but their power must have evaporated rapidly. Decision passed to the reviving aldermen, who were already plying the king with supplicatory letters. By the end of September they had won. The intransigents fled, Ferrun going into an exile which was to last twenty years, and fitz Thedmar, William fitz Richard, and John Adrien led a deputation to the king, taking Stephen Bukerel with them, probably by agreement. Roger Leyburn met them on the road and issued his instructions, and on 3 October the mayor, his friends and forty of the leading citizens set out for Windsor, under safe-conduct, to present the surrender. At Windsor, the safe-conduct was broken and all were imprisoned. Fitz Thomas, Puleston, Bukerel, Tovy and John le Chapler were handed

[1] On the crisis, see *Lib. de Ant. Leg.*, pp. 74-7, 114-15; K.R.M.R. 40, m.12; Cur. Reg. Roll 175, m. 25, 25d; 177, m.4, 22; 184a., m. 12; A.R. 1207, m.4; *C.P.R. 1258-66*, p. 434; F. M. Powicke, *op. cit.*, 498 ff.

over to Lord Edward and Henry entered the city in triumph.
London lay at his mercy.[1]

Mercy was at a premium in the autumn of 1265. The royalists
came back thirsting and Henry gave them their head, unleash-
ing an orgy of confiscation and private revenge which plunged
the country into two miserable years of guerilla war. London
was the object of a particular hostility. A pardon for the city,
drawn up on the eve of its surrender, was immediately cancelled.
The list of Montfortian leaders prepared by city royalists was
received, acknowledged and forgotten. Scores of Londoners
were arrested, sixty taken as hostages. When most of the men at
Windsor were released on the 20th, five were detained as hostages for the whole city, three of them men who had remained
loyal to the king throughout the troubles.[2] It was symbolic.
Royal wrath was as indiscriminate as it was savage.

Two days after the surrender, the confiscations began.[3] The
Bridge was granted to Queen Eleanor who was to mismanage it
for ten years and more, Queenhithe reverted to Richard of
Cornwall and Walter de Merton annexed a great tract of Moorfields to his prebend of Finsbury. Lands, houses, tenements
were snatched from sixty citizens and distributed among the
hungry victors. Beneficiaries ranged from Henry of Almaine
and Roger Mortimer to the royal baker, but it was the friends
and dependants of Lord Edward who profited most, Otto de
Grandson, Robert Tybetot, Pain de Chaworth, the Lestrange
family seizing important properties, and clerks and serjeants
making hay among the *mediocres*. The popular leaders lost all
as a matter of course, but their opponents suffered almost as
badly. Philip le Tailor, Simon de Hadestok, Nicholas de Basing
and many other patricians lost houses and rents. The names of

---

[1] *Lib. de Ant. Leg.*, pp. 77–9; *Waverley*, p. 367; *Ann. Lond.*, pp. 70, 71; K.R.M.R.
40, m.11; *C.P.R. 1258–66*, pp. 457, 461, 463.

[2] *C.P.R. 1258–66*, p. 469; *Lib. de Ant. Leg.*, pp. 79, 80; *Waverley*, p. 367; *Wykes*,
p. 177.

[3] Confiscations of city property may be found in *C.P.R. 1258–66*, pp. 460–99,
with occasional examples in pp. 499–624; for supplementary information, see
C.P.R. 1266–72, pp. 14–630; *C.P.R. 1272–81*, pp. 275–381; *C.R. 1264–72, passim*;
C.Ch.R. 1257–1300, pp. 55–180; *Cal. Inq. Misc.*, i, 113–34; Cur. Reg. Rolls 175–98,
passim; A.R. 1207; K.R.M.R. 40; Chanc. Misc. 109/1; Hust. Roll (Land) 1;
Weinbaum, ii, 144, 149; *Hundred Rolls*, i, 403–33; *Cal. Letter-Bks. B, C,* and *Cal. of
Wills*, i, *passim*; *Lib. de Ant. Leg.*, pp. 120–1, 141–2.

fifty victims are known. Sixteen were certainly rebels and another six may well have been. In ten cases it is impossible to say, but nine men were certainly and nine others almost certainly royalists. Of the men despoiled after Evesham, over a third had been loyal supporters of the king.

If Henry failed to discriminate, what could be expected of his followers in the counties? 'Offence—a Londoner', curtly states the Suffolk plea-roll recording the expropriation of a city magnate in 1265. 'Londoner and enemy of the king', was warrant enough for John Renger to plunder the city royalist Gilbert le Quilter. A man in Derbyshire was driven from his lands simply because he had been in London on business when war broke out.[1] No fine distinctions clouded these minds. The losses of Tovy and Puleston in Northamptonshire and Surrey were dwarfed by the fury of spoliation which engulfed their former opponents. John de Gisors himself was expelled from his Kentish manor of Crayford. Thomas de Basing, Richard de Walbrook, Robert de Meldebourne were among the dispossessed.[2]

Londoners everywhere were at the mercy of the spoilers. At Ipswich they were flung into prison; at Lynn their goods were seized. The Isleworth bailiffs confiscated Stephen Eswy's river-borne corn as 'wreck'. Richard de Walbrook dared not claim his land at Horton, 'for fear of Windsor Castle'. The autumn months of 1265 were anarchic. And while the lands of royalists like Thomas de Cumbe were being plundered, William Makerel, one of fitz Thomas's right-hand men, was quietly taking wine to Windsor under safe-conduct.[3]

Before the end of October, Westminster Abbey's liberties had been restored and respect for them was written into the oath of city bailiffs. The Exchequer expelled John Juvenal from the shrievalty of Middlesex and for two years made a sustained attempt to prise the county free from its dependence on

---

[1] Cur. Reg. Roll 175, m.3; 177, m.3d; 181, m.6; 186, m.27d, and see A.R. 821 quoted in E. F. Jacob, *Studies in the Period of Baronial Reform and Rebellion 1258–67*, p. 325.

[2] See, for example, Cur. Reg. Roll 177, m.4, 22; 186, m.9; A.R. 59, m.1, 19d; A.R. 1207, m. 3d, 4d; *Cal. Inq. Misc.*, i, 208, 227, 247, 253, 269, 274; *C.P.R. 1258–66*, p. 586; *C.R. 1264–8*, p. 181.

[3] *C.P.R. 1258–66*, pp. 491, 520; *C.P.R. 1266–72*, p. 705; *C.R. 1264–8*, pp. 144, 145; A.R. 59, m.1; *Hundred Rolls*, i, 431.

London.[1] Within the city Henry appointed a bailiff to serve under the Constable of the Tower. He chose a newcomer, Walter Hervey, whose origins are impenetrably obscure. Hervey's brother was an Essex landowner, he himself had been a witness in Cheap and Vintry in 1253 and 1258, among aldermen and aldermen's sons. Before 1265 he cut no figure; it was in the harsh confusion of collapse that he began his brief and headstrong career in city politics. John Adrien the draper, an experienced royal agent, was appointed to assist him. In November royal wardens were appointed as well. The aldermen themselves were not restored until December, when Hervey succeeded fitz Thomas in Cheap and Adrien moved to Walbrook. Tovy's ward, Ludgate-Newgate, passed to Thomas de Arderne, to begin its curious fifty-year career as a private estate. The reality in this muddle was the power of Hervey, who came to exercise dictatorial authority.[2]

At last, on 5 December, the king ordered that Londoners were no longer to be molested, and on 10 January 1266 issued a formal pardon. The price was an enormous fine of 20,000 marks. All enemies of the king were to be expelled. In return all prisoners and hostages, except known enemies, were released and all goods restored. The king made a specific exception of Alderman Richard de Walbrook whose property had gone to Ebulo de Montibus. Henry wished the grant to stand, though he freely admitted that Walbrook had been loyal. In the end, the city paid 500 marks as the alderman's redemption.[3]

With the pardon, the threat of social disintegration was removed. But recovery was slow and painful. The dispossessed, in particular, faced a bleak future. London was excluded from the terms of the Dictum of Kenilworth and Henry evidently intended his grants to be permanent, as he made clear in a letter-patent as late as 1272.[4] In fact only nine restitutions of city property are documented, though probably many houses

---

[1] K.R.M.R. 40, m.8, 9d, 17, 18; 41, m.15; C.Ch.R. 1257–1300, pp. 238, 241; C.P.R. 1258–66, p. 588; W.A.M., Domesday, fo. 61, 66b.
[2] St. Paul's A/24/137, A/15/286; C.P.R. 1258–66, pp. 461, 463, 512, 576; Lib. de Ant. Leg., pp. 79, 80.
[3] C.P.R. 1258–66, pp. 519, 524, 530–1, 539; K.R.M.R. 40, m.15d; Lib. de Ant. Leg., pp. 80–2.
[4] C.P.R. 1266–72, pp. 14, 629–30.

were restored. They were a source of profit. Robert de Montpellier had to pay 100 marks for his, John de Warenne's fee
was £200.[1] Sales and bequests of the confiscated property
complicated the picture. Fitz Thomas's houses passed to an
abbey, Gratefig's to the Arras family. The victims, royalist and
rebel alike, had to face prolonged litigation. Not until 1269,
for example, did Richard Bonaventure get Hugh de Turberville
to accept his innocence. By this time, his houses had passed to a
goldsmith who resisted restitution, and though the case dragged
on into the seventies, Bonaventure got no satisfaction.[2] One of
Stephen Bukerel's houses was sold by Roger Mortimer to Walter
Hervey himself, then at the peak of his power, and Hervey refused to restore it to Stephen's mother Isabella. She ultimately
regained the property after Hervey's fall, but not until 1276,
after the case had been bundled to and fro between Husting and
Curia Regis for seven years.[3]

Outside the walls the confusion was worse. Not until 1267,
after the Dictum, did the royal courts seriously tackle the problems of restitution, which by that time were often incredibly
confused. The Londoners had to cut through a procedural
jungle of procrastination. Gisors, it is true, recovered Crayford
quite early, but Thomas de Basing seems to have lost his
Kentish property permanently, and men like Walbrook,
Meldebourne and John Norman regained their lands only
after long delays and stiff redemptions. Thomas Box, a Londoner who had been overseas buying stone for Westminster
throughout the troubles, found that his Yarmouth property
had been seized by William de St. Omer. He recovered it in
1269 only after an epic legal struggle and then had to pay
forty marks for the privilege.[4] Perhaps it was Alderman William
de Hadestok who savoured the full irony of all this. His father
had been one of the ardent royalists who met their deaths at

---

[1] K.R.M.R. 40, m.10; Cur. Reg. Roll 198, m. 20d.

[2] *C.P.R. 1258–66*, p. 463; *C.P.R. 1266–72*, p. 381; *C.R. 1268–72*, pp. 110, 134;
Chanc. Misc. 109/1(47); Cur. Reg. Roll 189, m. 16d; 191, m.1d.

[3] Cur. Reg. Roll 186, m.33; 189, m.10; Hust. Roll (Land) 1, m. 2, 10; 2, 3,
passim; *C.P.R. 1258–66*, p. 493; *C.R. 1268–72*, p. 102; *C.Ch.R. 1257–1300*, p. 177;
Cal. of Wills, i, 49–50.

[4] For the Box case, see Cur. Reg. Roll 185, m.12d; 186, m.27d; 191, m.6d;
193, m.16.

Lewes, but under Montfort he had entered easily into his inheritance. It was when his own party triumphed that he ran into trouble. His manor of Gravesend was seized after Evesham by Simon de Creye, and only in January 1269 did William win his case and the right to buy it back. Even so, the bishop of Rochester refused to admit Hadestok to the advowson of the church, and after fifteen months of haggling, the king suddenly annexed the advowson himself and amerced William for a false plea.[1]

'Needless to say, the atmosphere in the city remained poisonous. Even as the Legate and the Westminster courts fled to the Tower from the Disinherited, prisoners had to be moved from London because of its perilous insecurity.[2] The situation was explosive. In April 1266 the weary Londoners begged for the restoration of elective sheriffs. Henry allowed them to choose one bailiff, provided he had been a loyalist and swore to respect the liberties of Westminster. As soon as the news reached the city there was a Montfortian riot. Demonstrations continued all week and when the aldermen chose William fitz Richard on 6 May, a great crowd invaded Guildhall, shouting for Thomas fitz Thomas. The aldermen lost control and order was restored only when Roger Leyburn moved in with an armed force to clear the streets and round up the ringleaders.[3]'

The riot was crushed none too soon, for during this spring the rebels of 1263 began to filter back into public life. The first recorded release was on 1 March 1266, when a plumer who had been one of the leading figures of the popular commune was freed. Others followed, singly and in batches, and by September 1267, procedure had been formalized. A general order was then issued for the delivery of the remaining prisoners who were to pay a redemption and find sureties for good behaviour. Some, however, were still in prison in 1268.[4]

The rebel leaders had been handed over to Lord Edward and had to buy their freedom from him. The first was Stephen Bukerel, on 5 April 1266. John le Chapler followed three days

---

[1] *C.R. 1261-4*, p. 344; Cur. Reg. Roll 184a, m.9, 21; 189, m.16d; 193, m.1d, 33; 197, m.3; 198, m.2.

[2] K.R.M.R. 40, m.10, 13; *Lib. de Ant. Leg.*, p. 84; *C.R. 1264-8*, p. 157.

[3] *Lib. de Ant. Leg.*, pp. 84-6; *C.P.R. 1258-66*, p. 588; *C.R. 1264-8*, p. 191.

[4] *C.R. 1264-8*, pp. 174, 422, 428 and *passim*; *C.P.R. 1266-72*, p. 157.

later; Michael Tovy in June 1268. Chapler paid 500 marks, Tovy £200, and all were received into Edward's household as a protection against further punishment. Bukerel, however, had a hard time warding off his former victims. John Renger in particular pursued him throughout 1267, until the Londoner found final sanctuary in death in March 1268.[1]

John Renger was only one of a number of aggrieved royalists who sought recompense for the raids of 1263-4. He was soon joined by Peter of Savoy, Walter de Merton, the abbot of Westminster, and through 1266 and 1267 their pleas before the Curia Regis fill the rolls, giving brief glimpses into the reality of a bewildered and dislocated society. Time after time, the hearings are postponed as sheriffs fail to find the wanted men. Officers hunt for men already in prison; writs solemnly order the arrest of Earl Gilbert de Clare, his name buried in a motley horde of fishmongers and cordwainers; witnesses cannot reach Westminster because the roads are blocked by bands of the Disinherited; scores of Londoners run to the guerillas in Ely, to the pirates of the Cinque Ports, vanish into thin air. The lists of the accused and their pledges grow longer and longer until the cases, hardly any of which reached definite settlement, splutter out in a series of individual fines.[2]

These man-hunts could be ruinous. Walter de Moulsham, a small property-holder in Southwark, was so bludgeoned by claimants that by the seventies he figures as a footloose vagrant among the city gangs.[3] Other rebels lived through kaleidoscopic changes of fortune. William le Flaoner, a rebel mercer, for example, was imprisoned in October 1265, his property passing to Robert de Cornevill. Sometime in 1267 he was released and redeemed his houses, but in 1268 he was outlawed and his property was granted to one of Edward's serjeants. Pardoned in 1269, he was expelled from the city shortly afterwards in a general proscription of former Montfortians. In November 1273 he reappeared, suing for his houses in the

---

[1] *C.P.R. 1258-66*, p. 579; *C.P.R. 1266-72*, pp. 237-8; *C.R. 1264-8*, p. 543; Cur. Reg. Roll 181, m.27; 182, m.21d; A.R. 1207, m.9d.

[2] Cur. Reg. Rolls 175-85 and A. R. 1207, *passim.*

[3] A.R. 1207, m.3d, 4, 4d, 5, 9d; Cur. Reg. Roll 187, m.16; 197, m.10; *C.P.R. 1258-66*, p. 468; *C.P.R. 1266-72*, p. 273; *Cal. Letter-Bk. B*, 1-3.

Husting, but in 1274 he was again in prison. He was free in 1276, but never recovered his property.[1]

Punishment was the harsher because it was haphazard; some escaped scotfree. The very fabric of social life was corroded. Nor was settlement any nearer in the counties. The Dictum of Kenilworth brought no immediate relief despite the efforts of the Legate. The dreary guerilla war dragged on into the spring of 1267. The deadlock seemed unbreakable.

It was at this point that Gilbert de Clare, earl of Gloucester, decided to resolve it by an armed demonstration.[2] Mobilizing his men, he marched on London and early in April was at the gates. The Legate, his accomplice in the early stages at least, advised the bemused aldermen to admit him. No sooner was his army within the walls than John d'Eyvill and a band of Disinherited from Ely, evidently acting in collusion, swept into Southwark.

The response was instantaneous. The *populares* broke into insurrection. Seizing those of the patricians who had not fled, they handed them over to the earl and confiscated their property. The Newgate prisoners were freed, the aldermen deposed. The exiles returned and a Folkmoot elected two old enemies of the king to serve as bailiffs under Gloucester's warden.

For two months the rebels held the city. They dug great ditches around the walls, fortified Southwark, besieged the Tower. The Disinherited raided Kent and Surrey, and plundered the royal palace. Jews fled in panic to the Tower as the siege degenerated into a series of skirmishes in Middlesex and on the Thames. But this was not war, it was blackmail. Moderate opinion seized the opportunity and by the end of June Gloucester had made his peace. Royal power was re-established, bailiffs and aldermen reinstated.

Brief and inhibited though it was, the outbreak of 1267 was an authentic expression of the spirit of 1263. Within a few weeks

[1] *C.P.R. 1258–66*, p. 467; *C.P.R. 1266–72*, pp. 244, 378, 447; *Cal. Inq. Misc.*, i, 326; *Hundred Rolls*, i, 431; Hust. Roll (Land) 1, m. 2, 4; *Lib. de Ant. Leg.*, pp. 120–1; Misc. Roll BB, m.3.

[2] For this episode, see *Lib. de Ant. Leg.*, pp. 90–5; *Wykes*, pp. 199–203 (who construes the execution of looters by drowning as a 'massacre'); *Flores*, iii, 14–16; *C.P.R. 1266–72*, pp. 71–222. Beaven, i, 369, errs in relating the keeping of wards by two royal appointees in 1265–66 to this rising.

of the rising, tailors and cordwainers were fighting in the streets against their rivals, the goldsmiths and parmenters, to be silenced only when thirty-six of them were imprisoned and thirteen hanged.[1] The menace of a popular revolt seemed more real than ever. The immediate consequence of Gloucester's coup, however, was the re-establishment of aldermanic power by a chastened king. For the adventure succeeded. The Disinherited made their peace, and the country relaxed. In London, royal policy mellowed, and in March 1268 a charter confirmed many of the traditional liberties. When Lord Edward took control of the city in Lent 1269, the pace of recovery quickened.[2] It was at this juncture, however, that the beckoning horizon was clouded. For in April 1269 the king, in response to complaints, appointed a commission of enquiry into the tallages levied to raise the great fine of 20,000 marks.[3]

The fine had caused trouble from the beginning. Henry needed 30,000 pounds Tournois to redeem his rights in the Limousin, sold to Louis of France during the wars, and over 10,000 marks was gouged out of the Londoners by February 1266, within a month of the pardon, some of it being paid in halfpennies. Since Louis renounced his damages, the money passed to Lord Edward, who used it to settle his debts and reward his friends.[4] The remainder of the fine was spent on all manner of objects, the duke of Brunswick's marriage to the king's niece, the maintenance of the Tower, payments to the merchants of Douai and Ghent.[5]

To raise such sums at such speed, the king resorted to forced loans from individuals, covered by recognizances executed in the name of the city. This caused endless trouble. For the payment to Louis, Thomas de Basing and Geoffrey de Winton handed over £1,428 and the city haggled over repayment. Distraint encountered boycott, arbitration failed, creditors called in their loans, and the envenomed dispute lasted for years.[6]

---

[1] *Lib. de Ant. Leg.*, pp. 98-9; parmenters were a subsidiary tailoring craft.
[2] *C.Ch.R. 1257-1300*, p. 98; *Lib. de Ant. Leg.*, pp. 102-5, 108-10.
[3] *C.P.R. 1266-72*, p. 335.   [4] *C.P.R. 1258-66*, pp. 548, 554, 650, 658, 662, 667.
[5] *C.P.R. 1258-66*, pp. 567, 594, 613; *C.P.R. 1266-72*, pp. 10, 35, 467; K.R.M.R. 41, m.13; 42, m.20.
[6] K.R.M.R. 40, m.13d, 14; 42, m.17d; see also Cur. Reg. Roll 186, m.25d; 193, m.3.

Hasty assessment was another grievance. For the Brunswick donation the bailiffs levied £560 from eight men without normal inquest, according to fitz Thedmar. The chronicler himself suffered. Having paid four marks on his house and then twenty-five marks by inquest of his neighbours, he was assessed at no less than 100 marks in the Brunswick tallage, followed later by half a mark and fifteen shillings on his rent. He claimed that royalists were singled out by the collectors.[1] This may have been true. They were rich. They were also articulate and before the end of 1266, their plaints had forced the appointment of a commission of enquiry. Many were excused further payment. Purchases of exemption multiplied. The familiar pattern reappeared. The purchasers were all magnates, Philip le Tailor, fitz Thedmar, the Cornhills, the Basings. The popular reaction was no less familiar. There were angry demands that the 'arrears' be raised from these men.[2] It was in response to this clamour that the new commission was appointed in April 1269.

It could not have come at a worse moment. For within a few days Thomas fitz Thomas was free, paying a redemption of £500. He was released to twenty-eight sureties and admitted to Edward's household.[3] The resurrection of the old tax grievance and the reappearance of the popular champion galvanized the council. With full power within their grasp, they did not hesitate.

Working in close harmony with the Court, they enforced rigorous police measures and ordered a special watch against treason. The old proscription lists of 1265 were dug out and brought up to date, fitz Thedmar adorned his chronicle with atrocity stories of the popular commune, and finally, on 21 December, the roll of nearly sixty former rebels was read out in Guildhall, the royal warrant proclaimed, and two days before Christmas, the Montfortians were expelled from the city, threatened with death if they returned. This Draconian measure was followed, early in 1270, by a special letter to the king in which the city pledged its absolute fidelity and obtained a

[1] *Lib. de Ant. Leg.*, pp. 239, 240; *C.P.R. 1266-72*, p. 590.
[2] *C.P.R. 1266-72*, pp. 126 and *passim*; K.R.M.R. 40, 42, *passim*; *Hundred Rolls*, i, 403-33, *passim*; *Lib. de Ant. Leg.*, pp. 240-2.
[3] *C.R. 1268-72*, pp. 103-4; *C.P.R. 1266-72*, p. 328; *Ann. Lond.*, p. 80.

R

promise that if treason were committed, individual traitors, not the commune as a whole, would be punished. It was in this harsh climate that London regained its liberty. The citizens made a 'gift' of 600 marks, raised the farm to £400 a year, and at Whitsun 1270, elective mayor and sheriffs were restored. After an irregular term of a few months, John Adrien was formally elected mayor on the traditional date of 28 October.[1]

The dynasties, however, faced a problematical future. After twelve years of complete abnormality, their hold on the city was broken. Obedience was no longer instinctive and the turmoil after Evesham had distorted the pattern of civic loyalties out of all recognition. The great quarrel had dissolved into a multiplicity of private discontents and disaffection had spread upward. There was a new spirit abroad, too, a weariness of communal disorder, a novel readiness to welcome the intervention of a Crown all too ready to intervene. For as the aldermen began to rebuild their broken commune, they did so in the shadow of the strongest king medieval England had yet seen.

[1] *Lib. de Ant. Leg.*, pp. 114, 115, 119–21, 124, 127, 128–30.

CHAPTER IX

The Intervention of Edward I 1270–99

ALDERMANIC authority was restored in 1270. Within two years, it was challenged by a sudden resurgence of popular hostility. This, the last crisis of the time of troubles, centred on the personality of Walter Hervey. His appointment as bailiff in 1265 had catapulted him from obscurity to headship of the council. In 1267 he was made royal escheator in the city; his wife was a recipient of Henry's bounty. For five years he had exercised virtually dictatorial power and he was slow to adopt the modesty proper to the new situation. Fitz Thedmar is full of complaints against his wilfulness. He was, however, an alderman and an influential figure and after Adrien's term, his colleagues duly elected him mayor. Thereafter relations deteriorated rapidly. His protracted dispute with Isabella Bukerel over Stephen's tenement was the subject of unfavourable comment, his attitude to the victuallers was suspect. In July 1272 a second royal commission was appointed to look into the 'arrears' of the great fine, for the first had completely failed to stem the mounting tide of popular protest. Hervey served on it and the joyful zest with which he pursued the exemption-purchasers was the last straw. In October the aldermen decided to replace him with Philip le Tailor.[1]

They underestimated their man. Hervey would not relinquish power so easily.[2] The 'arrears' gave him a perfect campaign issue, and he mobilized the *populares*. More, he organized them more effectively than ever before. On election day, a great crowd burst into Guildhall and forcibly installed Hervey in the

---

[1] *C.P.R. 1258–66*, pp. 504, 576; *C.P.R. 1266–72*, pp. 93, 126, 166, 287, 334, 435, 506–7, 705; *C.R. 1264–8*, pp. 185, 245, 280; *Lib. de Ant. Leg.*, pp. 118, 119, 122, 142, 145, 239, 240.

[2] For the election of 1272, see *Lib. de Ant. Leg.*, pp. 148–53.

mayoral chair, and when the aldermen fled to Westminster, where the king lay dying, they followed, on foot and horseback. Hervey organized a virtual siege of the palace, with crowds demonstrating every day for over a fortnight, chanting, 'We, we are the commune of the city. To us belongs the election of the mayor!' He imposed fines on absentees, raised a political levy of forty marks to finance the campaign, kept up the pressure until the nonplussed Council referred the issue to arbitration. Philip le Tailor's arbitrators were all patricians, Hervey's, significantly, included not only the brother of the former Montfortian sheriff William Gratefig and a girdler who had been a rebel in 1263, but three substantial merchants who had been royalist during the troubles. When the arbitrators failed to agree, there was talk of an uprising to coincide with Henry's death, a coup forestalled by the speedy proclamation of Edward's peace and the dispatch of Gloucester to the city. When Gloucester arrived, he encountered a well-organized demonstration by the Hervey men and at a Folkmoot on 18 November, gave his decision in favour of the *populares*. Having promised immunity to his opponents, Hervey was proclaimed mayor.

Once more a radical, or one who passed for radical, sat in Guildhall.[1] The banished rebels of 1269 streamed back. The 'arrears' were pursued, the Husting of land pleas suspended. This time the crafts dominated the scene. Hervey set the civic seal to the coveted ordinances of cordwainers, girdlers, woolpackers, joiners; enemies claimed that he was paid a salary by the fishmongers, that he let the bakers go unsupervised, that his sheriffs had been bought by the gilds. Whatever the truth of these charges, it is certain that under Hervey, the identification of the popular movement with the crafts was carried a stage further.

He was riding high. He held the mayoralty by warrant of the Council, acted as soke-reeve for Westminster, Holywell and Bermondsey Priory, served as attorney to Henry's widow herself. His action and oratory won him the crafts and captured the imagination of the populace. The Hundred juries a few

---

[1] For Hervey's mayoralty, see *Lib. de Ant. Leg.*, pp. 160–70; Hust. Roll 6(52)(53); 19(44); Hust. Roll (Common Pleas) 1, m.1; *C.R. 1268–72*, p. 201; *C.C.R. 1272–9*, p. 527; *C.P.R. 1272–81*, pp. 32, 70; *Hundred Rolls*, i, 403–33, *passim*.

years later were full of his doings. But it could not last. There was no continuity of confidence. The tough royal bailiff of 1265 was, after all, a paradoxical leader for a popular movement. Charges of bribery were frequent and sustained. He was accused of fraud over the appointment of attorneys, of suspending the land pleas in order to escape Isabella Bukerel. Within a year his support was fading and in October 1273 there was no repetition of the scenes of the previous year.

The aldermen turned anxiously to another of the strong-willed outsiders of the post-Evesham period and installed Henry le Waleys as mayor.[1] Waleys, certainly an immigrant and possibly a Welshman from the Chepstow district, had prospered in the wine trade, averaging some £230 a year in sales to the Household between 1259 and 1263. An attempt to make him bailiff in 1265 foundered on his ambiguous record during the wars, for he had been involved in the raids of 1264, but in 1269, after massive property purchases in London and Kent and a marriage to Joan daughter of Adam de Basing, he became alderman of Cordwainer. By 1270 he had bought his tallage-exemption, served as sheriff and become thoroughly respectable.

He liquidated the popular movement with a swift and authoritarian brusqueness which was to become characteristic of the man. He rounded up the returned exiles and threw them into Newgate, arrested Hervey's sheriffs for corruption. He re-established control over the victuallers and in December, when litigation over one of Hervey's craft-charters was referred to the aldermen, seized the opportunity to undo the popular movement's prime achievement. Powerfully supported by Gregory de Rokesle, he denounced the charters in council. Hervey countered with a public meeting at St. Peter's in Cheap and for two days moved from meeting to meeting, rallying the craftsmen. Waleys had him attached by writ and in January 1274 the aldermen formally annulled the charters.[2]

Waleys went on to reimpose the trade regulations and bully the negligent bakers. At Whitsun, Edward arrived in England

---

[1] An outline of Waleys's career, with references, is given in the biographical notes of the Appendix.

[2] *Lib. de Ant. Leg.*, pp. 159, 162, 163, 164–6, 171; *Hundred Rolls*, i, 404.

and to greet him, Waleys put through a project always near to the heart of the Court. With fearful abruptness he swept away the butchers' and fishmongers' stalls which cluttered Cheap, in open defiance of the lease they had bought with contributions to the city farm. Once more Hervey moved to the attack and the streets were loud with protest. Guildhall was invaded and the relevant Husting roll breaks off abruptly after the terse entry 'Walter Hervey came with a great crowd. . . .' On 28 May the ex-mayor stirred up the fishmongers against Waleys in the Husting itself.[1]

The mayor, however, who had been among the first to greet Edward on his arrival, saw the Council, and with royal backing for every step he took, summoned Hervey to Guildhall and formally arraigned him. The charges ranged over the whole period from 1265, covering Walter's alleged misdeeds, not only as radical mayor but as royal bailiff. After a ceremonial recitation of his sins, he was deposed from his aldermanry and excluded for ever from the counsel of the city.[2]

So ended the public career of this, the most enigmatic of London's mayors. For Waleys, his was just beginning.[3] He had made his mark on a mind more important than Hervey's. This imbroglio was Edward's first contact, as king, with the turbulent politics of London. His immediate response was to make the incisive Waleys his man. Before the autumn he transferred the Londoner to another trouble spot, Bordeaux, where in 1275 he presided over the warring clans as royal mayor. For the rest of his days, Waleys lived as a king's officer, travelling on Edward's intimate business from Berwick to Bayonne, serving as his personal liaison officer with the merchants and the Seneschal of Gascony, helping to plan towns and administer commercial edicts. He served on judicial commissions, witnessed deeds among those high officials of the Exchequer whom his son, Augustine de Uxbridge, was shortly to join as one of Edward II's keepers of Exchange. Edmund, earl of Cornwall, and Henry III's widow were his patrons; the Burnells were his

---

[1] *Lib. de Ant. Leg.*, pp. 164-6; Hust. Roll (Land) 1, m.4; (Common Pleas), 2, m.8.

[2] *Lib. de Ant. Leg.*, pp. 168-70; Hust. Roll (Common Pleas) 2, m.6, 8.

[3] All references for his career may be found in the biographical sketch in the Appendix.

friends. With houses in Boston and Berwick, two manors in Essex, another in Kent, and property clustered thickly in Westminster and fifteen London parishes (three pieces alone worth 140 marks a year), he moved easily among the Court retinue he entertained so magnificently in his mansions. In March 1299, the Great Council summoned after Edward's return from Scotland actually assembled in the Londoner's hall in Stepney.

Edward soon had need of such a man on his home ground. After Waleys's departure, the aldermen inaugurated the sedate seven-year mayoralty of Gregory de Rokesle. The Rokesles were a family of Kentish franklins.[1] Gregory himself held the manors of Rokesley and Lullingstone as demesne land, and in the sixties and seventies he and Robert, possibly a brother, served as aldermen, to be followed in a few years by four kinsmen on the council, with half a dozen others among the assembly-men. For two generations the Rokesles peopled the political society of London. Gregory, alderman of Dowgate for twenty-six years from 1265, was by far the most successful. Nominally a goldsmith, he exported wool, dealt in corn, fish and cloth, and was one of the great men of the wine trade, with interests ranging from Bruges to Bordeaux and Dublin. Royal butler from 1266, he became Master of Exchange in 1279, working closely with the king's Italians and Gascons, Poncius de Mora, Orlandino de Podio, the Pulci, the Bardi. Active in the royal service, planning towns, collecting taxes, lending money, serving as commissioner for the Anglo-Flemish dispute in 1275, he was one of the few Londoners to enjoy Edward's bounty—a wardship worth £200 a year in 1273, a marriage three years later, gifts, quittance of common summons, tax-exemptions. Between 1276 and 1291, no fewer than thirty-two judicial commissions were issued to him. His city estate, centring on a great mansion in Cornhill and embracing the entire patrimony of William Hardel, extended over twelve parishes and was acquired almost in its entirety in the five years after 1278, while outside he held eight manors, five of them in Kent. On his death in 1291, the chronicler Andrew Horn saw no ambiguity in placing his obituary next to that of the queen-mother.

[1] An outline of Rokesle's career, with references, is given in the biographical notes of the Appendix.

Gregory's nephew inherited and the Rokesles disappeared from the patriciate within two generations of their entry, but the man himself was outstanding, perhaps the last Londoner to play the grand patrician in the peculiar thirteenth-century style.

His administration was no less traditional. Rokesle was content to govern in the accepted empirical and practical spirit, the spirit which informed the appointment of a staff of official scavengers at this time. It was during his mayoralty that the former dissidents of 1263 were readmitted to society. At the Iter of 1276, it is true, the aldermen had Michael Tovy hanged for 'robberies', but this was an exception.[1] The old popular leaders were in any case a spent force. Bukerel died in 1268. Fitz Thomas himself was dead by 1276, leaving one son burdened with debt, another living outside the city.[2] It was 1275 before Puleston emerged from prison, to die within two years; 1285 before Alexander le Ferrun returned.[3] By 1280, old rebels like John de Stepney and William May were serving as councillors.[4]

Consolidation was the hallmark of the régime. In 1275, for example, the council redefined citizenship. The three lawful methods were specified and enforced and civic record made the ultimate warrant. As a corollary, Rokesle subjected city custom to a detailed re-examination, embodying the final decisions in his *Assizes*. From this mayoralty comes the only record of an administrative assembly of earlier date than 1285. City archives register the first indications of that marked improvement in administrative technique characteristic of the reign. The class of professional clerks and legists began to establish its virtual monopoly of administrative jobs, to acquire a distinctive personality. It was in 1280 that a gild of lawyers was established by mayoral decree. In 1280, too, Ralph Crepyn, the first recognizable

---

[1] *French Chronicle*, p. 14.

[2] Misc. Roll BB, m. 3, 5; Recog. Roll 1(187); Hust. Roll 12(96)(97)(102)(103); 14(158d); 15(10); 18(98d); *Cal. Letter-Bk. A*, 51, 53, 70, 139, 159.

[3] *C.P.R. 1272-81*, pp. 92, 94, 140; *C.P.R. 1281-92*, p. 151; *Cal. Letter-Bk. B*, 59, 202; *Cal. of Wills*, i, 31, 32.

[4] For former rebels holding official positions, see, for example, Hust. Roll (Common Pleas) 1, m.1; 2, m.1d, 4; Hust. Roll (Land) 1, m.1, 7; Misc. Roll BB, m.4, 5; St. Paul's A/12/1128.

Common Clerk, reached the aldermanic council, the first specialized civic administrator to do so.[1]

Crepyn, however, was better known for a less reputable reason. He was locked in vendetta with Laurence Duket. Duket was a goldsmith of good family, a friend of the Gisors, his supporters drawn from a respectable milieu of goldsmiths and vintners. In 1273 his sister had sold houses to the clerk and the feud may have originated in a loan. For Crepyn was a moneylender and, though connected with the cadet branch of the Gloucester family, a new man in the patriciate. There was a woman involved, Ralph's 'amisia', Alice atte Bowe, who apparently kept a tavern in Mark Lane. She was a member or dependant of the Laufare family, a clan of cutlers and cordwainers destined to produce an alderman in the next generation but one which had been prominent among the rebels of 1263. They were active supporters of Crepyn; so was his nephew Peter, another cordwainer, and John Tolosan, grandson of one of the aldermen deposed in 1258. Both sides resorted to force and their clashes disturbed the peace. But while both employed professional thugs from the underworld, Crepyn, it seems, could rely on fellow clerks within the administration to cover his tracks.[2] Indeed, in another case in 1279, a woman plaintiff claimed that he had for ten years used his Clerkship to shield himself from the law.[3]

In the envenomed atmosphere of the years after Evesham feuds had multiplied and it is distinctly possible that London was suffering from something akin to livery and maintenance. Certainly in the last years of Rokesle's mayoralty there were signs of mounting dissatisfaction. The Hundred juries were still loud for Hervey. In 1280 there was a special watch against buckler-play. Royal denunciation of lax administration grew more frequent, and more striking still, Londoners in increasing number began to appeal to the king against their own magistrates. Between 1277 and 1281, in an unprecedented volume

---

[1] For these aspects of Rokesle's mayoralty, see *Ann. Lond.*, pp. 85-6; *Cal. Letter-Bk. A*, 183-4, 211-12, 217-19; *Lib. Cust.*, pp. 99-100, 280-3; *Lib. Albus*, pp. 570-2; Beaven, i, 376.

[2] For the feud, see *Ann. Lond.*, pp. 92-3; Hust. Roll 5(2)(3); 14(9); *Cal. Letter-Bk. A*, 156, *B*, 1, 2, 3, 81, 261, 263-4.

[3] *C.P.R. 1272-81*, pp. 285, 339-40.

of complaint, no fewer than ten citizen appeals to Westminster, one levelled against a kinsman of the mayor himself, accused the Husting of sheltering delinquent aldermen.[1]

'Nulla inquisicio recte facta est in Civitate Londoniarum'— the protest of the justices in 1244 was the perennial complaint of monarchy.[2] In writ after writ in the eighties it was voiced by Edward with increasing asperity. Criminals were escaping, the assizes were not properly kept, inquests were faulty, city law full of quirks and oddities. The sheriffs, his officers, feared legal reprisal, an abomination which could exist only within the suspect sanctuary of the franchise.[3] It is difficult to assess the truth of his charges. The earliest surviving presentments for breaches of the peace date from the autumn of 1281 when, over a few weeks, sixty-nine men were accused of crimes ranging from murder to 'setting up games'. Twenty-six were acquitted, a large number of youths, often of good family, found guilty of minor but noisy offences. Over a dozen, however, went about armed to the teeth after curfew and eight were found to be professional 'Roarers' available for hire.[4] There was evidently some demand for their services. It is doubtful, however, whether disorder was exceptional. The novelty lay, probably, not in the situation, but in the king's reaction to it.

For it echoed a deeper dissonance. Edward's reign represents the apogee of kingship in medieval England, as the Crown, using its prerogative to the limit, tried to shape and direct the processes of social growth, to give legal definition to the national community. The struggles with Wales, Scotland and France transformed the English economy. Edward mobilized the merchants, established the first recorded wool-staple in the Low Countries. The Italian bankers occupied the centre of the new system. The traditional commercial practice of London patricians was out of phase with the new rhythms of royal policy; Edward, dependent on his Italian creditors and anxious to tap the wealth of England, found the franchise of a jealous citizenry a major obstacle to the free flow of trade. No less productive of

---

[1] *C.P.R. 1272–81*, pp. 99, 239, 406, 407, 409, 411, 414, 456, 460, 472, 474.

[2] Misc. Roll AA, p. 12.

[3] Among many examples, see *Cal. Letter-Bk. C*, 15–17; Lib. Ordinationum, fo. 197.

[4] *Cal. Letter-Bk. B*, 1–12.

friction was his sweeping legislative activity, for to the author of the great statutes London's juridical peculiarity was a flaw in the pattern of the new community he and his officers were consciously shaping.[1]

He was no stranger to urban contentiousness. In Bordeaux he permitted free elections for only ten years; in Bayonne, he confined the mayoralty to three loyal families. Feuds had undone these communes as they ruined Dax, Libourne and La Réole. In England, Lincoln lost its liberty in 1290, after petitions against misgovernment from lesser citizens and the new charter of Hull in 1299 expressly ordered government by royal agents. Royal administrative policy, the introduction of a higher borough rate in national taxation, the tightening-up of the police system in the Statute of Winchester, tended to reduce the number of free boroughs, while in those which remained, Edward tried to reassert royal control over those functions, such as the administration of the food assizes, which he considered the peculiar preserve of monarchy. Acutely aware of the wealth and talent of the towns, the king was determined that they should be applied to the national welfare as he saw it. In practice this implied the imposition of as much royal control as townsmen would stomach, generally in the form of indirect rule by a nominated mayor or one prepared to take orders, with destruction of the franchise as a final sanction.[2]

In London the process was eased by an abrupt change in the character of aldermanic service in the royal administration. From 1272, gone were the happy days of six oaks from this forest and six bucks from that. Only Waleys and Rokesle enjoyed patronage comparable to that which had nourished a score of their predecessors under Henry III. Royal generosity dried up and the greater posts passed to Gascons and Italians. Aldermen's service became more specialized. They found a humbler niche for themselves in the Customs, the wool-staple, in prisages and levies, and the number of mercantile aldermen

---

[1] On the reign of Edward I see, in particular, F. M. Powicke, *The Thirteenth Century*, and T. F. T. Plucknett, *Legislation of Edward I* (Oxford, 1949).

[2] For his urban policy, see C. Petit-Dutaillis, *Les communes françaises*, bk. ii, especially pp. 159–67; J. W. F. Hill, *Medieval Lincoln* (London, 1948), pp. 213–16, 239–40; J. Tait, *The Medieval English Borough*, pp. 201–13.

who entered the king's service fell by a tenth.[1] On the other hand, there was a sharp increase in the number of royal officers who acquired aldermanries, men like Joce l'Akatur who married into the former rebel family of Heyrun, a Wardrobe buyer who entered the council in the last years of his life.[2] Bartholomew de Castell, alderman of Cripplegate, was a Household official and financier, served as clerk to Burnell himself, drew Edward's livery, and ended his days as a canon of Wells.[3] Without law-schools of its own, the city drew so heavily on those outside the walls that the patriciate tended increasingly to crystallize around a Westminster-Guildhall axis.

Public attitude responded, for many were weary of faction. In 1303 the irascible councillor Peter de Berneval prayed aloud in the mayor's court for the end of the commune and the return of the royal warden, 'because business was dealt with speedily under him'.[4] He voiced an opinion which was without doubt prevalent in the eighties, when a 'king's party', at least in the passive sense, was a reality in the city. This confluence of royal and popular discontents finally submerged the hesitant traditionalism of Rokesle. In October 1281 Henry le Waleys returned to the mayoralty.[5]

The most ardent disciplinarian could not have foreseen the result. Waleys launched a drive for order and efficiency such as London had never experienced in peace-time. A great series of peace ordinances was promulgated. Inns, hostels and their inmates were enrolled; the trades were to keep lists, all over twelve were to be registered. Sweeping police action followed, experiments with the watch, a drive against curfew-breakers. There was a massive enquiry into the trades, revision of craft ordinances. Cheap was cleared again. The placid confines of Guildhall

---

[1] See table of aldermanic interests in the Appendix; for some examples of typical aldermanic service, see K.R. Acc. V. (Army and Navy) E101/5/13, 14; C.C.R. 1302-7, pp. 137, 147; C.P.R. 1281-92, pp. 3, 58, 81 and passim.

[2] For l'Akatur, see Lib. Roll 48, m.12; 51, m.6; Misc. Roll BB, m.1; K.R. Acc. V. (Alien Merchants) E101/126/27, m.3; Hust. Roll 5(64); 9(51)(52); 12(4) (109); St. Paul's A/14/1184; C.C.R. 1272-9, p. 118; C.C.R. 1279-88, p. 470; C.P.R. 1281-92, pp. 118, 287.

[3] The key references for Castell are: Hust. Roll 16(125); 22(104); 24(57); 27(2); Chanc. Misc. 3/21(18); Lib. Roll 50, m.6; C.R. 1231-4, p. 90; C.R. 1264-8, pp. 262, 399; C.P.R. 1266-72, pp. 596, 651; C.P.R. 1272-81, p. 301; Cal. of Wills, i, 128.

[4] Cal. E.M.C. Rolls, pp. 146-7.   [5] Beaven, i, 375.

were enlivened by edicts remodelling juries, forbidding the leasing of Middlesex, calling for the utmost despatch in executive action. Waleys tried a bold and imaginative experiment in civic estate-building, creating a new victuals market at the Stocks and a new housing project near St. Paul's to finance the maintenance of Bridge. And all legislation was enforced by a virtually continuous process of inquest and presentment.[1]

'No mayor could act in this manner without some warrant stronger than communal precedent. Within a month of his election, a royal writ instructed him to take extraordinary measures to restore good order, and in 1283 Edward expressly ordered justices not to molest the mayor for his new methods and penalties. Forty years later the Londoners were to claim that Waleys acted throughout on royal orders.[2] It is this which explains the furious controversy which attended two of his edicts in particular. The mayor created an entirely new prison for curfew-breakers, the Tun on Cornhill, and, setting up weigh-beams for the pesage of corn en route to the mills, inflicted novel and harsher penalties on scores of convicted bakers and millers. Only eight aldermen attended the council which promulgated these ordinances and controversy over them runs like a red thread through the next twenty years.[3] For they touched the nerve of the franchise. Keeping of the peace and of the food assizes was at once the hallmark of a free borough and the special preserve of monarchy.[4] That the mayor's edicts should encounter such resistance is itself adequate testimony to the real meaning of his mayoralty.'

For three years he had enough support to override the opposition of the traditionally minded. But the Stocks created a new interest and disturbed the balance in the victualling trades; his new houses rose around St. Paul's only to the accompaniment of litigious outcry, and with every edict his following

---

[1] Numerous copies of his edicts exist; see, for example, *Cal. Letter-Bk. A*, 184, 206, 221, *C*, 6, 55, 84-5, and *passim*; Lib. Ordinationum, fo. 225 ff.; *Lib. Cust.*, pp. 91, 95, 96, 120, 213, and *passim*; Hust. Roll 14(10); *C.P.R. 1281-92*, pp. 23, 24, 193-4, 226.

[2] *C.P.R. 1281-92*, p. 80; *Cal. Letter-Bk. A*, 213; *Lib. Cust.*, pp. 328-9.

[3] For these ordinances and the controversy, see, for example, *Cal. Letter-Bk. A*, 120, 121, 208, 211, 213, *B*, 13, 14, 241, 243-4, *C*, 15-17, 84, 85 and *passim; Lib. Cust.*, pp. 82-3, 213, 292, 326; *Ann. Lond.*, p. 90.

[4] See J. Tait, *op. cit.*, 208.

dwindled. In October 1284 the aldermen restored Gregory de Rokesle to the mayoralty.[1]

Their timing was singularly unfortunate, for at the end of July, the feud between Ralph Crepyn and Laurence Duket had erupted into armed conflict in the middle of Cheap. Duket wounded the alderman, and pursued by Crepyn's supporters, fled for sanctuary to St. Mary le Bow. He found none. At midnight his enemies broke in and hanged him in the church. As additional horror, they tried to disguise the murder as suicide. The outraged king demanded action. Crepyn was deprived of Clerkship and aldermanry and sent to the Tower. With him went his fellow clerks, the rector of St. Mary and Jordan Godchep the sheriff. There were hangings and Alice atte Bowe was burned alive.[2] But hard on this shock came the rejection of Waleys and the reassertion of patrician independence. Events must have made an ominous conjuncture in Edward's mind.

It was after a winter loud with echoes of the Duket murder that he made his decision. Early in the summer of 1285 he announced that he was sending John de Kirkby and a special commission of judges to the Tower to examine the state of public order in London. On 10 June, nineteen days before their coming, he issued a letter-patent. The area around St. Paul's, he asserted, had become the haunt of thieves and vagabonds and he empowered the cathedral to enclose and incorporate it in the churchyard.[3] The 'area around St. Paul's' was nothing less than the site of the Folkmoot and the Muster. The moot was the primal city assembly, the muster the characteristic expression of communal patriotism. By this time, neither was much more than an institutional fossil, but both were integral and basic components of civic tradition. The sites were the city's freehold and there had been no preliminary inquest of any kind. As late as the Iter of 1321, when Hamo de Chigwell tried to reverse the decision, the insult still rankled.[4]

Among the aldermen, Stephen Eswy took the lead. Nephew to the chronicler fitz Thedmar and a friend of John de Gisors,

---

[1] *Ann. Lond.*, p. 93; Beaven, i, 374.
[2] *Ann. Lond.*, pp. 92, 93.
[3] St. Paul's A/70/1756; *Ann. Lond.*, pp. 94-5; *Lib. Cust.*, pp. 338-44.
[4] See *Lib. Cust.*, pp. 338-44.

Eswy, with his manors in Kent and his impeccable pedigree, was a fit spokesman for the dynasties.[1] On 30 June, at his prompting, Gregory de Rokesle resigned the mayoralty and presented himself before Kirkby as an ordinary citizen, in protest and rebuke. Royal reaction was swift. Eswy was banished to Windsor, eighty Londoners were detained at Westminster and a few imprisoned. The city was taken into the king's hands and Sir Ralph de Sandwich moved into Cornhill to occupy Crepyn's confiscated houses. On 1 July he was appointed royal warden and the king's officers took control.[2] It is difficult to avoid the inference that Edward acted deliberately, in full awareness of the inevitable consequences. As with the Welsh three years earlier, his opponents had been induced to become the authors of their own destruction.

The new régime was launched with irresistible éclat. The king's men moved in with a zeal for organization and a sense of mission quite alien to civic tradition. They worked through Rokesle's *Assizes*, clause by clause, and finally published their decisions in a formal proclamation, the *Ordinances*. This was a complete code of city government. The premier city of the realm was to be subjected to the direct authority of royal officers operating on a basis of consent. In their peace regulations, the *Ordinances* echo the statutes of Westminster and Winchester, in their commercial clauses, they foreshadow *Carta Mercatoria* of 1303. They were the manifesto of a model régime.[3]

The multitudinous police regulations, which bulk largest, were a development of Waleys's edicts, and with their stress on deterrent and swift punishment, not novel in themselves, but the crisp, strong clauses were all directed at the massive reinforcement of the executive arm and the bludgeoning of the public into a sense of responsibility. More striking were the commercial edicts. With a stark and shattering simplicity, one revolutionary clause ordered the immediate admission of alien merchants to full citizenship rights. At one stroke, in theory at least, the

---

[1] For Eswy, see W.A.M. 9, 42, 52, 80; A.R. 543, m.10; A.R. 538, m.7; St. Paul's A/25A/1731; *Cal. of Wills*, i, 22, 122, 435.

[2] *Ann. Lond.*, pp. 94, 95; *C.P.R. 1281–92*, pp. 182, 357; *Lib. Cust.*, p. 240.

[3] The *Ordinances* were copied, in part or entirety, into several city custumals, e.g., *Lib. Albus*, pp. 280–97; the fullest version and the basis of this section of the text, is found in Lib. Ordinationum, fo. 197–202b.

whole laborious edifice of monopoly was broken and citizenship itself drained of one vital meaning. Aliens were empowered
to inspect city balances, their lands and debts were protected,
they were to have a piepowder court daily and to provide
half the jury in cases which concerned them. Similarly, the most
detailed regulations shielded peasant importers from the sharp
practice of city victuallers and every opportunity was taken to
pare down citizen immunity. Intransigence and inertia blunted
the operation of these decrees. There was a running fight with
Arnold de Hispannia and his Gascons and a violent revulsion
under Edward II, but many proved permanent and they profoundly modified the commercial structure and climate of
London.

City law was no more immune. Writs of customs and services and devised lands were to be pleaded according to old
usage, but every other judgment in the Husting was henceforth
to be by the common law of England, and that strictly. All
juries were now to be sworn, trespass was to go to inquest not
compurgation, new actions were provided where city law had
supplied no remedy. Court procedure was reformed, all rolls
duplicated. In all fields much more attention than ever before
was paid to system and record.[1] Assemblies became regular,
records multiplied. London was integrated more fully into the
national system.

It was an abrupt modernization whose cumulative effects
were far-reaching. But there was a price. 'Et le Roy veult que
touz entendent qe nule fraunchise ne aucune usage eit lu per
quei cest establisement ne seit tenu', proclaimed the *Ordinances*.[2]
Elective mayor and sheriffs were gone. Kings had done this
before, but Edward went much further. For aldermen themselves were now to be appointed in the Exchequer and sworn
to his ordinances. London's oldest autonomous, perhaps auto-
genous, magistrates, its doomsmen, were transformed into
royal agents. After 1285 royal judicial commissions penetrated
without hindrance into the city. In 1289 the court of the Exchequer itself was installed at Guildhall, draining the city
tribunals of vitality, and the Treasurer came to exercise an

---

[1] See *Cal. Letter-Bk. A, B, C, passim*.
[2] Lib. Ordinationum, fo. 197.

increasing measure of control over the daily lives of citizens.[1]
Not for centuries, perhaps never, had the city been so subject, in
such detail, to the royal power.

It was over five years before opposition became vocal, an
oblique indication, perhaps, of the strength of that civic opinion
which found no cause for alarm in the events of 1285. In 1289,
however, the Exchequer intruded its irritating presence and
Edward on his return from Gascony launched his drive against
administrative abuse, with its purges and state trials. The atmosphere seemed favourable. The old families took the lead—
Philip le Tailor had already been amerced for refusing to serve
as sheriff in 1286[2]—and in 1290 the city petitioned for a restoration of its elective sheriffs.[3] The petition succeeded, and in the
following year, during the hearing of *querelae* against officials,
Londoners, led by two prominent merchants, crowded forward
to assail the wardens.[4] Finally, in December, an assembly decided formally to petition the king for the restoration of the
mayoralty. It seemed reasonable. There had been frequent sus-
pensions under Henry III but they had been of brief duration.
That which followed Evesham had been exceptional and in
any case had been surpassed. London's autonomy was hardening into an accepted tradition. But the Londoners deceived
themselves. Edward answered with a blank refusal.[5]

It was now, perhaps, that full awareness of the king's purpose penetrated London minds. Particular grievances focused
their dismay. They squabbled with Waleys over the St. Paul's
houses, and in the summer of 1293 suffered a series of local tallages levied for sheriffs' arrears.[6] Above all, there was the meteoric
rise of the Common Clerk John de Bauquell. The royal régime
was a fillip to the growth of a civic bureaucracy and the Clerk
was the chief beneficiary. Bauquell was a professional of obscure

[1] Lib. Ordinationum, fo. 197; *Select Cases before the King's Council 1243–1482*,
ed. I. S. Leadam and J. F. Baldwin, Selden Society (Cambridge, Mass., 1918),
liii; T. Madox, *The History and Antiquities of the Exchequer of England*, 2nd. ed.
(London, 1769), ii, 9.
[2] This information comes from a fourteenth-century enquiry—Chanc. Misc.
68/6 (92).
[3] *Cal. Letter-Bk. A*, 198; see F. M. Powicke, *The Thirteenth Century*, pp. 361 ff.
[4] A.R. 541a, m.42d; A.R. 541b, m.7d, 11, 11d, 23, 26, 30, 31, 34d.
[5] *Cal. Letter-Bk. C*, 3, 4.
[6] *Ann. Lond.*, p. 101; K.R.M.R. 66, m.7, 7d.

origin, his kinsfolk cordwainers and skinners of lesser degree. In time, with his loans and his marriage to Cicely de Ludlow, sister of the greatest wool-merchant of England, he entrenched himself in the financial hinterland of city trade, but he owed his position primarily to the king. In 1286, at the first opportunity, the Exchequer placed the clerk in an aldermanry, and appointment to the custody of the merchants' seal under the statute of merchants followed. Within a few weeks he had leap-frogged over the heads of his senior colleagues to become virtually a deputy-warden.[1] This was bad enough, but in 1293, shortly after the sheriffs' tallages, the king proposed to confer upon him the great hall which Roger de Clifford had bequeathed to the city.[2] Alderman Wolmar de Essex, a woolmonger so heavily indebted to Bauquell that he was later driven into bankruptcy and Alderman Thomas Box, the husband of Essex's sister-in-law, organized a protest.[3] The machinery of government ground to a halt as revolt and dissension paralysed the council.

The warden retaliated with radical action. He deposed the entire council and put through a general election under strict supervision. Essex and Box were duly displaced, the grant to Bauquell confirmed, and the wards told to see to it that there would be no more 'challenge or opposition' in the future. The Exchequer followed up with an attempt to restore royal control over the appointment of sheriffs, but this foundered on a citizen boycott.[4]

The troubles of 1293 were crucial. Royal government was running into thickening resistance. The very dynamism of the new order had recoiled upon itself. Within eight years, it had exhausted its fund of consent. Edward was thrown on the defensive. Time and erosion were to be his allies. Already, before

---

[1] See *Cal. Letter-Bk. A*, 161 and n.3; *C.C.R. 1279–88*, pp. 297, 301, 361; *C.P.R. 1281–92*, p. 245; A.R. 541b, *passim*; Beaven, i, 376.

[2] Hust. Roll 19(19)(20); *C.P.R. 1272–81*, p. 381; *Cal. Letter-Bk. A*, 227; *Ann. Lond.*, p. 89; on the later history of the hall, see H. A. Harben, *A Dictionary of London*, p. 83 (Bakewell Hall).

[3] For Essex and Box, see Recog. Roll 1(234); Hust. Roll 34(106); St. Paul's A/14/1185; *Cal. Letter-Bk. C*, 131, 132.

[4] *Cal. Letter-Bk. C*, 11, 12, 13; *Ann. Lond.*, p. 102; *Lib. Cust.*, p. 293; *Cal. Letter-Bk. A*, 198.

1293, novel figures had appeared on the aldermanic council.[1] Adam de Fulham, one of the first fishmongers to get there, did so in 1291. Of the ten sheriffs appointed by the Exchequer, six belonged to crafts not hitherto represented in the patriciate. Before 1293, however, it was still possible for a dynast like John Blund to take office, for Adam de Rokesle to succeed in Langbourn. But from 1293 to the final collapse of the royal régime, not a single member of the old dynasties took office and hardly any of the new aldermen represented a traditional trade or combination of interests. The only man to approximate to the conventional was the pepperer Thomas Romeyn and he was an Italian. To find his officers, Edward turned away from the established families. He found them, of course, among those very groups whose growing strength had been a factor in the 1263 revolt. The men deposed in 1293 were replaced by the skinner Dunstable and the fishmonger Cros, both of solidly middle class antecedents. Within a year they were followed by Solomon, a cutler from the old rebel family of Laufare. A merchant-potter and a cornmonger replaced a Blund and a Gisors in 1295-6, and in 1297 a Basing, a Rokesle and a Hereford were succeeded by the Westminster lawyer Geoffrey de Norton and two skinners, one of them a prominent craft-leader. Several were direct descendants of rebels of 1263. Under the royal régime, the patriciate was, quite abruptly, thrown wide open, a factor of crucial significance in the development of the crafts and the newer mercantile interests.

The new men, however, were new in terms of origin and occupation. Politically they could be as prickly as fitz Thedmar and Edward's problem resolved itself into the dismally familiar conflict between royal bureaucracy and recalcitrant burgesses. All hope of governing with some measure of consent was abandoned. 'It is an evil thing to fall into the hands of the king, so beware!' wrote Andrew Horn.[2] The Treasurer exhausted every ingenuity to make the system pay. Debts as old as Magna Carta were dug up and with the war came the 'maltolte', the confiscation of money from St. Paul's, the wool-seizures. Citizen

---

[1] For these aldermen, see Beaven, i, 376-8; their careers have been reconstructed from a variety of sources—see Appendix for tables and biographical notes; several individuals were treated in Chapters IV and V.   [2] *Ann. Lond.*, p. 71.

after citizen was caught in the toils of the Exchequer. John de Gisors II, refusing to acknowledge its jurisdiction over a city tenement, suffered severe distraint. Osbert le Laner, wool-monger and councillor, sued the Treasurer William de la Marche as Dean of St. Paul's, over a free holding. De la Marche refused to answer outside the Exchequer but Osbert tried to summon him before the Husting and the aldermen supported his case in face of royal thunders. In the first few months of the war the Londoners' anger again boiled over and they went before the King's Council with a long list of grievances against the Exchequer. They begged for the mayoralty and the restoration of their franchise. But Edward would not let go.[1]

It was the national crisis of 1297 and that crisis alone which broke his hold.[2] From the first outbreak in July, Londoners gave Bohun and Bigod their mass support, added their voice to the demand for *Confirmatio Cartarum*. Who would resent more the favour shown to aliens, the levies and the wool tax? Magna Carta was widely regarded as the city's mainstay and the events of 1285 were a flagrant violation of its letter and spirit.[3] 'Ne ils ne ount lur fraunchises les queux ils solayent avoir mes sount mys hors voluntriement . . .'—whole passages of the *Monstraunces* could have been written by the Londoners themselves.

Yet London was the last to benefit from the earls' movement and its success hung by a thread to the final moment. The charters were confirmed on 10 October. Nothing was said of London. On 5 November Edward set his reluctant seal to the agreement, but there was still no word on the city's future. Not until 30 November did the shadow lift. On that day, the warden announced to an assembly at Guildhall that Edward of Caer-narvon, the Barons of the Exchequer, Bohun and Bigod had ordered him to 'bear himself in all things as if he were mayor',

---

[1] *Select Cases before the King's Council*, pp. 8-18 and li-lvi; *Cal. Letter-Bk. B*, 74, *C*, 4, 7, 9, 10; *Ann. Lond.*, p. 98; *Dunstable*, iii, 390; F. M. Powicke, *The Thirteenth Century*, pp. 523 ff., 628 ff., 644 ff.

[2] On the crisis, see J. G. Edwards, 'Confirmatio Cartarum and baronial grievances in 1297', *English Historical Review*, lviii (1943); H. Rothwell, 'The Confirmation of the Charters, 1297', *English Historical Review*, lx (1945); F. M. Powicke, *op. cit.*, 678 ff.

[3] *Lib. de Ant. Leg.*, pp. 87-8; F. Thompson, *The First Century of Magna Carta; why it persisted as a document* (Minneapolis, 1925), pp. 21-2, 38-9.

to maintain the liberties of the city, to abolish Waleys's Tun prison and annul his corn-trade edicts. 'Nota bene et lege', added the Husting clerk.[1] Londoners needed no reminder. A riotous crowd, led by eight aldermen, marched to the Tun, broke it and freed the prisoners.[2] In one dramatic gesture, they were ridding themselves of the incubus not only of Edward's wardens but of his mayor Waleys as well.

They were over-optimistic. Edward was desperately slow to yield. Not until April 1298, after his return to England, did he give way. By the 11th, he restored the mayoralty. But within a few weeks he was threatening an enquiry into the breaking of the Tun and insisting ominously on the need to reimpose Waleys's edicts. In an atmosphere heavy with uncertainty, the Londoners elected Henry le Waleys mayor, even though he had resigned his aldermanry four years previously, a procedure without precedent and evidently a measure of reinsurance.[3] During 1298, however, the aldermen rapidly consolidated their position. Within a few days of the restoration, Bauquell was ejected from his aldermanry, to begin a new career as a royal officer which was to make him Seneschal of Ponthieu and Baron of the Exchequer, and in an unprecedented reshuffle of seats, seven new men reached the council, among them Ralph de Honilane who had impleaded the warden in 1291 and Nicholas Picot who had led a brief resistance to military service in 1296. An attempt to elect Waleys was quashed.[4]

Their base secure, the aldermen tried for a settlement with the king. They tried to buy a charter with £1,000 in August and failed. In March 1299 they tried again. In the end they were forced to pay 2,000 marks, which they borrowed from seven Italian companies, covering a settlement of the fine of 1266, Osbert le Laner's case, the breaking of the Tun and the restoration of self-government. On 17 April Edward finally issued a

---

[1] *Cal. Letter-Bk. B*, 243–44 and marginal note.

[2] See J. Stow, *A Survey of London*, ed. C. L. Kingsford (London, 1908), i, 189, ii, 303, confirmed by references to the consequences of the incident in *Cal. Letter-Bk. B*, 75, 76, *C*, 37, 38; Dr. Sharpe, in his calendar, reads 'a tun' for 'The Tun'.

[3] *Cal. Letter-Bk. B*, 212, 213, 215; *C.C.R. 1296–1302*, p. 164; Beaven, i, 378.

[4] Hust. Roll (Common Pleas) 24, interlocutaria, m. a, b, b dorse, c; Beaven, i, 375–80; for Picot, see *Cal. Letter-Bk. C*, 21, 23–4; *Lib. Cust.*, pp. 72–3, 74–5.

comprehensive *inspeximus*.[1] It remained only to displace Waleys in a brief flurry of hostility in October and London was free again.[2]

The effects of Edward's rule, however, were revolutionary. For, paradoxically, he succeeded where the *populares* had failed. He destroyed the old patriciate as a political force.[3] Under his wardens, dynastic representation in the aldermanic class was decimated, and once the political hold of the dynasties was broken, they dwindled to insignificance with remarkable speed, for in the new world of syndicate finance and war purveyance, with its multiplying trade groups and new breed of merchant, they found no place. The old monopoly was gone, the old battles were over. Moreover, as the leaders of the newer trades penetrated the patriciate, the craft movement itself gained irresistible impetus. The wardens' insistence on registration, their use of the crafts as police units strengthened their corporate spirit and sense of identity. More important, Edward's free trade policy sharpened their most vivid apprehensions and drove them forward into social and political action. In a radically transformed political climate and under a patriciate open to all the trade winds, they made a renewed attempt to win a place for themselves in the civic constitution. That constitution itself had assumed coherent form in the same seminal period. After the order and regularity of the wardens, there could be no return to the *ad hoc* informality of the old régime. The assemblies were beginning to think like an estate. They, too, were acquiring a political personality.

The reign of Edward I, in short, was a watershed in the history of London. It completely refashioned the modes of political life in the city. Under Edward, the Crown succeeded in integrating London more fully than ever before into the life of the nation, and the effect, paradoxically enough, was to give free play to those social forces which had first manifested themselves in the days of Montfort. By breaking the political monopoly of the dynasties Edward radically changed the structure and

---

[1] *Cal. Letter-Bk. B*, 74–6, *C*, 37, 38, 43–4, 107; *C.C.R. 1296–1302*, p. 303; *C.Ch.R. 1257–1300*, pp. 477–8.

[2] *Cal. Letter-Bk. B*, 88, *C*, 29, 77–8; Beaven, i, 377.

[3] See tables on the aldermanic class in the Appendix.

climate of the commune. The year 1285, in fact, marks the end of that commune. The community which emerged in 1298 was a new and unstabilized political society in course of formation. Stability London was to find amid the crises, coups d'état and executions of the reign of Edward II.

CHAPTER X

The Making of the Constitution 1299–1319

THE last mayor to hold office under Edward I was John Blund. He was also the last man from the traditional twelfth-century dynasties to serve as mayor. For, under him, the new order in city politics rapidly took shape.[1] Half the new aldermen of the first decade of the fourteenth century came from those rising middle class families who had entered into their political inheritance under the royal wardens. Second to them in number, and often superior in importance, were the new thrusting merchants from the provinces, beginning their swift climb to pre-eminence. Dynastic representation went into its last steep decline as population, commercial expansion and trade competition alike mounted to a peak.'

Under this open and fluid patriciate, novel forces refashioned the political community. The Londoners had been taught the necessity of self-defence, the need to equip themselves with the legal establishment Edwardian society demanded. As soon as the wardens had gone, they created the recordership, appointed attorneys at the central courts. The city's administrative offices were professionalized, Waltham and Kelsey launched on their brilliant careers. The new bureaucracy established itself as a permanent feature of the civic landscape, a disconcerting phenomenon to a middle class citizenry already perturbed by the growing cost and efficiency of government.

No less disconcerting was the threat to the rights and perquisites of citizenship and citizen monopoly of the retail trade. For in 1303 *Carta Mercatoria* made general the free trade imposed on London in 1285. Throughout the early decades of the new

---

[1] For the background to what follows, see tables on aldermanic class in the Appendix and Chapter XII. Aspects of the period were treated in Chapters IV, V and VI.

century the city tried doggedly to reimpose its regulations and it was now that a running guerilla against aliens, particularly Gascons, became a constant theme in London politics.[1] No-one was affected more directly than the developing mercantile crafts. With numbers multiplying and competition growing, the impulse to organize and control focused on citizenship and its management. The misteries were stung into action. This time they encountered little resistance. Fishmongers, corders, ironmongers were on the council. The skinners had won recognition in the days of the wardens, the gilds of the Baltic trades were among the most powerful in the city. The greatest of the newer crafts were already establishing themselves alongside the rapidly changing former patrician gilds in the new oligarchy of the city. In these circumstances, the charters which had occasioned such controversy thirty years earlier were reissued without a murmur. The cordwainers got theirs in 1303, the joiners in 1308.[2] By the reign of Edward II, lesser colleagues were organized, active, and protected by the courts.

The movement could not be contained. In 1299 the carpenters held a 'parliament' at Mile End. The first journeymen's organizations were reported by cordwainers and skinners, the first journeymen's strike by tilers. Between 1298 and 1307 the mayor's court rolls record an effervescence of craft formation, among brewers, coopers, smiths, chandlers, spurriers, barbers, fruiterers.[3] Their spirit of solidarity was ferocious. In 1305 a fishmonger, John de Ely, prosecuted some of his colleagues on behalf of the king. A few years later they killed him.[4]

Parliaments of carpenters were a sign of the times. As soon as the shadow of Edward I was dispelled, the crafts moved into political action. In October 1309 enrolments of new citizens appear for the first time in the letter-books. They run on without a break to December 1312, ending three days before the first general assembly of city crafts ever officially convened.

---

[1] For some examples, see *Cal. Letter-Bk. C*, 13, 31, 32, 65, 75, 126–7, 135.

[2] *Lib. Cust.*, pp. 80, 81, 83, 84.

[3] *Cal. E.M.C. Rolls*, pp. 1, 2, 16, 18, 19, 25, 33, 34, 49, 52, 67; *Cal. Letter-Bk. C*, 7, 165 and n. 3; *C.P.R. 1281–92*, p. 519.

[4] *Cal. E.M.C. Rolls*, pp. 228, 229, 233; *Ann. Paul.*, p. 278; see also *Ann. Lond.*, pp. 221 and *passim*; Weinbaum, ii, 176.

Evidently they were considered worthy of special record. For their number was without precedent. New admissions were running at a rate well over double what was normal in the twenties and thirties. In 1311 they were treble. In three years, not far short of a thousand new citizens were enrolled. Many of them took up the franchise in trade groups, as the leading misteries made an organized drive for control.[1]

The relatively sudden advent of hundreds of new citizens transformed the political situation. The commonalty, already strengthened by the practice of the royal wardens, grew rapidly in stature. Its assemblies became politically formidable. For they bristled with grievances. The most immediate was the perennial, discontent with the daily friction of government. Plaints made later at the Iter of 1321 strike the keynote.[2] The sheriff Stephen de Abyndon extorted money from victuallers, sheriffs' clerks like Robert de Wengrave took bribes, lawyers like Kelsey were 'ambidextrous'. On and on the complaints run, covering membrane after membrane of the closely written judicial records, the same protest which echoes from generation after generation, the characteristic relic left by medieval town government. Government was a painful business at the best of times and, under Edward II, resentment was immeasurably sharpened by the existence of a novel class of professional administrators as suspect as it was necessary.

The reformers, beginning in a small way, went on to evolve the most complex and comprehensive scheme of constitutional control London had yet seen. In the process, all the old demands of the commons reappeared. They were strengthened by newer ones, ultimately by a revolutionary attempt to make the craft the basic unit of government in place of the ward. For the crafts were the backbone of the movement. The more important of them must have been functioning as political clubs. The logic of their own economic and social policy demanded the most sustained political action, for implicit in it was the ultimate identification of citizenship with craft-membership. Crafts and

[1] *Cal. Letter-Bk. D*, 35-179; compare with the admission fees in the chamberlains' accounts for 1326-35 in Letter Book E, fo. clxxiib-clxxiii, ccib-ccii, ccxxixb-ccxxx, ccxliiib-ccxliv (*Cal. Letter-Bk. E*, 216-17, 247-8, 270-1, 292).

[2] See the extracts from A.R. 546, 547a and 553 in Weinbaum, ii, 154-96, also *Lib. Cust.*, pp. 285-432.

commonalty became increasingly interpenetrated as, now separately, now in concert, they moved to an attack on oligarchy.

In response, the patriciate splintered into factions. It is no longer a question of measuring fishmongers against pepperers. This newer patriciate was a much more complex organism than the old, more fully integrated into the national pattern, more susceptible to the tug of popular discontent, the ebb and flow of those baronial crises which convulsed the reign. At the Iter of 1321, for example, the ward juries charged five important groups with organized conspiracy.[1] The charge was proved in only one case, that of the recorder John de Wengrave and his small circle of clerks and lawyers, but the presentments included such a wealth of circumstantial detail—exact times of meeting in the Leadenhall of Cornhill in one instance—that the existence of organized factions can scarcely be doubted. There was a group of merchants with the Common Clerk Hugh Waltham and most of the aldermen, the hard core of the patriciate, under the leadership of the reforming mayor Richer de Refham; a much smaller group clustered around John de Gisors III who took the reformers' pay and gave them their head. William de Hakford led an influential association of mercers said to be masters of the art of manipulating elections, while fishmongers and merchants of the Baltic connexion gathered about the enigmatic figure of Hamo de Chigwell, foremost leader of the commons. All these groups represented different degrees of reforming zeal, different attitudes towards the national contestants, and the presence of all of them may be dimly discerned behind the terse official records of decree and annulment.

For the *populares*, however revolutionary their ends, operated within the framework of the constitution. Writs obtained by their enemies in years of reaction speak of clandestine meetings and conspiracies, of lobbying during elections, of organized tumult and heckling in Guildhall. Men were enrolled as citizens *en masse*, assemblies were packed.[2] The commons were turning the Husting into a hustings. Little of this percolates through the

[1] See A.R. 547 in Weinbaum, ii, 171–9; *Cal. Letter-Bk. E*, 11, 111, 121, 122, 124, 138, 139; *Ann. Paul.*, p. 287; *French Chronicle*, p. 40; *Ann. Lond.*, pp. 175, 176; *Lib. Cust.*, pp. 371–4.

[2] See, for example, *Cal. Letter-Bk. D*, 24–6 and compare with the situation described by Miss Bird in *The Turbulent London of Richard II*.

bald formality of records, which register only *faits accomplis*, but behind the sudden and inexplicable reversals, the abrupt ebb and flow of election and deposition, one senses for the first time something of the spirit of the organized struggle of parties, in what was, without doubt, the most sustained and successful reform movement in the history of medieval London.

It was unleashed by the victory of the Ordainers. The accession of Edward II, greeted by Andrew Horn with an assortment of hair-raising prophecies culled from the more lurid pages of Geoffrey of Monmouth, plunged England into twenty confused and bloody years. The resentment accumulated under Edward I broke over the head of this strange uncomfortable king with his bizarre mechanic tastes and waspish Gascon counsellor Piers Gaveston, as Lancaster, Warwick and the baronage led a frontal assault on the Edwardian system, setting in train a dismal succession of crises which was to culminate in the revolutionary deposition and murder of a king.[1]

The London plebs was wholeheartedly Lancastrian, canonizing Earl Thomas as the true heir of St. Simon, but the situation was never clear-cut. Every crisis had its own chain of action and reaction and the interplay of civic and national faction gave to the texture of London's political life a complexity unknown in former days. At the beginning, however, the pattern was simple. The Londoners, upon whom Isabella had already made a much more favourable impression than her unorthodox spouse, heartily endorsed the first exile of Gaveston and, on his return, successfully blocked a royal attempt to install one of his nominees as Common Serjeant.[2] When the crisis broke in the spring of 1310 and the great retinues of Lancaster and Hereford camped in the suburb, they rallied to the barons, made sporadic attacks on the Gascon vintners.[3] As the Ordainers took control and moved into the city, the lesser citizens gave voice. Piecemeal

---

[1] The most useful sources for the reign are T. F. Tout, *The Place of the Reign of Edward II in English History*, 2nd. ed. rev. by H. Johnstone (Manchester, 1936) and J. C. Davies, *The Baronial Opposition to Edward II, its Character and Policy* (Cambridge, 1918).

[2] *Cal. Letter-Bk. C*, 65, 66, *D*, 209; Lib. Ordinationum, fo. 190b; for freedom-admissions sponsored by the king or the magnates, see *Cal. Letter-Bk. D*, 35–159, *passim*.

[3] *Cal. Letter-Bk. D*, 211, 212, 213–14; *Ann. Paul.*, p. 268.

reforms were wrung from the aldermen and in October, Richer de Refham was elected mayor.[1]

Refham, a powerful mercer who dealt heavily with the French and Italians and shipped wool to the Netherlands, was a man from Norfolk, where his family held land in chief of the Bigods.[2] He was typical of the ambitious provincials who were coming to dominate the aldermanic council. Acquiring land in Somerset and a knighthood by 1321, he built up his civic estate from the disintegrating patrimonies of older families, Basings, Hardels, Bukerels. He leased the lands of Henry le Waleys, married his son to the daughter of John le Blund, and got much of that dynasty's inheritance as well. By 1304 he owned property in twenty-five parishes. Two years earlier he had been restored to the aldermanry he had lost in a quarrel with Waleys in 1299, and his election as mayor in 1310 inaugurated the reform drive.[3]

For he was 'austerus', in the words of the friendly Andrew Horn, 'et celer ad justitiam faciendam'. 'Karissimi concives mei', he addressed the commons on election, in words not heard for a generation, and at a great assembly, presented a new codification of city custom, vowed there would be no more misgovernment in future. Like Puleston before him, he made a formal circuit of the city, destroying all purprestures. He resumed the attack on disorder, improved procedure in tax-assessment, in a well-staged display which eased the operation of government without in any way altering its essential character.[4]

Popular aspirations could not be so easily contained. There were renewed attacks on the Gascons and excitement mounted as the Ordainers neared the completion of their task. Finally in August the Ordinances were proclaimed in a blaze of publicity. Revolutionary though they were in their attempt to impose permanent baronial control on the royal household, they touched London directly in only one instance. The New Custom levied from aliens as a tribute for *Carta Mercatoria* was

[1] See, for example, *Cal. Letter-Bk. D*, 284.

[2] An outline of Refham's career, with references, may be found in the biographical notes in the Appendix.

[3] *Cal. Letter-Bk. B*, 88, *C*, 28, 29, 77, 78; *Ann. Lond.*, p. 104.

[4] *Ann. Lond.*, pp. 175, 176; *Cal. Letter-Bk. D*, 242, 262–8, 285–6; Riley, *Memorials*, pp. 86–9.

abolished and the charter declared contrary to Magna Carta
and the city franchise. The citizen monopoly was restored, at
least in theory.[1] This, and the second exile of Gaveston, gave a
fillip to the commons. It was on 16 August that the mayor,
aldermen and *probi* took the oath to the Ordinances before
parliament. In eleven days, they were meeting again for a
more immediate purpose. For on the 27th twelve men from
every ward assembled in the presence of the Ordainers themselves to consider the state of the city.[2]

The meeting, presided over by Refham, issued a series of
edicts regulating the watch, imposing fines on defaulters, ordering citizens to assist law-enforcement officers under threat of
amercement. Aldermen were formally instructed to consult
regularly with their wardmoots on pain of dismissal. Though
these ordinances embody the first official recognition that aldermen were personally responsible to their electors, they were in
no sense revolutionary and probably represented the limit of
the patriciate's capacity for reform on its own initiative.

Within a few weeks that question was no longer theirs to
decide. Refham's political career came to an abrupt end. The
mayor clashed violently with his own mercers' fraternity over a
wardship debt-recognizance. According to Horn, the mercers'
leader William de Hakford was actually imprisoned and in
retaliation organized a party which secured Refham's deposition from the mayoralty and later from his aldermanry as well.
Official records are silent on the point, but they do confirm that
Refham quitted the mayoralty in 1311, never to return, and
that he ceased to be an alderman in 1312.[3] He was succeeded
by John de Gisors III. This man, however, was cast for a role
vastly different from his grandfather's. For in the first month of
his mayoralty the commons took control. The detail of events is
now completely lost. It is not clear whether there was a struggle.
But in four decisive weeks the balance of power in London was
radically displaced, and at a great assembly on 20 November
1311 the reform drive swept forward to its first climax.

---

[1] *Cal. Letter-Bk. D*, 226–9, 232, 256, 268–9, 286–7; *Ann. Paul.*, p. 270; see J. C.
Davies, *op. cit.*

[2] *Cal. Letter-Bk. D*, 286.

[3] *Ann. Lond.*, pp. 175, 176; *Cal. Letter-Bk. D*, 182, 183, 188, 228, 275, *E, passim*;
Weinbaum, ii, 178, 179; Beaven, i, 378.

In essence the commons won control over the executive service, the personnel of city administration and vital sectors of the revenue. Every important executive office was declared elective, its incumbent to be chosen by the commonalty, mayor and aldermen retaining only the power of confirmation. All officers were to submit themselves for re-election every year. Under this rule on the 20th the commonalty elected the chamberlain, Common Clerk, wardens of Bridge, muragers, auditors for the chamber and auditors for Bridge. To ensure continuous daily supervision of fiscal administration, they appointed a comptroller of the chamberlain and soon set him to inspect the city prosecutor as well. The commons, further, took over one whole class of revenue, the fees for the enrolment of deeds, wills and 'writings' in the chamber. Control of this, the source of those vital perquisites which supplemented the salaries of civic officials, was vested in the permanent body of elected auditors.[1] There may have been other edicts. It is from this date that the association of ordinary citizens with professional officers in administrative committees becomes a regular practice. A stray record from 1316 reveals that, by that date, selection of the staff of city paviours had passed to the craft of masons. About this time, too, the various official designations of the city as a political entity yield to the stock formula, 'Mayor, Aldermen and Commonalty'.[2] The edicts of November 1311, in short, carried through a constitutional revolution. The commonalty got its hands on the innermost levers of power and won for itself permanent and formal association with the aldermanic council in the government of London.

In the following year, the reform drive gathered momentum, spurred on by the crisis precipitated by the return of Gaveston. On Lancastrian London, royal writs ordering mobilization in the king's cause made no impression. The Londoners refused to maintain the Tower, as the barons made St. Paul's their base and turned the suburb into an armed camp. By February the king was pointedly reminding Londoners of their letters of fealty to Henry III.[3] As tempers grew heated, the commons

[1] *Cal. Letter-Bk. D*, 275; also 18, 79, 276, 289; the evidence for the taking over of enrolment fees was examined in Chapter IV.

[2] *Cal. Letter-Bk. E*, 55, 56; see the constantly recurring patterns in *Cal. Letter-Bks. C-F.*   [3] *Ann. Paul.*, p. 271; *Cal. Letter-Bk. D*, 278, 279, 282, 284.

once more took power into their own hands. On 22 March an assembly met at Guildhall in the presence of Gisors and a few aldermen and drew up three further articles of reform. No letter which committed the city in any way was to be sealed without the prior and unanimous consent of a communal assembly. The city seal, henceforth, was to be kept in a chest under six keys, three to be held by the aldermen, three by nominees of the commonalty. The commons probably had the immediate political situation in mind, were anxious to avoid having the city committed to Edward's cause, but their action was a logical extension of the policy of the previous November. The third ordinance was less novel. No alien was to be admitted to the franchise without the assent of the commonalty. On 15 April the assembly met again and compelled the aldermen to ratify its decisions. Within three days the mayor summoned every alien merchant in the city and warned them not to stay longer than the statutory forty days, and on the 19th a royal request for the admission to the franchise of the king's Genoese financier Antonio di Passano was flatly rejected. Gisors was earning the £40 the commons had awarded him 'for his household' in March.[1]

Meanwhile the crisis worsened about their exultant heads. The hunted Gaveston surrendered and in June was treacherously murdered. In a sharp revulsion of feeling, Pembroke and his allies rallied to the king. Writs ordered the mayor to seize and hold the city for the Crown and in July, Edward, with Pembroke and the Council, turned south and, in a terrifying display of force, marched his army straight through the heart of London. Camping at Blackfriars, he summoned the mayor and aldermen.[2] Edward addressed them in person. 'Le secle se mene mervylousement', he said. His barons were in arms against him, and he ordered them to consult their fellow-citizens and give a definite pledge to hold the city for him. If they were unable or unwilling to do so, he added ominously, the king's men would undertake the task themselves.

The circumstances of Gaveston's death, the presence of Pembroke and the army, even the fact that the king had spoken to

---

[1] *Cal. Letter-Bk. D*, 280–4.
[2] *Ann. Paul.*, pp. 271, 272; *Ann. Lond.*, pp. 207, 208; *Cal. Letter-Bk. D*, 290, 295.

them 'de bouche . . . en sa propre persone' had their effect.
Even so, there was discussion for a whole day before mayor,
aldermen and the entire commonalty went before the king, and
in the person of their law officer Kelsey, undertook not to open
the gates to the king's enemies.[1] The honeymoon was brief indeed. As the barons massed threateningly at Ware and French
lawyers arrived for an attempt at mediation, relations abruptly
deteriorated. The Constable of the Tower suddenly swooped
on William de Hakford and his friends and imprisoned them in
the fortress, alleging a plot to open the gates to Lancaster. Public
opinion rallied to their support and on 20 September, when
Pembroke and Despenser rode to Guildhall at the head of an
armed troop and proposed to transform the general under-
taking of July into a thoroughgoing security scheme to be
operated under the orders of the Council, they ran into fierce
resistance. A general assembly gathered at Guildhall and the
recorder John de Wengrave loudly protested that their word
was enough. No-one would find them guilty of sedition, said the
lawyer, a shade disingenuously, and they would do nothing at the
order of men coming to the city in arms and without warrant.
The assembly broke into applause, thronged round the magnates, demanding the release of Hakford and the fulfilment of a
royal pledge to curb the court of the Marshalsea. A rumour ran
through the streets that the king's men had arrested the aldermen. Huge crowds flocked to Guildhall and would not be paci-
fied until they had seen Gisors in the flesh. The harassed magnates rode out through hostile crowds, and in the evening a troop
from the garrison raided Tower ward. The Londoners rounded
them up and threw them into prison, as an angry Council
accused the mayor of sedition.[2]

No action was taken but, once more, external hostilities
stimulated activity within the walls. In the autumn of 1312, as
the national contestants moved clumsily towards a temporary
settlement, the reform movement took a new and decisive turn.
The crafts emerged from the shelter of the commonalty and
struck for direct power. In October, Gisors was re-elected

---

[1] These proceedings are described in Lib. Ordinationum, fo. 191b–192b; a version
is published in Weinbaum, ii, 102–4; see also *Ann. Lond.*, pp. 208, 209.

[2] *Ann. Lond.*, pp. 215–18; *Ann. Paul.*, p. 272; *Cal. Letter-Bk. D*, 297, *E*, 102.

T

mayor and on 1 December presided over a general assembly of the city crafts, which 'for the commonalty' proposed a number of articles 'for the common weal'. For the benefit of ignorant city youth, all civic usages were to be enrolled and read in public assembly once or twice a year, and copies made available to any who wanted them. All aldermen were to be more diligent in future under penalty of loss of office; the activities of sheriffs and clerks were to be scrutinized. Finally, since the city ought always to be governed by the aid of men engaged in trade and handicrafts, no stranger was to be admitted to the franchise until men of the trade he wished to pursue had ratified his entry.

The assembly followed up with a brisk attack on aliens. Two Italian merchants and the Gascon Gerard Dorgoyl, brother to a former alderman, were struck from the register of citizens. Eight days later all the executive officers of the city came up for re-election under the ordinances of November 1311. The assembly which elected them was one of four or six delegates from every craft in the city. Gisors himself may have been formally re-elected, for when Pembroke presented him to the king on 16 December, he was introduced as a 'newly-elected' mayor.[1]

In the spring of 1313 the reform movement was at its zenith. Power passed to the organized misteries. Had the transfer proved permanent, the consequences would have been incalculable. In February 1313 the fishmongers staged a dazzling pageant as they escorted the queen to Eltham, gorgeous with liveries and mounted squadrons, long remembered for its miraculously engineered ship-float. They had cause to rejoice. In March, when John Vanne of Lucca and John de Triple were admitted to the franchise, the two Italians renounced their tax-exemptions and were received only by permission of a mass-assembly of representatives from every mistery in the city.[2] The *populares* had crossed the line between reform and revolution.

In so doing, they conjured up forces which overwhelmed them. For in the summer of 1313 the reform drive was halted in its tracks. By the end of the year its edicts were a dead letter, and for six years the movement went into eclipse. The root

---

[1] *Cal. Letter-Bk. D*, 21, 276, *E*, 12–14.
[2] *Cal. Letter-Bk. E*, 16; Riley, *Memorials*, p. 106.

cause, without doubt, was the excessive ambition of the crafts. The pattern was now established which became characteristic of all similar situations in later years.[1] The moment the crafts stood out from the commonalty and strove for direct authority, they provoked a resistance which frequently cost them even their easily-won initial gains. The threat of total mistery rule frightened many outside the patriciate. The prospect of unlimited power in the hands of the victuallers, in particular, touched an old nerve of fear. It was not so much the formation of an anti-victualling interest as an almost instinctive rally of non-victuallers, which proved politically decisive at every crisis to the burning of Jubilee Book and beyond. Besides, the transfer of power raised more problems than it solved. Assemblies were to be drawn from 'every craft', but what were the crafts? What were the criteria of selection? City records are silent. A great mercantile gild like the skinners had little in common with a mistery such as the coopers. The one common feature was an employers' front against employees; there were too many conflicts, too few points of contact. The switching of the reform drive to craft lines robbed it of impetus. On the tide of reaction the patriciate rode back to power.

There may have been other factors. The reformers never penetrated into parliamentary elections.[2] The establishment of the compulsory staple in May 1313, setting up new combinations of interests and new patterns of conflict, may have distracted attention. The *populares* found it difficult to recover from a check, and in the summer, they were divided by the celebrated Brandeston case. Henry Brandeston murdered a man in the church of St. Mary at Hill but, before the justices, claimed, as a citizen, the privilege of release to twelve pledges. The Londoners were obliged to support him in the interest of the franchise, but even the sheriffs' record speaks of a 'reluctant' replevin, and what made matters infinitely worse were sinister charges that Brandeston had bought the franchise after the murder by bribing the mayor John de Gisors.[3]

---

[1] See, for comparison, R. Bird, *op. cit.*
[2] See, for example, *Cal. Letter-Bk. D*, 289, 292.
[3] *Cal. Letter-Bk. D*, 93, 312–13; *Lib. Cust.*, pp. 371–4; Weinbaum, ii, 112–13 (quoting B.M. Addit. Ms. 38131).

The mayor's position was in any case anomalous in the extreme, for the same Gisors who had led the reform assemblies now presided over their destruction. At a meeting of the mayor and twelve aldermen in September 1313, patrician control was re-established over shrieval elections. To avoid 'certain perils', only nominated electors were to be summoned in future.[1] This decree was the first overt symptom of a reaction which gained ground with the recovery of the Lancaster faction. The disaster at Bannockburn in 1314, which sent Andrew Horn into a fit of gloomy moralizing, shattered the royal position and Lancaster's men climbed back to power.[2] The tone of city record and chronicle suddenly alters. No more is heard of craft assemblies and reform edicts. Gisors' name now is linked ever more frequently with that of William de Leyre, an alderman cordially hated by the commons. In October he was rewarded with the mayoralty, and by the spring of 1315 succeeded in establishing friendly relations with the Lancaster administration. Royal writs curbed the court of the Steward and Marshal, regulated prises and purveyance, and in May the city was granted the murage for two years.[3]

Lancaster's benevolence no doubt pleased those whose conception of reform was primarily extramural, and it strengthened the hand of the aldermen at a crucial moment. In May, John de Ely was killed by his fellow fishmongers and within a few weeks the council took the decisive step. On 4 July they published a special writ from the king. In forceful language it ordered that mayoral and shrieval elections in future were to be conducted in the traditional manner. Any 'plebeian' who intervened would be imprisoned and released only by special command of the king.[4] Never had the royal power intervened so decisively on the aldermen's behalf. St. Thomas was showing a cloven hoof. Under his dispensation the reform movement withered, and in October 1316 reaction reached its logical culmination when the recorder, John de Wengrave, was elected mayor. Three years later it took a minor revolution to dislodge him.

---

[1] *Cal. Letter-Bk. D,* 22, 23.
[2] *Ann. Lond.*, p. 231; see T. F. Tout and J. C. Davies, *op. cit.*
[3] *Cal. Letter-Bk. D,* 24, *E,* 24, 30, 40–5, 63–7; *Ann. Paul,* pp. 275–6; *Ann. Lond.*, pp. 232, 233, 237.
[4] *Cal. Letter-Bk. D,* 24–6, *E,* 53; *Ann. Paul.*, p. 278.

Under Wengrave, effective power passed to the professional administrators. It was, perhaps, inevitable that the clerks should be residuary legatees. They had been the irritant in 1310, they represented government itself, their trained talent was at a premium.[1] But they were unpopular. Their three-year hegemony ended in a violent resurgence of popular radicalism, the purchase of a royal charter directed largely against themselves and a barrage of organized accusation at the Iter of 1321 notable even for that institution.

Wengrave's personal authority was novel. With his first election in 1316, he held simultaneously the offices of mayor, recorder and coroner. In 1317 he was re-elected by the aldermen, 'with one consent, without any scrutiny being made among them', and in the following year his election was carried in the teeth of intense popular hostility.[2] A faction formed around him.[3] His closest colleagues were two fellow alderman-administrators, the lawyer Robert de Kelsey and the clerk John de la Chambre, both self-made immigrants and skilful manipulators of lands and loans.[4] With them was William de Leyre, an Essex pepperer and more of a traditional establishment figure, but one who seems to have specialized in small debts. No creditor's name recurs more frequently on the recognizance rolls, a fact which may account for his unpopularity.[5] All four belonged to the city élite. In the Twelfth of 1319, Leyre's forty marks was the second highest assessment; Wengrave and Kelsey, both of whom received licence to crenellate their houses, followed at £20. With them were associated Alderman Simon Corp, a Sopers Lane pepperer assessed at £10 in 1319 and linked to the clerical family of Durham; Michael Myniot, a younger man who became a

---

[1] See the constant appearance as parliamentary representatives of John de la Chambre and Henry de Durham, clerks, Wengrave and Kelsey, lawyers—*Cal. Letter-Bk. D*, 273–4, 289, 291, 307, *E*, 20, 30, 33, 39, 54, 99 and *passim*.

[2] *Cal. Letter-Bk. D*, 27, 28; *Ann. Lond.*, p. 240; *C.C.R. 1313–18*, p. 355.

[3] For this group, see Weinbaum, ii, 154–62, 172–7; Ekwall, *Two Early London Subsidy Rolls*, pp. 48, 105, 106, 107, 113–15, 222, 261, 275, 276.

[4] For an outline biography of Kelsey, see Chapter IV and biographical notes in the Appendix; for Chambre's lands and debts, see Recog. Roll 6, 7, 8; *C.C.R. 1313–1318*, pp. 309–464, *passim; C.C.R. 1318–23*, pp. 326–82, *passim*; Hust. Roll 33–53, *passim*; Misc. Roll CC, m.1d, 21d; *C.P.R. 1307–13*, pp. 278, 593; *Cal. of Wills*, i, 328.

[5] Recog. Rolls, *passim*; Ekwall, *Two Early London Subsidy Rolls*, pp. 163, 275.

warden of the vintners and royal butler under Edward III; and more characteristically, a group of followers drawn from the regiment of city administrators, two city serjeants who were kinsmen of the recorder, the bailiff of Queenhithe, the gaoler of Newgate. It was this group, with the professional administrators as inner caucus, which was convicted of conspiracy at the Iter of 1321.

The charges levelled against them are revealing. Particularly obnoxious was the unprecedented concentration of legal power in the hands of Wengrave. He was said to have drawn sheriffs' cases into his own court and to have stepped up the fees. Amercements for default had risen from 6d. to 6s. 8d. All fees had gone up; clerks and sheriffs assessed them at their own will. Court officers influenced jury verdicts, clerks threatened to sabotage cases unless they were paid. Underlings were illegally retained, staffs had increased beyond reason. There were the usual charges of personal corruption.[1] What the commons were bewailing, in effect, was the increased cost and efficiency of government, with its customary and concomitant vexations. It was asking a great deal of men like Wengrave and Kelsey to be content with their official fees. These men could command high salary anywhere. By mid-century the recorder's stipend had risen to 100 marks. Their administrative assistants were probably underpaid.

The collapse of the popular movement in 1313 thrust the professionals into power. Wengrave and his group remodelled the administration to a pattern closer to the professional ideal; the clerks would run the city as it ought to be run. But, inevitably, with an increase in efficiency went an increase in fees. To the commons, the very sins against which they had preached were being committed on an unheard-of scale, their heinousness aggravated, perhaps, by a certain legalistic and *arriviste* ruthlessness on the part of the new rulers. The role of clerks and lawyers in the patriciate, indeed, seems to have been analogous to that of the crafts in the commonalty. In assuming direct power, they provoked a reaction which destroyed them.

Hostile forces, rooted as they were in powerful victualling and entrepreneurial interests, remained strong despite the setback

[1] For the charges, see A.R. 547a and 553, Weinbaum, ii, 155-62, 172-6.

of 1313. The irritant of Wengrave's mayoralty set them in motion. Their leader, appropriately enough, was a fishmonger. Hamo de Dene, an immigrant from Essex, had served as factor to Richard de Chigwell, greatest of the new alderman-fish-mongers of the reign of Edward I, and had assumed his master's surname. He had followed him, too, into the complex triangular traffic in fish, corn and Baltic products which flowed between London, East Anglia and Holland. He, his kinsmen and his agents were established figures among the granaries and curing-sheds of Henley and Yarmouth, and with his own 250-mark ship *La Nicholas*, he was a prominent merchant in the wine trade. His property, centring on a mansion in St. Mary Monthaut and spread over three parishes, was solid rather than impressive and he was no estate builder. Assessed at £2 in 1319, he was a man of substance rather than affluence, but, a friend of the family of the coroner Robert de Gunthorp, he had been trained in his youth, indeed had taken minor orders, and throughout his chequered career he displayed political talents of a high order. He must also have been a man of commanding personality, for no matter how chequered the career, he retained to the end the loyalty and affection of large numbers of Londoners which ultimately won him a place in the select circle of city heroes.[1]

In 1319 he drove to power at the head of an unstable coalition of interests marshalled into a momentary unity of purpose. His buttress was the revived spirit of 1311, his main supporters Andrew Horn and Edmund Lambyn the fishmongers, Roger le Palmer the influential cornmonger, John de Preston and William de Boddele, wealthy and powerful figures in the corders' and vintners' misteries. But he was able to command support from wider circles. One of his intimates was Hamo Godchep the Wardrobe merchant. Godchep was a mercer, and the number of mercers who rose to prominence during Chigwell's campaign is striking. One reason, perhaps, was the decision which Chigwell made shortly after he became mayor, for he settled the vexed

---

[1] The key references for Chigwell are: K.R. Customs Acc. E122/69/9; *C.C.R. 1313-1318*, pp. 594, 595; *C.C.R. 1318-23*, pp. 162, 398; *C.P.R. 1321-4*, p. 162; *P. and M. Rolls*, i, 34, 35, 62, 64, 86, 110; *Cal. Letter-Bk. D*, 23, 24, 30, 31, *E, passim; Cal. of Wills*, i, 329, 383.

wardship dispute which had undone Refham, and settled it in Hakford's favour. If Hakford and his men were really the election-mongers the jurors of 1321 believed them to be, this alliance alone could have been decisive.[1]

External factors assisted the fishmonger. In 1318 controversy over the wool-staple became overt. Its siting at St. Omer pleased few. The Bardi purposed its abolition, many overseas merchants favoured Bruges. In 1318 the mayoralty of the staple fell to the Londoner John Charlton. Another mercer, Charlton was a colleague of Chigwell's companion Roger le Palmer and, backed by a substantial body of London opinion, favoured home staples, with the city an obvious centre. In April 1319, a few weeks after Chigwell's faction won power, the Londoners made a determined effort to carry this policy, and its defeat rallied the bulk of them around Charlton in defence of the St. Omer staple as a *pis aller*, notably in a stand against the Bardi at the classic Westminster debate of April 1320.[2] Conspicuously absent from this rally were the leading city pepperers, Richard de Bethune, John de Gisors and Benedict de Fulsham. In later years, Bethune was to emerge as a partisan of the Bruges staple and a bitter enemy of Charlton. All three, moreover, were to be in a few years equally bitter enemies of Chigwell in the political field. The names of the Londoners backing Charlton in 1320, on the other hand, are the names which dominate the London scene during Chigwell's rise to power—Godchep himself, John de Causton, Hakford, Henry Nasard, Richard de Hakeney. Indeed, it was in these years that the contemporary generation of great city merchants achieved public office.

There need have been no direct, causal connexion. Apart from Godchep, neither Chigwell nor his friends were closely involved in the staple except in an official capacity. But the hard core of his faction had little interest in the Bruges con-

---

[1] For the allegiance of Chigwell's allies, see the records of his mayoralty in *Cal. Letter-Bk. D, E; Ann. Paul., passim* and the pattern of aldermanic elections in Beaven, i, 381-3; on the mercers' wardship dispute, see Weinbaum, ii, 178, 179; *Cal. Letter-Bk. D*, 182, 183, 188, 228, 275.

[2] On the staple controversy, see, in particular, T. F. Tout, *op. cit.*, chapter 7; *C.P.R. 1307-13*, p. 591; *C.C.R. 1318-23*, pp. 234-5; *Cal. Letter-Bk. E*, 18, 54, 58, 105; A. E. Bland, 'The establishment of home staples, 1319', *English Historical Review*, xxix (1914); Charlton left little impression on the London records, see *Cal. Letter-Bk. B*, 49, *D*, 103; Ekwall, *Two Early London Subsidy Rolls*, p. 289.

nexion; Godchep and Causton were allies of both mayors; the enemies of the one were enemies of the other. Evidently, controversy over the staple played its part along with the general reaction against Wengrave and the horse-trading with the mercers in making Chigwell's success possible. And across the scene swept the chill winds of the bitter national conflict. For the rise to power of both Chigwell and Charlton coincided with the rise of Pembroke and the middle party.

In London, Lancastrian zeal survived even Lancaster, but never again could Earl Thomas count on the almost unanimous support of 1311. The years of his supremacy were years of famine, private war and a virtual interregnum in government. When Pembroke began to build his party, he found a ready response. By the spring of 1318 the king was under his hand, by August Lancaster was bated, and in October the triumphant earl consolidated his position at the parliament of York.[1]

The rise of Pembroke, he who had countenanced the reforms of 1311, transformed the situation in London. In October, Wengrave retained the mayoralty only by ruthlessly overriding the popular will.[2] But the news from York was of the wholesale displacement of sheriffs and of commissions of enquiry. It was probably in this winter that the coalition against the recorder took shape, for the coup which followed in the spring bore all the hallmarks of careful preparation. When the promised commission arrived at Guildhall in February 1319, it was greeted by an organized campaign of *querelae* against the city's officers. The commission brushed aside the mayor, deposed the gaoler of Newgate and other officials. The commons kept up the pressure and the commission withdrew to refer the matter to higher authority.

This was the decisive moment. The commons marshalled for the assault. They promptly made the king a loan of 2,000 marks and on 24 March an even weightier commission arrived. Pembroke was there in person, with the Treasurer Sandale and the Earl Marshal. They summoned Wengrave before them in the Chapter House of St. Paul's. Whereupon, in the words of the

---

[1] For the rise of Pembroke, see especially J. C. Davies, *op. cit.*, 439 ff.
[2] *French Chronicle*, p. 40; *Cal. Letter-Bk, D*, 28, *E*, 99.

St. Paul's annalist, the whole city rose against him. They deluged Pembroke with plaints and pleas, petitioning for control of the election of aldermen as well as mayors and sheriffs. Caught between commons and commission, Wengrave was helpless. He surrendered.[1] A draft charter was immediately prepared and taken to the parliament at York. There, for 1,000 marks, Edward issued an *inspeximus* confirming all ancient liberties and a letter-patent and charter embodying the new provisions. On 20 June the new charter was proclaimed and under it, in October, Chigwell swept triumphantly to the mayoralty.[2]

The bland generalities of chroniclers cannot conceal the fact that this was a revolution. For the charter of 1319 represents the highest peak of achievement that a popular movement ever attained in medieval London. Many of its terms were obviously inspired by the Wengrave interlude. The mayor was to hold no other office nor draw sheriffs' pleas to himself. He was to hold office for one year only and he and the recorder were to be content with their fees. Common Clerk, Common Serjeant, chamberlain were to be elected by the commonalty and removable at will; no sheriff was to have more than two clerks and two serjeants; no officials were to draw salary save those elected by the commonalty; no legal business was to be delayed beyond the third court.

Other clauses re-enacted, sometimes in modified form, earlier reforms. No alien was to be admitted to the franchise except by the authority of six men of his craft or full Husting; no non-citizen was to trade retail and annual enquiries were to enforce the ban. All executive officers were to be elected and removable by the commonalty. This thinking was now carried to its logical conclusion. City tallages were to be controlled by four auditors elected by the commonalty and aldermen were to be taxed as other citizens. The common seal was committed to two

---

[1] *Ann. Paul.*, pp. 285, 286; *Cal. Letter-Bk, E*, 37, 38; J. C. Davies, *op. cit.*, 456–8; see Kelsey's sour comment at the Iter of 1321 on his group's helplessness in Weinbaum, ii, 176.

[2] *French Chronicle*, p. 41; *Ann. Paul.*, p. 286; *Cal. Letter-Bk. D*, 29, 30, *E*, 104, 105; the *inspeximus* is set out in Letter Book E, fo. 109–11b and is most readily available in *Lib. Cust.*, pp. 255–68; the additional articles are in *Lib. Cust.*, pp. 268–73; there is a summary in *Lib. Albus*, pp. 141–4.

aldermen and two commoners; no aldermen were to be wardens of Bridge. Control of weights and measures passed to the commonalty, election of brokers to the misteries. Finally, aldermen were to be removable annually and were not to have a second consecutive term.

These measures, radical though they were, represented a sensible compromise. Executive officers were to be removable at will, not annually. The more extreme demands of the crafts were dropped. The attempt to curb administrative costs was a pious hope rather than anything else and annual election of aldermen was a dead letter from the start. Indeed, the whole charter tended to be overshadowed by the immediate local consequences of the desperate national crisis. But nothing can detract from its general significance. This was the most effective communal order yet devised. The very abatement of popular ambitions ensured that the charter's terms, in their essentials, would be permanent. The crafts had won that measure of control over citizenship which was to colour the whole history of late medieval London, and looking to the Crown as the ultimate sanction in a manner which was to become common, the citizens tried to make their charter the basis of a permanent civic order. In this they largely succeeded. Throughout the later Middle Ages, the charter of 1319 was the Magna Carta of the London commonalty. They called it *The Constitutions*.[1]

For, in a very real sense, it closed a period of transition. In constitutional terms, it represents the resolution of those issues which were raised with such violence in 1263. Chigwell's people themselves were aware of the qualitative change in the character of London's public life which the charter effected. 'At this time, many of the people of the trades of London arrayed themselves in livery', proclaimed the author of the *French Chronicle*, adding in cheerful defiance of demonstrable fact, 'and a good time was about to begin.'[2]

The fact that events were so swiftly to prove him wrong has tended to obscure the real achievement of 1319. In the turmoil

[1] For this valuable piece of information on city tradition, I am grateful to Mr. Philip E. Jones, Deputy-Keeper of the City of London Records Office. Special measures were taken to keep city copies of the charter in good preservation.

[2] *French Chronicle*, p. 41.

which followed there was certainly plenty of faction strife and not a little bloodshed, but internal constitutional issues were never at stake, because in a fundamental sense they had been settled. What was at stake henceforth, implicitly if rarely explicitly, was London's status in the national community.

CHAPTER XI

The City and the Kingdom 1319–37

HAMO DE CHIGWELL reached the mayoralty in October 1319. Within a month, he went into action against Wengrave. On 20 November he summoned the recorder, Robert de Kelsey, John de la Chambre and William de Leyre to Guildhall and accused them of inflating the assessments made for the Twelfth authorized at York in order to curry favour with the king. Public opinion was mobilized, a petition sent to Edward, and in January 1320 all four were deposed from their aldermanries. There was clearly a political motive, for while the council retained the Westminster pleader Geoffrey de Hartpol to replace Wengrave, it was Roger le Palmer, Chigwell's ally, and two mercer colleagues of Hakford who succeeded the others.[1]

The very success of this violent attack broke one bond of unity between the disparate allies of 1319. At about the same time, staple affairs worsened. After the failure of the April conference, Charlton was empowered to enforce the St. Omer staple by judicial action. He laid about him with a will, fining Swanland and Conduit and throwing Henry Nasard into prison.[2] With this multiplication of personal and commercial hostilities, political fortunes fluctuated during the summer. The king, on his return from France, was greeted by a splendid display of craft liveries, but at parliamentary elections in September, while the commons chose a fishmonger and a cornmonger,

[1] *Ann. Paul.*, p. 287; *Cal. Letter-Bk. E*, 106, 109, 111, 121, 122, 124; Weinbaum, ii, 175–7. No official record of the depositions survives, but they may be reconstructed from the Iter of 1321 inquisition in Weinbaum, ii, 175–7 and the election of replacements in *Cal. Letter-Bk. E*, 11; see also Beaven, i, 381–2 and Ekwall, *Two Early London Subsidy Rolls*, pp. 105–275, *passim*.

[2] K.R. Acc. V. E101/120/14, 15; *C.P.R. 1317–21*, pp. 477, 489 and *passim*; *C.C.R. 1318–23*, pp. 253, 254; T. F. Tout, *op. cit.*, chapter 7.

the aldermen picked Nicholas de Farndon and Anketil de Gisors, traditional patricians to their fingertips, and in the following month, after what had evidently been a troubled time, it was Farndon who became mayor, 'all the Commons sitting in Guildhall and silence being demanded for the said election'. Farndon, however, had no hope of an equally quiet term. In three weeks he received a royal writ ordering him to prepare for an Iter in January.[1]

The Iter of 1321 was the last and the worst the city had to face.[2] The justices, led by Hervey de Stanton, sat at the Tower on 14 January, and the first day set the tone. 'William Denom vint a la barre et les pria, qille volleient escuter de ceo qil voleit dire pur la communalte de Londres. Hervi: A quei parlez vous? W. Denom: A vous justices. Hervi: Uncore ne savet vous si nous seoms justices ou noun, et pur ceo atendez tanqe nous savoms si nous seoms justices ou noun.' So it went on, with the inimitable Geoffrey le Scrope, prosecuting for the Crown, thrusting in on every possible occasion with his reiterated 'Par qeu garant?' and 'Nous prioms qe cele franchise seit pris en main le Roi.'[3] Stanton and Scrope in a matter of days acquired an unpopularity in London which lasted their lifetime and indeed in 1326 bid fair to shorten it.

The barons claimed that the Iter was the brainchild of Hugh Despenser, now rising to power in Westminster and Wales. It seems likely. Its professed object, after the Wengrave depositions, was to enquire into illegal confederacies. Wengrave and Leyre were in fact mulcted of £40 each, Chambre of £20, Simon Corp of twenty marks, and all were driven out of public life, at least until 1326. Several other groups were presented. But the eyre went much further. Quo Warranto proceedings were launched against every franchise in the city. London's own liberties were combed through, clause by clause, and finally,

---

[1] *Ann. Paul.*, p. 290; *Cal Letter-Bk. D*, 30, 31, *E*, 130, 134, 138.

[2] There is a London journal of the Iter in *Lib. Cust.*, pp. 285-432. The main royal records are two enormous rolls A.R. 546 and 547a. Extracts from these rolls, together with pleas against officials from A.R. 553, which overlapped, are given in Weinbaum, ii, 154-96. In Weinbaum, ii, 114-27, there is an extremely entertaining journal of the opening days of the Iter, apparently verbatim, derived from B.M. Harl. Ms. 453. See also *Ann. Paul.*, pp. 290 ff.

[3] Weinbaum, ii, 114 ff.; *Ann. Paul.*, pp. 290, 291.

many of the citizens' cherished privileges were suspended and referred to the Council for examination.[1] Over a hundred articles of inquest were presented to the ward juries. The administrative record of the past fifty years was raked through. Organized attacks on the fishmongers' gilds by petty traders, on Waleys's edicts by the bakers were tolerated, indeed encouraged, and the justices went on to probe into the affairs of weavers, chaplers, vintners and other crafts. Crown pleas and private suits ground on, day after day.[2] Because of the Brandeston case and other offences, Gisors and three other aldermen were deposed. Personal grievances aggravated the communal. The Iter ran for over twenty-four weeks; sometimes sittings were prolonged till dusk. The summoning of officers, the daily service of juries, the closure of city courts, the endless hearings, paralysed municipal life. The king seemed bent on prising every privilege and penny out of the city. And as soon as the Iter was under way, Farndon was deposed and a royal warden appointed.[3] This, together with the reference of liberties to the Council, meant the virtual suspension of the franchise. Until the end of the reign, Londoners lived under an emergency régime of dubious legality. There can be little doubt that it was the impact of this Iter which turned London irrevocably against Edward and Despenser.

With the displacement of Farndon, it was Hamo Godchep who came to act as deputy to the warden, and his party rapidly gained ground. The city rallied, moved to a counter-attack on the Constable of the Tower and on St. Paul's over the Folkmoot site. Hamo de Chigwell and Andrew Horn emerged as its champions. Their aggressive leadership at this time proved politically decisive. For the justices, who had raged like lions before the Easter recess, were as very lambs after it.[4] In Wales, Despenser's empire-building had recoiled on his head. Hereford and the Mortimers rose in arms against him. Dissidents everywhere rallied. On 28 April Chigwell and his friends went

---

[1] A.R. 546, m. 84–5; *Lib. Cust.*, pp. 308–26; Weinbaum, ii, 124 ff.

[2] See A.R. 547a especially for many private suits and note a whole series of commercial cases, mainly over partnership, in A.R. 546, m.2d–24d.

[3] For the depositions, see *Lib. Cust.*, pp. 371–4, 378; Weinbaum, ii, 112, 113; *Cal. Letter-Bk. E*, 138, 139; *Ann. Paul.*, pp. 290–1.

[4] *Lib. Cust.*, pp. 338–44, 383–4, 385–406, 407–9; *Cal. Letter-Bk. E*, 139.

before the king with a petition for the ending of the Iter. In May fighting broke out in Glamorgan, and on the 21st Edward 'replevied' the city to the fishmonger. Four days later, Lancaster formed a northern league and on 28 June, at Sherborne, the barons issued a manifesto against Despenser. They may already have made contact with the city, for the Iter was denounced as a sin of the king's 'evil counsellor'. Three days later, Edward asked whether the mayor was prepared to hold London against his enemies. The citizens pledged their loyalty, but begged relief from the Marshalsea and permission to handle the misteries in their own way. On 4 July the Iter was formally closed. The citizens put a plan of defence into operation, but at the end of July, baronial armies were at the gates and Chigwell was receiving an emissary from Waltham, bearing 'salus et chers amities' from Hereford and Mortimer.[1]

In the fortnight which followed, the fishmonger's skill was tested to the utmost. The city seethed with sedition, but Chigwell's men had few fond memories of Lancaster. At this point, however, Pembroke returned. In secret sympathy with the Marchers, he worked for moderation, and Chigwell's policy followed his in every particular. The king at first banned all discourse with the barons, but offered no opposition to a conference at Lancaster's Inn on 29 July, where Hereford spoke softly to the city delegates, stressing Despenser's responsibility for the Iter. Edward's reply to the London emissaries, transmitting the earl's message, was ambiguous, but contained a promise to punish all enemies. This was enough for Chigwell. A letter to the barons on 1 August assured them of London's good will and indifference to the fate of Despenser. Hereford was satisfied and Godchep led the city delegation to the parliament which coerced the king into the exile of his favourite.[2]

Chigwell had ridden the crisis without alienating king, barons or populace. At every single step, he took care to associate a common assembly with him. Indeed, it was at his prompting that the commonalty met in October to decide its policy on

[1] *Cal. Letter-Bk. E*, 139, 141–4; *Ann. Paul.*, pp. 292–4; *C.C.R. 1318–23*, p. 301; *Lib. Cust.*, p. 409; R. R. Sharpe, *London and the Kingdom* (London, 1894), i, 148; J. C. Davies, *op. cit.*

[2] *Ann. Paul.*, pp. 293–6; *Cal. Letter-Bk. E*, 143, 145.

defaulters from the *congregatio*. No doubt his action was elementary self-insurance, but Chigwell's handling of the commonalty throughout 1321 helped to make the 1319 charter a reality. On 28 October, he had his reward when the citizens, 'pro rege placendo', allowed him to continue in the mayoralty without a new election. On the following day, when he went to Westminster to take the oath, he established another precedent. He went by barge.[1]

Already, however, he was in the throes of a more desperate crisis. The insult to the queen at Leeds Castle in Kent gave Edward his chance. By swift mobilization and exploitation, he was able to destroy his enemies in detail. In the winter of 1321-2, the revitalized king crushed Badlesmere, the Marchers, the Northerners in turn, recalled Despenser, and celebrated his triumph with a wholesale slaughter of the men who had plagued him so long. A force of 500 Londoners had served with the royal army at Leeds, but when the king turned against Mortimer and the Marcher Contrariants in November, Chigwell was faced with a situation worse than that of July. Pembroke rallied to the king; the mayor followed. His city, however, did not, and a brief exchange of letters in mid-crisis throws vivid light on the realities of the situation.[2]

'Edward was trying to impose a charter of service on London, a sealed military indenture to formalize its allegiance. On 17 November the king wrote an angry letter demanding compliance and complaining that Contrariants had been received in the city. Chigwell replied with two letters. One, under the commonalty seal and omitting all reference to the mayor, respectfully refused to give security under a common seal which would burden the 'good' with the sins of the 'bad'. The other, under the mayor's seal, promised a hunt for Contrariants and asked for a commission to deal with them. As for the military indenture, the king was referred to the commonalty letter. Edward gave Chigwell his commission, but repeated his military demands. On 3 December the mayor reported that a common assembly, feeling their assurances to be enough, had promised

[1] *Cal. Letter-Bk. E*, 147; *Ann. Paul.*, p. 298.
[2] For these letters and their background, see *Cal. Letter-Bk. E*, 151-6; *C.P.R. 1321-1324*, p. 36; *Ann. Paul.*, pp. 299-301.

U

a force of 300, but had refused the indenture and petitioned for a restoration of the franchise. The citizens 'took the King's affairs less to heart than they were accustomed', replied Edward and he ordered them all to join the army immediately. Chigwell hurriedly promised a force of 500 men and Edward was mollified.'

The mayor's extraordinary policy of dissociating himself from the commonalty, upon whom he thrust full responsibility, no doubt reflects the cleavage in the city, for in following Pembroke, Chigwell was isolating himself from civic opinion. But it was also a political exercise of considerable dexterity. By acting almost as a mediator between king and commons, he won for divided London a security it otherwise could not have hoped to enjoy in face of the resurgent monarchy. Not that there is any reason to doubt his sincerity. He owed his position to Pembroke. On 27 December he was appointed to the custody of the Contrariants' lands.[1] But he enabled suspect London to make its voice heard, even after the restoration of the Despensers. Throughout the campaigns in the west and the north, the Londoners kept pressing for a return of their franchise. When the king permitted Chigwell to remain in office until after Easter, they pressed him again.[2] This time, Edward was not disposed to listen. In March came the victory of Boroughbridge and the massacre of the Lancastrians. The rule of the Despensers began.

Five years later, it ended in an explosion of hatred. In the revolt against this detested government, London played a vital role. The events of 1321-2 were enough to form city opinion. The character of Despenser's régime inflamed it beyond endurance, for in a reign where treachery, selfishness and brutality were common form, Despenser, Arundel and Baldock were notorious for cynical abuse of power. The moral opacity at Westminster was equalled by that at Guildhall, where a popular mayor held office at the will of men whom the city considered its worst enemies. Its public life became a shadowy half-world, peopled with mysterious figures like John le Marshal of Walbrook, Despenser's *secretarius*, widely believed to be a betrayer

---

[1] *Cal. Letter-Bk. E*, 159–60; *C.C.R. 1318–23*, pp. 517, 518, 538, 539 and *passim*.
[2] *Cal. Letter-Bk. E*, 150, 155, 156, 163, 164, 166; *Ann. Paul.*, pp 301 ff.

of civic counsel and the real power in London, or Arnold de Hispannia, the Gascon leader, suspected of wielding occult influence. The ambivalence of Chigwell's régime bred widespread contempt for government itself. In the revolution of 1326, even Mortimer's partisans were appalled at the destructive nihilism of the city's young men.[1]

Almost every faction was driven into opposition. The middle class reform charter lost its meaning. Petty traders returned to the attack on civic ordinances. Towards the end of the period, a petition against clerks, usurers, and the purchase of expensive charters which were no benefit to common people, voiced the bitterness of the inarticulate. In 1326, journeymen rose against their masters.[2]

The patriciate was equally discontented. The friends of Wengrave, of Gisors and the men deposed in 1321 were bitterly hostile. There were even sharper compulsions. Alderman Stephen de Abyndon acted as surety for Henry Nasard in a recognizance of 1,000 marks to the earl of Arundel. The money was paid, or at least the recognizance was cancelled, but Arundel forced Abyndon to execute a further recognizance for 600 marks, an act of extortion annulled after enquiry in 1327.[3] Abyndon was but one of a group. For between 1318 and 1323, and particularly during 1321, a number of Londoners were entangled in a bewildering web of recognizances to the leading members of Despenser's faction.[4] The most heavily involved was Henry Nasard, the Wardrobe draper. With him were members of the Abyndon family, the fishmonger Hugh Matefry, Simon de Swanland the draper, and Richard de Bethune the pepperer, with his brother Thomas. All the recognizances were for large sums. Some of Despenser's victims, like the prior of St. John Jerusalem, were involved with them, and though Arundel

---

[1] See *Ann. Paul.*, pp. 315, 321, 322; *P. and M. Rolls*, i, 11 ff.

[2] *P. and M. Rolls*, i, 1–5, 15, 16; Weinbaum, ii, 255, 256; *Ann. Paul.*, pp. 321–2.

[3] *C.C.R. 1327–30*, pp. 47, 50.

[4] After the fall of Despenser, the Exchequer listed the recognizances made out to his group. Three rolls survive among the Exchequer Miscellanea—E163/3/4, 3/6, 4/29. All recognizances listed there may be found on the Chancery enrolments, but the Exchequer rolls are incomplete. Many others may be traced in the Chancery rolls. The more important of those here considered may be found in: *C.C.R. 1313–18*, pp. 480, 559, 615; *C.C.R. 1318–23*, pp. 228, 236, 356, 360, 372, 373, 479, 705; *C.C.R. 1323–7*, p. 161; see also Wardrobe Debentures E404/482/310.

was the chief beneficiary, Despenser's agents, John le Marshal
and Oliver de Ingham, were prominent in the transactions. It
is impossible to say what these interlocking recognizances represent. Probably they were the sanctions for other, hidden agreements. It was one of Despenser's favourite methods of compulsion. There were some other points of contact. Stephen de
Abyndon was deprived of his aldermanry in 1321; Swanland
ceased to be active in the royal service between 1320 and 1326;
Nasard and Swanland were victims of Charlton, mayor of the St.
Omer staple; Bethune was Charlton's rival. Other great city
merchants, men like Oxford, Conduit, Darcy, swift to adapt
their enterprise to every shift in royal policy, were never caught
in this recognizance web. Stephen de Abyndon certainly suffered in consequence. Probably the others did, too, for in 1326,
Bethune and his allies suddenly emerged as familiars of Roger
Mortimer in his attack on the régime.

The conversion of some of the city's most influential men into
ardent Mortimer partisans, coupled with the furious disaffection of the plebs, made Chigwell's position extremely uncomfortable. These years are the central enigma of his career.
He was in no sense Despenser's man. He would hardly have
survived 1326 if he had been. But he could never have been a
partisan of Mortimer. After Boroughbridge, Chigwell, as mayor,
was immediately involved in the proscription of rebels. On 23
March 1322 he served on the commission which condemned
Henry Tyeys and John Giffard of Bromfield. More important,
on 14 July he was one of the five men appointed to try the
Mortimers themselves, and as Mortimer's judge, he had condemned him to death.[1] The mutual hatred of Mortimer and
Chigwell was the central feature of city politics from 1323 to
1330. Chigwell's star was Pembroke, and had been since 1319.
When Pembroke's influence waned in 1323, the fishmonger got
into trouble, and the earl's death left him without a sense of
direction. He found it later in an alliance with Henry of Lancaster, Earl Thomas's brother—once more the anti-Mortimer
faction—and was able to exploit London's Lancastrian myth
to his own advantage. Certainly he retained sufficient hold on
city loyalties not only to survive 1326, but to re-emerge as a

[1] *C.P.R. 1321-4*, pp. 148, 249; *Ann. Paul.*, p. 303.

power as soon as the dust had settled, a remarkable achievement in the circumstances. But from 1322 to 1326, as he trod a desperate tightrope between the avarice of the Despensers and the anger of the Londoners, he was a living anomaly. 'Many said, he is a good man; but others, no, no, he deceives the people.'[1]

The sparse annals of London under the Despensers, therefore, chronicle a lurching progress towards disaster. In October 1322, 'to obtain the king's grace', the citizens confirmed Chigwell in the mayoralty, and in February 1323 he and Conduit were purveying wheat for the Crown, but in April he was in trouble. Rebels seized Wallingford Castle in an attempt to liberate imprisoned Lancastrians, and when the earl of Kent asked the city for fifty arbalesters, the commonalty refused, saying their prime duty was to hold London for the king, as surety for which the queen and her children were living amongst them. The Court already suspected Londoners of complicity in the affair; this reply was the last straw. In April, special commissions of enquiry were sent in and Edward abruptly deprived Chigwell of the mayoralty. The citizens begged Despenser and Baldock to exercise mercy, but the fishmonger and his close allies, Godchep, Roger le Palmer and Edmund Lambyn, were taken into custody and followed the Court as prisoners.[2]

Nicholas de Farndon took office, and it was he who had to cope with the renewed attack of the street-traders, with royal orders to search Bishop Stratford.[3] He had bigger problems, for in August, Mortimer made his celebrated escape from the Tower. Londoners were implicated up to the hilt, for the whole adventure was planned with the help of citizens. From the Tower, Mortimer and his men were ferried across the Thames to John de Gisors' mills, where horses were waiting to take them to Portsmouth. There, agents of Ralph de Bokton, a London merchant, transferred them to a ship which Bokton had brought from Normandy, and they sailed for France. Personal relations between Mortimer and some of the patricians, the leading pepperers in particular, were evidently close. Bethune's name

---

[1] *Ann. Paul.*, p. 346.
[2] *P. and M. Rolls*, i, 1; *French Chronicle*, pp. 45, 46; *Ann. Paul.*, pp. 304, 305; *Cal. Letter-Bk. D*, 31, *E*, 31–2, 112, 161, 174, 178, 179.   [3] *P. and M. Rolls*, i, 1–4.

was mentioned.[1] The king reacted. On 5 September he pardoned Chigwell and his friends. Rumours of secret letters passing through the staple from Mortimer to his London allies multiplied; in November the city gates were suddenly closed against treason. On the 29th Edward formally committed the custody of London to Chigwell, and on 7 December the fishmonger was sworn at the Exchequer by the king himself.[2] Against Mortimer at least, Chigwell was a Londoner to be trusted.

He at once began to root out plotters, and throughout 1324 and 1325 was active on royal commissions.[3] His fellow mayor, however, came to grief. The truce with Flanders and the war with France finished the St. Omer staple. In 1323, Charlton ceased to be mayor of the merchants. His successor occupied himself with the transfer to Bruges, a policy which reached its logical culmination in May 1325 when Richard de Bethune, despite his suspected role in Mortimer's escape, was made mayor and ordered to set himself up in the Flemish city.[4] His posting abroad at this date was probably a political error of the first magnitude. For the last crisis of the reign was at hand. The estranged queen, refusing to return to Edward, joined Mortimer and preparations for an invasion and a rising accelerated. Despenser and Baldock made strenuous efforts to save themselves. On 1 May 1326, probably in an attempt to win popularity, they completely reversed their staple policy, established home staples at eight centres throughout the kingdom, and on 12 June Charlton won his long-delayed triumph, when representatives of the staple towns elected him their mayor.[5] Chigwell was associated with the new policy. With Charlton, Conduit and Darcy, he headed the steering committee which established the staples; it was he who warned the king that Flemings were buying up all the teasles in the kingdom.[6] The home-staple policy, indeed, may have strengthened his position at a critical moment.

[1] See the detailed account in *Ann. Paul.*, pp. 305–6.
[2] *C.P.R. 1321–4*, pp. 342, 351; *Cal. Letter-Bk. D*, 31, 32, *E*, 182, 183; *Ann. Paul.*, p. 306.
[3] *C.P.R. 1321–4*, p. 358; *C.P.R. 1324–7*, p. 48; *C.C.R. 1323–7*, p. 228; *P. and M. Rolls*, i, 24, 66, 67.
[4] *C.C.R. 1318–23*, p. 9; *C.C.R. 1323–7*, pp. 307, 308, 378; *C.P.R. 1321–4*, p. 13; *C.P.R. 1324–7*, p. 134.
[5] *C.P.R. 1324–7*, p. 269; *C.C.R. 1323–7*, pp. 571, 585; *C.P.R. 1327–30*, pp. 98, 99.
[6] *C.C.R. 1323–7*, pp. 564, 565; *Cal. Letter-Bk. E*, 210, 211; *Ann. Paul.*, p. 312.

The moment, however, was critical in the extreme. The staple ordinance itself was probably the final stage in the formation of the Mortimer faction in London, for Edward immediately proclaimed Bethune his enemy and confiscated his estates. Charlton was ordered to search for Mortimer's correspondence in staple merchandise, and throughout the summer, city levies were moving to the coast. In September the crisis broke. When the newly elected sheriffs presented themselves at the Exchequer, they could not be sworn, the Husting clerk reports, 'because the King was engaged owing to the arrival of the Queen from France'.[1]

Isabella and Mortimer landed at Harwich on 24 September. Magnates flocked to join them. Among the first was Henry of Lancaster. He took London's loyalties with him. On the 28th, the king's proclamation against Mortimer was read to a sullen city. Archbishop Reynolds's publication of an old Bull against the invaders was greeted with open hostility. A letter from Isabella had already reached London, and Edward's nerve broke. On 2 October he fled to Wales. Scrope was left to mobilize the royal forces. He was still there on 9 October, but on that day, Isabella's second letter came. It ordered the Londoners to arrest Despenser immediately, so that she should 'not have cause to punish the city'. Copies suddenly appeared on the Cross in Cheap, on house windows all over London.[2] On the morning of 15 October, Chigwell went to Blackfriars to consult with the unpopular Treasurer, Bishop Stapledon and with Stephen Gravesend, bishop of London, who was trying to mediate between Isabella and her husband. In his absence, evidently at a given signal, the populace rose in arms.[3]

Huge crowds poured into the streets, shouting for Isabella and the blood of her enemies. They smashed the houses of the king's men, marched to the Tower, broke in and freed John de Eltham

[1] *C.C.R. 1323-7*, pp. 607, 608; *French Chronicle*, pp. 55, 56; *Ann. Paul.*, p. 313; *Cal. Letter-Bk. D*, 33.

[2] *P. and M. Rolls*, i, 41, 42, for the second letter; see also *Ann. Paul.*, p. 315; *French Chronicle*, pp. 51, 52; *Cal. Letter-Bk. E*, 213; E. L. G. Stones, 'Sir Geoffrey le Scrope, Chief Justice of the King's Bench', *English Historical Review*, lxix (1954), 4, n. 1.

[3] This account of the rising is based mainly on *Ann. Paul.*, pp. 316-22 (narrative) 345-50 (penance of Stapledon's murderers); *French Chronicle*, pp. 51-3; *P. and M. Rolls*, i, 14-19; *C.P.R. 1327-30*, p. 240; *Cal. Letter-Bk. D*, 253, *E*, 224, 225; I am indebted to Dr. E. B. Fryde for information on the London raids on county estates.

and the Lancastrians. John le Marshal, Despenser's *secretarius*, they caught at his house and in a sudden access of fury, they dragged him into Cheap and cut his head off. The killing crazed them. They took fire and sword through the city. Mobs sought Scrope and Stanton down burning streets. Baying out towards Blackfriars, they caught Chigwell, dragged him back to Guild-hall, wringing his hands and crying for mercy, forced him to swear allegiance to the invaders. They turned against Staple-don's palace. At this point, the bishop himself rode in through Newgate on his way to lunch. At St. Michael le Quern, the crowd was on him, yelling 'Traitor!'. He and his two squires raced frantically for St. Paul's, but at the north door they were cornered. A butcher called Hatfield grabbed the bishop, ham-mered him half-conscious and heaved him from his horse. 'Kill! Kill!', shouted the crowd, closing in. They dragged him through the Churchyard into Cheap and hacked off his head with a bread-knife.

With the corpse of a bishop and royal counsellor lying head-less in Cheap, the city collapsed into anarchy. Crowds broke into Holy Trinity, Arundel's treasury. John Charlton and William de Clif were plundered, the Bardi stripped. Baldock's treasure was looted from St. Paul's, the man himself torn from Gravesend's house by an enraged crowd, led by the sheriff, who threw him into Newgate, where he died 'in torment'. Journey-men rose against their masters, hunted down aliens. Arnold de Hispannia, the Gascon leader, was taken out to No-Man's-Land and beheaded. Robber gangs of 'Roarers' pullulated. John Coterel, a leatherseller, organized raids and distributed loot as Londoners swarmed out to Despenser's estates. Extor-tioners battened on visiting magnates; there were gang-killings in broad daylight. County victuallers dared not venture within the walls. The courts closed. There was a naked terror.

The maddened Londoners were an instrument made for Mortimer's hand. John Giffard rode in to take the city's alle-giance; Isabella commended the citizens, hastened to throw her protection over Bishop Gravesend, whose life was in danger. The young prince announced the restoration of the franchise and on 15 November, John de Stratford arrived with letters appointing Richard de Bethune and John de Gisors joint keepers of the

Tower. On the same day Chigwell was deposed and Bethune took the mayoralty. With Mortimer's men in power, the way was clear. A stream of urgent proclamations flowed from Guildhall as the council tried to restore order. An assembly of crafts re-enacted the old radical doctrine on freedom admissions. The personality of Bethune emerges from an order permitting all who had fled to return, 'except John Charlton'.[1] Gradually a new note of political purpose sounds.

London had rejected Edward II and the murder of Staple-don committed the city to deposition.[2] Already, when Stratford came on 15 November, he had been sworn to the city's liberty and cause. This became general practice. The Londoners com-pelled every man of importance who came to the city to swear an oath to maintain their liberties and the cause of Isabella, which were invariably linked. It was physically dangerous to refuse. The city rapidly assumed an ominous national import-ance. Guildhall proclamations promised safety to Geoffrey le Scrope, invited by letter under the common seal to come to London, and to others who came, all 'in order to be in accord with the good men of the city for the common profit of the King and the land'. The crucial parliament was to be held at West-minster in the shadow of the mob; all attempts to have it trans-ferred elsewhere were overridden. The writs were issued on 2 December, the day before Despenser's head was paraded through the streets to cheers and the blowing of horns. By Christmas, the Lancastrians Stratford and Lord Wake were closeted with the mayor and aldermen on business 'touching the king'.[3]

What the Londoners did, in effect, was to create a sworn commune to depose Edward II.[4] On 30 December every citizen was sworn in his ward under compulsion. An oath to the new

[1] *P. and M. Rolls*, i, 14–19, 42, 43; *Cal. Letter-Bk. E*, 214; *Ann. Paul.*, p. 318.

[2] On the general background to the deposition, see M. V. Clarke, 'Committees of Estates and the deposition of Edward II', in *Historical Essays in honour of J. Tait*, ed. J. G. Edwards, V. Galbraith, E. F. Jacob (Manchester, 1933) and M. McKi-sack, 'London and the succession to the Crown during the Middle Ages', in *Studies in Medieval History presented to F. M. Powicke*, ed. R. W. Hunt, W. A. Pantin, R. W. Southern (Oxford, 1948).

[3] *P. and M. Rolls*, i, 17; *Cal. Letter-Bk. E*, 215; *Ann. Paul.*, pp. 318, 322, 323.

[4] For London's role in the deposition, see, in particular, *P. and M. Rolls*, i, 11–19; *Ann. Paul.*, pp. 322–4.

régime, in which London's liberties were accorded a premier
place, was prepared for the magnates and the parliament. The
city took under its wing the rebellious burgesses of Bury and St.
Albans, paraded itself as the leader of the movement. Parliament met on 7 January 1327. The strong city contingent was
led by Gisors and from the start, proceedings were overshadowed by the London crowds. They manhandled the fasti-
dious bishop of Rochester, growled at the wavering Gravesend,
and, heated by Orleton's harangues, parliament agreed to
replace Edward. But the captive king turned stubborn. So
Mortimer played his trump.

On 12 January Bethune sent a commonalty letter to Westminster. It was virtually an ultimatum. It demanded to know
whether the assembly was 'willing to be in accord with the
city' in deposing Edward. On the next day, in response, the
magnates rode to Guildhall and after great meetings and fiery
sermons from Orleton and Stratford, took the oath to the new
king and London's liberties. For three days the swearing-in
continued, until four earls, a couple of dozen barons, over
seventy knights, two archbishops, twelve bishops, abbots,
priors, clerks, barons of the Cinque Ports, burgesses of Bury and
St. Albans were sworn. Never in its history had the country
witnessed scenes as bizarre as those enacted at Guildhall in
January 1327, with the baronage and prelacy of England marshalled by the mayor and the chamberlain Andrew Horn and
drilled in solemn oath by the sheriff's clerk Roger de Depham,
with his minatory forefinger and loud command of 'You will
swear!'; with a tearful archbishop of Canterbury prostrating
himself before the citizens, buying their forgiveness with fifty
tuns of wine, while outside, the mob which had murdered one
of his suffragans held the lawless streets to ransom.

On the 13th it was decided. Parliament was swung into action
again, and Gisors led the city deputation which attended the
final pitiful scene at Kenilworth. Magnates and prelates had
deposed a king in response to the 'clamour of the whole people'.
That clamour had a distinct London accent.'

London's liberties had been built into the new order. In the
spring, they were formalized. On 28 February Edward III
pardoned the citizens; on 4 March, released them from all debts

owed the late king. They were exempted from the prise of wine, granted the privilege of being taxed at the lower county rate. On 6 March the vill of Southwark was given to the city, and on the next day, Edward issued a comprehensive charter of liberties, which Andrew Horn expounded to a Guildhall mass-meeting on the 9th, 'in English'.[1] This charter, concerned in the main with the detail of Crown-city relationships, represented the widest measure of administrative freedom London had yet attained. All the ancient liberties, in their pre-1321 purity, were restored and confirmed. The city was never again to be subjected to royal wardens. The Marshalsea was to have no jurisdiction within the franchise. One royal confirmation of the charters was to be sufficient to any reign. There were to be no more forced prisage and purveyance; the citizens were to be taxed only with the rest of the kingdom; their sheriffs were to be amerced no more heavily than others and were not to be held responsible for sanctuary. The forty-day rule for aliens and all the old city claims over the trade regulations, the sokes, the Thames were expressly confirmed. These were all matters which had been in dispute during the previous century. There were additional comforts. The city farm was reduced to its old, and increasingly nominal, figure of £300; the mayor was to be ex officio justice of gaol delivery and the right to hang hand-having thieves was officially guaranteed. Finally, no market was to be held within seven leagues of the city—with the grant of Southwark, a formidable theoretical monopoly.

/The charter of 1327 closed an epoch in London history, put an end to 150 years of existence as a struggling, insecure commune in a developing feudal kingdom. It signalized London's integration into the new national community. With its shield against royal power, its assuagement of the city's administrative irredentism, it accorded political recognition to social fact. The city was fast becoming the focus of the power of the realm, its patriciate in truth 'a mirror to all England'. In that same March of 1327 royal charters went to its goldsmiths, skinners, girdlers and tailors, giving them rights of search

---

[1] The charter is set out in full, with several of the other privileges, in *Ann. Paul.*, pp. 325–32; see also *Lib. Albus*, pp. 144–8; *Lib. Cust.*, pp. 435, 436; the charter is preserved at Guildhall.

throughout the kingdom.[1] Within the city, the crafts were dominant powers, their control over citizenship confirmed. Here, too, there was decision, as the *Constitutions* of 1319, suitably softened by ritual and convention, settled into permanence. As the echoes of the 1326 revolution died away, so did political warfare of the old kind. Compared with the almost continuous turmoil of the troubled years from 1263 to 1330, the succeeding generations were silent.[2] The charter of 1327 symbolized a new synthesis, a new balance. With it, the history of London the commune ends, that of London the capital begins.

Synthesis and balance, however, were not immediately apparent to the men of 1327. Their bloody revolution brought no easement to that state of political tension which had become a permanent condition of the lives of most of them. At first Mortimer's men carried all before them. Benedict de Fulsham, the pepperer ally of Gisors and Bethune, reached the council; so did Swanland. Even Wengrave's old allies reappeared. William de Leyre's son Thomas became an alderman and the irrepressible lawyer Kelsey bobbed up again on the surface of political life.[3] But Chigwell was no less indestructible. In terror of his life on 15 October, he was acting as Bethune's deputy by the new year.[4] He was, after all, the *Constitutions'* author. Soon he was gaining ground. Bethune failed to prevent the removal north of the Exchequer and Common Pleas; he was involved in an unseemly squabble with his old rival Charlton at the abortive staple conference at York. In October 1327 Bury rose against its overlord and appealed to London, which was emerging as a leader of the towns, as a recipient of letters from Oxford, seeking advice 'as from a daughter to a mother'. In Chigwell, the men of Bury found a sympathetic listener. The trend of opinion strengthened. The fishmonger's kinsman, Thomas, reached the parliamentary panels, and in October Hamo himself returned to the mayoralty.[5]

---

[1] *C.P.R. 1327-30*, pp. 29, 34, 40, 42.

[2] For the later period, see especially, S. L. Thrupp, *The Merchant Class of Medieval London* and J. Tait, introduction to R. Bird, *The Turbulent London of Richard II*.

[3] Beaven, i, 383, 384; *Cal. Letter-Bk. E*, 222, 223 and *passim*; *P. and M. Rolls*, i, 25, 30, 51, 60, 63, 70.   [4] *Cal. Letter-Bk. E*, 220; *P. and M. Rolls*, i, 33 and *passim*.

[5] *Cal. Letter-Bk. E*, 223; *P. and M. Rolls*, i, 25-30, 31-59, 169; *Ann. Paul.*, pp. 333, 345, 346.

He was sustained by a strong resurgence of Lancastrian feeling. For Mortimer was proving a second Despenser. His exclusiveness and wanton terrorism finally united Henry of Lancaster, several bishops led by Stratford and Gravesend, and, for a while, the royal earls of Kent and Norfolk, in a demand for action. The peace with the Scots was the final goad. The parliament called for Salisbury on 16 October was to be the battlefield and through the summer, the opposition rallied its forces. London swung solidly back to its old allegiance, with Chigwell whole-heartedly leading the campaign against Mortimer.

By 28 August 1328 Chigwell and the Lancastrians were in contact, and in September Wake and Stratford arrived at Guildhall to 'talk over affairs of state'. The king was not living of his own, they complained to the mayor, neither was he consulting his proper counsellors. Remedies must be sought at the next parliament. When news of the meeting reached the Court, Mortimer at once sent Oliver de Ingham and Bartholomew de Burghersh to demand an explanation. Chigwell's reply was worthy of a man who had served under Despenser. He outlined his visitors' complaints and said he had replied that 'if these things were so, it would be well that they should be amended in parliament'. He asked for the parliament to be held at London or Westminster, rather than Salisbury, and denied a plot.[1]

This reply, to say the least, was disingenuous. Immediately after Stratford's visit, city clerks drafted and enrolled whole series of letters, to the king, Archbishop Melton of York, several bishops and earls, asking for the parliament to be transferred to London or Westminster. All were cancelled after Ingham's coming, but with the precedent of 1327 in mind, the purpose is clear. The mayor was soon in contact with Gravesend, and trying to influence the new archbishop. Co-operation was the order of the day. On 10 October, at the request of Henry of Lancaster himself, Chigwell entered into the city records the original deed of transfer conveying the New Temple to the house of Lancaster.[2]

More important, when Stratford left the city he took with him a fully equipped force of London men-at-arms which

[1] P. and M. Rolls, i, 66, 68, 69.
[2] P. and M. Rolls, i, 36, 67, 68, 70, 71; Cal. Letter-Bk. E, 229.

joined Lancaster's retinue. The nucleus was a force which the city had raised in July 1327 for service against the Scots, when John de Bedford, an important farrier, took north 100 horsemen in the city's pay with twenty men-at-arms and 160 archers whom he had raised independently. Indeed, Bedford in these years was pursuing a brief but profitable career as a mercenary.[1] As close companions, he took with him two fishmongers, a cordwainer, and John Chaucer, father of the poet Geoffrey Chaucer, a young man at the time. Many of the men who rode out to join Lancaster were old companions in arms. Of the sixty-three known by name, sixteen had served in a city contingent sent north in 1318, twenty-one were to serve in another of 1334. Most of them were *populares*, most, if not all, mercenaries. But they had been supplied and equipped by wealthy fellow-citizens, at least fifty of them, according to royal investigators, and with Bedford and Chaucer among them and two of their own armourers to service them, they were virtually an official city contribution to Lancaster's livery and cause. And, despite the mayor's disclaimer to the king, at their head rode the powerful warden of the fishmongers, his own kinsman Thomas de Chigwell.[2]

In October the crisis came to a head. The Salisbury parliament broke up in anger, with Mortimer, now earl of March, breathing threats and Lancaster's men, including the Londoners, under arms at Winchester. A riot broke out in Bury, and in the confusion, some of Bedford's men, acting in collusion with an alderman of the town, kidnapped the abbot. They hid him in London, robbed him and eventually even shipped him overseas. John Coterel, prominent in the enterprises of 1326, was equally prominent in this, and suspicion fell on Chigwell.[3] He

---

[1] Lists of the men who joined Lancaster may be found among the Exchequer Miscellanea in E163/4/27, the record of an inquisition in London, and E163/4/28, a duplicate with a few additional names; see also *P. and M. Rolls*, i, 41; *Cal. Letter-Bk. F*, 206; V. B. Redstone, 'Some mercenaries of Henry of Lancaster', *Trans. Royal Hist. Soc.*, 3rd. ser. vii (1913).

[2] For Bedford and his colleagues, see A.R. 551, m. 2; *Ann. Lond.*, p. 245; *Ann. Paul.*, p. 346; *Cal. Letter-Bk. E*, 2–5 (expedition of 1334), 93–6 (expedition of 1318); the Exchequer lists may be collated with these, with Ekwall, *Two Early London Subsidy Rolls*, and *Cal. Letter-Bk. D, E, passim*; John Chaucer is called the 'brother' of Thomas Heyrun (E163/4/28); Thomas de Chigwell heads all lists.

[3] A.R. 551, m.2; *P. and M. Rolls*, i, 35, 73; *Ann. Lond.*, p. 245; *Ann. Paul.*, pp. 333, 345, 346.

had already given offence by launching judicial proceedings against a fellow-alderman, the skinner John Cotun, who was alleged to have denounced the mayor in 1326 as 'the vilest worm to have come to London for twenty years', and to have advocated his immediate decapitation as a cure for the city's ills.[1] At the mayoral election, when the aldermen announced that their choice had again fallen on the fishmonger, an organized claque broke into a chant of 'Fulsham! Fulsham!' —Bethune's ally. Uproar ensued and weapons were drawn. To avert disaster, the aldermen decided on a compromise candidate and the pepperer John de Grantham took office.[2]

He took pains to lower the city's voice. With Mortimer's armies scouring the country, the mayor hastened to welcome Scrope and Walter de Norwich and to assure the king of London's loyalty. A propagandist letter from Lancaster on 5 November, hinting darkly at rumours that Edward II was still alive, kept partisan feeling on the boil, and on the 13th a royal writ summoned a citizen deputation to Windsor. Men hostile or indifferent to Chigwell—Fulsham, Thomas de Leyre, John Pulteney, Kelsey—dominated its counsels, and on the 18th Grantham promised Edward that Bedford's troopers would be punished.[3] Early in December, however, the king left for the north, and as soon as he had gone, the Lancastrians came flocking to the city.

This was the climax. The archbishop rallied to their cause, and after preaching at St. Paul's, joined with Gravesend, Kent, Norfolk and the Lancastrians to issue a summons to the baronage. The king reacted with an unprecedented exercise in public relations. A letter went to Guildhall begging for assistance from the city 'which he regarded as the king's chamber'. With it was a full and frank account from the royal standpoint of the whole quarrel, Lancaster's arguments challenged, point by point. This apologia, which fills two membranes of the city record, was to be proclaimed in public. Never before had such intimate detail of high policy been so bandied about the market place.[4]

Grantham was acutely embarrassed, for the letter came before

[1] *P. and M. Rolls*, i, 69, 70.   [2] *Ann. Paul.*, p. 342; *r. and M. Rolls*, i, 72, 73.
[3] *P. and M. Rolls*, i, 71-4.   [4] *C.C.R. 1327-30*, p. 422; *P. and M. Rolls*, i, 77-83.

a Guildhall assembly on the 20th, when Wake and other Lancastrians were present on a mission from the barons at St. Paul's. No-one wanted war and the patriciate was divided. The Lancastrians asked for time, and the Londoners begged Mortimer for an ending of hostilities. This was followed, on 23 December, by two letters from the city and the archbishop, couched in similar terms, cautioning the king, with references to Magna Carta, against proceeding in arms against Lancaster. The London letter, unusually frank, added that the writers felt bound by their allegiance to Edward 'to warn him of the dangers which would ensue if he persisted in his intentions'.[1]

Edward's reply, on the 29th, was a declaration of war and in the new year Lancaster, with Thomas de Chigwell, John de Bedford and over 600 Londoners in his train, marched out. But this was a paper tiger. Kent and Norfolk lost their nerve and were lured back to the king's side. At Bedford, the disorganized Lancastrians caved in. By 15 January Lancaster had surrendered and his men were in flight.

The earl of March closed in for the kill. His intention, clearly, was to isolate, discredit and destroy the London leaders. The mayor was ordered to hold inquest. Chigwell's enemies rose to the bait. It proved necessary to amerce one goldsmith for evading service on the panel of inquisitors, but among the rest, familiar names reappear—Bethune, Gisors, Leyre, Pulteney, the inevitable Kelsey. It was these men who listed Lancaster's Londoners and prepared charges. On 5 February Grantham and the Despenser-trained Oliver de Ingham were ordered to begin the trials.[2] Enquiry soon ranged far beyond the question of the city men-at-arms. Charge after charge, generally of extortion, was levelled, some bearing little apparent relevance to the Lancaster crisis. Bedford and his men were condemned. So were two important leather merchants, two wardens of the fishmongers, a prominent vintner. Of twenty accused men whose names are known, eleven were fishmongers from the substantial middle class. Mortimer was after bigger prey. John Coterel, for his part in the Bury affair, was hanged, and the court went on to bracket Thomas de Chigwell's name with his.

---

[1] *P. and M. Rolls*, i, 83–5.
[2] *Ann. Lond.*, pp. 241–3; *Cal. Letter-Bk. E*, 234; *P. and M. Rolls*, i, 85–6.

Finally, on 13 February, Hamo himself was brought to trial on the same charge. Mortimer at last settled his account. Chigwell was condemned to death.

This was dangerous. The London chroniclers virtually accuse the jury of personal animosity against the fishmonger; the continuator of Andrew Horn goes so far as to list their names. John Cotun, who thought Chigwell such a vile worm, was one; Simon Corp, the alderman deposed as a Wengrave supporter in 1321, was another; Richard de Bethune's brother Thomas a third. But Hamo's following was large. The populace was Lancastrian and the fishmonger could claim benefit of clergy. The authorities yielded. Chigwell was committed to Bishop Gravesend, who lodged him honourably at Orset.[1]

The opposition had been blunted but in no sense disarmed. In May special precautions were needed during Edward's absence in France and the new year brought a startling demonstration of hostility to Mortimer. For in January Chigwell made purgation at Orset and Gravesend released him. The Londoners seized the opportunity and Chigwell's return to London was a triumph. Aldermen and commoners, on horse and foot, thronged out to meet and escort him with full honours through the city. The shocked Isabella immediately ordered his arrest, but the Londoners connived at his escape. Hamo de Chigwell survived the régime, to die in bed sometime in 1332.[2]

His old enemy's time was now running out. A month after the fishmonger's release, Mortimer lured the earl of Kent to his death in a futile revolt to restore a mythical Edward II. Once more, inquest in the city unearthed yet more dissidents, among them, ironically enough, John Hauteyn, city representative at the renunciation of fealty at Kenilworth in 1327. At the Winchester parliament, Mortimer was threatening London for its reception of his enemy John Charlton. In July there was another scare, when the mayor was summoned to Woodstock, asked for yet another declaration of loyalty, yet another security scheme. But the Londoners had not long to wait. In the autumn,

---

[1] *Ann. Lond.*, pp. 243–6; *Ann. Paul.*, pp. 346, 347.

[2] *Ann. Lond.*, pp. 246, 247; *Ann. Paul.*, p. 347; debts to Chigwell were recorded in 1331—*C.C.R. 1330–3*, p. 313; his will was dated 16 June 1332, enrolled 22 February 1333—*Cal. of Wills*, i, 383.

Edward at last broke free from his tutelage and, with virtually unanimous support, turned on Mortimer. On 29 November, the earl of March died on the scaffold.[1]

The destruction of Mortimer ended the time of troubles. The old quarrels were finally stilled. There was a new generation, a new England was taking shape. The settlement which had been achieved in 1319 and 1327 began to take effect as the generation which had achieved it passed away. The very names of these years spell out the new age. Swanland was mayor in 1329, Preston in 1332, Conduit in 1334. Above all, there was John Pulteney, mayor three times in the decade.[2] A new generation looked to new enterprises as the great conflict with France approached. In 1336 Oxford, Hakeney and their fellows were summoned to the wool merchants' assembly; the syndicate formed. In 1337, the year of the comet, men massed, ships gathered and Pulteney was knighted. The city braced itself for the struggle which was ultimately to make it the metropolis of England.[3] On 12 July 1338 Edward sailed. With him, from the London wharves, went the *La Jonette*, the *Cogge of All Hallows*, the *Sainte Marie Cogge* of William Hansard, sheriff and warden of the fishmongers, heading for glory at Sluys.[4] With him, too, London entered the Hundred Years' War and a new era.

[1] *Ann. Lond.*, pp. 247-51; *Ann. Paul.*, p. 349; *Cal. Letter-Bk. E*, 222, 245-6.
[2] Beaven, i, 382-4.
[3] *Cal. Letter-Bk. E*, 299, 300, *F, passim*; *Ann. Paul.*, p. 366.
[4] R. R. Sharpe, *London and the Kingdom*, i, 182.

CHAPTER XII

The Capital

'AND Lowys, yf so be that I shewe the in my light Englissh as trewe conclusions touching this mater, and not oonly as trewe but as many and as subtile conclusiouns, as ben shewid in Latyne in eny comune tretys of the Astrelabie, konne me the more thank. And preie God save the King, that is lord of this language.'[1] Under an umbrella of modest disclaimers, Geoffrey Chaucer, in the 1390's, was advancing English into the realm of science, and if the *Equatorie of the Planetis* is really his, the deprecatory prologue to the *Treatise on the Astrolabe* must be discounted even more decidedly. For who can miss the note of patriotic achievement? It is appropriate that a Londoner, moving in a London circle of writers, Gower, Strode and Thomas Usk, should pen them. Two generations earlier, city clerks were carrying English into administration, Andrew Horn expounding the charters in the vernacular.

The charter which Horn took such pains to make clear to the *vulgus*, the great charter of 1327, defines an epoch in London's history. Its terms were liberal enough. More important was its meaning. It was a formal renunciation of all those weapons which English monarchs had used against the city since 1216. In so far as it were possible, Edward III guaranteed that London would be for ever free. Reality, of course, was not so rosy, but, even in the reign of Richard II, the city's liberties were not put to the question in anything like the manner of Henry III and Edward I. With the charter of 1327, the medieval English monarchy reconciled itself to the idea of an autonomous London.

For the city was no longer a fractious liberty under the harrow

---

[1] *The Works of Geoffrey Chaucer*, ed. F. N. Robinson, 2nd (New Cambridge) edn., p. 546 (Prologue to *A Treatise on the Astrolabe*).

of a monarchy wrestling with the problems of a feudal kingdom. The community of the realm had taken shape and London had been integrated into it.ʹ That community finds its clearest reflection in the new patriciate. Its fundamental characteristics were unaltered.[1] The aldermen were still merchants, officials and landowners. The apparent increase in the number of county landowners among them is in part illusory, a product of more abundant documentation.ₗ If anything, there was a decline in the quality of ownership, as the big estates and the plurality of manors became rare under Edward I. The reign of his successor witnessed a distinct recovery. English county immigrants assumed social leadership in London, many of them rooted in the franklin and knightly classes of the shires. Consequently, the distribution of aldermanic estates broadened to embrace much of England, though the south-east and the midlands remained the core. In the more fluid society of the fourteenth century, transition to and from the county knighthood was common. A Pole and a Pulteney could effect an entry into the aristocracy.[2]

Royal service itself bore witness to the same process of fusion. The decline in numbers under Edward I, with power passing to the aliens, and general royal familiars of the old type disappearing, was real enough, but, on the other hand, there was an increase in the number of specialized royal officers on the council, and aldermanic service in general became more specialized, urban and mercantile in character. They were customs collectors and town planners, and towards the end of Edward's reign, became increasingly important as purveyors and controllers of purveyance.[3] Under his son, this kind of service became so frequent and heavy that comparison with earlier days is quite meaningless. In fact, there was a qualitative change in the character of aldermanic service in the early fourteenth century. The settlement of the Great Wardrobe at London, and the needs of war and royal finance created a new pattern. Far more important than tenure of office was the almost

---

[1] See the tables on the aldermanic class in the Appendix, which should be read in conjunction with the text.   [2] For Pole and Pulteney, see *D.N.B.*

[3] For some examples, see K.R. Acc. V. (Army and Navy) E101/5/13, 14; *C.P.R. 1281–92*, pp. 3, 58, 81 and *passim*; *C.C.R. 1302–7*, pp. 137, 147; *C.P.R. 1301–7*, pp. 262, 312, 454; *Cal. Letter-Bk. C*, 25, 98.

continuous process of contractual service in goods, money, and function, in which nearly every merchant of substance was involved. The syndicates of Edward III were merely the most striking institutional expression of this social reality, itself a measure of the country's growth.

Growth, diversity and sophistication are reflected more sharply still in the range of aldermanic interests.[1] The abrupt expansion which began in the reign of Edward I is exaggerated by a greater abundance of evidence, but the documents mirror a reality. Numbers in the wool trade more than trebled, in spice and corn trebled, in cloth doubled. The inflow of clerks and professional administrators was sustained and there was a vastly increased representation of victualling and industrial trades based on the German connexion. The number of aldermen drawn from the latter increased tenfold. Men without a trade designation virtually disappeared, and there was a dramatic increase in the number of crafts represented on the council. Before 1263 seven trades can be identified among aldermen, and for most of the period, only five were effectively represented. By 1340 the number was twelve.[2]

It was, of course, the fishmongers, skinners, corders and their kind who were the newcomers. Before 1250 they never appeared; as late as the third quarter of the thirteenth century, they were no more than a tenth of the aldermanic class. Under the royal wardens, between 1285 and 1298, however, representation of the older trades plummeted to less than 50 per cent; newer men, including the clerks, rose to become an actual majority. This phenomenal increase broke the mould. In the years which followed, the pendulum swung back, and through to 1340, representation of older and newer trades remained in the ratio of five to three. This is a quantitative assessment. Qualitatively, the older trades produced greater merchants, but the representation of the newer had nevertheless increased in remarkable measure, and the fixity of the ratio suggests that it was a fairly accurate index of social reality.

In the process, the dynasties dwindled to insignificance.[3]

---

[1] For land-ownership, office and commerce, see the table of interests in the Appendix. [2] See the table of designations in the Appendix.
[3] See the tables of origins in the Appendix.

Viewed as a whole, their decline over the period from 1200 to
1340 has the inevitability of a historical trend. Closer examination dispels this impression. 'Paramount before 1263, they held
their own into the seventies, despite the pressures of social
change and political interference. Once more, the period of
direct royal rule between 1285 and 1298 was the crux. The fall
in their representation then was dramatic, and the breach
in continuity was never repaired. The immediate result was an
inflow of leaders of the newer trades, who were mostly men of
long-established citizen families. Representation of this type of
rooted, non-dynastic, London family was at its peak in the
years from 1290 to 1310. 'The inevitable dynastic recovery
after 1298 was a minor affair, with so many new families entrenched. Aliens remained an element, though their representation tailed off sharply after 1320. The true inheritors were
immigrants from the English counties. Running at a fifth of
the new aldermen in the third quarter of the thirteenth century,
they, like all other groups, lost ground before the sudden rise
of citizen families under the royal régime, but, thereafter, they
moved forward rapidly to achieve overall supremacy, the flood
of newcomers from Norfolk and the east Midlands even effect-
ing a change in city dialect. By the mid-fourteenth century,
their position was analogous to that of the dynasties themselves
in the mid-thirteenth.

Political power was the key. The dynasties' political monopoly had evidently stemmed and delayed what would have been
the natural consequences of economic and social growth. Once
it was broken, change was swift. Hardels can still be traced in
the early fourteenth century, in relatively humble station,[1] but
most of the great families simply vanish from the London
records. Unable, perhaps, to adapt themselves to the new
modes of commerce, and with their familiar political world
transformed out of recognition, they disappeared, probably
following those established routes of dispersion, into the Church,
the law, and the county gentry, which were always open and
always attractive.[2]

No successor dynasties took shape. The long-lived Gisors

[1] See Hust. Rolls, *passim*, with occasional appearances in St. Paul's and W.A.M.
[2] See S. L. Thrupp, *The Merchant Class of Medieval London*, chapter 5.

were an exception.[1] Seven sons followed their fathers in aldermanic office in the years between 1307 and 1340, but the line
of succession rarely stretched further. The Rokesles were probably the nearest approach to a dynasty the period could produce. They gave five members to the aldermanic council over
two generations or so after 1270, as well as a number of important merchants to the councillor group, but then vanished. The
change was not necessarily abrupt. Many of the newcomers
married dynastic heiresses. Nicholas le Fevre married a Farndon
and took the family's name. Sometimes there was a form of
affiliation, as when Hamo de Dene adopted his master's surname of Chigwell. But there was nothing comparable to the
survival pattern of the dynasties of Arras.[2] Possibly, English life,
under a strong monarchy, was at once too complicated, too
open, and yet too subject, to permit such urban survival. Certainly, by the fourteenth century, nothing lasted long in London.
Cosyns and Combemartins passed into and out of the patriciate
between father and son, and this became characteristic, as
provincial immigrants took the leading role. Now was established that three-generation cycle typical of the patrician
families of late medieval London.[3]

ʹFor the roots of the new patriciate lay in the aspiring provinces of England. It was a change which falls into place with
the rising curve of an immigrant-fed population, with London's
climb to pre-eminence in most branches of commerce, with the
reception of the Great Wardrobe, the concentration of government agency near the city, and with its assumption of leadership over daughter towns. The changes in the aldermanic class,
in the last resort, were a by-product of London's rise to capital
status. The city had become in truth the *King's Chamber* and *a
mirror to all England.*[4] ʹ

The charters won by the leading city crafts in the same period
were a symptom of the process. They testify to the victory of the
craft form within the city. Merchant company and mistery
stem from this same root, from that fusion of citizenship and

[1] S. L. Thrupp, *op. cit.*, 345–6.
[2] The men named were treated in earlier chapters; see, in general, Beaven, i and ii;
compare with J. Lestocquoy, *Les dynasties bourgeoises d'Arras du xie. au xve. siècle.*
[3] See S. L. Thrupp, *op. cit.*, especially chapter 5.
[4] See the royal use of such expressions in, for example, *P. and M. Rolls*, i, 77–83.

craft-membership which was the most distinctive legacy of the struggles of Edward II's reign. In those struggles, the civic constitution was shaped, with its nice balance of election and co-optation, of professional and amateur, of a tightly knit executive and an assembly responsive to currents of opinion among the politically important. For not until the great charter of 1319, and the contemporary settlement with the Crown, does London assume the character of a stabilized community. That its society was then stabilized, its political, economic and social institutions brought into phase, is evident from the longevity of the new order, which proved sufficiently resilient to counter the powerful oligarchic tendency inherent in all medieval urban societies, and which enabled London, after the testing time under Richard II, to enter modern times unfettered by the shackles of the closed corporation.[1]

For it retained at its heart that active and continuous participation of the conscious citizenry in government and administration, which was the guarantee that the new oligarchy would not lose all effective contact with social reality. The core of the régime was the reciprocity of function and responsibility between the aldermanic court and that *congregatio* which grew into Common Council—the 'counsail des prodes-hommes de la vile que mieux scierent les constituciouns' of Brunetto Latini.

It is characteristic that it was Latini's treatise on town government, his *Trésor*, which Andrew Horn carefully copied in *Liber Custumarum*, thoughtfully inserting the title *mayor*, unknown to the original.[2] The treatise, a product of Florentine experience, shrewdly and calmly sifted by the man who was the city's Orator and the teacher of Dante, is basically conservative, larded with quotations from the Fathers and the philosophers and adorned with a typically Thomist analysis of the distinction between a king and a tyrant. The concepts of natural law, a stratified society and the organic nature of the political unit govern it; harmony and reciprocity are the keynotes. The mayor must protect the weak, 'mais noun pas en tiele maniere qe les puissauntz perdent lour dreit pur les lermes

---

[1] See J. Tait, introduction to R. Bird, *The Turbulent London of Richard II*, especially xxiii-xxiv.

[2] *Lib. Cust.*, pp. 16–25.

des fiebles'; he must hold the balance between 'les grauntz, les petiz et les meynes . . . donez a chescun ceo qe soen est'.

The book is freshened, however, by a broad liberality of spirit, a bourgeois grasp of reality and a wry sense of humour. On no account, writes Latini, is the mayor, in his annual report, to omit to mention the many improvements which have taken place during his term of office. He must be honest, rich enough to be independent, old in sense rather than years, and prefer the reality of power to its appearance. He must avoid too much laughter, for it is written that laughter is in the mouth of the fool. Above all, proclaims the Orator, he must be a good speaker, better than all others, 'pur ceo qe touz li moundes tient a sage celui qi sagement parole'. On the other hand, he must guard against talking too much, 'car qi parle bien et poy len le tient a sage, et mout parler rest ja saunz peche'.[1] Small wonder that this book appealed to the London clerk and fishmonger whose name has been linked to the *Mirror of Justices*.

The easy learning and sureness of touch of Latini find their reflection in the writing of Londoners. The careful yet imaginative work of Horn and Waltham turns the city custumals into a mirror for lively minds, makes fitz Stephen seem bombastic and fitz Thedmar sound shrill. These men of the mid-fourteenth century seem infinitely more self-confident than their predecessors, much less conscious of any need for aggressive self-assertion. According to Froissart, it was a rooted belief among the London plebs in the late fourteenth century that the entire 1326 revolution had been engineered by the city. The Frenchman himself describes them as men 'par lesquels tout le royaulme d'Angleterre se ordonne et gouverne'.[2] The quarrel of Hardel and fitz Mary seems as remote as Ansgar the Staller. We are in a new climate, a new world, the world of the easy confidence of the London poets, of the superb and quiet mastery of Chaucer.

For the change in London's status was not merely quantitative. The transformation of the prickly commune into the self-confident capital was far more than a matter of ledgers and fees,

[1] For the quotations, see *Lib. Cust.*, pp. 21, 18.
[2] Quoted in M. McKisack, 'London and the succession to the Crown during the Middle Ages', *Studies in Medieval History presented to F. M. Powicke*, ed. R. W. Hunt, W. A. Pantin, and R. W. Southern, p. 81.

of a thickening of population and a multiplication of men and money. Mutations of the mind and spirit lie too deep for our plumb-lines. They are easy to forget, as we follow London's citizens through their age of iron, watch the Heyruns shouting for fitz Thomas and marching out to Lewes, trace their descendants rising in the wine trade as their society is transformed around them under Edward I, and observe John Chaucer ride out with Henry of Lancaster. But as we move on from John to his son, we cross the shadow-line, to the turret above Aldgate and 'the lyf so short, the craft so long to lerne'.[1] For Chaucer's roots lie here, among those very families, groups and classes, whose hopes and ambitions were the driving force of change. Nothing could be more appropriate. After a hundred and fifty years of vigorous growth, it was London which gave England a voice in the community of the European spirit.

[1] *The Parlement of Foules*, line 1, *The Works of Geoffrey Chaucer*, ed. F. N. Robinson, p. 310.

APPENDICES

A

Note on the Population of London

There are no *global* figures; there is no statistical base to start from. On general grounds, there is reason to believe that London was at least comparable with Brussels or Ghent, which were around the 30,000–40,000 mark in the early fourteenth century.

According to Miss Thrupp, the poll tax returns of 1377 point to a resident population of some 33,000, though a higher total seems more probable.[1] This was in the plague era, but Professor Postan believes that London may not have lost population during the pestilences; it may have stagnated, may even have gone on increasing, though at a slower rate.[2] The 1377 figures will probably do for 1340, if they will do at all.

One point of departure is Professor Russell's stimulating, if sometimes startling, work.[3] He claims that the rate of increase was more or less uniform for the whole country, and estimates an English population of 1,100,000 in 1086, 3,700,000 in 1348. There are no Domesday returns for London, so he presses 'average parish settlement' figures into service, to give an estimated city population of 14,000–18,000 in 1086. Using a uniform rate of increase, or applying a calculated national rate, one arrives at estimates of 25,000–28,000 in 1200, and 32,000–36,000 in 1300. Professor Russell himself allows for a considerable reduction in the period from 1340 to 1377, and guesses at a London population of 30,000 in 1200, rising to 60,000 by 1340.[4] These figures seem too high, though the doubling of population over a century is plausible. No warrant can be offered for support or rejection of Professor Russell's figures, other than an intuitive sense of proportion derived from familiarity with the records.

This sense is strengthened by an attempt to tackle Miss Thrupp's estimates. What lends power to her argument is the close attention she has devoted to one sector of the city population, the merchant class.[5] No-one

[1] S. L. Thrupp, *The Merchant Class of Medieval London*, p. 1.

[2] M. M. Postan, 'Some economic evidence of declining population in the later Middle Ages', *Economic History Review*, 2nd. ser. ii (1950); see also J. Saltmarsh, 'Plague and economic decline in the later Middle Ages', *Cambridge Historical Journal*, vii (1940), and, for general theory, H. J. Habakkuk, 'English population in the eighteenth century', *Economic History Review*, 2nd. ser. vi (1953).

[3] J. C. Russell, *British Medieval Population* (Albuquerque, 1948).

[4] J. C. Russell, *op. cit.*, 285–7, and my own calculations from his figures.

[5] S. L. Thrupp, *op. cit.*, 41–52 (numerical estimates of the population), 191–206 (survival of merchant families in the male line).

can quarrel with her general conclusion—that the class was extremely fluid, that it barely reproduced itself, and was dependent on immigration. But this was in the plague period. It is essential to remember that before the last quarter of the thirteenth century, the opposite was true. The class was characterized by stability and immobility. The changes between 1290 and 1340 were, in part, and perhaps mainly, the product of a peculiar constellation of social and political forces; purely demographic factors become important in the ensuing period.

To arrive at her conclusions, Miss Thrupp uses testamentary evidence, grouping 'merchants' (uncategorized) in thirty-year generations, and searching their wills for male descendants. For 1288–1317, for example, ninety-nine will-making merchants, followed through to their grandsons in the direct male line, yield a reproductive ratio of 1.3. An attempt to assess the proportion of young males who survived to maturity reduces this ratio to a still lower figure. That for 1318–47, before the incidence of plague, falls to 1.1. The class simply could not renew itself. With this equipment, she estimates the size of various groups, trying to allow for fertility (or survival) differentiation between classes, and other factors, in her multipliers, to arrive at an estimate of 33,000 for 1377, and, by inference, for 1340.[1]

These ratios cannot be accepted.

1. Many wills were not enrolled in Husting.

2. More important, wills frequently omit children, and, indeed, often omit the chief heir. To take aldermen alone, from the 1288–1317 group, Walter Hauteyn, Robert de Rokesle, Robert de Basing, Reginald de Frowyk, Fulk de St. Edmund, Walter de Finchingfield and Henry de Gloucester, each omitted one son from his will, and, in four cases, the son omitted was the eldest.[2] Miss Thrupp herself states that a surprisingly large proportion of her merchants seemed to die without leaving any heirs at all in the male line.[3] It seems more probable, in view of the quite massive evidence of omission from wills, and of the often puny bequests to known eldest sons, that a settlement on the heir was frequently, perhaps even customarily, made before any testament was drawn up.

Testamentary evidence, in short, understates the number of children in general, and of sons in particular.

3. Moreover, the same evidence can be made to yield quite different results. If the twenty-six *alderman* testators of the period 1288–1317 are traced through forty sons to six grandsons in the direct male line, the ratio which results is 2.19. Professor Ekwall has made his own analysis of Miss Thrupp's figures. If his twenty *merchants* are added to these aldermen, the ratio rises to 2.3 at least.[4]

---

[1] S. L. Thrupp, *op. cit.*, 41–52, 200, 204.

[2] See their wills in *Cal. of Wills*, i; cross-reference with their sons' wills in the same volume is in most cases sufficient to place the omitted sons and identify heirs; Hust. Rolls, Recog. Rolls and *Cal. Letter-Bk. A-E*, yield abundant evidence on the omitted; for Basing, see also *Cal. Letter-Bk. D*, 57.   [3] S. L. Thrupp, *op. cit.*, 200.

[4] Professor Ekwall criticizes Miss Thrupp's estimates, along similar lines, with great thoroughness. I have tried to combine my own aldermanic material with his broader but looser categories. See Ekwall, *Two Early London Subsidy Rolls*, pp. 71–81.

4. Similarly, the number of foreigns and people outside the tax-returns is under-estimated. Apprentices alone could be numerous. One poor chandler had four in 1310. A cordwainer could employ eight *serjeants* in his shed.[1]

If the taxpayers are taken as representative of a substantial sector of the population, we are left with the incredible situation that in Lime Street and Aldersgate wards in 1319, there were only four, three, or even two, families to a parish. These were wards of the poor. The sheer number of London parishes is itself a warning against too conservative an estimate of the city population.[2]

Furthermore, there were wholesale changes in personnel among the lesser taxpayers over the relatively short period between the subsidies of 1319 and 1332. This suggests that a large number of people must have lived on the taxable border, that the number of *technical* paupers was big. Dr. A. H. Thomas estimates that foreigns could be four or five times as numerous as citizens, and were probably more numerous still.[3]

In brief, current estimates, at least of the pre-plague population, are certainly too low.

We are back to guesswork. The number of taxpayers in 1292, 1319 and 1332 remained fairly uniform at 1,700, 1,900, and 1,600. Applying Miss Thrupp's multipliers to the 1319 returns, and adding an allowance for under-estimation, we get a total of around 38,000–40,000 for that year. It seems reasonable to suggest, therefore, that London's population increased from some 20,000 in 1200 to some 40,000 in 1340. If anything, these guesses err on the side of conservatism.

Peter de Blois, in 1199, told Innocent III that London had 120 churches and 40,000 people. It is some consolation to think that he probably knew little more than we do.

B

The Aldermanic Class, circa 1200 to 1340

I. The Structure of the Class: Illustrative Tables

NOTES

1. *Trade designations.* Sometimes variant, these are scattered all over the records. The most fruitful sources were *Cal. Letter-Bks.*, Recog. Rolls, and P.R.O. King's Remembrancer's Accounts, Various.
2. *Main Interests.* Based on the totality of collected evidence. The most useful sources were the records of trade and purveyance in K.R. Acc. V. and

---

[1] Lib. Horn, fo. 339b; *Cal. Letter-Bk. D,* 119.   [2] Ekwall, *op. cit.,* 79.
[3] A. H. Thomas, *P. and M. Rolls,* ii, lxi-lxiv.

K.R. Customs Acc., Wardrobe Debentures, and the mass of Exchequer records, with a good deal of information coming in from the published Chancery enrolments, Recog. Rolls, Hust. Rolls and *Cal. Letter-Bks.*, *P. and M. Rolls*, and *Cal. E.M.C. Rolls.*

Long-term periods, rather than decades, have been used, but evidence for the early thirteenth century is very scarce and derived almost entirely from royal records. Non-aldermanic sheriffs were few in the period 1307–1340, but there were fourteen of them in 1200–63, and twenty-five in 1265–1307. They have been included in the two earlier columns in the interests of reality. Omission of these men would leave the period 1200–63 unchanged in general pattern, but would exaggerate the rapidity of the rise of new interests between 1265 and 1340.

3. *Origins.* Again, based on total evidence. Particularly useful were *Cal. of Wills* and the indication of marriage and kin relationships frequently found in Hust. Rolls. Deeds and wills in St. Paul's and W.A.M. were invaluable, especially for the earlier men.

4. *Dynasty.* I have put a man among dynasts, before 1263, if his family had been established in the aldermanic class by the mid-twelfth century; after 1265, if it had been established for two generations on his arrival. It is often extremely difficult to distinguish between established London (non-dynastic) families and those of immediate or recent immigrant antecedents. An element of speculation inevitably enters, and there is plenty of room for error. The possibility of error, however, is made less terrible by the inescapably marginal nature of such errors as may have been committed. The main tendencies are so well documented and the main trends so marked, that confusion on the fringes will not touch the central argument. The quantity and quality of the relevant material ensure that the results of research survive even the clumsiness of the researcher.

In tracing some of these families, I have found W. Page, *London, its Origin and Early Development* (London, 1929) of the utmost value.

5. *Intermarriage.* Based mainly on W. Page, *op. cit.*, and Hust. Rolls, with some reference to St. Paul's. The three most inclusive groups of *lignages* have been selected to demonstrate the character of dynastic society. Evidence is scarce, and it is impossible to construct these tables according to the strict canon. There is no significance, for example, in the lateral order of names of children. The cohesion of the class, however, is abundantly displayed, and an attempt has been made to visualize it in the schematic diagram, where *connecting lines* indicate marriage relationship, and *figures* the number of aldermen supplied by a family out of its natural members.

TABLE 1: Trade Designations of the Aldermanic Class circa 1200–1340

Trade-Designation	Pre-1230	1230–40	1240–50	1250–63	1265–75	1275–85	1285–98	1298–1307	1307–17	1317–27	1327–40	Total
Drapers	5	3	8	2	2	5	4	4	3	4	4	44
Mercers	2	2	2	1	2	1	1	4	2	8	4	29
Vintners	4	1	4	3	2	1	1	1	1	2	2	22
Goldsmiths	3	0	2	1	4	1	3	2	2	0	2	20
Pepperers	1	0	1	2	0	2	2	2	2	5	2	19
Woolmongers	0	0	0	0	3	2	0	1	0	3	0	9
Clerks	0	0	0	0	0	1	2	3	2	4	1	13
Fishmongers	0	0	0	1	1	0	3	2	2	1	4	14
Skinners	0	0	0	1	0	0	3	0	0	2	2	8
Cornmongers	0	0	0	0	0	0	2	1	0	1	1	5
Corders	0	0	0	0	0	1	1	0	0	2	0	4
Cutlers	0	0	0	0	0	0	1	0	0	0	0	1
Potters	0	0	0	0	1	0	0	0	0	0	0	1
Leathersellers	0	0	0	0	0	0	0	0	0	1	0	1
Dyers	0	0	0	0	0	0	0	0	0	1	0	1
Butchers	0	0	0	0	0	0	0	0	0	0	1	1
No Designation	18	7	3	4	0	1	0	2	1	0	1	37
Total	33	13	20	15	15	15	23	22	15	34	24	229
Total Number of Trades	5	3	5	7	7	8	11	9	7	12	10	

Note: Column totals indicate the number of new aldermen elected between the dates given.

319

TABLE 2: Main Interests of the Aldermanic Class circa 1200–1340

Interes	circa 1200–63	1265–1307	1307–40
Wool	11	38	30
Cloth	14	28	23
Wine	29	19	17
Rope, Canvas, Timber and Hanse Goods	—	16	19
Spices	5	14	16
Fish	—	12	14
Furs, Hides, Leather	—	14	9
Goldsmiths' Work	—	13	9
Corn	5	14	11
Ironmongery, Pottery, Metal-Industry	—	7	4
Law and Administration	—	7	7
Finance	—	7	14
Land-ownership in the Counties	45	57	54
Royal Service	35	33	58
Total Number of Aldermen	*95*	*100*	*73*

Non-Aldermanic Sheriffs: these are included in the first two columns, 14 for the period 1200–63; 25 for the period 1265–1307; for 1307–40, there were only a few cases and these have been omitted.

TABLE 3: Origins of the Aldermanic Class circa 1200–1340

Origin	Pre-1230	1230–40	1240–50	1250–63	1265–75	1275–85	1285–98	1298–1307	1307–17	1317–27	1327–40	Total
Dynasties	27	9	17	7	7	5	4	4	3	1	1	85
London Families	0	0	0	2	2	4	11	11	4	11	8	53
Probable London Families	1	1	0	0	2	1	0	0	0	0	1	6
English Immigrants 2nd generation descendants	1	0	0	1	2	2	1	4	3	14	8	36
English Place-names as Surnames	1	2	1	2	1	1	3	1	2	5	6	25
Alien Immigrants	2	0	0	0	1	1	1	1	2	1	0	9
Alien 2nd generation descendants	0	0	1	1	0	0	2	0	0	1	0	5
Alien Place-names as Surnames	0	1	1	2	0	1	0	0	0	0	0	5
Totally Unknown	1	0	0	0	0	0	1	1	1	1	0	5
Total	*33*	*13*	*20*	*15*	*15*	*15*	*23*	*22*	*15*	*34*	*24*	*229*

TABLE 4: Proportional Representation of Origin-Groups in the Aldermanic Class circa 1200–1340

Origin-Group	Pre-1230	1230–40	1240–50	1250–63	1265–75	1275–85	1285–98	1298–1307	1307–17	1317–27	1327–40
Dynasties	82	62	85	47	47	33	17	18	20	3	4
London Families	3	9	0	13	27	33	48	50	27	32	38
English Immigrants	5	18	5	20	20	20	17	25	33	56	58
Alien Immigrants	6	9	10	20	6	14	13	4	13	6	0

Figures expressed as percentages of the decennial totals; occasional discrepancies resulting from existence of persons of totally unknown origin.

322

II. Biographical Notes

Documented outline biographies of ten of the leading patricians, who were given extended biographical treatment in the text.

Adam de Basing	Richard Renger
Andrew Bukerel	Gregory de Rokesle
John de Gisors	Philip le Tailor
Robert de Kelsey	Henry le Waleys
Richer de Refham	Hugh de Waltham

For their official careers, see A. B. Beaven, *The Aldermen of the City of London*, i, 371–81.

A. = Alderman. S. = Sheriff. M. = Mayor.

ADAM DE BASING

A. Cheap 1247–60; S. 1243–4; M. 1251–2.

Draper. Sold rich cloths and vestments to the Household. As payment, in 1244, granted the entire wool production of the bishopric of Winchester; by June 1245, had received £203 of the issues. In 1251, bought March wool from the king.[1] In 1252 and 1253, royal payments were made to his agents in Dublin, and in 1258, he went surety for the executors of the archbishop of Tuam.[2] In 1258, he bought 245 quarters of corn in Herts., to be delivered at Queenhithe. In 1242, he went bail for Rouen merchants and in 1245 bought wax for the king in the Norman city.[3]

Primarily, he was a Household merchant, supplying the Court with larest, cloth of gold, chasubles, mitres, copes, vestments, banners, and, occasionally, precious metals.[4] In 1251, 1256 and 1260, he made up such cloths, at times supervising the work of the royal artist-craftsman Edward of Westminster.[5] Between 1238 and 1260, in such transactions, he was paid £1,733. In 1243–5, the annual average was £233; in 1251–2, £262. Over twenty-two years, his annual average was £78. His dealings with the Crown were probably the heaviest individual transactions on record for the period.

He paid the wages of the royal serjeants and made loans to the king in 1248–51, and in 1253, was declared quit of tallage.[6]

[1] *C.R. 1242–7*, p. 181; *C.Lib.R. 1240–5*, p. 308; *C.Lib.R. 1245–51*, pp. 341, 354.
[2] *C.Lib.R. 1251–60*, pp. 36, 39, 40, 113; *C.R. 1256–9*, pp. 251, 468.
[3] *C.R. 1237–42*, p. 467; *C.R. 1256–9*, p. 330; *C.Lib.R. 1240–5*, p. 302.
[4] See *C.Lib. R. 1226–40*, pp. 356–493; *C.Lib.R. 1240–5*, pp. 8–286; *C.Lib.R. 1245–1251*, pp. 14–56; *C.Lib.R. 1251–60*, pp. 1–517; Chanc. Misc. 3/29, m.3.
[5] *C.R. 1247–51*, pp. 445, 451, 458, 494; *C.Lib.R. 1251–60*, pp. 1, 8, 336, 337, 516.
[6] *C.Lib.R. 1245–51*, pp. 187, 188, 240; *C.Lib.R. 1251–60*, p. 8; *C.P.R. 1247–58*, p. 196; *C.R. 1247–51*, p. 449; *C.C.R. 1302–7*, p. 202.

In 1247, he bought the Aldermanbury soke, a capital messuage, with six shops, the advowsons of three churches and rents which totalled £43 a year.[1] He acquired the fitz Alulf selds from his mother-in-law, and bought property in Cheap and Wood Street. He built the Basing mansion in Aldermanbury and his family gave its name to Basinghall Street, Basing Lane and Bassishaw. He held property in at least eight parishes, with holdings outside at Hendon and Kentishtown.[2]

His family had been established in the aldermanic class since the early twelfth century. His grandfather, Solomon, had been one of the great mayors of an earlier generation, and Adam himself married Desiderata, daughter of Arnulf fitz Alulf and Dyonisia Viel. Adam's son Thomas was an important woolmonger, who died young. His nephew Thomas became one of the leading city wool merchants. Adam's grand-daughter Avice married William de Hadestok and their daughter into the Bedyks. Adam's grandson Peter married into the Frowyks and founded an important family.[3]

ANDREW BUKEREL

A. Cripplegate 1223–37; S. 1223–5; M. 1231–7. Died in office.

Pepperer. Exported hides. Sold hides to an alien in 1230 and seized eighty-two tuns of wine in default of payment. In the same year, was shipping hides from north in vessel arrested at Hull.[4] Had agents in Dublin in 1220 and tried to arrange for repayment of royal loan in that city.[5] Bought safe-conducts for incoming and outgoing vessels in 1224 and 1225.[6] In June 1227, was paid £10 for six tuns of Anjou wine sold to the Court. Sold wool to a merchant of Caen in 1238.[7]

Was serving as royal chamberlain of London at Henry III's coronation, the expenses of which he covered.[8] Sub-keeper of Exchange before 1218. Leased the Exchange for 4,000 marks, 1218–21.[9] In 1234, served on commissions enquiring into Peter des Rivaux's activities and was present at Peter's surrender of Treasury.[10]

Property in St. Laurence Jewry; walled in a garden in Cripplegate and bought up property of a dead Jew in 1228.[11] Manor of Delce, Kent, other

---

[1] C.Ch.R. 1226–57, pp. 313, 314; St. Paul's A/16/141, 1206, 1282.

[2] Ancient Deeds B 4356, D 3160, 3806, 7729; W.A.M., Domesday, fo. 385; St. Paul's A/66/41, A/71/1818; Hust. Roll 2(90)(101); Misc. Roll AA, p. 78; Hundred Rolls, i, 403, 405, 407 and passim.

[3] See W. Page, London, its Origin and Early Development, p. 142 and genealogical tables above.

[4] C.R. 1227–31, p. 356; C.R. 1231–4, pp. 79, 148.

[5] Pat. Rolls 1216–25, p. 275.

[6] Pat. Rolls 1216–25, p. 467; Pat. Rolls 1225–32, p. 4.

[7] C.Lib.R. 1226–40, p. 38; C.R. 1237–42, p. 27.

[8] C.Lib.R. 1226–40, p. 158.

[9] L.T.R.M.R. 4, m.4d, 5; Pat. Rolls 1216–25, p. 322.

[10] C.P.R. 1232–47, p. 53; C.R. 1231–4, pp. 581–3.

[11] Misc. Roll AA, p. 80; C.Ch.R. 1226–57, p. 68.

land, same county, land at St. Pancras; croft and sixteen acres at Westminster.[1]

Family established in patriciate since the Conquest. Andrew's father, Andrew I, sheriff, pepperer and benefactor of St. Bartholomew's, alienated family soke of Bucklersbury to Hasculf de Tania and died on pilgrimage to Jerusalem in 1183. Andrew II's brothers Thomas and Stephen became aldermen; third brother, Walter, married daughter of Alderman Andrew Nevelun. Andrew died without issue; brother Thomas inherited.[2]

JOHN DE GISORS

A. Vintry 1243–c.1263; S. 1240–1, 1245–6, bailiff, 1254; M. 1246, 1258–9.

Pepperer. November 1236, sold almonds, dates, grapes and gingerbread to Court.[3] Owned shipping. In 1236, prises taken from his craft in Gascony; and he bought wine worth £86 from Arnold de Perigord. In 1242, his ship carried merchandise from Scotland to London. 1253, brought shipload of wine to city; 1254, his ship at Sandwich helped to carry queen and her retinue to Gascony. 1265, his ships carried food from his Essex manor of Moze to London.[4] 1259, supplied lead to roof queen's new chamber at Windsor. Visitor at Boston Fair; went surety for executor of a Rouennais. Acted as surety for abbot of Missenden, Bucks.[5]

Important wine merchant. In 1245 sold wine to Bishop William of Carlisle, in 1253, to Philip Lovel and bishop of London; in 1257 to Aylmer de Valence.[6] Between 1236 and 1261 sold wine to Household to value of £1,280; 1253–60, annual average was £120; 1253–5, £250. Annual average over twenty-five years was £53.[7]

Appointed royal butler in 1236; reappointed in 1253, serving until 1256. Succeeded by his brother Peter, 1256–60, whom he assisted. Took wine to Household in own carts.[8] 1250, made protector of House of Converts. 1262, appointed keeper of exchanges, but resigned because of ill-health the following year.[9]

[1] Ancient Deeds B 4410, 4416; *C.R. 1231–4*, p. 26; *C.R. 1234–7*, p. 26; *C.Ch.R. 1226–57*, pp. 193, 194.

[2] W.A.M., Domesday, fo. 493b; L.T.R.M.R. 14, m.3d; Misc. Roll AA, p. 67; W. Page, *op. cit.*, 240–1. [3] *C.R. 1243–7*, p. 397.

[4] *C.R. 1234–7*, pp. 359, 485; *C.R. 1251–3*, pp. 318, 471; *C.R. 1253–4*, p. 24; *C.R. 1264–8*, pp. 38, 39; *C.P.R. 1232–47*, p. 304.

[5] K.R.M.R. 42, m.26d; *C.R. 1272–9*, p. 120; *C.P.R. 1266–72*, p. 688; *C.Lib.R. 1251–60*, p. 466; *Cal. Letter-Bk. A*, 35.

[6] *C.R. 1242–7*, p. 282; *C.R. 1251–3*, pp. 318, 471; *C.R. 1256–9*, p. 172.

[7] *C.Lib.R. 1226–40*, pp. 256–503; *C.Lib.R. 1240–5*, pp. 39–247; *C.Lib.R. 1245–51*, pp. 10–191; *C.Lib.R. 1251–60*, pp. 106–514; Lib. Roll 37, m.13; *C.P.R. 1232–47*, pp. 136, 185; *C.P.R. 1247–58*, pp. 178, 402; *C.R. 1251–3*, pp. 448, 449.

[8] *C.P.R. 1232–47*, p. 167; *C.P.R. 1247–58*, p. 180; *C.R. 1256–9*, p. 37; *C.R. 1259–61*, p. 116.

[9] *C.R. 1247–51*, p. 260; *C.R. 1261–4*, p. 198; *C.P.R. 1258–66*, pp. 197, 219, 227, 249.

1240, found falcon for Henry III; 1245, bought 500 quarters of wheat for Household. 1246, made king loan for liveries of royal serjeants; 1250, sold him palfrey for gift to count of Toulouse. 1251, paid wages of royal serjeants and 1256, paid royal debt to King's Goldsmith. 1256, went on royal mission to Amiens; 1258, lent king £100.[1]

June 1246, his wines were exempted from prise; confirmed in 1253. 1237, king, in repeated writs, ordered sheriffs to protect Gisors' seisin of manor of Great Baddow, Essex. 1256, pardoned for monetary offences and exempted from tallage for life.[2]

Much property in St. Thomas and St. Michael Paternoster, in the Vintry. Held great messuage on the Thames in St. Martin Vintry, land near the river in All Hallows Haywharf (worth forty marks), tenements and rents in St. Mary Abchurch, rents in Walbrook and messuage in Bread Street.[3] In Middlesex, owned property at Edmonton; in Kent, leased manors of Postling, Fleet and Morehall from William de Valence and Philip de Columbariis, and held land in Crayford; in Essex, owned manor of Moze, leased manors of Great Baddow and Walthamstow from the Earl of Chester and Ralph de Tony; held an estate in Sacomb, Herts.[4]

Called a Norman by chroniclers. His father was Peter de Gisors, dead by 1247; his nephews Rostand de Bordeaux and William Bidau, were Gascons. In 1224–7, a John de Gisors, sometimes called Junior, was selling wine and buying land in London.[5] Alderman John's brother Peter sold wine worth £400 to Household, 1255–61, served as butler in the same period. His two daughters became nuns at Kilburn and his son Dennis married into the Bukerels.[6] John de Gisors married a sister of the chronicler Arnold fitz Thedmar, and his son John II, and grandsons John III, Anketil and Henry all served as aldermen. The family lived in London for three hundred years.[7]

ROBERT DE KELSEY

A. Billingsgate 1315–20. Parliamentary representative 1312, 1314, 1316, 1327, 1328.

Lawyer: An immigrant from Lincs, he bought a house in London in 1298,

[1] *C.R. 1237–42*, p. 253; *C.R. 1242–7*, pp. 445, 534; *C.R. 1254–6*, p. 427; *C.P.R. 1232–47*, pp. 452, 484; *C.P.R. 1247–58*, p. 97; *C.Lib.R. 1240–5*, p. 387; *C.Lib.R. 1245–51*, pp. 231, 271; *C.Lib.R. 1251–60*, pp. 35, 456.

[2] *C.R. 1234–7*, pp. 452–3, 567, 568; *C.R. 1237–42*, p. 10; *C.R. 1242–7*, pp. 314, 432; *C.R. 1251–3*, p. 316; *C.R. 1256–9*, p. 1; *C.P.R. 1247–58*, p. 529.

[3] Hust. Roll 2(41)(56); 4(12); Hust. Roll (Common Pleas) 2, m.9; W.A.M., Domesday, fo. 99; St. Paul's A /1 /727, 728 (fifteenth century copy); *Cal. of Wills*, i, 57.

[4] *Cal. Inq. Misc.*, i, 227; W.A.M. 9; *C.P.R. 1232–47*, pp. 185, 476; *C.P.R. 1247–58*, p. 74; *C.R. 1264–8*, pp. 38, 89, 90.

[5] *Gerv. Cant.*, ii, 231; Hust. Roll 1(36); *C.R. 1251–3*, p. 471; *Pat. Rolls 1216–25*, p. 448; *Pat. Rolls 1225–32*, p. 5; *C.Ch.R. 1226–57*, p. 55.

[6] *C.Lib.R. 1251–60*, pp. 234–521; Lib. Roll 37, m.2, 13, 14; 50, m.2; Hust. Roll 1(36); 9(4:25); 14(132); W.A.M., Domesday, fo. 485b; *Cal. of Wills*, i, 122.

[7] See S. L. Thrupp, *The Merchant Class of Medieval London*, pp. 345–6.

became a citizen, and practised in the city courts. 1300, he served as junior to the royal pleader Gilbert de Toutheby, and was accused of malpractice. 1302, he was attorney to Sir Ralph de Montchensy. 1305, became one of the sworn pleaders of the city.[1]

From this period a great mass of debt-recognizances and deeds cluster about his name. Debtors and creditors include the Riccardi, the king's clerk Henry de Guildford, merchants of Dinant, Lincs. men, and many city mercers. Sums of eighty marks to £150 were involved. Probably he was a moneylender.[2] In 1304, the mercer Robert de Bery owed him £4; in 1312, Bery's widow transferred a shop and a messuage in St. Laurence Jewry to the lawyer; 1314, a shop in Aldgate followed.[3] He acted as executor of Alderman William de Combemartin from 1318; entered into a maze of reciprocal recognizances with his fellow-executors, and secured a good proportion of the alderman's property.[4] Between 1309 and 1315, he acquired fifteen properties in eight parishes, many from the fitz Ailwins.[5] In 1315, he was licensed to crenellate his mansion.[6]

He served as councillor, had his salary trebled and was elected alderman in 1315.[7] In 1320, he was deposed by Hamo de Chigwell, ostensibly over a tax scandal, as one of the recorder Wengrave's party. His financial transactions continued and in 1322 he acted as executor to Alderman John de Burford.[8] After the revolution of 1326, he was restored to favour and was a city delegate on six occasions in 1327-8.[9]

Robert was the younger son of a family of small landowners in North Kelsey, Lincs. His brother Richard inherited. Sir Robert de Kelsey, the Chancery clerk, seems to have been a kinsman.[10] Robert married a woman of the Boteller family of mercers, Juliana.[11] His son Sir Thomas became a clerk at Westminster; a younger son entered the goldsmith's trade, but died in the plague. Robert's brother died young, and, in 1331, the lawyer received the family estate at Kelsey from the hands of his sister-in-law, a

---

[1] Hust. Roll 27(109); *Cal. Letter-Bk. B*, 119, *C*, 147-8, 185-7.

[2] See Recog. Roll 6 and 7, *passim*; Hust. Roll 31-58, *passim*; St. Paul's A/17/101, 1269, A/20/1532; W.A.M. 13907; *C.C.R. 1313-18*, pp. 225, 459; *C.C.R. 1318-23*, p. 338; *C.C.R. 1323-7*, pp. 334, 339, 353, 376, 401; *C.P.R. 1307-12*, p. 339; *Cal. Letter-Bk. B*, 128, 129, 134, 137, 168, 170, 201, 230, *C*, 203, 169.

[3] Hust. Roll 38(89)(90); 39(150); St. Paul's A/22/1635; *Cal. Letter-Bk. B*, 109.

[4] *C.C.R. 1313-18*, p. 540; *C.C.R. 1323-7*, pp. 353-4; Hust. Roll 40(103), 47(34); 54(46)(64).

[5] See Hust. Roll 37(88); 38(109); 57(53).

[6] *C.P.R. 1313-17*, p. 292.

[7] *Cal. Letter-Bk. D*, 228, 257, 262, 269, 289, 291, 314, *E*, 30, 33.

[8] *Cal. Letter-Bk. E*, 11, 12, 54, 94, 121, 124; *Ann. Paul.*, p. 287; *French Chronicle*, p. 40; W.A.M. 25372; Ekwall, *Two Early London Subsidy Rolls*, p. 275.

[9] *C.C.R. 1327-30*, p. 167; *C.C.R. 1330-3*, pp. 57, 384; *Cal. Letter-Bk. E*, 168, 169, 222, 226; *P. and M. Rolls*, i, 25, 30, 51, 60, 63, 70, 74.

[10] *C.C.R. 1330-3*, p. 420; *Cal. Letter-Bk. E*, 168-9; for the Chancery man, see, for example, *C.P.R. 1321-4*, pp. 56-370 and *passim*.

[11] *Cal. of Wills*, i, 511; Hust. Roll 37(70).

transfer witnessed by Sir Robert of the Chancery. Robert's own death four years later left his widow and sons well endowed with properties in twelve parishes, including the Tanners' Seld and a great hall in St. Laurence Jewry.[1]

RICHER DE REFHAM

A. Langbourn 1298–1300, Bassishaw, 1302–6, Langbourn, 1306–8, Dowgate, 1308–12; S. 1298–9; M. 1310–11.

Mercer. Norfolk immigrant. The interest of his career is twofold. Firstly, there was its political ebullience. Elected to replace Bauquell in the purge of 1298, he quarrelled with Waleys and was deprived of his aldermanry. Restored after Waleys's death, he emerged in 1310 as the first leader of the reform movement under Edward II, only to come to grief in the violent quarrel with his own mercers' company led by William de Hakford.[2]

Secondly, he is a prime example of the ruthless drive of immigrant enterprise in the period. One of the new Norfolk mercers, he climbed swiftly to pre-eminence over the ruins of dynasties, but left no dynasty ensconced behind him.

A mercer, he shipped wool to the Low Countries, Winchester wool worth 174 marks in one transaction in the 1290's. Scores of debts ranging up to £70 were owed him by a variety of knights and merchants. In 1294, he and his three factors had bought mercery worth nearly £300 from the Bellardi and two other Parisian merchants when the royal confiscations occurred. In 1304, he was made keeper of the New Custom in London and by 1321, he had been knighted.[3]

A central feature of his activity was the building up of a civic estate from the disintegrating patrimonies of older families. He began to buy in 1295 and goes on without cease to 1309. The last Hardels sold out to him an estate which, by this time, included the central property of the Bukerels. In 1302–3, he bought most of the property of the newly deceased Henry le Waleys; in 1304–5, he acquired lands from the Basings and Northamptons. In 1305, it was the turn of the Bethunes, the Rokesles and the survivors of the Duc dynasty. He married his son John to the daughter of Alderman John Blund, last mayor to be drawn from the old families, and got much of the Blund property as well.

In Norfolk, his family held land in chief of the Bigods, and he acquired estates in Somerset. In London, over fourteen years, he bought properties in

[1] *C.C.R. 1330–3*, p. 420; *Cal. of Wills*, i, 412–13, 511, 518–19; *P. and M. Rolls*, i, 259; Hust. Roll 56(160).

[2] *Cal. Letter-Bk. B*, 88, *C*, 28, 29, 77, 78, *D*, 182, 183, 188, 228, 275, *E, passim*; *Ann. Lond.*, pp. 104, 175, 176; Weinbaum, ii, 178.

[3] K.R. Acc. V. (Alien Merchants) E101/126/8; K.R. Customs Acc. E122/156/15; *C.P.R. 1301–7*, pp. 223, 262, 454; *C.C.R. 1296–1302*, pp. 532, 543; *C.C.R. 1302–7*, pp. 137, 147, 347; *Lib. Cust.*, p. 303; *Cal. Letter-Bk. B*, 21, 96, 113, 117, 160, 180, 181, 198, *C*, 117, 118, 214, 216, *D*, 16.

twenty-five parishes. His son John became a fishmonger and an alderman, but the family disappeared in less than two generations.[1]

RICHARD RENGER

A. Bridge 1217–39; S. 1220–2; M. 1222–7, 1238–9. Died in office.

Safe-conduct for overseas trade 1224. In 1225, sent two ships abroad for wine; paid £37 for twenty-one tuns sold to the Court in 1227; safe-conduct for Dunwich ship sent to Anjou for wine in 1230. In May 1225, he and John Travers shipped corn from the Marshal estates in Ireland to London. In 1230, confiscated goods of Cahorsin Peter Beraud handed over to Renger's agents in Bristol; in 1237, Renger and Arnold Beraud chartered a ship which was wrecked off East Anglia. Renger was in debt to Jews (118 marks) in 1218, and was owed £26 by Master of St. Bartholomew's at his death.[2]

Master of Exchange 1226–8; appointed to supervise exchanges of London and Canterbury at salary of 700 marks a year, 1229–33. In 1238, was keeper of the Thirtieth at Tower.[3] Six judicial commissions 1229–30; found three horses for king's gift to Simon the Norman in 1238.[4] Attorney for Robert fitz Walter in 1218; witnessed the deeds of Earl William Marshal and the archbishop of Canterbury. Attended at Peter des Rivaux's surrender of Treasury.[5] In 1232, given the goods of arrested Flemings by king; in 1238, royal gift of six deer. In 1241, king's debts to Renger allowed his son in account with Exchequer.[6] In early civic deeds, precedes sheriffs; in 1228, precedes mayor and sheriffs. In 1232, acted as surety for royal bond at express demand of creditor, the Italian, Guala de Nonetus.[7]

Inherited much property. On death of Alderman Richard fitz Reiner, the friend of John, in 1191, his property divided between his brothers. Henry fitz Reiner took manor and church of Shenley, Herts., and Duston, Northants (honour of Peverel of Nottingham) and Brainford, Essex. William fitz Reiner, father of Renger, received rest of property from John, then count of Mortain— lands at Edmonton, Newland, Wittlesham, Ham, and Newton.[8] Renger added property at Saffron Walden and Debden, Essex, and Elmingham,

---

[1] See Hust. Roll 25(30); 27(85); 31(3)(4)(35)(43); 32(15)(51)(75)(116)(117); 33(1)(34)(39)(49)(50)(58)(111); 34(58)(59)(117); 35(22)(23)(24); St. Paul's A/22/1633, 1635, 1647, A/25/1415; Ancient Deeds E 326; *Cal. of Wills*, i, 339, 472, 480, 655.

[2] *Pat. Rolls 1216–25*, pp. 470, 514, 526; *Pat. Rolls 1225–32*, pp. 418, 419; *C.R. 1227–31*, pp. 555, 556; *C.R. 1234–7*, p. 410; *C.R. 1242–7*, p. 327; *C.Lib.R. 1226–40*, p. 38; L.T.R.M.R. 5, m.8d.

[3] *C.R. 1227–31*, pp. 213, 214, 299, 478, 577; *C.R. 1231–4*, pp. 89, 197; *C.P.R. 1232–47*, pp. 209, 217, 218, 230; *C.Lib.R. 1226–40*, pp. 4, 29, 77, 113, 126, 326, 327.

[4] *Pat. Rolls 1225–32*, pp. 285, 293, 367; *C.R. 1227–31*, pp. 229, 241, 317; *C.R. 1237–42*, pp. 97, 101.

[5] K.R.M.R. 2, m.2; *C.Ch.R. 1226–57*, pp. 79, 197; *C.P.R. 1232–47*, p. 53.

[6] *C.R. 1231–4*, p. 53; *C.R. 1237–42*, pp. 51, 267.

[7] Ancient Deeds B 4410; St. Paul's A/4/709; *Pat. Rolls 1225–32*, p. 482.

[8] *Cat. Anc. Deeds*, ii, 148; W. Page, *op. cit.*, 246.

Suffolk. Within city, held capital messuage in Vintry, the cellars of the *Lorraine* merchants, land in St. Alphege and many rents.[1]

Family descended from Berengar, Norman servant of first Norman bishops of London. Established in patriciate from Conquest. Renger's family intermarried with Bukerels. Daughter Idonea married 1. Alderman Richard de Hadestok, whose children married a Bukerel and a Hardel, 2. Sheriff Henry de Cookham. Son John became an Exchequer official, with property in Enfield, Edmonton, Mimms and Stepney in Middlesex, Plumstead in Kent, Leyndon, Fobbing and Eastley in Essex.[2]

GREGORY DE ROKESLE

A. Dowgate 1265–91; S. 1263–4, 1265, 1270–71; M. 1274–81, 1284–5.

Goldsmith. 1258, sold wax to the Household. 1273, export licences for 110 sacks of wool; 1277, for fifty sacks. In 1274, claimed compensation for seventeen sacks of Cotswolds wool shipped to Bruges. He took corn to Gascony in 1274; arranged for fish to be supplied to the Court in 1282. He sold burels to the Household in 1274 and dealt with the Riccardi.

In 1285, he was bracketed with Waleys by the men of the Cinque Ports as the leading wine merchant of England. One contract, in 1281, records the purchase of 100 tuns for £150 cash from a Delsoler of Bordeaux. In 1290, his agent took Bergerac and St. Emilion wine direct to Boston Fair. In 1285, he was the leading spirit in a move to reduce the brokerage rate on wine in London by two-thirds.[3]

In 1266 he served as taker of the royal wines at Southampton and was drawing livery as Edward's retainer on his accession. He was formally appointed royal butler in 1275, with the Gascon Poncius de Mora as colleague. He resigned in June 1278, but was almost immediately made Master of Exchange. Orlandino de Podio of the Riccardi was his companion and he was heavily involved with the Italian companies in the royal fiscal service. In 1280, he administered thirty-one loans, totalling over £30,000. He and Iter Angoulême audited the Irish Exchange accounts in 1283, and his control was extended over the entire kingdom. Reappointed in 1285, he served until his death in 1291.[4]

---

[1] W.A.M., Domesday, fo. 99, 483b, 490; *C.Ch.R. 1226–57*, pp. 197, 269; *C.R. 1251–3*, p. 510.

[2] A.R. 1187, m.9d; K.R.M.R. 42, m.24; L.T.R.M.R. 14, m.2d; Misc. Roll AA, pp. 57, 70, 80; Cur. Reg. Roll 178, m.15d; 181, m.12d; 182, m.19, 21d; 184, m.13d; 185, m.6, 15d; 186, m.6.

[3] For his trade, see Lib. Roll 50, m.4; Excheq. Misc. 5/17; *C.Lib.R. 1251–60*, p. 429; *C.P.R. 1266–72*, pp. 651, 702; *C.P.R. 1272–81*, pp. 15, 23, 26, 437; *C.P.R. 1281–1292*, p. 168; *C.Chanc.R.*, pp. 2, 250; *C.C.R. 1272–9*, pp. 123, 137; *C.C.R. 1279–88*, p. 127; *C.C.R. 1288–96*, p. 97; *Cal. Letter-Bk. A*, 214, *C*, 86; *Lib. Albus*, pp. 490–2.

[4] Chanc. Misc. 3/21(18); Lib. Roll 49, m.2, 3; *C.P.R. 1266–72*, p. 267; *C.C.R. 1272–9*, pp. 93, 365; *C.P.R. 1272–81*, pp. 126, 301, 358, 401; *C.P.R. 1281–92*, pp. 72, 168, 358. The royal rolls are full of his activities; see, in particular, *C.P.R. 1272–92*, *C.C.R. 1279–96, passim*.

In 1275, he was a commissioner for the Anglo-Flemish dispute, in 1276, scrutinized the chirographers of the Jews. In 1277-8 he acted as tax collector and in 1283, as commissioner for the coinage decrees. In 1290, he presided over the sale of the houses of expelled Jews. He was the financial agent of the Dominicans in the building of Blackfriars.[1] Between 1276 and 1291, thirty-two judicial commissions were issued to him.[2]

In 1280, he ranked third after Hugh fitz Otto and Ralph de Sandwich as witness to a grant to an Exchequer official; Barons of the Exchequer witnessed his own deeds. His personal proctor Walter de Maidstone was kinsman to a royal clerk. He lent the king £250 in 1279, £1,000 in 1290. In 1273, he was granted a wardship worth £200 a year, in 1276, a marriage. He was given bucks, quittance of common summons and exemption from taxation.[3]

He already held the manors of Rokesley and Lullingstone in Kent as demesne land when he came to London. Between 1278 and 1286, he acquired the bulk of his city property, which extended over twelve parishes and embraced the entire estate of William Hardel. The bishop of Ely was his tenant in Holborn.[4] Outside, at his death, he held five manors in Kent, town houses in Canterbury and Rochester and other scattered property. In Sussex, he held two manors, in Surrey, one, with other land totalling five knights' fees.[5]

The Rokesles were a Kentish family. Gregory, the leading figure, moved to London sometime in the fifties. He had leased Rokesley itself to a dependant by 1264. Robert, possibly a brother, served as alderman with him; they were followed by Walter, a nephew, Adam, Robert and John Vivian in the court, while William, Simon, Roger and others figured among the councillors. For two generations, the city records are full of Rokesles. Gregory died on 13 July 1291, leaving chantries in St. Mary Woolnoth and All Hallows Haywharf, but no direct heir. His sister's son inherited and, within two generations of their entry, the Rokesles disappeared from the patriciate. Andrew Horn placed the report of Gregory's death next to that of the queen-mother's.[6]

[1] See *C.C.R. 1272-9*, pp. 230, 441; *C.P.R. 1272-81*, pp. 81, 158, 240, 286, 287; *C.P.R. 1281-92*, pp. 81, 82 and *passim*.

[2] *C.P.R. 1272-81*, pp. 183-474; *C.P.R. 1281-92*, pp. 94-456; *C.C.R.1272-9*, p. 478; *C.C.R. 1279-88*, p. 404.

[3] Lib. Roll 51, m.7; *C.C.R. 1272-9*, pp. 80, 81, 258, 379, 456, 549; *C.C.R. 1279-88*, pp. 24, 50, 92, 162, 173; *C.C.R. 1296-1302*, pp. 242, 243; *C.P.R. 1272-81*, pp. 163, 273, 378, 389, 400; *C.P.R. 1281-92*, p. 358; *C.Ch.R. 1257-1300*, pp. 215, 246; Ancient Deeds D 2151.

[4] Hust. Roll 9(8:39, 40); 11(67); 12(28)(72); 14(32)(106); 16(134); *C.P.R. 1272-1281*, p. 435; *Cal. Letter-Bk. A*, 202-3; *Cal. of Wills*, i, 98-9.

[5] *C.R. 1261-4*, p. 376; *C.Ch.R. 1257-1300*, p. 215; *Cal. Inq. P.-M.*, ii, 322-3, 504-5; *C.P.R. 1281-92*, pp. 3, 269; *C.C.R. 1288-96*, p. 95; Weinbaum, ii, 145.

[6] *C.R. 1261-4*, p. 376; *Cal. Inq. P.-M.*, ii, 504-5; *Ann. Lond.*, p. 99. It is almost literally impossible to turn a page of the civic records of this period without coming across some member of the family.

PHILIP LE TAILOR

A. Billingsgate c. 1260–92; S. 1261–2, 1270; Aldermanic candidate at disputed mayoral election, 1272.

Mercer. 1276, sold thirty quarters of corn to the king and twenty marks of barley to some Londoners. 1275, he was selling cloth.[1] He was primarily a wine merchant. In November 1253, he and his partner, a man of Hamburg, were declared quit of prise on a shipload. 1255, he was quit of prise on a cargo of 120 tuns, and in 1258, brought 150 tuns from Gascony in a Winchelsea ship. In 1262, he was quit of withernam in Gascony.[2] From 1259, knights like Adam Despenser and John de Burgh were his debtors. Ten of them were indebted to him fairly heavily in the period 1267–90. In 1276, the earl of Oxford owed him £93; in 1282, William de Valence paid him £34 for sixteen tuns and in 1283, there was merchandise of Philip's in Roger de Clifford's manor of Morton, Lincs.[3]

In 1256, he began selling wine to the Household, earning £70 in the year. In 1259, he topped the £100 mark. Between 1256 and 1280, he was paid £1,624. From January 1261 to May 1263, he sold the Court well over 300 tuns and received an annual income from this source of £260 a year. His annual average over the twenty-four years was £68.[4]

He served as keeper of the Jews in 1266 and was a collector of the Fifteenth in Surrey-Sussex in 1280. In 1267, he was declared quit of all prise and his tallage was fixed at a nominal one mark.[5]

He began to buy property in 1259 and went on buying to 1287. There is no record of any sale. His marriage into the fitz Ailwins brought in a block of property in five parishes in 1264–5. By the end of his life he owned property in at least twenty-three parishes, some individual pieces worth £4 a year.[6] In Kent, he leased the manor of Crayford and another near Dartford. He held much property, including two shops, at Erith, and some holdings in Lessness. By 1297, the Kentish property sold by his executors was worth £6 a year.[7]

[1] Lib. Roll 48, m.8; K.R. Acc. V. (Alien Merchants) E101/127/2; *Cal. Letter-Bk. A*, 11, 19.

[2] *C.R. 1253–4*, p. 187; *C.R. 1256–9*, p. 238; *C.P.R. 1247–58*, p. 449; *C.P.R. 1258–66*, p. 227.

[3] K.R.M.R. 42, m.5d, 7; Recog. Roll 3(119); Ancient Deeds A.S. 163; *C.R. 1256–9*, pp. 471, 482, 483; *C.C.R. 1272–9*, pp. 356, 418, 421; *C.C.R. 1279–88*, pp. 190, 201; *C.C.R. 1288–96*, p. 185.

[4] Lib. Roll 37, m. 2, 7, 9, 14, 18; Chanc. Misc. 3/7(29)(32)(35); K.R. Acc. V. (Butlerage) E101/77/1; *C.Lib.R. 1251–60*, pp. 267–505; *C.P.R. 1258–66*, pp. 162–411; *C.P.R. 1266–72*, pp. 91–317.

[5] *C.P.R. 1258–66*, pp. 279, 577; *C.P.R. 1266–72*, pp. 99, 100, 464; *C.C.R. 1279–88*, p. 31; *Lib. de Ant. Leg.*, p. 49.

[6] Hust. Roll 7(5:49)(8)(9)(16); 8(4); 9(27); 11(49); 12(11)(49)(87); 16(39)(60); 18(1); 29(7); W.A.M., Domesday, fo. 495; St. Paul's A/18/1444; *Cal. of Wills*, i, 107, 244–5; *Cart. S.M. Clerkenwell*, pp. 259, 260; *Cal. Letter-Bk. B*, 221; *C.P.R. 1272–1281*, pp. 291, 407.

[7] *C.P.R. 1266–72*, p. 464; *C.P.R. 1281–92*, p. 404; *C.C.R. 1302–7*, p. 262; *Select Excheq. Pleas*, p. 155.

He came of substantial but non-patrician London stock. In his early years, he was often known as 'the cousin of Martin le Tailor'.[1] He married Sabine, daughter of Peter fitz Alan, who was the great-grandson of Alan, brother of the first mayor Henry fitz Ailwin. Peter's other daughter Matilda married Alderman Ralph Blund; another was known as Dame Elizabeth; a son became a canon of Holy Trinity.[2] Philip's sons Henry and John married into the Paris and Picard families; three of his daughters became nuns at St. Mary Clerkenwell.[3] A fourth, Matilda, married Philip de Beauvais, son of Master Simon the King's Surgeon, who by 1293, had succeeded his father in royal office. Their daughter married John le Riche, a knight of Pentlow in Essex.[4] Philip le Tailor's fifth daughter Sabine married John le Mire, the draper, master of the Yorkshire immigrant Henry Darcy, who became one of the important Wardrobe drapers of Edward II's reign.[5] Philip's widow was owed several debts 1296–1302, and bought land in the same period. She had her own chaplain, Sir Henry de Scaldwell, and in 1292, was the third highest taxpayer in London.[6]

HENRY LE WALEYS

A. Cordwainer 1269–94; S. 1270–1; M. 1273–4, 1281–4, 1298–9.

An immigrant, he entered the wine trade, made his first small sale to the Household in 1252. He became one of the foremost vintners of England. Contracts recorded in 1284 and 1298 register individual purchases of 300 tuns and 250 tuns from merchants at St. Emilion and Libourne. In 1285, he was singled out by name by men of the Cinque Ports as a leader in the trade.[7] From 1259 to 1277, he sold wine regularly to the Household, ceasing to do so in the early eighties. Between 1259 and 1263, his sales totalled £1,157; in 1261 he was paid £548 in a single year. His annual average over these years was some £300, and over twenty years it ran at around £100 a year.[8]

An attempt to make him royal bailiff after Evesham failed, because he had

---

[1] Hust. Roll 3(75)(76)(77)(82).

[2] See, for example, Cal. of Wills, i, 126; C.Ch.R. 1257–1300, p. 79; W. Page, op. cit., passim.

[3] C.C.R. 1288–96, p. 442; C.C.R. 1302–7, p. 262; Cart. S.M. Clerkenwell, pp. 259, 260; Cal. of Wills, i, 107, 275.

[4] C.C.R 1279–88, p. 111; Recog. Roll 2(239); 3, m.5; K.R. Acc. V. (Wardrobe) E101/354/5, fo. 5; Hust. Roll 13(37); Cal. of Wills, i, 244–5.

[5] Cal. of Wills, i, 244–5; Cal. Letter-Bk. D, 119.

[6] Cal. Letter-Bk. B, 61, 62, 114, 115; Hust. Roll 30(4); Weinbaum, ii, 214.

[7] See C.P.R. 1281–92, pp. 148, 168; Cal. E.M.C. Rolls, pp. 38, 39; for his trade in general, see Lib. Roll 47, m.6; 48, m.7; K.R.M.R. 40, m.5; 42, m.26d; Recog. Roll 1(68)(120); 3, m.1; C.C.R. 1279–88, p. 183; Cal. Letter-Bk. A, 33, 51, B, 13, 69, 90, C, 241; K.R. Acc. V. (Army and Navy) E101/13/39, m. 1d.

[8] Lib. Roll 37, m.7, 11, 13, 14; 47, m.10; Chanc. Misc. 3/7(36); C.Lib.R. 1251–60, pp. 80–499; C.P.R. 1258–66, pp. 198, 262; C.P.R. 1266–72, pp. 89–396; C.P.R. 1272–1281, pp. 139, 212.

taken part in the Montfortian raids, but in 1266, he was exempted from tallage. Alderman in 1269 and sheriff in 1270, he became a fully-fledged royal agent. He acted in intimate concert with Edward during his first mayoralty in 1273–4, and before it was over he was transferred to Bordeaux on the king's 'special affairs'. He served as royal mayor of the Gascon city in 1275.[1] He went to Rouen for the king in 1286, went overseas on Edward's 'special affairs' again in 1288. In 1291, he went to Gascony as personal aide to the Seneschal and in 1299, went to Berwick on Edward's personal business.[2] He assisted in the planning of Winchelsea, the administration of fiscal ordinances, and between 1280 and 1286, received seven judicial commissions.[3]

He became an intimate member of the inner circle of royal servants. He witnessed grants to Robert Burnell and his kinsmen, ranking fifth among high Exchequer officials after the Treasurer; acted as go-between for the king in his dealings with the merchants in 1298; he was given the wardship of the heir of John de Nevill by the queen-mother and Amadeus of Savoy in 1283. Edmund of Cornwall gave his kinsman Andrew an annuity. Henry was an executor of Luke de Tany, bought cloth for Hugh Despenser, and took custody of the archbishop of Canterbury's houses in Lambeth during repairs to the chapel. In 1299, a Great Council actually met in his hall in Stepney.[4]

In 1267 he bought the manor of Beckenham in Kent, adding its dependent block of city property worth forty marks a year. In 1268, he acquired the entire estate of the former sheriff Henry Walemund, including a mansion in St. Mary le Bow, Cordwainer. Marriage into the Basings brought him the Aldermanbury soke.[5] He held a cluster of properties in Westminster and Middlesex, acquired two manors in Essex, lands in Bucks, liberties in Boston and a quay and houses in Berwick.[6] Within the city, he held properties in fifteen parishes, three of them alone worth 140 marks a year gross.[7]

Waleys was an immigrant and may have come from Striguil, near Chepstow.[8] He married Joan, daughter of Adam de Basing. His son, Augustine de

[1] *C.P.R. 1272–81*, p. 126; *C.C.R. 1272–9*, pp. 87, 142; C. Bémont, 'Les institutions municipales de Bordeaux au moyen âge', *Revue Historique*, cxxiii (1916), 50.

[2] *C.P.R. 1281–92*, pp. 227, 291, 431, 446; *Cal. Letter-Bk. B*, 89.

[3] *C.P.R. 1272–81*, p. 371; *C.P.R. 1281–92*, pp. 3–256, *passim*.

[4] *C.C.R. 1272–9*, pp. 73, 74, 364, 579; *C.C.R. 1279–88*, pp. 242, 346, 423; *C.P.R. 1266–72*, p. 8; *.C.P.R. 1272–81*, p. 421; *C.P.R. 1281–92*, pp. 64, 334; *Cal. Letter-Bk. A*, 119, *B*, 69; Hust. Roll 19(28)(29); *V.C.H. Middlesex*, ii, 22.

[5] Ancient Deeds E 220; *C.P.R. 1266–72*, pp. 112, 208; *Cal. Letter-Bk. A*, 163; Hust. Roll 4, 5, *passim*.

[6] *C.P.R. 1272–81*, p. 421; *C.P.R. 1281–92*, p. 64; *C.C.R. 1272–9*, p. 114; *C.C.R. 1279–1288*, p. 364; *C.Ch.R. 1257–1300*, p. 403; *Cal. Letter-Bk. A*, 2; Hust. Roll 27(44); Unwin, *Gilds*, pp. 56, 57; A.R. 543, m.6d, 30; *Cal. Inq. P.-M.*, ii, 478.

[7] Hust. Roll 4(159); 5(54); 12(129); 14(73)(80)(81)(82)(87); 16(125)(126); 23(12)(26)(28); St. Paul's A/15/140, A/18/155, 1425, 1433; Ancient Deeds E 214, 220, 271, 579; *C.P.R. 1272–81*, p. 244; *Cal. Letter-Bk. A*, 112, 155, *C*, 198.

[8] No other known Londoner of this period had the surname, other than two kinsmen, and in 1282 a William from Striguil (Chepstow) bequeathed Aldgate property, which later appeared among the mayor's holdings, to a kinsman Henry le Waleys (*Cal. of Wills*, i, 57).

Uxbridge, became keeper of Exchange under Edward II, and after Waleys's death in 1301, the family disappeared from the patriciate.[1]

HUGH DE WALTHAM

Common Clerk. pre-1311–35.

Clerk. Clerk to the sheriffs by 1290. Around 1300, married Agnes, daughter of Alderman Hugh Pourte, the fishmonger.[2] After Pourte's death in 1308, Waltham acted as his executor and raised a chantry to his memory. Much of his father-in-law's property, in three concentrated holdings at the Tower, in Vintry and around Gracechurch, fell to the clerk.[3]

For eight years, he was active in financial and land transactions. He owned cellars in the Vintry, well stocked in 1290, and in 1310, sold wine worth £20 to a taverner.[4] Many debts were owed him by a variety of merchants, and he bought land heavily.[5]

In 1312, almost immediately after the death of his first wife, Waltham married Juliana, daughter of Alderman Nicholas Picot the mercer. By this marriage he acquired the great mansion in Cornhill, formerly the residence of the revolutionary mayor Thomas fitz Thomas, which became his home.[6]

In 1311, his Common Clerkship was confirmed by the reforming assemblies and he held office until his death in 1335.[7] Elected a parliamentary representative in 1319, he continued to buy land, and in the last few years of his life, bought and exchanged properties on a large scale and made munificent settlements on his son and married daughter. In the twenty-five years from 1310 to 1335, he acquired forty-eight properties in fifteen parishes.[8]

Hugh's father Adam was an ironmonger; his uncle Alexander de Waltham, also an ironmonger, had been a leader of the revolt of 1263.[9] Hugh was a friend of John de Oystergate, fishmonger, grandson of another rebel leader. The clerk's first wife was the daughter of a fishmonger. His daughter married another, Philip Lucas. Hugh's son, Stephen, also a clerk, married into the corder family of Box. A second daughter became a nun at St. Helen's. His brother John, formerly a Chamber serjeant, became vicar of Windsor,

---

[1] See T. F. Tout, *The Place of the Reign of Edward II in English History*, p. 325.

[2] *Cal. Letter-Bk A*, 124, 150, *B*, 184, 226, *D*, 147, 168; *Cal. E.M.C. Rolls*, pp. 38, 221, 258.

[3] Hust. Roll 29(87); 32(63)(64); 37(16); Ancient Deeds E 501, 509; *Cal. of Wills*, i, 399–400; *Cal. of Wills. Bk. B*, 160.

[4] *Cal. Letter-Bk. A*, 124, *B*, 252.

[5] See Recog. Roll 9, m. 3, 4; Hust. Roll 37–48, *passim*; *Cal. Letter-Bk. B*, 17, 31, 43, 44, 52, 124, *D*, 260, *E*, 96, 103, 105.

[6] Hust. Roll 32(82); 33(96); *Cal. Letter-Bk. B*, 17, 24; *Cal. of Wills*, i, 233–4.

[7] *Cal. Letter-Bk. D*, 275, 304–5, *E*, 5, 6, 12, 21, 236; *Cal. E.M.C. Rolls*, p. 38, n. 2; *Lib. Cust.*, pp. 137 ff.

[8] Hust. Roll 48–60, *passim*; *Cal. Letter-Bk. E*, 104–5, 235–6.

[9] *Cal. of Wills*, i, 399–400; *Cal. Letter-Bk. B*, 59; on the family, see also Hust. Roll 2(124); 3(11); *C.C.R. 1272–9*, pp. 26, 50–1; *C.P.R. 1281–92*, p. 151; Cur. Reg. Roll 191, m. 6d; *Cal. Letter-Bk. B*, 202; *Cal of Wills*, i, 31.

another, Ralph, rector of St. Michael Bassishaw. Hugh built a burial vault in St. Peter Cornhill and endowed chantries in St. Magnus and St. Mary Southwark.[1]

C
Communa Mediocris Populi

Biographical notes on some of the leading rebels of 1263

The rebels of 1263, dissident patricians excluded, are shadowy figures, but it is possible to get a general impression of their social standing. To illustrate this, brief outlines of a dozen of them are given, together with other general indications of status.

JOHN DE STEPNEY

Fishmonger. Held land in three parishes; made a purpresture in 1276. Owned a ship and employed several agents. Closely connected with the Treyere family, fishmongers, officials and councillors. He married Cecilia, widow of the revolutionary mayor Thomas fitz Thomas.[2]

ROBERT STERRE

Fishmonger, Bridge Street. Had great house in Candlewick Street and several shops in Bridge Street. In the nineties, towards the end of his life, was busy buying more shops in the same area. His son John acquired property at Plumstead, Kent and was a friend of Adam de Fulham, one of the earliest alderman-fishmongers and the leader of the city trade.[3]

WILLIAM DE BIXLE

Fishmonger, Old Fish Street. His father, Thomas, married into the Pelham family of cordwainers and girdlers. William held property in three parishes and a tenement in Surrey. His customers included men of Middlesex and a clergyman from Shropshire. His first wife was a tailor's daughter, his second was Agnes, widow of John de Northampton, first skinner to reach the aldermanic council.[4]

[1] Hust. Roll 64(51); Ancient Deeds E 501, 509; *Cal. Letter-Bk. B*, 226, *C*, 168, 172, *E*, 75, 76; St. Paul's A/23/1728; *Cal. of Wills*, i, 233–4, 399–400.
[2] Misc. Roll BB, m.6; Hust. Roll (Common Pleas) 2, m.4; K.R. Acc. V. (Sheriffs Accounts) E101/571/3, schedule; *Cal. E.M.C. Rolls* and *Cal. Letter-Bks.*, *passim*.
[3] Hust. Roll 27(51); 31(32); 35(95); W.A.M. 5183; *Cal. of Wills*, i, 342.
[4] Hust. Roll 4(105); 10(2:15); A.R. 543, m.20d; Recog. Roll 1(64); *C.C.R. 1272–9*, p. 66; *Cal. of Wills*, i, 476–7.

WILLIAM MAY

Skinner. Appears to be the son of Henry May, an immigrant from St. Pol, who owned property in St. Michael le Quern around 1240. William sold £205 of silver to the Mint in 1263, and, in 1272, bought an export licence for wool. He held property in two parishes. His son, William junior, married Matilda of the Cornwaleys family, which rose to aldermanic status by the end of the century; his grandson, John, became a clerk, councillor, and reeve of Battersea manor. William junior was a founder-member of the skinners' gild in 1288.[1]

SIMON DE POURTEPOLL

Weaver. Held much property in the suburb at Holborn, in a street which bore their family name. Bought property in three parishes from goldsmiths and fishmongers. His family intermarried with the aldermanic family of Paris. His son was a warden of the weavers' gild and his daughter married Richard de Chigwell, greatest of the alderman-fishmongers.[2]

WALTER DE WATFORD

Goldsmith. In 1273 bought a wool-export licence for twenty sacks. In 1276, sold silk cloths to the alderman-goldsmith John de Blakethorne. In 1275, sent Bartholomew de Durham, cadet of an aldermanic family, to Ireland as his factor. Held land in Kent. Owned a seld in St. Peter Wood Street and bequeathed much of his property, in All Hallows Haywharf, to Solomon de Laufare, a cutler of rebel family who became an alderman. Shops in Smithfield sold to John de Laufare and to the lawyer Reginald de Oundle, by his son-in-law, Thomas Basset, an armourer.[3]

RICHARD LE BRET

Goldsmith. After his pardon, served on juries and inquisitions in 1284 and 1292. Owned property in St. John Zachary and, in 1288, leased a messuage and fifty acres in West Ham. His son Robert owned shops in Goldsmiths' Row and Friday Street. His brother Robert owned a seld and property in

---

[1] St. Paul's A/7/890, A/19/294; W.A.M. 27500–27502; K.R. Acc. V. (Mint) E101/288/6, m. 7; K.R. Acc. V. (Alien Merchants) E101/126/7, m. 3; Hust. Roll 7(4:32); 14(176); 24(23)(43)(48); 34(17); Misc. Roll AA, p. 80; *C.P.R. 1266–72*, p. 693; *Cal. Letter-Bk. A*, 220.

[2] St. Paul's A/2/611, 613, A/12/1128, 1130, A/17/406; *Cal. Letter-Bk. B*, 17, 116, *C*, 56, 60; *Cal. of Wills*, i, 48.

[3] Hust. Roll 28(72); 31(36); 32(41); *C.C.R. 1272–9*, p. 188; *C.P.R. 1272–81*, pp. 22, 106; *Cal. Letter-Bk. A*, 7; *Cal. of Wills*, i, 66.

Z

three parishes, and his niece Isabella was a nun at Stratford. The rebel's father, Robert, had been a draper who supplied the Court.[1]

WILLIAM DE BASING

Mercer. Connected to the aldermanic family of the same name. In 1275, was left property in Boston by Peter de Basing, kinsman of Adam de Basing the alderman. William traded at the fairs and was arrested at Northampton in 1252. In 1255, bought property in two parishes, including a mansion in Riders Street, from the goldsmiths de la More, who intermarried with the Basings. He also dealt in wool, and his son, woolmonger and Weigher at the King's Tron, was elected sheriff in 1308.[2]

ROBERT BAYNARD

Draper. Sold cloth to Eleanor de Montfort during the protectorate. Owned thirty-six acres arable, six acres woodland, four acres meadow and ten shillings rent in Salinges, Essex. His brother Roger witnessed a grant by Baldwin Fillol of Essex of land to the widow of John, brother of the rebel alderman Alexander le Ferrun.[3]

IVO LE LINENDRAPER

Linendraper. Imported French linen and exported wool. Married Alice, daughter of Roger de Harwe, of an important family of civic officials. Owned property in three parishes. His daughter married one of the leading tailors.[4]

JOHN CROS

Girdler. Known as John de Preston. Owned much property in Sopers Lane, St. Laurence Jewry and two other parishes. Married Mariota la Bokelere of the Buckler family. After the wars, sold horses. Closely connected with the corder family of Box, which entered the aldermanic council after 1285. His sons became corders and served as councillors. His grandson John de Preston became an alderman.[5]

---

[1] St. Paul's A/12/1188, A/18/1441, A/20/304; Hust. Roll 20(58); 21(56); 22(15); 30(88); 32(62); *C.Lib.R. 1251–60*, p. 103; *Feet of Fines for the County of Essex*, ii, 61; *Cal. Letter-Bk. A*, 87, C, 7; *Cal. of Wills*, i, 34, 110–11, 217.

[2] Hust. Roll 2(1)(2); 33(21); W.A.M. 24695; *C.Lib. R. 1251–60*, p. 75; *Cal.Letter-Bk. C*, 113, 170, 172, 179; *Cal. of Wills*, i, 20.

[3] *Feet of Fines for the County of Essex*, ii, 4; *C.C.R. 1272–9*, p. 51.

[4] Hust. Roll (Land) 1, m.4; Hust. Roll 12(83); 24(10).

[5] St. Paul's A/22/1630, 1631, 1634; Hust. Roll 17(24); *Cal. Letter-Bk. A*, 56, 58, 118, 119; *Cal. of Wills*, i, 435–6, 669–70; Ekwall, *op. cit.*, 163, 217, 218.

JOHN PATRIK

Cutler. Family originated in Edmonton, and held large properties there and elsewhere in Middlesex. John and brother Geoffrey were sons of another cutler William, and on intimate terms with the rebel Bixles and Heyruns. John seized Simon de Montfort's old city house after the war. His widow Matilda married William de Garton, a prominent pepperer of aldermanic stock. The family was connected to the aldermanic Caustons.[1]

Some further indications of status[2]

RICHARD LE ORBATUR: goldbeater, son of a goldbeater; held two shops in Cheap.

JOHN ELILAND: family had produced aldermen in the early years of the century; was a friend of Alderman Walter de Finchingfield, and married his daughter to the son of Alderman John de Blakethorne.

WILLIAM LE FLAONER: mercer: owned property in Vintry and tenements in Herts; had a factor, Guy.

OSBERT LE POULTER: poulterer? in 1268, acted as *serviens* to William de Grandcourt, Baron of the Exchequer, and the Exchequer collected his debts; property in two parishes; hundred-jury for Cornhill ward.

JOHN ALBYN: fishmonger; property in three parishes; son held land in Lambeth.

THOMAS DE ST. MARTIN: sold wine to Household; owned 120 acres arable in South Mimms, Middlesex.

WALTER CARBONEL: owned a row of houses in Pentecost Lane.

ALEXANDER AND WILLIAM LE POTTER: potters; owned shops at Bury, Boston and Winchester, and were cousins to Alderman Walter le Potter.

MICHAEL DE PARIS: owned property in five parishes.

GUY LE TAILOR: called *Master*; his son Ralph was a factor of Alderman Stephen de Cornhill.

GILBERT LE ARMOURER: had clientele of county knights; served as councillor.

JOHN AND ROBERT HEYRUN: property-owners; served as chirographers of the Jews.

---

[1] W.A.M. 155, 250, 262, 319, 332, 335, 342; Hust. Roll (Common Pleas) 2, m.1d; Hust. Roll 27(86); 31(64); *Hundred Rolls*, i, 427, 433; *Cal. Letter-Bk. B*, 274; *Cal. Inq. Misc.*, i, 134.

[2] For these instances, see St. Paul's A/12/1128, A/18/134; W.A.M. 4216, 4236, 13417; W.A.M., Domesday, fo. 237b–238b; Hust. Roll 13(44); 20(27)(28); A.R. 543, m.10d; K.R.M.R. 40, m. 15d; 42, m. 12; Ancient Deeds D 4635; Recog. Roll 1(75)(136)(219); Misc. Roll BB, m.1; *C.P.R. 1258–66*, p. 467; *C.P.R. 1272–81*, p. 414; *C.C.R. 1272–9*, pp. 2, 137; *C.Lib.R. 1251–60*, p. 301; *Cal. Inq. Misc.*, i, 326; *Cal. Letter-Bk. A*, 124, *B*, 4, 5, *C*, 2; *Cal. of Wills*, i, 12, 27, 52, 54, 80, 105, 166, 289.

Relationships[1]

John de Preston leased property to Walter de Watford.

William Albyn owned house occupied by Arnold le Tailor, whose son William Arnold joined the rebels.

Hubert le Orfevre, rebel, witnessed sales of property to Michael Tovy and Simon de Pourtepoll.

Walter de Watford bequeathed property to the Laufares; Suffolks witnessed the deeds of Enfields; Oystergates those of Ferruns.

The rebels Richard de Coudres, William May and William de Basing lived next door to each other in the same street.

The rebels John l'Affeyte, Robert le Treyere, John le Chapler, John de Fleet, William le Clerk, Walter de Watford and John de Blakethorne were related to each other by marriage.

[1] For these instances, see St. Paul's A/7/891, A/14/678; Hust. Roll 9(2:6), 14(38); A.R. 543, m.19; *C.C.R. 1272–9*, p. 51; *Cal. Letter-Bk. A*, 7, 91, 92, 101, 102, 168, 169; *Cal. of Wills*, i, 12, 66, 150, 151.

PRIMARY SOURCES
I. Royal Records

(i) MANUSCRIPT

Public Record Office

CHANCERY
Chancery Miscellanea.
Chancery Warrants.
Liberate Rolls.

EXCHEQUER
Exchequer Miscellanea.
Exchequer Plea Rolls.
Great Wardrobe Debentures.
King's Remembrancer's Accounts, Various.
   Alien Merchants, Army and Navy, Butlerage, Mint, Miscellaneous,
   Sheriffs' Administrative Accounts, Wardrobe.
King's Remembrancer's Customs Accounts.
King's Remembrancer's Memoranda Rolls.
Lord Treasurer's Remembrancer's Enrolled Accounts.
Lord Treasurer's Remembrancer's Memoranda Rolls.

LEGAL RECORDS
Assize Rolls.
Coram Rege Rolls.
Curia Regis Rolls.

SPECIAL COLLECTIONS
Ancient Deeds.
Ancient Petitions.

(ii) PRINTED

GENERAL COLLECTIONS
Royal and other historical letters illustrative of the reign of Henry III, ii, ed. W. W.
   Shirley (London, 1866).
*Select charters and other illustrations of English constitutional history from the
   earliest times to the reign of Edward I*, ed. W. Stubbs, 9th edn. rev. by
   H. W. C. Davis (Oxford, 1913).

CHANCERY
Calendar of Close Rolls preserved in the Public Record Office, 1272–1360, 18 vols.
   (London, 1892–1908).

Calendar of Chancery Rolls, Various, preserved in the Public Record Office, 1277–1326 (London, 1912).

Calendar of Chancery Warrants preserved in the Public Record Office, 1244–1326 (London, 1927).

Calendar of Charter Rolls preserved in the Public Record Office, 1226–1417, 5 vols. (London, 1903–16).

Calendar of Fine Rolls preserved in the Public Record Office, 1272–1368, 7 vols. (London, 1911–23).

Calendar of Inquisitions, Miscellaneous, preserved in the Public Record Office, 1219–1377, 3 vols. (London, 1916–37).

Calendar of Inquisitions Post-mortem and other analogous documents preserved in the Public Record Office, 1216–1347, 8 vols. (London, 1904–13).

Calendar of Liberate Rolls preserved in the Public Record Office, 1226–60, 4 vols., vol. iv printed but not published, at the P.R.O. (London, 1916–1937).

Calendar of Patent Rolls preserved in the Public Record Office, 1232–1361, 23 vols. (London, 1893–1913).

Close Rolls of the reign of Henry III preserved in the Public Record Office, 1227–1272, 14 vols. (London, 1902–38).

Excerpta è Rotulis Finium 1216–72, 2 vols., ed. C. Roberts (London, 1835–1836).

Patent Rolls of the reign of Henry III preserved in the Public Record Office, 1216–1232, 2 vols. (London, 1901–3).

EXCHEQUER

Great Roll of the Pipe for 14 Henry III: Michaelmas 1230, ed. C. Robinson, Pipe Roll Society (Princeton, 1927).

Inquisitions and Assessments relating to Feudal Aids 1284–1431, with other analogous documents preserved in the Public Record Office, 6 vols. (London, 1899–1920).

Memoranda Roll of the King's Remembrancer 1230–1, ed. C. Robinson, Pipe Roll Society (Princeton, 1935).

Select Cases in the Exchequer of Pleas, ed. H. Jenkinson and B. E. R. Formoy, Selden Society (London, 1932).

LEGAL RECORDS

Curia Regis Rolls of the reign of Henry III preserved in the Public Record Office, 1219–26, 5 vols. (London, 1938–57).

Select Cases before the King's Council, 1243–1482, ed. I. S. Leadam and J. F. Baldwin, Selden Society (Cambridge, Mass., 1918).

Year Books of Edward II, i, ed. F. W. Maitland, Selden Society (London, 1903).

SPECIAL COLLECTIONS

A Descriptive Catalogue of Ancient Deeds in the Public Record Office, 6 vols. (London, 1896–1915).

Rotuli Hundredorum temp. Henry III et Edward I, i, (London 1836).

II. Records of the City of London

(i) MANUSCRIPT

Corporation of London Records Office

CUSTUMALS
Liber de Assisa Panis.
Liber Horn.
Liber Memorandorum.
Liber Ordinationum.

CITY COURTS
Court of Husting:
Rolls of Common Pleas.
Rolls of Pleas of Land.
Rolls of Deeds and Wills.
Miscellaneous Roll CC: Sheriffs' Court 1318–20.

ADMINISTRATIVE RECORDS
Miscellaneous Roll DD: Assize of Nuisance.
Recognizance Rolls: Statute of Merchants.

RECORDS OF ROYAL COURTS
Miscellaneous Roll AA: Iter of 1244–6 (transcript by H. M. Chew).
Miscellaneous Roll BB: Iter of 1275–6.

BRIDGE HOUSE ESTATES
Deeds: Portfolio, Large Register, Miscellaneous.

Guildhall Library Muniment Room

PAROCHIAL CHARITIES DEPOSITED DEEDS
Series: St. Mary Magdalen Milk Street; St. Mary the Virgin Aldermanbury; St. Michael Wood Street.

ADDITIONAL MANUSCRIPTS
Miscellaneous Deeds.

COLLECTANEA
J. J. Stocken: Collection towards a biographical account of the Lord Mayors, Aldermen and Sheriffs of the City of London.
B. I'Anson: Collection of mayors' pedigrees.

Note: For a brief guide to the archives, see P. E. Jones and R. Smith, *A Guide to the Records in the Corporation of London Records Office and the Guildhall Library Muniment Room* (London, 1951).

Reference: On a few rolls, every entry is numbered individually; reference given in form Hust. Roll. 1(1); for the remainder, the reference is to membrane number.

(ii) PRINTED

RECORD SERIES

Calendar of Coroners' Rolls preserved among the archives of the Corporation of the City of London, 1300–1378, ed. R. R. Sharpe (London, 1913).

Calendar of Early Mayors' Court Rolls preserved among the archives of the Corporation of the City of London, 1298–1307, ed. A. H. Thomas (London, 1924).

Calendar of Letter-Books preserved among the archives of the Corporation of the City of London, 1275–1498, Books A–L, 11 vols. ed. R. R. Sharpe, (London, 1899–1912).

Calendar of Letters from the Mayor, Aldermen and Commonalty of the City of London preserved among the archives of the Corporation of the City of London, 1350–70, ed. R. R. Sharpe (London, 1885).

Calendar of Plea and Memoranda Rolls preserved among the archives of the Corporation of the City of London, 1324–1457, 5 vols., ed. A. H. Thomas (i–iv) and P. E. Jones (v) (London, 1926–54).

Calendar of Wills proved and enrolled in the Court of Husting, London, 1258–1358, 2 vols., ed. R. R. Sharpe (London, 1889).

Munimenta Gildhallae Londoniensis, i, *Liber Albus,* ii, *Liber Custumarum,* ed. H. T. Riley (London, 1859–62).

COLLECTIONS

M. Bateson, 'A London municipal collection of the reign of John', *English Historical Review,* xvii (1902).

E. Ekwall, *Two Early London Subsidy Rolls,* with an introduction, commentaries and indices of taxpayers (Lund, 1951).

Historical Charters and Constitutional Documents of the City of London, ed. W. de G. Birch, rev. edn., (London, 1887).

Memorials of London and London life in the XIII, XIV, and XV Centuries, 1276–1419, ed. H. T. Riley (London, 1868).

M. Weinbaum, *London unter Eduard I und II, Verfassungs und Wirtschaftsgeschichtliche Studien,* 2 vols. in one cover, vol. ii a collection of documents (Stuttgart, 1933).

III. Miscellaneous Records

(i) MANUSCRIPT

Archives of St. Paul's Cathedral: Chapter Library

Deeds and Wills.

Archives of Westminster Abbey: Muniment Room

Cartulary of St. Martin-le-Grand.
Westminster Abbey Domesday: cartulary.

Westminster Abbey Muniments: deeds, bonds, and wills.

Note: *St. Paul's:* reference to class, box and number, in form A/1/1.

Westminster: Domesday is in typescript: reference in form W.A.M., Domesday, fo. 1. The deeds are indexed in manuscript: reference in form W.A.M. 1.

There is some account of the archives of St. Paul's in the *Ninth Report of the Historical Manuscripts Commission.*

(ii) PRINTED

ECCLESIASTICAL

Cartulary of St. Mary Clerkenwell, ed. W. O. Hassall (London, 1949).

Chartulary of the Hospital of St. Thomas the Martyr, Southwark, 1213–1525 (London, 1932).

Early Charters of the Cathedral Church of St. Paul, London, ed. M. Gibbs (London, 1939).

Registrum Roberti Winchelsey Archiepiscopi Cantuariensis, ed. R. Graham (London, 1917–42).

The Records of Merton Priory, ed. A. Heales (London, 1898).

LOCAL

A Calendar of the Feet of Fines for London and Middlesex, 2 vols., ed. W. J. Hardy and W. Page (London, 1892–3).

Feet of Fines for the County of Essex, 2 vols., ed. R. Kirk (Colchester, 1899).

Henry of Pytchley's Book of Fees, ed. W. T. Mellows (Northampton, 1927).

The Pipe Roll for 1295: Surrey Membrane, ed. M. H. Mills (Guildford, 1924).

SOME GILD RECORDS

Facsimile of the first volume of the Ms. Archives of the Worshipful Company of the Grocers of the City of London, 1345–1463, 2 vols. (London, 1883–6).

Memorials of the Goldsmiths' Company, 2 vols., ed. W. S. Prideaux (London, 1896–7).

Memorials of the Guild of Merchant Tailors, ed. C. M. Clode (London, 1875).

The Charters, Ordinances and Bye-Laws of the Mercers' Company, ed. W. D. Selby (London, 1881).

Note: For a full list of London gild records and histories, see G. Unwin, *The Gilds and Companies of London*, rev. edn. by F. J. Fisher (London, 1938).

MISCELLANEOUS

G. P. Cuttino, *English Diplomatic Administration 1259–1339*, appendix of mercantile documents (London, 1940).

The Coventry Leet Book, 2 vols., ed. M. D. Harris (London, 1907–13).

The Records of the Borough of Northampton, 2 vols., ed. C. Markham (Northampton, 1898).

The Records of the City of Norwich, i, ed. W. Hudson and J. C. Tingey (Norwich, 1906).

IV. Chronicles

LONDON GROUP

Annales Londonienses and *Annales Paulini* in *Chronicles of the reigns of Edward I and II*, i, ed. W. Stubbs, Rolls Series (London, 1882).

Croniques de London depuis l'an 44 Henry III jusqu'a l'an 17 Edward III (*French Chronicle of London*), ed. G. J. Aungier, Camden Society (London, 1844).

Great Chronicle of London, ed. A. H. Thomas and I. D. Thornley (London, 1938).

Liber de Antiquis Legibus seu chronica maiorum et vicecomitum Londoniarum, ed. T. Stapleton, Camden Society (London, 1846).

ST. ALBANS GROUP

Chronicon de duobus bellis apud Lewes et Evesham in *Walsingham's Ypodigma Neustriae*, ed. H. T. Riley, Rolls Series (London, 1876).

Flores Historiarum, ii and iii, ed. H. R. Luard, Rolls Series (London, 1890).

Johannis de Trokelowe et Henrici de Blaneforde, chronica et annales, ed. H. T. Riley, Rolls Series (London, 1866).

Matthaei Parisiensis Chronica Majora, iv and v, ed. H. R. Luard, Rolls Series (London, 1877–80).

Thomas Walsingham, Historia Anglicana, 2 vols., ed. H. T. Riley, Rolls Series (London, 1863–4).

ANNALES MONASTICI

Series: *Annales Monastici*, ed. H. R. Luard, Rolls Series: all volume numbers refer to volumes in this series.

Monasterii de Burton, i (1864).

Monasterii de Oseneia, iv (1869).

Monasterii de Theokesberia, i (1864).

Monasterii de Waverleia, ii (1865).

Monasterii de Wintonia, ii (1865).

Prioratus de Dunstaplia, iii (1866).

Prioratus de Wigornia, iv (1869).

Chronicon vulgo dictum Chronicon Thomae Wykes, iv (1869).

MISCELLANEOUS

Adae Murimuth, Continuatio Chronicarum, ed. E. M. Thompson, Rolls Series (London, 1889).

Bartholomei de Cotton, monachi Norwicensis, Historia Anglicana, ed. H. R. Luard, Rolls Series (London, 1859).

Chronica Johannis de Oxenedes, ed. H. Ellis, Rolls Series (London, 1859).

Chronicles of the reigns of Edward I and II, ii, ed. W. Stubbs, Rolls Series (London, 1883).

Chronicon Walteri de Hemingburgh, i, ed. H. C. Hamilton (London, 1848).

Continuation of the Gesta Regum in *Historical Works of Gervase of Canterbury*, ii, ed. W. Stubbs, Rolls Series, (London, 1880).

Nicholas Trivet, annales sex regum Angliae, ed. T. Hog (London, 1845).

SELECT BIBLIOGRAPHY

This bibliography is strictly selective. Standard texts and basic reference works have been omitted. So have highly specialized studies, reference to which may be found in the footnotes. A full bibliography has been deposited at the University of London with the thesis upon which this book is based— G. A. Williams, 'London, 1216–1337: a study of the main factors in the social and constitutional development of the city', Ph.D., University of London, typescript, 1960.

The aim of this bibliography is to list those works which were most influential, directly or indirectly, in shaping the present study.

GENERAL SOCIAL AND POLITICAL CONTEXT

Social

CARUS-WILSON, E. M., *Medieval Merchant Venturers; collected studies*, with introduction (London, 1954).

COHN, N., *The Search for the Millennium* (London, 1957).

DARBY, H. C., *The Domesday Geography of Eastern England* (Cambridge, 1952).

DARBY, H. C. (ed.), *An Historical Geography of England before 1800* (Cambridge, 1936).

HABAKKUK, H. J., 'English population in the eighteenth century', *Economic History Review*, 2nd ser. vi (1953).

HOBSBAWM, E. J., *Primitive Rebels* (Manchester, 1959).

KOSMINSKY, E. A., 'Peut-on considérer le xive. et xve. siècle comme l'époque de la décadence de l'économie européenne?' *Studi in onore di Armando Sapori* (Milan, 1957).

PIRENNE, H., 'Les périodes de l'histoire sociale du capitalisme', *Bulletin de l'Académie Royale de Belgique*, v (1914). *Histoire économique de l'occident médiéval*, collected works (Bruges, 1951).

POSTAN, M. M. and RICH, E. E. (eds.), *Cambridge Economic History of Europe*, ii (Cambridge, 1952).

Rapports du ixe. Congrès International des Sciences Historiques 1950 (Paris, 1950).

RUSSELL, J. C., *British Medieval Population* (Albuquerque, 1948).

347

SALTMARSH, J., 'Plague and economic decline in the later Middle Ages', *Cambridge Historical Journal*, vii (1940).

UNWIN, G., *Studies in Economic History:* collected works, ed. R. H. Tawney (London, 1927).

Political

DAVIES, J. C., *The Baronial Opposition to Edward II, its Character and Policy* (Cambridge, 1918).

DENHOLM-YOUNG, N., *Richard of Cornwall* (Oxford, 1947).

JACOB, E. F., *Studies in the Period of Baronial Reform and Rebellion 1258–1267* (Oxford, 1925).

MCKISACK, M., *The Fourteenth Century*, Oxford History of England (Oxford, 1959).

PLUCKNETT, T. F. T., *Legislation of Edward I* (Oxford, 1949).

POWICKE, F. M., *King Henry III and the Lord Edward*, 2 vols. (Oxford, 1947).

—. *The Thirteenth Century*, Oxford History of England (Oxford, 1953).

SOUTHERN, R. W., *The Making of the Middle Ages* (London, 1956).

TOUT, T. F., *The Place of the Reign of Edward II in English History*, 2nd. edn. rev. H. Johnstone (Manchester, 1936).

TREHARNE, R. F., *The Baronial Plan of Reform 1258–63* (Manchester, 1932).

—. 'The knights in the period of reform and rebellion 1258–67: a critical phase in the rise of a new class', *Bulletin of the Institute of Historical Research*, xxi (1946–8).

SOME SPECIALIZED STUDIES

Social

D'ALAUZIER, L., 'Achats d'étoffes d'une dame du Quercy au xiiie. siècle', *Annales du Midi*, lxx (1958).

BIGWOOD, G., 'Un marché de matières premières: laines d'Angleterre et marchands italiens vers la fin du xiiie. siècle', *Annales*, ii (1930).

BOUTRUCHE, R., *La crise d'une société. Seigneurs et paysans du Bordelais pendant la Guerre de Cent Ans* (Paris, 1947).

BRIDBURY, A. R., *England and the Salt Trade in the later Middle Ages* (Oxford, 1955).

DAENELL, E. R., *Die Blütezeit der deutschen Hanse*, 2 vols. (Berlin, 1905–6).

DOEHAERD, R., *L'expansion économique belge au moyen âge* (Brussels, 1946).

ESPINAS, G., *Sire Jehan Boinebroke, patricien et drapier douaisien* (Lille, 1933).

FRYDE, E. B., 'Materials for the study of Edward III's credit operations 1327–48', *Bulletin of the Institute of Historical Research*, xxii (1949).

—. 'The deposits of Hugh Despenser the Younger with Italian bankers', *Economic History Review*, 2nd ser., iii (1951).

—. 'The English Farmers of the Customs 1343–51', *Transactions of the Royal Historical Society*, 5th ser., ix (1959).

GRAS, N. S. B., *The Early English Customs System* (London, 1918).

—. *The Evolution of the English Corn Market* (Cambridge, Mass., 1926).

JAMES, M. K., 'The fluctuations of the Anglo-Gascon wine trade during the fourteenth century', *Economic History Review*, 2nd ser., iv (1951).

—. 'Les activités commerciales des négociants en vins gascons en Angleterre durant la fin du moyen âge', *Annales du Midi*, lxv (1953).

—. 'The medieval wine dealer', *The Entrepreneur*, papers of the annual conference of the Economic History Society (Cambridge, 1957).

KERLING, N. J. H., *Commercial relations of Holland and Zeeland with England from the late thirteenth century to the close of the Middle Ages* (Leiden, 1954).

POSTAN, M. M., 'Credit in medieval trade', *Economic History Review*, i (1928).

—. 'Some economic evidence of declining population in the later Middle Ages', *Economic History Review*, 2nd ser., ii (1950).

—. 'Italy and the economic development of England in the Middle Ages', *Journal of Economic History*, xi (1951).

—. 'Partnership in English medieval commerce', *Studi in Onore di Armando Sapori* (Milan, 1957).

POWER, E. E., *The Wool Trade in English Medieval History* (Oxford, 1941).

POWER, E. E. and POSTAN, M. M. (eds.), *Studies in English Trade in the Fifteenth Century* (London, 1933).

RENOUARD, Y., *Les hommes d'affaires italiens au moyen âge* (Paris, 1949).

REYNOLDS, R. L., 'In search of a business class in thirteenth-century Genoa', *Journal of Economic History*, v (1945).

SCHAUBE, A., 'Die Wollausfuhr Englands vom Jahre 1273', *Vierteljahrschrift für Sozial und Wirtschaftsgeschichte*, vi (1908).

SIMON, A. L., *A History of the Wine Trade in England*, 3 vols. (London, 1906–1909).

STURLER, J. DE, *Les relations politiques et les échanges commerciaux entre le duché de Brabant et l'Angleterre au moyen âge* (Paris, 1936).

UNWIN, G. (ed.), *Finance and Trade under Edward III* (Manchester, 1918).

VERLINDEN, C., 'The rise of Spanish trade in the Middle Ages', *Economic History Review*, x (1940).

Political

COHEN, H., *A History of the English Bar and Attornatus to 1450* (London, 1929).

CLARKE, M. V., 'Committees of Estates and the deposition of Edward II', *Historical Essays in honour of James Tait*, ed. J. G. Edwards, V. Galbraith and E. F. Jacob (Manchester, 1933).

EDWARDS, J. G., 'Confirmatio Cartarum and baronial grievances in 1297'. *English Historical Review*, lviii (1943).

FOSS, E., *The Judges of England*, iii (London, 1851).

HOYT, R. S., *The Royal Demesne in English Constitutional History* (New York, 1950).

LEES, B. A., 'The Statute of Winchester and Villa Integra', *English Historical Review*, xli (1926).

MITCHELL, S. K., *Studies in Taxation under John and Henry III* (New Haven, 1914).

—. *Taxation in Medieval England*, ed. S. Painter (London, 1951).

ROTHWELL, H., 'The Confirmation of the Charters, 1297', *English Historical Review*, lx (1945).

STONES, E. L. G., 'Sir Geoffrey le Scrope, Chief Justice of the King's Bench', *English Historical Review*, lxix (1954).

WILLARD, J. F., *Parliamentary Taxes on Personal Property 1290 to 1334* (Cambridge, Mass., 1934).

CRAFTS, GILDS AND COMPANIES

General

COORNAERT, E., *Les corporations en France avant 1789* (Paris, 1941).

—. 'Les ghildes mediévales', *Revue Historique*, cxcix (1948).

ESPINAS, G., 'Groupe économique; groupe religieuse: les tisserands de Valenciennes au xive. siècle', *Annales*, ii (1930).

KRAMER, S., *The English Craft Gilds: Studies in their Progress and Decline* (New York, 1927).

KULISCHER, J., *Allgemeine Wirtschaftsgeschichte*, i (Berlin, 1928).

MEYER, E., 'English craft-gilds and borough governments of the later Middle Ages', *University of Colorado Studies*, xvi, xvii (1929–30).

MICKWITZ, G., *Die Kartellfonktion der Zunfte und ihre Bedeutung bei Entstehung des Zunftwesens* (Helsinki, 1936).

POWER, E. E., 'English craft-gilds of the Middle Ages', *History*, iv (1919–20).

THRUPP, S. L., 'Medieval gilds reconsidered', *Journal of Economic History*, ii (1942).

UNWIN, G., *Industrial Organisation in the XVI and XVII Centuries* (London, 1904).

VERRIEST, L., *Les luttes sociales et le contrat d'apprentissage à Tournai jusqu'en 1424* (Brussels, 1912).

London

CONSITT, F., *The London Weavers' Company* (Oxford, 1933).

HERBERT, W., *History of the Twelve Great Livery Companies of London*, 2 vols. (London, 1836–7).

JOHNSON, A. H., *History of the Worshipful Company of Drapers of London*, i (Oxford, 1915).

THRUPP, S. L., *A Short History of the Worshipful Company of Bakers of London* (London, 1933).

—. 'The Grocers of London, a study of distributive trade', *Studies in English Trade in the Fifteenth Century*, ed. E. E. Power and M. M. Postan (1933).

UNWIN, G., *The Gilds and Companies of London* (London, 1908).

VEALE, E. M., 'The London Fur Trade in the later Middle Ages, with particular reference to the Skinners' Company', Ph.D. dissertation, University of London, typescript (London, 1953).

WELCH, G., *History of the Worshipful Company of Pewterers of the City of London*, 2 vols. (London, 1902).

Note: Of the large number of gild histories which exist, few, other than those named, are useful for social analysis. For a good bibliography, see the revised version of Unwin's great book—G. Unwin, *The Gilds and Companies of London*, rev. edn. by F. J. Fisher (London, 1938).

URBAN HISTORY

General

CLARKE, M. V., *The Medieval City State* (London, 1936).

DICKINSON, R. E., *The West European City: a Geographical Interpretation* (London, 1951).

FRANCESCO, E., *Dal commune al principato* (Florence, 1929).

GANSHOF, F. L., *Étude sur le développement des villes entre Loire et Rhin au moyen âge* (Paris-Brussels, 1943).

LAVEDAN, P., *Histoire de l'urbanisme*, 3 vols. (Paris, 1926–52).

LESTOCQUOY, J., *Les villes de Flandre et d'Italie sous le gouvernement des patriciens* (Paris, 1952).

LOT, F., *Recherches sur la population et la superficie des cités remontant à la période Gallo-Romaine*, 3 vols. (Paris, 1945–50).

MUNDY, J. H. and RIESENBERG, P., *The Medieval Town* (Princeton, 1958).

PETIT-DUTAILLIS, C., *Les communes françaises* (Paris, 1947).

PIRENNE, H., *Les villes et les institutions urbaines*, collected works, 2 vols. (Paris-Brussels, 1939).

TAYLOR, T. G., *Urban Geography* (London, 1949).

VERGOTTINI, G. DE, *Arti e popolo nella prima metà del secolo xiii* (Milan, 1943).

La Ville: première partie: Institutions administratives et judiciaires, recueil de la Société Jean Bodin, vi (Brussels, 1954).

Comparative

BÉMONT, C., 'Les institutions municipales de Bordeaux au moyen âge', *Revue Historique*, cxxiii (1916).

CHAPIN, E., *Les villes de foire de Champagne des origines au debut du xive. siècle* (Paris, 1937).

FAVRESSE, F., *L'avènement du régime démocratique à Bruxelles pendant le moyen âge, 1306–1423* (Brussels, 1932).

LESTOCQUOY, J., *Les dynasties bourgeoises d'Arras du xie. au xve. siècle* (Arras, 1945).

SAYOUS, A. E. and COMBES, J., 'Les commerçants et les capitalistes de Montpellier au xiiie. et xive. siècles', *Revue Historique*, clxxxviii–clxxxix (Brussels, 1940).

WERVEKE, H. VAN, *Gand: esquisse d'histoire sociale* (Brussels, 1946).

WERVEKE H. VAN, *Gand: esquisse d'histoire sociale* (Brussels, 1946).

England

BALLARD, A. and TAIT, J. (eds.), *British Borough Charters 1042–1307*, 2 vols. (London, 1913–23).

BATESON, M. (ed.), *Borough Customs*, 2 vols., Selden Society (London, 1904–1906).

DAVIS, H. W. C., 'The Commune of Bury St. Edmunds', *English Historical Review*, xxiv (1909).

HEMMEON, M. DE W., *Burgage Tenure in Medieval England* (Cambridge, Mass., 1914).

HEWITT, H. J., *Medieval Cheshire* (Manchester, 1929).

HIBBERT, A. B., 'The origins of the medieval town patriciate', *Past and Present*, iii (1951).

HILL, J. W. F., *Medieval Lincoln* (London, 1948).

LOBEL, M. D., *The Borough of Bury St. Edmunds* (Oxford, 1935).

MAITLAND, F. W., *Township and Borough* (Cambridge, 1898).

MURRAY, K. M. E., *The Constitutional History of the Cinque Ports* (Manchester, 1935).

STEPHENSON, C., *Borough and Town, a study of urban origins in England* (Cambridge, Mass., 1933).

TAIT, J., *The Medieval English Borough* (Manchester, 1936).

London and Londoners

AHRENS, F., 'Wilhelm Servat von Cahors zu London', *Vierteljahrschrift für Sozial und Wirtschaftsgeschichte*, xi (1913).

BEAVEN, A. B., *The Aldermen of the City of London*, 2 vols. (London, 1908–13).

BIRD, R., *The Turbulent London of Richard II*, with introduction by J. Tait and map of London by M. B. Honeybourne (London, 1949).

BRETT-JAMES, N. G., 'John de Drokensford, Bishop of Bath and Wells', *Transactions of the London and Middlesex Archaeological Society*, n.s. x (1951).

BUTLER, L. H., 'Archbishop Melton, his neighbours and his kinsmen, 1317–40', *Journal of Ecclesiastical History*, ii (1951).

CHEW, H. M., 'Mortmain in medieval London', *English Historical Review*, lx (1945).

—. 'The office of Escheator in London in the Middle Ages', *English Historical Review*, lviii (1943).

EKWALL, E., *Early London Personal Names* (Lund, 1947).
—. *Street-names of the City of London* (Oxford, 1954).
—. *Studies on the Population of Medieval London* (Stockholm, 1956).
—. *Variation in surnames in Medieval London* (Lund, 1945).

GOSS, C. W. F., 'History of the parish of St. Mary the Virgin, Aldermanbury', *Transactions of the London and Middlesex Archaeological Society*, n.s. ix (1944–7).

HARBEN, H. A., *A Dictionary of London* (London, 1918).

JAMES, M. K., 'A London merchant of the fourteenth century', *Economic History Review*, 2nd ser. viii (1955–6).

LOFTIE, W. J., *History of London*, 2 vols. (London, 1887).

MACKENZIE, B. A., *The Early London Dialect* (Oxford, 1928).

MCKISACK, M., 'London and the succession to the Crown during the Middle Ages', *Studies in Medieval History presented to F. M. Powicke*, ed. R. W. Hunt, W. A. Pantin and R. W. Southern (Oxford, 1948).

PAGE, W., *London, its Origin and Early Development* (London, 1929).

REDSTONE, V. B., 'Some mercenaries of Henry of Lancaster, 1327–30', *Transactions of the Royal Historical Society*, 3rd ser. vii (1913).

REDSTONE, V. B. and L. J., 'The Heyruns of London: a study in the social origins of Geoffrey Chaucer', *Speculum*, xii (1937).

REYNOLDS R. L., 'Some English settlers in Genoa in the late twelfth century', *Economic History Review*, iv (1933).

ROUND, J. H., *The Commune of London and other studies* (Cambridge, 1899).
—. *Geoffrey de Mandeville* (London, 1892).

SHARPE, R. R., *London and the Kingdom*, 3 vols. (London, 1894–5).

STENTON, F. M., *Norman London*, with a translation of William fitz Stephen's description by H. E. Butler and a map of London by M. B. Honeybourne (London, 1934); new and revised version in G. Barraclough (ed.), *Social Life in early England* (London, 1960).

STOCKEN, J. J., 'The Briklesworths of London and Northampton', *The London and Middlesex Notebook*, ed. W. P. W. Phillimore (London, 1892).

STOW, J., *A Survey of London* (temp. Elizabeth), 2 vols., ed. C. L. Kingsford (London, 1908).

TAIT, J., 'Two unknown names of early London wards', *London Topographical Record*, xv (1931).

THOMAS, A. H., 'Some recent contributions to the early history of London', *History*, n.s. ix (1924–5).
—. 'Illustrations of the medieval municipal history of London from the Guildhall records', *Transactions of the Royal Historical Society*, 4th ser. iv (1921).

THRUPP, S. L., *The Merchant Class of Medieval London, 1300–1500* (Chicago, 1948).

2A

TOUT, T. F., 'The beginnings of a modern capital: London and Westminster in the fourteenth century', British Academy Raleigh Lecture 1923, *Proceedings of the British Academy*, xi.

WEINBAUM, M., *Verfassungsgeschichte Londons 1066–1268* (Stuttgart, 1929).

Victoria County History of the Counties of England: London, i, *Middlesex*, ii, ed. W. Page (London, 1909–11).

INDEX

Abingdon, 128
Absolon, Adam, dyer, 176
Abyndon, Alderman Simon de, 128
—, Alderman Stephen de, 128–9, 266, 291–2
—, Thomas de, 132, 151
— family, 128–9, 291
Administrative class, in London, **95–105**, 248–9, 264, 277–8, 320, 335–6; *see also* LONDON: ADMINISTRATION
Adrien, Alderman John, 61, 62, 112, 211, 212, 232, 235, 242, 243
—family, 66n; *see also* Eswy, Leipzig
l'Affeyte, John, rebel, 340
Agenais, 146
Aguillon, Robert, 61
— family, 73
Aid, *see* Tallage, royal
l'Akatur, Alderman Joce, 252
Albyn, John, rebel, 339
—, William, rebel, 340
— family, 229–30
Aldermanbury, Alderman Gervase de, 71
Aldermanic class, dynasties, 9–10, 53, **73–5, 321–2**, genealogical tables, 322ff; eclipse of dynasties, 310–11, **321–2**; landed property, **53–8**, 308, **320**; royal service, **62–72**, chapter V, *passim*, 251–2, 308–9, **320**; commercial interests, **60–7, 115–48, 157–167, 319–20**; importance of monarchy, **66–72**, 251–2, 308–9, and *passim*; rise of professional administrators, **96–105**, 248–9, 264, 277–8, 320, 335–6; rise of provincial merchants, 14, 18, 108–9, 121, **133–48**, 310–11, 321–2; fluidity of class, 73–4, 310–311; the class and capital status, 308–312; *see also* Patriciate
Aldermen, *see* LONDON: CONSTITUTION
Aldgate, William de, 93

Almaine, Henry of, 233
Amanati company, 92
Amiens, 11, 62, 69, 122
Andreu, Peter, Montpellier, 142
— family, 135
Anglesey, 121
Anglo-Saxon thegnhood, and London aristocracy, 4, 5, 9, 74; *see also* Aldermanic class
Ansgar the Staller, 1, 313
Antwerp, 112, 127, 137, 159; ships leased from, 164
Appleby, Roger de, 88
Apprentices, 18, 22; *see also* LONDON: CONSTITUTION, CRAFTS
Arderne, Thomas de, acquisition of Ludgate-Newgate ward, 32, 235
Armentiers family, 129–30
Armourer, Gilbert le, rebel, 339
Arnold, William, rebel, 340
Arras, 129, 311
— family, 236
Articles of the Barons (1215), 6–7
Artois, 127
Arundel, earl of, 120, 129, 290–2, 296; and London debtors, 291–2
Ashbourne family, 185
Ashridge abbey, runaway bondman as city joiner's apprentice, 180
Assemblies, city, *see* LONDON: CONSTITUTION
Aubrey, Alderman Andrew, 134
Audley, James de, 61, 98, 224
Aumbresbury, Martin de, 28
Aungier family, 64
Auverne, Alderman Anketil de, 66, 200
Aylsham, 134, 137–9, 140
— family, 138

Bache, Anthony, Genoa, 134
Badlesmere, Bartholomew de, 113, 120, 289

355